PERSONAL AUTONOMY, THE PRIVATE SPHERE AND THE CRIMINAL LAW

Personal Autonomy, the Private Sphere and the Criminal Law

A Comparative Study

edited by
PETER ALLDRIDGE
and
CHRISJE BRANTS

HART
PUBLISHING
OXFORD – PORTLAND OREGON
2001

Hart Publishing
Oxford and Portland, Oregon

Published in North America (US and Canada) by
Hart Publishing c/o
International Specialized Book Services
5804 NE Hassalo Street
Portland, Oregon
97213-3644
USA

Distributed in the Netherlands, Belgium and Luxembourg by
Intersentia, Churchillaan 108
B2900 Schoten
Antwerpen
Belgium

Hart Publishing Ltd is a specialist legal publisher based in Oxford, England. To order further copies of this book or to request a list of other publications please write to:

Hart Publishing Ltd, Salter's Boatyard,
Folly Bridge, Abingdon Road, Oxford OX1 4LB
Telephone: +44 (0)1865 245533 or Fax: +44 (0)1865 794882
e-mail: mail@hartpub.co.uk
WEBSITE: http//www.hartpub.co.uk

British Library Cataloguing in Publication Data
Data Available
ISBN 1–901362–82–5 (hardback)

Typeset by Hope Services (Abingdon) Ltd.
Printed and bound in Great Britain by
Biddles Ltd, www.biddles.co.uk

Preface

This book is the result of long-standing collaboration between Cardiff Law School, University of Wales, and the Willem Pompe Institute for Criminal Law and Criminology of the University of Utrecht. It is the fifth book to appear since our first research contacts in 1986.[1] Since those early days, our field of collaborators has broadened considerably. Some of the original group have moved on to work elsewhere, but have nevertheless remained sufficiently involved to want to contribute to this volume. We have also sought to interest researchers from other universities and institutes, both in and outside the United Kingdom and The Netherlands, in our continuing and widening comparative studies.

Our thanks to the British Council, the Departments of Law at Cardiff and Utrecht, Hart Publishing and the University of Wales facility at Gregynog itself for help in putting on a weekend-colloquium at Gregynog, during which we were able to discuss the first versions of the contributions that appear in this book.

Finally, a short note on our system of case law citation: for cases in the European Court of Human Rights we have given the EHRR citation, the name and the date of the decision plus the application number; this should allow anyone accessing the website of the Council of Europe at <http://www.dhcour.coe.fr>, which has an excellent search engine, easy access to all of the case law. For decisions by national courts, we have used the method of citation usual in the jurisdiction in point.

[1] See also Phil Fennell *et al.* (eds), *Criminal Justice in Europe. A Comparative Study* (Oxford: Clarendon Press, 1995; Christopher Harding and Bert Swart (eds), *Enforcing European Community Rules. Criminal Proceedings, Administrative Procedures and Harmonization* (Aldershot: Dartmouth, 1996); Chrisje Brants and Stewart Field, *Participation Rights and Proactive Policing. Convergence and drift in European criminal process* (Deventer: Kluwer, 1995); S.A. Field and C.M. Pelser (eds), *Invading the Private: State Accountability and New Investigative Methods in Europe* (Aldershot: Dartmouth, 1998).

Contents

Contributors

Peter Alldridge is Senior Lecturer in Law at Cardiff Law School and Director of Cardiff Centre for Crime, Law and Justice.

Leonard Besselink is Senior Lecturer in Constitutional Law, University of Utrecht.

Lois Bibbings is Lecturer in Law at Bristol University.

Chrisje Brants is Professor of Criminal Law and Criminal Procedure and Director of the Willem Pompe Institute, University of Utrecht.

Richard Collier is Professor of Law at the University of Newcastle.

Constantijn Kelk is Professor of Criminal Law, Criminal Procedure and Penology at the Willem Pompe Institute.

Martin Moerings is Senior Lecturer in Criminology and Criminal Law at the Willem Pompe Institute.

Caroline Pelser is Lecturer in Criminal Law at the Willem Pompe Institute.

Koen Raes is Professor of Law and Legal Philosophy at the University of Ghent, Belgium.

Paul Roberts is Reader in Law at the University of Nottingham.

Bert Swart is a judge at the Court of Appeals in Amsterdam, Professor Extraordinary at the University of Amsterdam and formerly Professor of Criminal Law and Criminal Procedure at the Willem Pompe Institute.

Table of Cases

1. INTERNATIONAL

2. EUROPEAN COURT OF HUMAN RIGHTS

3. EUROPEAN COURT OF JUSTICE

4. NATIONAL COURTS

Belgium

France

Germany

Netherlands

United Kingdom

United States

Table of Legislation

1. INTERNATIONAL

2. COUNCIL OF EUROPE

3. EUROPEAN COMMUNITY AND UNION

4. NATIONAL LEGISLATION

United Kingdom

Introduction

PETER ALLDRIDGE AND CHRISJE BRANTS

THE COMPARATIVE EXERCISE

AT THE MOST general level, this book will attempt to highlight a number of differences in legal cultures and underlying assumptions with regard to the private sphere, personal autonomy and the supposed justifications for state interference by means of (the implementation of) substantive criminal law. The essays in this volume are mainly concerned with England and Wales on the one hand and continental Europe – notably, although not exclusively, the Netherlands – on the other. The major differences between the common law and civil law systems that these countries exemplify, are often simply accepted as the inevitable and everlasting result of the forces of history. And yet, in theory at least, Europe as a whole increasingly shares a common culture of basic individual rights and of standards against which to measure the legitimacy of state interference with them, expressed in and reinforced by the European Convention on Human Rights and Fundamental Freedoms. At the same time, the development of a supra-national European economic and social order is pushing national criminal justice systems ever further in the direction of a shared instrumentalist perception of criminal law. An important issue in comparative studies therefore becomes to what extent such developments will lead, or have perhaps already led, to convergence or even harmonisation of legal systems and legal culture.

This immediately raises questions as to the nature of the comparative exercise which is contemplated here. Comparative studies of common law and civil law systems, and of the legal culture that derives from and sustains them, have usually concerned the most visible differences, which are to be found in styles of criminal procedure (most commonly distinguished as adversarial and inquisitorial respectively).[1] In our view, however, this often fails to take into consideration the more fundamental cultural, political and social context within which legal traditions and practice develop. Moreover, comparisons of procedural traditions and practices are usually made against the background of a broad consensus as to substantive law, although it is in the area under consideration –

[1] And see Mirjan Damaska, *The Faces of Justice and State Authority* (New Haven, CT: Yale University Press, 1986).

intervention in the private sphere and the limits of personal autonomy – that some of the most interesting differences between legal cultures could be expected to arise, and where we have assumed that common and civil law countries might, or indeed do, attempt to find different solutions for similar problems.

A first step to tracing such differences is through questioning the assumptions that justify the right of the state *per se* to intervene by means of criminal law in individual behaviour. A second is to examine the actual provisions of substantive law with regard to issues of privacy and autonomy in jurisdictions from the different traditions. A third, and by far most interesting, step is to compare the findings against each other and against a more general background of difference in cultural and legal tradition, economic and social arrangements, and possible harmonising supra-national effects. A truly comparative study requires that we take all of these steps. We have, in any event, attempted to go further than what David Nelken[2] calls comparison by mere juxtaposition, although close examination of the provisions of law that actually apply in different jurisdictions is an indispensable pre-condition of understanding how exactly they differ, and why that should be so. At the same time, it is important that we keep an open mind as to the implications of the findings.

Comparative studies sometimes include attempts to prove that, although the rules in different jurisdictions appear to be different, they are really the same and embody some deep truth about the human condition.[3] In our case, for example, it could well be that what appear at first sight to be major differences in substantive law, are in fact not attributable to essential differences in the underlying norm or moral standards in given jurisdictions, but to differing styles of, and (historically conditioned) social expectations with regard to law enforcement. Another approach, that formed the backbone of classical comparative law, is to compare with a view to saying that the rules of one system are better than those of the other, and that their adoption should be considered in the other jurisdiction. This approach is fraught with the dangers now known to attach to "transplants", but nevertheless, if that is borne in mind, can be helpful, if only because it requires that we explicitly justify what we consider to be "the better rule", and why.

Conversely, while different jurisdictions may share norms and values and yet have widely divergent solutions in positive law, it is by no means certain that harmonisation of law in a wider context such as the European Union rests on shared perceptions of normative issues. This is not to deny the discursive power of law over a long period of time, but harmonising mechanisms – for example the Maastricht and Amsterdam Conventions (especially with regard to the so-

[2] David Nelken, "Understanding Criminal Justice Comparatively" in Mike Maguire, Rod Morgan, Robert Reiner, *The Oxford Handbook of Criminology* (Oxford: Oxford University Press, 2nd edn, 1997) 599.

[3] Joseph M. Perillo, "Abuse of Rights: A Pervasive Legal Concept" (1995) 27 *Pacific Law Journal* 37.

called third pillar of the European Union) and the case law of the European Court of Human Rights – may actually leave so much room for difference that their practical effect can be overstated.

The very problems inherent in comparative work[4] have meant that in this volume we have sometimes been unable to progress further than the second step of examining differences in substantive law in a number of countries. To identify common problems and at the same time to rise above our own legal culture in tracing essential differences, is a process that advances by stages. It will take many joint studies of the problems of privacy and autonomy in different jurisdictions, before we can say that we are really able to draw conclusions as to the fundamental differences and similarities between the legal systems and cultures in which such concepts function.

Above all it takes time and repeated attempts to find a common language that is truly mutually understood. It is, of course, necessary to be conscious that notions of autonomy and privacy have widely divergent values and meanings in different (legal) cultures. Similarly, the word "right" may have connotations that derive from our own legal cultural tradition, yet it is possible to continue a discussion at cross purposes for quite some time without realising that the one is referring to a cultural heritage of negative freedom and the other to a positive and legally entrenched demand that may be made upon the state – to say nothing of the implicit judgments as to the value of rights that we automatically make in the wake of connotative assumptions.

And finally, the use of the English language as a common means of communication has its own specific problems. Even if all concerned are equally fluent in English, the very fact that legal concepts from very different traditions are expressed in the same English words will mean that English readers and listeners will assume them to be used in the sense that they have in the common law tradition. One important example is the term "adversarial", often used by continental lawyers to denote oral proceedings in open court, which however, on the continent, fall far short of what a lawyer from the UK or USA understands by it. Another is the German word *Rechtstaat*, which English speakers are inclined to translate as "rule of law". Given that there is, in the common law tradition, no such legal concept as that embodied by the word *Rechtstaat*, the translation is at best an approximation, at worst a serious handicap to understanding.[5]

These are formidable hurdles and we have no doubt that we have failed to clear any number of them in the course of compiling this volume. While it is certainly not our first joint comparative exercise, it is the first time that we have

[4] See on the many pitfalls of comparative legal work: David Nelken (ed.),*Contrasting Criminal Justice. Getting from here to there* (Aldershot: Ashgate, 2000), esp. chapters 1 and 2.

[5] See for an attempt to overcome the difficulties inherent in the cultural contingency of meanings of particular legal concepts and notions: Chrisje Brants and Stewart Field, "Legal Cultures, Political Cultures and Procedural Traditions: Towards a Comparative Interpretation of Covert and Proactive Policing in England and Wales and The Netherlands" in David Nelken (ed.), *op.cit.* n 4.

compared substantive law in general and the issues of privacy and autonomy in particular. Moreover, comparisons of substantive criminal law upon which to build or take further comparative theory or empirical knowledge are few and far between. That is no excuse, but the reader will, we hope, forgive us that, as a first attempt, this book too is far from comprehensive.

WHY PRIVACY NOW?

There are several reasons why privacy takes on particular significance now. First, the ***effect of technology*** in providing challenges to the relationship between privacy and criminal law is not restricted to dealing with new mechanisms for surveillance.[6] In the areas of genetic and information technology, the questions which have arisen are whether the classical doctrines of the criminal law (homicide and assault law in the case of genetic technology, criminal property law in the case of computer crime) are sufficient, or whether a new *corpus* of law is appropriate to either case. In either event, there are significant privacy implications.

Developments in information technology make it far easier to obtain and disseminate information about peoples' pasts. Moreover, the Internet has radically altered the force of "the public domain" by allowing the collection and dissemination of materials that, while formally public, were not widely available. It has given rise to claims to privacy of information. It has now also generated claims from law enforcement agencies to encryption keys to decode encrypted emails and prohibitions upon anonymous and pseudonymous Internet use.

The second important precipitation has arisen from concern for the ***legality of police behaviour*** in combination with a ***move from reactive to proactive policing***,[7] striking most specifically at drugs but more generally, increasingly, at "organised crime". Reactive policing takes place in response to reports of crime. It involves the traditional policing techniques of interrogation, searches, seizures and so on of which the suspect is immediately aware, and by police officers whose status and identity the suspect knows. In a system of reactive policing the traditional guarantees of rights to the suspect may or may not in fact be available, but it is fairly clear what they would involve. In adversarial systems, due process provides an argument for the right to be informed of one's rights, for access to legal advice, some knowledge of the prosecution case, the right to have interviews recorded and the right to know when an interview is taking place and when it is being recorded. In inquisitorial systems too, the suspect has the right to remain silent, although legal aid may not be immediately available (in the Netherlands, for example, a suspect has no automatic right to have a lawyer present during police interrogation). Nevertheless, there are guarantees

[6] And see Roberts, *infra* at 52 *et seq*.

[7] And see S.A. Field and C.M. Pelser (eds), *Invading the Private: State Accountability and New Investigative Methods in Europe* (Aldershot: Dartmouth, 1998) 253–75.

that the case which is gradually being built up by the authorities (including statements by witnesses, evidence from search and seizure procedures, etc.), will – more or less in its entirety – be available for scrutiny by the defence at a specified time before the case is brought to court. Indeed, in such systems, full knowledge of the prosecution case is a necessity for the defence – for it is the prosecution that will compile the one and only *dossier* upon which the court will base the trial. What may remain secret during inquisitorial pre-trial investigation, must therefore be brought into the open in due time for the defence to prepare for the trial stage.[8]

In both adversarial and inquisitorial systems, these guarantees simply cannot be available in a system of policing that is directed towards the secret securing of evidence against an accused, before and at the time of an offence. Secret surveillance is incompatible with reading the suspect a statement of his/her right to remain silent or to legal advice, or with the implementation of a right that interviews be tape-recorded.[9] If every interaction between police and suspect must be prefaced by the same warnings that would take place at a police station after an arrest has been made, there could be no undercover police work.[10] Similarly, there is much in undercover work that must, forever, remain secret: the names of (threatened) witnesses or informers, the exact location of observation posts, the number of telephone taps against persons other than the suspect, information gleaned about others that may or may not be useful in future, but which nevertheless may be stored – just in case. Such secrecy precludes disclosure or providing complete access to a trial *dossier* – or, as is more likely, precludes that the dossier itself will be complete. If defence lawyers are kept ignorant of certain police activities, they are prevented from being able to ask the court to examine the legality of such action.

Consequently, within a system of proactive policing, arguments for rights for suspected persons are not arguments for due process, but rather are arguments for regulating access to the suspects' private time, space and information or that of others who may or may not be involved, and for storing the data that such access provides. In this sense, privacy is to proactive policing what due process is to reactive policing. As proactive policing increases in importance, consequently, so should attention be devoted to the claims of privacy in criminal procedure.

Arising partly at least from the fiction of the English policeman as a "citizen in uniform", there was no discrete law of criminal procedure in the United Kingdom.[11] In contrast to the civil law jurisdictions, there has never been

[8] See for a comparison of pre-trial procedure in England and Wales and The Netherlands: Stewart Field *et al.*, "Prosecutors, Examining Judges and Control of Police Investigations" in: Phil Fennell *et al.*, *Criminal Justice in Europe. A Comparative Study* (Oxford: Clarendon Press, 1995) 227–50.

[9] *R v. Smurthwaite* 98 CAR 437; [1994] 1 All ER 898.

[10] See C. Brants and S. Field, *Participation Rights and Proactive Policing*, Preadvies uitgebracht voor der Nederlandse Vereniging voor Rechtsvergelijking No 51, (Amsterdam: Kluwer, 1995) esp. at 46–7, and S.A. Field and C.M. Pelser (eds), *Invading the Private*, *supra* n 7.

[11] And see J.R. Spencer, "The Case for a Code of Criminal Procedure" [2000] *Criminal Law Review* 000.

anything resembling a *Code* of Criminal Procedure in England and Wales. Such rules as did govern police behaviour at common law grew out of two major sources – the law of criminal evidence and the civil law of interference with persons and property. What a discrete law of criminal procedure would acknowledge is that the role of the police sets them apart from the common run of humanity, and that a separate set of rules is appropriate.

The Netherlands, of course, does have a Code of Criminal Procedure (dating from 1926), which enumerates police powers to invade privacy and the conditions under which these may be used. With the exception of telephone tapping (regulated by law for the first time in 1973) however, these powers were typical products of an era in which there not only was little technological scope for secret proactive policing, but in which reactive policing was the norm. As concerns both about (organised) crime and the new technical means of policing it through surveillance and information-gathering increased, the Dutch police employed ever more far-reaching and extra-legal methods of investigation, in many cases at the instigation of, and trained by, the American DEA. (Typically, American police agents were unable to understand why the Dutch police should – at least originally – be wary of methods for which there was no basis in law).[12] When this came to light in the 1990s, there was serious public and political concern in the Netherlands that the police were somehow "out of control", the more so since some high-ranking Dutch police officers and public prosecutors were now openly doubting the necessity of a legal basis for police powers that would only serve to undermine an effective fight against organised crime. While such concerns therefore focused primarily on the issue of legal policing rather than privacy, nevertheless, the debate on new legislation on proactive policing methods (which entered into force in February 2000) brought the problem of privacy and the storing of secretly gathered data into the open.

Finally, underlying concerns about privacy in all jurisdictions are also developments in which claims to a right to procedural guarantees against infringements of informational privacy, or of private space, have been extended to include an **all-encompassing claim to a right of personal autonomy**. This is what impacts most importantly on substantive criminal law, for it is here that we find provisions that have lasting implications for the way in which people are allowed to live their lives. Increasingly, such provisions have come under criticism, for they reflect a supposedly shared, but in our late modern and atomistic society no longer automatically valid, social morality.

John Major's mythical golden age of warm beer, cricket and old maids on bicycles – and, it should be added, of leaving your door open, trusting your neighbour, putting the money in the box on the counter, letting the children walk to school – has gone forever. The same applies to the Netherlands, even if

[12] Cf. E.A. Nadelmann, *Cops Across Borders. The Internationalization of U.S. Criminal Law Enforcement* (University Park PA: Pennsylvania State University Press, 1993).

no Dutchman would ever long for warm beer or cricket. Here too there is said to have been a time when bicycles could be left unlocked, when football was sport not war, when most people went to church, when the red-light district of Amsterdam was a nice place to be on Saturday evening and when (a potent image, this, after the devastation of the Nazi occupation) the Dutch were concerned with social solidarity – with rebuilding their country together and then with enjoying, together, the fruits of the tolerant welfare state they had achieved.

Whether or not such apparently collective memories bear any resemblance to the realities of the past is not the point. In both countries they reflect a sense of loss of shared identity and of (moral) security. However, at the same time and despite the appeals to "citizenship" that figure in most sound-bites of the past years, few are prepared to countenance giving up their private – read: autonomous – lifestyle because some, or even a majority, in society believe it to be immoral. This has profound implications both for the social function of the criminal law and for its enforcement, for it has engendered increasing public debate (at the very least) about the legitimacy of using criminal law to regulate and if necessary enforce "private" moral choice. Yet it is in the sphere of private moral choice that some of greatest demons of crime are constructed. This is especially true of such areas as drugs (the "drugs-baron") and sexuality (the "paedophile").

Although a degree of social consensus, both national and international, appears to exist on the necessity of tackling the drugs trade, putting away the traffickers "and throwing away the key", nevertheless individual citizens wish to be free to indulge in the recreational use of drugs which, at present and in almost all of the countries of Europe, can only be obtained through the illegal drug trade (the Netherlands being an exception only with regard to soft drugs and even these not entirely). At the same time, although there is also a burgeoning consensus that citizens should not be prohibited from leading the sexual life of their choice, some forms of sexuality have given rise to what could almost be called a moral crusade.

Such contradictions are, in themselves illustrative of the fragmentation of morality in late modern society, and of the contradictory demands and fears to which it gives rise. On the one hand, people welcome both the expanding, international order and the dissipation of old moral certainties, demanding the right to use their freedom and autonomy as they see fit – including the right to withhold solidarity, not to be beholden to any one nation state or to the society in which they live and to develop their own moral convictions and norms, even if these fly in the face of what the rest consider to be moral and normal. On the other hand, there is an almost nostalgic longing for small-scale, national space, where morality, social solidarity, security and – especially – law and order are self-evident and where people are "true citizens". It is the national governments that must respond to such appeals and, increasingly it is the instrument of criminal law to which they turn.

JUSTIFICATIONS FOR STATE INTERVENTION

Broadly speaking, it is commonly thought that state intervention in common law countries is characterised by legal moralism – using the power of the state to enforce a particular moral code – and in civil law countries by paternalism – using its power to protect people from their own choices – with greater state intervention in the common law states. This observation has been made with explicit reference to the United Kingdom and the Netherlands. A second relevant distinction concerns conceptions of the relationship between the individual and the state, which is reflected in economic, social and legal arrangements. Common law cultures proceed from the notion of the "state at arms length" (and even have no legal conception of "state" as understood in continental Europe) and from a concept of autonomy as *conditio sine qua non* for the realisation of self-sufficiency and independence from the state. Civil law cultures are based on the notion of "the common good", that is to be upheld and reinforced by an essentially benevolent state and in which, for that reason, the autonomy of the individual may "disappear". There is also an important constitutional distinction: under common law, state interference, or interference by anybody else, is allowed so long as not expressly forbidden, while civil law requires an explicit basis in law for any state interference with the individual. It is to be expected that such differences will logically result in distinctive notions of the legitimacy of state interference.

The right of the state to intervene is the subject of the first two contributions to this book: *Raes* and *Roberts* both attempt to identify underlying assumptions about the nature of privacy/autonomy and state intervention from a broadly liberal approach. The perspectives of these authors however differ, in the first instance because *Raes* explicitly seeks to compare, historically and philosophically, continental Europe with the United States, while *Roberts* appears to be concerned with an abstract complex of rights, privacy and autonomy that is unrelated to specific legal systems. But the reader will discover that the perspectives of these authors differ too by virtue of the fact that their initial frame of reference derives from the value-systems of different legal cultures: that of *Roberts* from the English common law tradition, that of *Raes* from the continental (Belgian) civil law tradition.

Roberts argues for a moral right to privacy that is, in essence, an individual right to personal autonomy and that, in principle, precludes interference by the state for the purpose of sustaining the common good. While he concedes that there are justifiable reasons for state intervention that derive from the rights of others, his primary interest is in establishing the value of privacy, its nature and significance as a moral right of autonomy, and the necessity of privacy rights entrenched in law that will allow the development of specifically recognised areas of autonomous space where the state cannot interfere. *Raes*, on the other hand, takes both the value of autonomy in itself and the existence of privacy rights in law as given and is more concerned with establishing a case for a "European" egalitarian concept of autonomy, which, of necessity, implies searching inquiry into the possible justifications for state interference.

INTERNATIONALISATION AND HARMONISING TENDENCIES

In speaking of *justifiable* state interference in the private life of the autonomous individual, relating it, as we have done, to matters of substantive criminal law and assuming substantial differences between jurisdictions, we are assuming democratic structures within which state power is curtailed, regardless of the philosophical and/or constitutional basis for such curtailment. We are also assuming a sovereign nation-state with few external influences. Indeed, from an international perspective, freedom in the setting of its own criminal law is usually invoked as one of the identifying criteria of the sovereignty of the nation-state. Nonetheless, we must question whether stereotypes flowing from old models of criminal justice should be re-appraised in the light of an emerging European Union of states, and other international movements that are increasingly pushing towards the harmonisation of criminal law.

International developments

The internationalisation of criminal law and its potential for harmonisation concerns both substantive law and law enforcement procedures. At first sight it might seem that sexual crimes are not an area in which to expect international convergence, but there are two major forces militating towards their being adopted. First, the internationalisation of criminal law is strongly linked to globalisation of markets and to its expression in criminal law. This is a development that goes far beyond the enforcement of economic arrangements between states (such as the communal European market) by means of criminal law, although supra-national social-economic criminal law forms a growing body of legislation. *Alldridge* views substantive criminal law as being, increasingly, the regulation of *criminal* markets, and considers the relationship between the market and the private/public dualism. What is, when performed as a private act for reasons other than financial gain, neutral or even noble behaviour (for example, organ donation, surrogate motherhood, adoption, the "giving of oneself" in sexual encounters, helping desperate refugees to cross a border),[13] is transformed into – serious – crime when money changes hands. This is true at both a national and international level. The distinction, between,

[13] In the face of the demonisation, not only of the paedophile, but also of the international and organised trafficker in human beings that currently colours the discourse on the asylum problem, it is all too easy to forget that there are groups who actually help refugees for altruistic and/or humanitarian reasons.

on the one hand, the limits of freedom of contract, where the parties make their own rules, and on the other the assertion of privacy in excluding the state, will take on growing importance as the criminal law is directed increasingly against (globalised) markets.

Where the market in question deals in sexual tourism, generally by alleged paedophiles, it gave rise to an international movement for extraterritorial legislation.[14] In the United Kingdom the consequent legislation reversed, so far as concerned a small group of sexual offences against minors, the rule that conspiring in England and Wales to commit a crime elsewhere was no crime.[15] Two years later the rule was reversed in its entirety, using many of the same legislative expressions that had been deployed in the sexual tourism legislation.[16] In this way, sexual offences provided a "leading edge" to a wider change in notions of criminal jurisdiction. A similar movement may be discerned with regard to the "trade in human beings" that involves both women seeking work in the prostitution business and asylum seekers (the categories may overlap), and with regard to organ donation by (poor) citizens of third world countries.

The second factor pushing towards internationalisation and convergence of a substantive law of "criminal markets" is the great media coverage that such crimes command. The *Dutroux* case in Belgium, for example, commands world-wide attention (and within this framework the construction of the paedophile as demon is critical). The smuggling of asylum-seekers, the buying of babies in Romania or of kidneys in Pakistan, all lend themselves for media attention in which sensation and moral outrage about this "trade in misery" reinforce a growing trend to invoke the criminal law as an instrument of regulation of immoral markets. Law enforcement activity directed against the proceeds of crime provides the last link between the internationalisation of criminal law, on the one hand, and attacks upon privacy, on the other. It has only been in the last twenty years that international efforts have breached the legal mechanisms (banking secrecy, corporate anonymity and the lawyer-client privilege) which have been deployed to protect the profits of crime from the attention of the authorities.[17] The change in enforcement law has come about upon an international scale.

The European Union

For the countries of the European Union, of course, the effects of internationalisation are even greater. There are strong forces at work in Europe that, if not

[14] World Congress Against Commercial Sexual Exploitation of Children, Stockholm, August 1996.

[15] *Board of Trade* v *Owen* [1957] AC 602, reversed by Sexual Offences (Conspiracy and Incitement) Act 1996.

[16] Criminal Justice (Terrorism and Conspiracy) Act 1998.

[17] United Nations Convention against Illicit Traffic in Narcotic Drugs and Psychotropic Substances, Vienna 1988.

entirely undermining the notion of sovereignty in the traditional sense, at least have the potential to change it substantially. In some respects, the instrumentalist approach to crime that emanates from "Brussels", means that harmonisation is most apparent in interstate police-co-operation and criminal procedure. The areas in which these pressures are most evident are those of transnational crime. That impacts upon personal privacy because of the powers of search involved, but also because of the degree of access to financial records which is required by the existence of crimes such as money laundering. However, questions of powers of investigation and law enforcement are not our main concern, although they certainly also have implications for substantive law (if only because, for example, a common policy on fraud requires at the very least compatible criminalisation of behaviour deemed to constitute fraud). There is, however, an important preliminary question: namely whether the process of European integration could eventually provide an alternative to the state institutions of criminal law that is both viable and legitimate in terms of social and political acceptability and democratic control.

In his essay on sovereignty, criminal law and the new European context, *Besselink* examines the significance of the burgeoning European order for concepts of sovereignty and for the legitimacy of interference in the private sphere of the European citizen, both within the Member States and within the wider context of the European Union. He sees ominous developments, most especially in the expanding use of *sui generis* instruments under the third pillar that could create rights and obligations for citizens in the sphere of (national) criminal law, but that lack effective democratic control. This in itself could have a harmonising effect, for it will take a strong national government to stand up for its own national legal culture and to resist pressure from other Member States to adapt. On the other hand, there is (as yet) certainly no common EU standard of public morality, so that the legitimacy of interference in the autonomous sphere of individual citizens by national governments (by means of the criminal law, because the EU so requires) is severely curtailed. Indeed, *Besselink* doubts whether the European Union is so very different in this respect from its constituent Member States.

The European Convention on Human Rights and Fundamental Freedoms

To the extent that they do impact on privacy ("criminal market" regulation is one such area), developments within the European Union have led to expanded use of the criminal law as an instrument of (supra-national) control. The European Convention on Human Rights and Fundamental Freedoms could, however, be expected to have a restraining influence on governments, and moreover to hold them to certain basic common standards of criminal procedure and substantive criminal law. It might be thought to be a source at least of convergence, if not harmonisation in the field under consideration here – intervention by the state in the private and autonomous sphere of the individual – in the sense that it imposes limits on when and how the state may intervene.

At a general level, it is true that the European Convention and the case law of the European Court oblige the signatories to the Convention to bring their criminal justice systems into line with a number of formal requirements of what could be called a decent and democratic society, requirements that derive from the rights and freedoms the Convention guarantees. This in itself brings the legal systems of the different jurisdictions closer together. The most obvious examples are Article 1, Sixth Protocol ("the death penalty has been abolished"), Article 5 (arrest, detention and examination of the grounds thereof by an independent judge), Article 6 (fair trial) and Article 7 (no retro-active penalisation or punishment). Articles 5 and 6, which concern the criminal process with its emphasis on formal rules of procedure, have had the greatest impact.[18]

When we come to look at substantive criminal law, however, the picture is very different. The Convention itself says little about substantive law. It does however guarantee fundamental rights and freedoms that derive directly from a concept of the free and autonomous individual: Articles 8, 9, 10 and 11 (right to respect of private life, freedom of religion and conscience, freedom of expression and freedom of association, respectively) all require that the state place no restrictions in the path of the citizen in their exercise, unless these are *prescribed by law and necessary in a democratic society*. Criminalisation of behaviour is one such restriction, and in this sense Articles 8, 9, 10 and 11 are directly linked to substantive law. We will return below to the problems of differentiating between privacy and autonomy. Suffice it here to say that, while both concern the right to be one's own uninhibited self (in the words of the Dutch Supreme Court), privacy perhaps refers primarily to an "introvert self" and autonomy to an "extrovert self".

The European Court does not make that distinction and regards a right of autonomy (to develop and express all of the aspects of one's personality) as part of the right to privacy (or *vice versa* – which only goes to illustrate the extent of the lack of conceptual clarity). For the purpose of this introduction, it is however possible to bring some order to the many decisions on Article 8, most of which are concerned with the impact of interference by the state in the private sphere for reasons of criminal investigation. As the use of technological and

[18] It should be noted that the European Court does not proceed from any standard style of procedure. Although it speaks, for example, of the opportunity to challenge the evidence in adversarial proceedings, what it appears to have in mind for those countries with essentially inquisitorial systems (the great majority), is something more akin to the French *contradictoire*, and it certainly does not require that such proceedings take place in open court. Likewise, equality of arms is a concept so bound up with true adversarial procedure that the Court appears to interpret it as "no unfair disadvantage for the defence" in inquisitorial systems that, by definition, do not have any concept of equal parties in a criminal case. If this means that the harmonising influence of the Convention is less than might be expected at first sight, there are nevertheless numerous examples, from all of the different jurisdictions, where criminal procedure has been changed in order to meet its requirements.

electronic methods of surveillance and investigation gathers momentum, privacy has become an ever greater issue in the European Court. At the same time, however, there is a growing body of European case law concerning privacy in the sense of autonomy.

LIMITING THE POWER OF THE STATE?

The first and foremost harmonising influence emanating from the European Convention on Human Rights and Fundamental Freedoms is, in any event, the requirement that any invasion of privacy for a legitimate reason (for purposes of criminal investigation, usually the prevention of crime) must have a basis in law, and that law – be it case law or statute – must be of a certain quality: foreseeable (sufficiently detailed) and accessible and providing remedies for the citizen. While in civil legal systems and culture it is regarded as self-evident that interference with the individual citizen by the state requires an explicit basis in law, common law systems take the opposite view: everything is allowed unless forbidden. It will be seen, therefore, that the European Convention requires of the United Kingdom a substantial cultural *volte face*,[19] at least as far as the rules governing police powers are concerned. But the states of continental Europe too, have been required to bring their procedural rules up to the quality standards that the European Court demands.

But what if the restrictions on the right of privacy are to be found in substantive law, so that criminalisation is the obstacle to the exercise of the right to privacy and therefore not procdure but the moral basis of criminal law is the contentious issue. If interference by the state is justified by a commonly agreed criminal policy, such as exists in the shadow of the third pillar of the European Union with regard to organised crime, money laundering, migration and a number of other matters, there will be few problems with the legitimacy of far-reaching police powers (provided they meet procedural norms) or the provisions of substantive law needed in order to realise that policy. It is where a right to respect for private life is equated with an individual right of autonomy that intractable questions arise. Here, Article 8 (2) of the Convention appears to make allowances for what the European Court of Human Rights calls the "moral climate" of a given society, for it contemplates the justification of regulation by a nation state of "morals".

Now, whatever "morals" may mean in this context (and it is an exceedingly hazy concept), the protection of morals as a legitimate aim of state intervention appears not only in Article 8(2), but also in Articles 9(2), 10(2) and 11(2). In any event, it is clear that we are not only talking about sexual morality, although most such cases with which the European Court deals concern sex in some way

[19] The events from *Malone* v. *United Kingdom* (1984) 7 EHRR 14 to the Regulation of Investigatory Powers Act 2000 is a *locus classicus*.

or another (and many involve the United Kingdom – "no sex please, we're British").[20] Taken together with the other requirement, that however legitimate the aim *in abstracto*, intervention must also be necessary in a given democratic society, we must surmise that this has something to do with holding together the (moral) fabric of society, if necessary by criminalising autonomous individual behaviour that threatens it. There are any number of exceedingly problematic issues here.

In their contributions to this book *Brants*, *Bibbings* and *Swart* all address, from different perspectives aspects of the problem of restricting the freedom of one person if it runs up against the freedom of another, and the role of "majority morals" in determining which should prevail and which should be defined as causing (moral) harm and therefore as criminal. *Brants* deals explicitly with the case law of the European Court on the criminalisation of sexual behaviour. The Court has two points of departure: the first is that the concept of privacy involved here extends far further than the geographical privacy of the bedroom, to include a right to express and develop all autonomous aspects of oneself, including one's sexuality; the second is that it is nevertheless legitimate for the state to limit that right through criminalisation for reasons of public morals. The question is, when is it necessary for the state to do so in a democratic society? As *Brants* points out, by its very definition the concept of autonomy in a democratic society stands in the way of establishing criteria for answering that question. They certainly cannot be found in public morals, for the significance of autonomy in a democracy is that individuals are free to be different in all aspects of life, without reference to whether that is appropriate in terms of mainstream beliefs and values. Nevertheless, it is from the morals of the majority prevailing in the society in question that the Court derives its criteria for establishing whether criminalisation is a justifiable, because necessary, restriction.

Bibbings is concerned with the relationship between the divergent claims of cultural relativism and human rights in respect of what was formerly known as female circumcision and is now, in international instruments and in far less neutral terms, referred to as female genital mutilation. The fact that in practice the latter term is reserved exclusively for non-Western practices involving alteration of the female genitalia, embodies all of the problems of the clash between autonomy and prevailing moral discourse. She deals with one of the areas of English law which have attracted significant attention internationally – the questions arising out of the law relating to body alteration in the wake of *Laskey*. She also shows that the French approach towards female genital mutilation derives at least in part from a legal culture arising from the indivisibility of France, guaranteed in the Constitution, that leaves little room for legal recognition of ethnic difference.

[20] And for the relation between privacy and the sexual *persona* in England see P. Alldridge, *Relocating Criminal law* (Aldershot: Dartmouth, 2000) 122 *et seq*.

Both *Brants* and *Bibbings* examine more closely the question of why majority beliefs and values apparently override the significance of consent by the individuals involved in putting into practice what appear to be autonomous decisions about lifestyle. *Swart* deals with an area where consent is irrelevant, but which also concerns the exercise of individual autonomy: the right to have opinions contrary to – the received opinion on – established historical facts of the Holocaust and to express such opinions. Increasingly in Europe, this is deemed harmful both to those who experienced the Holocaust and to contemporary political and social morals. He compares the law on the criminalisation of hate-speech and more in particular of denying Shoah in several jurisdictions, ascribing the differences between the approach to free speech in the United States (first amendment jurisprudence) and in a number of European countries, to the revolutionary, republican beginnings of American democracy. These are still traceable in the seminal decisions under the Warren Court. While Swart's preferred rules for Europe would be those of the US, he questions whether there is anything in the history of European countries that stands in the way of such a solution. The cases he discusses suggest that there is: collective memory of the Holocaust has left Europe singularly sensitive to the denial of Shoah, but it is a sensitivity that may, in the end, prove counterproductive.[21]

CRIMINAL LAW AS A SOLUTION FOR SOCIAL PROBLEMS

From the previous paragraph we may conclude that holding together the moral fabric of society is not only a sociological assumption with regard to the function of criminal law, but also, in human rights law, a legal justification for using it to intervene in the private sphere. This in its turn presupposes a certain instrumentalist notion of criminal law: namely that criminalisation, prosecution and punishment, with their attendant stigmatisation and possibilities of retribution and re-socialisation, will somehow prevent the collapse of a coherent society (or restore social coherence) and are in a sense the ultimate solution for social problems. It also implies that the "seamless web" can be identified and protected,[22] as we have seen, an increasingly difficult proposition in contemporary pluriform and multicultural society.

Where criminal law interferes with the private lives of autonomous individuals, a certain paradox arises when we look at the legal systems and culture of civil law states and common law states. In the latter, we find on the one hand, greater hostility to the state and scepticism of its right to interfere in the lives of

[21] The issue arose in the English libel trial *Irving v. Lipstadt* (2000), concerning the account of Irving in Deborah Lipstadt, *Denying the Holocaust* (New York City, NY: Free Press, 1993).

[22] And compare Dworkin's remark that what is shocking about Devlin's position is not that public morality counts but what counts as public morality (in Devlin's position, the criminal sanction can legitimately be imposed where reasonable people are "driven to feelings of intolerance, indignation and disgust", Ronald Dworkin, "Lord Devlin and the Enforcement of Morals" (1966) 75 *Yale Law Journal* 986.

individuals. Yet, on the other hand, it is in the "arm's length" state that greater intervention through the use of criminal law in the private sphere is usually to be found. Can it be that the "arm's length" state relies upon criminal law not only because of a different conception of (the relationship between the individual and) the state and the resulting absence of legal-theoretical barriers to state interference, but because it lacks, for precisely that reason, other, more subtle, mechanisms of intervention? And can it also be that, as the nation state declines (albeit slowly) in importance, as individuals redefine their relationship to state and society and demand greater autonomy in their own lives and yet more intervention by the state in the autonomous lives of others, the significance of those other mechanisms of intervention will also decline?

The Netherlands is often cited as a prime example of the paternalistic but essentially liberal state, where social control relies on a subtly enforced (moral) consensus by other means than the criminal law; and where the result is a tolerant society that is relatively relaxed about all things moral (drugs, sex, sexual preference, euthanasia, indeed, crime in general). In her contribution on the historic roots of criminal law and non-intervention in the Netherlands, *Pelser* traces the foundations of this approach to the essentially liberal (in the continental sense of the word) philosophy of the Dutch bourgeois *élite* who first drew up the Dutch Criminal Code, that is still in force today. Throughout the first half of the twentieth century, the same philosophy was to be found in the theoretical writings of legal scholars. Willem Pompe, professor of law at Utrecht University from 1928–1963, needed only ten words to describe the essence of morality and law: "morality is concerned with good people, law with good society". This would seem to be describing the difference between law and morality, but a closer look at Pompe's work reveals that he saw them as two sides of the same coin. The state must promote good society, among other things by enforcing criminal law. However, because criminal law implies curtailment of freedom while man is a free and autonomous being and freedom is the basis of good society, the state itself is curtailed by the rules of criminal procedure. This is a classic, continental concept of *Rechtstaat*, that is firmly rooted in Enlightenment philosophy. But it is a concept that is based on two implicit and interrelated assumptions. The first is a substantive concept of law, based on a system of shared values and beliefs. Here, law is very close to morality, or even synonymous with it: only norms of "good substance" can be accepted as law and as binding upon individuals. At the same time, this is precisely what gives the state the "right" to enforce them. The second assumption is that there is a shared and generally valid morality to which the good person in the good society considers himself bound as a matter of course, so that the need to enforce the criminal law must and always will be an exception.

This notion of a moral *Rechtstaat* is still reflected in the rules of Dutch criminal procedure, where the Public Prosecutor is required to combine a magistrate's impartiality with the mentality of an inquisitorial investigator and is, to that end, invested with supreme discretionary power to use or not use the criminal law, but in any event to use it sparingly – as an *ultimum remedium* – and always in accordance with procedural rules. At the same time, Dutch socio-political conditions were, again until the 1960s, extremely well suited to a legal philosophy of the shared moral foundation of criminal law and they reinforced a shared perception of there being no great need to use it.

Pelser draws attention, as others have done, to the politico-social arrangements in the Netherlands known as pillarisation, and their pervasive effect on all important, social, political and legal components of Dutch society. In political terms, the essence of pillarisation can be grasped in the terms compromise and consensus: Dutch society was a politically and religiously pluriform society, but one governed by the élite from the four main pillars (Protestant, Catholic, Socialist and Liberal), each with the same, very definite, stake in preventing social unrest and class struggle, and ensuring pacification of the "members" of divergent and internally cohesive segments of society.[23] This in its turn required flexible solutions to social problems (such as crime) that are less divisive and conflictual than criminal justice. For the implicit acknowledgement that criminal justice cannot solve social problems requires a flexible and pragmatic approach to rules and regulations and an attendant ideology that criminal law and criminal law enforcement should be the last resort.

The decline and relatively swift dismantling of pillarised society as such, and with it the breakdown of traditional values and informal modes of social control, have formed the lasting legacy of the turbulent years of the 1960s. Yet, as *Kelk*'s article on the significance of consent in Dutch criminal law shows, there is still much of the old philosophy around. There is, for example, a marked reluctance actually to decriminalise behaviour through legislation, especially where the legislative process would entail political discord and conflict, and *Kelk* discusses this at some length in relation to the issue of euthanasia. The preferred course of action is often still to rely on the wide discretionary powers of the public prosecution service and, in its wake, the police to refrain from prosecution and/or to look for alternative means of dealing with deviance. This allows for flexible policies on crime, adapted to the needs of the times, without having to take (irrevocable) legislative measures. It also explains the Dutch habit, so irritating and baffling to neighbouring countries, of not prosecuting a substantial number offences that are regarded as typically criminal matters elsewhere (drugs and euthanasia being prime examples), but rather of seeking alternative methods of regulation and control.

Gradually, however, the great changes implicit in a globalised world of unlimited information, in the unification and extension of Europe, in an increasing immigrant population, have led to irrevocable changes in Dutch society and in Dutch (thinking about) criminal law. And perhaps only now, has the

[23] See, for a comprehensive outline of pillarisation, the classic work by A. Lijphart, *The Politics of Accommodation* (2nd. rev. edn., Berkley and Los Angeles CA: University of California Press, 1975); and see also R. Andeweg, R. B. and G.A. Irwin, *Dutch Government and Politics* (London: Macmillan, 1993).

disappearance of the regulating capacity of pillarisation and (in the 1970s) of the benevolent welfare state, truly made itself felt. *Moerings* shows how substantive law in the Netherlands on the involvement of children and young people in sexual activity is gradually changing as a result of both international pressure and moral insecurity: harsher penalties, the demonisation of the paedophile, changes in the age of consent, a severe crackdown on child pornography, "moral panics" about children abusing children, all are now part of both common sense consciousness, political manoeuvring and new legislative measures or proposals. The classic criterion of "harm", in any sense, to the children concerned seems to have fallen by the wayside. Ministers of Justice and politicians speak explicitly of moral harm to the community, and this applies not only to children and sex, but to many areas with which the criminal law, increasingly, is concerned.

Unlike the Netherlands, the history of criminalisation in England and Wales cannot be said to have a consistent underlying premise as to the function of criminal law in society and the role of the state in using it when all else fails. Much legislation was, and still is, enacted on a "There oughta be a law . . ." basis[24] and little thought is given to possible alternatives. Consequently, the identification and definition of (new forms of) immorality are easily translated in terms of the protection of society against risky individuals by means of criminal law, harsher punishment, greater stigmatisation, etc.

Collier describes the way in which the paedophile was constructed as a demon in the domestic politico-legal discourse of the United Kingdom, by reference to a whole series of events centred around Cooke. The treatment of the paedophile in this manner is described in terms of the modernised theory of "moral panic", highlighting the particularly significant role of the media. At the same time, *Collier* draws attention to another lost mythical age, when children were children, and men were men and neither role within the nuclear family was confused or fraught with unknown danger. As with *Bibbings*' essay, confronting the cases which are more intuitively problematic than the laws upon whose (un)justifiability there is widespread agreement, gives insight into the relation between changing cultures and privacy.

Throughout the late twentieth century history of criminal legislation in almost all Western jurisdictions, two kinds of arguments resound, that are typical of the way in which criminal law has developed in many areas. The first hold that drugs offences, or terrorism offences, or offences involving organised crime, or paedophilia, are graver by an order of magnitude than any other category of offence and consequently that they require differential treatment, with more intrusive enforcement powers, reversed burdens of proof, higher penalties and so on. The second hold that other offences are very serious too and that it is important that they be treated as equivalent to drugs offences or terrorism

[24] The Prevention of Female Circumcision Act 1985 is such a piece of legislation, as is the Human Organ Transplant Act 1989 (and see, respectively, Bibbings and Alldridge, *infra*.

offences, or offences involving organised crime or whatever happens to be flavour of the week. The first set of arguments has typically been deployed to secure a breach in some liberal dam or other so far as concerns a selected offence, or enforcement power, and the second to bring all other offences to an equivalent position. In this way, the introduction of the paedophile panic influences two areas of legal development with a profound impact on privacy. The first is the maintenance and publication of registers of convicted persons. Until the development of searchable databases there were many forms of evidence – fingerprints are one – which were only useful once there was a suspect. The development of searchable databases and of the Internet will increase the amount of information that it is possible to accumulate and disseminate about an individual. The second is the internationalisation of enforcement, through putting in place provision for extra-territorial jurisdiction, for mutual assistance and recognition and in other ways for breaking down barriers between nation-states.

Although they highlight different aspects, both *Collier* and *Moerings* show the encroachment of criminal law on everyday existence in, and on attitudes towards, what most people regard as their most private sphere: their intimate personal development and relational/family life, and the well-being of their children. From other contributions we may learn that this encroachment is by no means limited to paedophilia or even to sexual matters. Criminalisation was always an easy option in the UK and is certainly no longer the last resort in the Netherlands. In both countries, it is frequently and with increasing ease justified both in government policy and in the media, as a means of holding citizens to their duties to society, of confirming the norms we take seriously, of promoting and eventually attaining "social cohesion" (a term that has started to creep into policy documents and invitations to apply for research grants),[25] and of protecting society from an increasing number of identifiable evils and risks, regardless of the consequences to both (potential) perpetrators and supposed or real victims. And regardless of whether the criminal law is actually capable of performing these functions. For, beyond the reiteration of instrumentalist ideology and populist notions of protecting and avenging the victim, there is no longer a coherent philosophy of criminal law upon which to found such sweeping statements. There is only the great paradox: there is no such thing as society, but woe betide whoever find themselves excluded from it.

WHY IS PRIVACY SUCH A WEAK RIGHT?

In conclusion, we must turn to another issue that runs through the contributions to this volume: in cases of conflicting rights and interests, it is the right of

[25] Nils Jareborg, "What kind of Criminal Law do we want?" (1995) 14 *Scandinavian Studies in Criminology* 17.

privacy that almost always gives way. It has become trite to announce that the problem with the right to privacy is not so much in locating it (which is not without difficulty), but in its lack of purchase.[26] When it comes into conflict with other widely recognised claims, whether based on individual rights (such as those deriving from freedom of speech), or dealing with a claim on behalf of the collectivity (typically criminal justice enforcement) privacy seldom prevails. The explanation for the apparent weakness of privacy rights is to be found in three areas – the equation of privacy with autonomy; the sorts of harm which are done by the violations of privacy which attract most attention; and the sorts of reasons which are held to be sufficient countervailing reasons to overcome a claim of privacy.

Where privacy in *substantive* criminal law (the law of criminal prohibitions) is under consideration, the question is whether the citizen has a *liberty* to behave in the manner proposed or a duty not so to behave. If s/he is prohibited from doing something which s/he wants to do there is a diminution in his/her freedom. The classical liberal position of J.S. Mill is that, so long as others are not affected, there is no right for the state to interfere. The private is frequently adopted as the model of the space where none but the willing participant is affected. Interference by the state in the private impacts upon self-fulfilment, and has undesirable long-term effects, whether or not its injunctions are obeyed. When, on the other hand, we talk of privacy in *procedural* criminal law what is generally in issue is an *immunity* – the asserted right of the accused person not to have particular things done to him/her as against a claimed power for representatives of the state to do them. There is an overlap between these cases and those dealing with the exclusion of evidence in order to discipline the police, or to preserve the rights of the citizen.[27] The immunity is almost always qualified, so that privacy claims during criminal investigation are seldom indefeasible (the lawyer-client privilege providing an interesting exception).

A question that will legitimately arise is as to the relationship between the two types of invasions of privacy (invasion by prohibition and invasion by enforcement mechanism) and the strength of their respective justifications. With arguments about evidence-gathering techniques, the question is to do with process-values, and the usual approach is to say that the more serious the invasion of the privacy, autonomy or dignity of the defendant, the higher the degree of formal scrutiny which is required before it can be invaded. There are some invasions which can be undertaken by anyone, some only by police officers, some which can be authorised only by senior police officers, and some invasions which require orders from magistrates, or by more senior judges. There are some invasions that cannot be made under compulsion, but from the defendant's refusal to be invaded can be drawn adverse inferences. Whether or not the additional constraints provide substantial checks or easily surmounted formal

[26] For a fuller exposition see P. Alldridge, *supra* n 24, 122 *et seq*.

[27] Andrew Ashworth, "Excluding Evidence as Protecting Rights" [1977] *Criminal Law Review* 723.

obstacles is not here in point: what is of concern is the value expressed by having such a body of rules.

In determining whether or not to authorise, permit or institute a particular violation of privacy, one important consideration is how serious an intrusion is made. Underlying the movement from physical to psychological accounts of privacy is a changing notion of what are to count as breaches of privacy rights, and what are to be their respective seriousness. In making this evaluation it might be possible to construct a model of the seriousness of an invasion of privacy. Jareborg and von Hirsch have constructed a "living standard" analysis for the gauging of criminal harms.[28] Employing the same kind of approach one could attempt to construct broad guidelines as to the degree of intrusion that is generated by a particular invasion of privacy. Inconvenience, embarrassment, pain and duration might all be important indices of the seriousness of invasions of privacy. Consider the following table:

Area of law involved	Typical case	Duration	Impact
Substantive law	Creation of "victimless crimes",restrictions upon absolute proprietary rights	Indefinite	Lifestyle alteration/constant fear
Proactive procedural law	Targeted surveillance	Finite	Variable
Reactive procedural law	Search	"One shot"	Isolated unpleasantness
Information storage and retrieval law	Database compilation/ financial monitoring	Indefinite	Pervasive

One of the reasons why privacy might be considered a weak(ish) right is that the focus of the literature on the right to privacy in criminal justice contexts has been largely on the second and third cases. The effect of a single search – even an intimate search – may not be too serious when compared with an interference with lifestyle that lasts far longer. Successive stops, searches or arrests may amount to a campaign of harassment, but that simply raises issues about their legality and legitimacy. Targeted surveillance that is unknown to the suspect, causes no direct interference with his/her lifestyle. Even the knowledge that at any given time the police might be engaged in targeted surveillance is not something which need impact tremendously upon the suspect's enjoyment of life. It is the endurance of the invasion that bears upon the seriousness of the invasion

[28] N. Jareborg and A. von Hirsch, "Gauging Criminal Harm: a Living-Standards Analysis" 11 *Oxford Journal of Legal Studies* 1.

far more than any transient indignity.[29] However strong the claim is that the kinds of police powers which would be necessary to enforce a policy of criminalisation of drugs are intrusive and unpleasant, even in this area it is the lifestyle impact which the legislation has upon the people both who obey and who do not that is the more significant issue. It is therefore critically important that the European Convention on Human Rights should generate examination of substantive as well as procedural law. Similarly emphasis in the US federal courts upon the notion of privacy[30] in the procedural cases compared with its slight and probably diminishing[31] influence in the substantive law cases is difficult to defend.

Thirdly, a distinction between information and autonomy rights generates different strengths in the claims of privacy which are made. The claim made by a person aggrieved in a system protecting a right of privacy focused upon information is "Mind your own business", "Don't be so nosey" or somesuch. The claim from autonomy is of a different moral order altogether. It is "Do not interfere with my exercise of my liberty". Surveillance of which the subject is aware is an inhibitor of action: but it is only an inhibitor, not a prohibitor. Again the argument is that by concentrating upon invasions of privacy which only indirectly impinge upon personal freedoms, the violation can be made to seem less serious.

In some ways autonomy, broadly defined, is not an enforceable right in any useful sense. It is the basis of all fundamental rights – namely to be able to behave and to be treated with the dignity that goes with being human, whatever one is, it is that self that commands respect. This underlies all of the rights of the European Convention. Privacy, freedom of expression etc., are the part-expression of this in positive law, for those situations in which the autonomous individual finds him or herself in the context of society. Then, the autonomy rights of one may clash with those of the other and one will give way. Given that it is the social context that will decide which right has the stronger claim, it must follow that many autonomy claims are unenforceable and privacy rights are weak.

Indeed, in those cases of claims of privacy that are rooted in autonomy, the very notion of autonomy is ambiguous, for in considering privacy in terms of autonomy we immediately run up against a preliminary question: what is the nature of the self to which autonomy is granted? Is it to be a socialised or an unsocialised self? The European Court of Human Rights is most definite: protection of autonomy rights is restricted to the socialised self. The debate surrounding the anonymity of Internet use is of particular interest to this issue, precisely because it is partly a debate about autonomy and the freedom to escape

[29] This is not to suggest that body cavity searches are trivial, or should be countenanced otherwise than with pressing grounds.

[30] William J. Stuntz (1995), "Privacy's Problem and the Law of Criminal Procedure" 93 *Michigan Law Review* 1016.

[31] *Bowers* v. *Hardwick* (1986) 478 US 186.

from the limits of social normalcy. Those who advocate protection for total anonymity in Internet access argue that only thus is "uninhibited" self to be given full rein. This is the self for whom the Dutch Supreme Court claims to seek vindication, but at the same time the ultimate freedom to be oneself that the virtual society of Internet could provide, is not what the Supreme Court has in mind for real Dutch society. In frequent references to what the majority of the Dutch population regard as immoral or to "the changing climate of public opinion", it recognises claims to personal autonomy in pornography, drugs and euthanasia cases for example, only insofar as a majority of the Dutch population accept that these are private spheres where autonomous decisions are legitimate. A law which only recognises the autonomy of the socialised self still asserts control, for reasons of paternalism, authoritarianism or moralism, but makes socialisation the principal mechanism of its instantiation.

1

Legal Moralism or Paternalism? Tolerance or Indifference? Egalitarian Justice and the Ethics of Equal Concern

KOEN RAES

1. USUAL PREJUDICES

DURING A STAY in the United States, in August 1998, I was once again struck by the huge number of homeless people I encountered in the streets and parks of any of the great cities I visited. Although the amount of people without a permanent shelter is growing in Europe as well, there is nevertheless a significant difference between both Western cultures in the way these people are treated by the state and by their fellow citizens. First, in most European countries, sleeping on the streets or in parks is simply forbidden as a criminal offence, while, for a long period of time being a vagabond itself was considered a crime.[1] Second, it is recognised as a primary duty of the state – and the towns – to provide shelter to homeless people. In the United States, people have the right to sleep in public places, while taking care of the homeless is, for the greatest part, a task performed by charity organisations. In public opinion, homelessness is mainly considered a choice, or at least a consequence of personal choice. It is a dimension of freedom, the freedom to be left alone, and to leave alone. Similarly, the "right to beg" is in American case law widely accepted as a fundamental dimension of freedom, while in many European countries, begging is a conditional right, in the sense that the towns may promulgate decrees to restrict begging (to certain streets, to certain periods of time, only with a licence etc.)

Different conceptions of what a state is and what its tasks are, as well as different conceptions of personal autonomy, are at the roots of these different approaches to homelessness.

[1] In Belgium, vagabondry ceased to be a criminal offence upon the introduction of a guaranteed national minimum income, which, at least legally, abolished the category of citizens without means of existence.

The fact that notions of personal autonomy and of privacy have widely divergent meanings and value in different cultures and in different periods of time, has been widely documented.[2] But let us here focus on differences between the Anglo-American "common law" and continental European systems. In both of these cultures personal autonomy and privacy are highly valued, yet they have rather different cultural meanings and implications in discourses about the relationship between the individual, society and the state, which resurface in differences between legal cultures as well. In sociological terms, American society is defined in terms of the predominance of utilitarian and expressive individualism,[3] while in continental Europe utilitarian individualism is for the greatest part a "second language" within a framework of thought that is largely collectivistic and egalitarian,[4] although more so in Catholic than in Protestant regions. In Europe, the concept of personal autonomy is therefore integrally related to the concept of egalitarian citizenship, while in the United States a libertarian concept of citizenship seems to be the primary point of reference.

Philosophically, Europeans seem to be the heirs of a Kantian approach to personal autonomy, with a focus on protection, while Mill's approach with its focus on self-determination is much more canonical in common law countries. While the latter consider personal autonomy as a fact about individuals in terms of a (negative) freedom-right, the former see it rather as an aim to be realised in terms of a right to protection of personal integrity, as a personality-right. In a sense, these differences can also be defined in terms of the two models of autonomy (more or less resembling Berlin's distinction between negative and positive liberty)[5] which Faden and Beauchamp[6] developed. According to the first model, the so-called "model of authenticity", an autonomous person is a being who has his life in his own hands, acts rationally, consistently and independently and is motivated by proper values and norms: he is able to control situations and to resist external power and hidden persuaders. According to the second model, the "model of liberty", persons are supposed to be autonomous and this imposes a prima facie requirement that we should not control the choices and actions of others, except when they harm others.

The first model sees personal autonomy as an ideal and will therefore more easily accept that we should not respect (a) irrational acts; (b) acts based on weakness of will; (c) acts based on wrong information ("erroneous preferences"); or (d) acts based on coerced, manipulated or even adaptive preferences.

[2] Barrington Moore Jr., *Privacy. Studies in social and cultural history* (New York City NY: Sharpe, 1984).

[3] Robert Bellah *et al.*, *Habits of the hearth: Individualism and commitment in American life* (New York City, NY: Harper & Row, 1986).

[4] M. Elchardus and A. Derks, "The consequences of individualistic challenges in a collectivistic culture" in Bart Pattyn (ed.), *Courageous or indifferent individualism* (Politeia Conference, May 1998, KUL, Leuven) 31–57.

[5] Isaiah Berlin, "Positive and Negative Liberty" in *Four Essays on Liberty* (Oxford: Oxford University Press, 1969).

[6] Ruth Faden and Tom Beauchamp, *A history and theory of informed consent* (Oxford: Oxford University Press, 1986).

State intervention, that is, is accepted in as far as it contributes to the development of an autonomous person and protects individuals against their powerlessness, poverty, irrationality etc. The ideal of personal autonomy is a "regulative idea" rather than an *a priori* norm.

Elements of the two models can be discerned in common law countries as well as in continental European countries. Yet they differ in the emphasis which is given either to personal autonomy as an ideal or as a *prima facie* norm. Thus the protection of labourers, women, consumers etc. is much more easily seen as *deriving from* the right to protection of personal autonomy, rather than as contradicting personal autonomy as a freedom-right. To give an example: the right to protection of motherhood in labour law is in Europe generally accepted, while it remains in the United States a highly debated issue (even in feminist circles): first, because it is a "special right" (contravening equal treatment by the law) and second, because pregnancy is considered as a personal autonomous choice, which should not give rise to special treatment.

That common law countries consider personal autonomy as a *prima facie* norm, does not mean that there is no ideal behind the concept. In the United States, personal autonomy means independence, the realisation of self sufficiency, Aristotelian *autarchia*, as it is evoked in the works, for instance, of Ayn Rand. Dependency is considered intrinsically wrong: it is better to be poor but independent than rich but "in slavery" (as, characteristically, socialism is for many libertarian Americans for whom even taxation by the state is already an expression of slavery). It is this over-emphasis on autonomy-as-autarchy which lies at the heart of recent communitarian critiques of liberalism[7] and of individual "rights discourse", as it is understood in terms of "individual rights against the rest of the world".[8]

The "embedded self" of communitarianism is much more common to European (legal) culture. *Inter*-dependence, not *in*dependence, is the central point of reference, while personal autonomy implies protection against abuse of power and abuse of dependency. Thus, welfare rights are not considered as rights installing dependencies of citizens from the state, but as rights, protecting citizens from abuse of (economic) power and from exploitation. Abuse of power and exploitation are an intrinsic wrong: it is better to be protected by the state (by means, for instance, of unemployment benefits) than to be the plaything of power holders (in consequence of lack of minimum income). State interference with the distribution of socio-economic goods is not seen as contradicting the requirement of ideological state-neutrality. It is, on the contrary, seen as

[7] Amitai Etzioni, *The spirit of community. The reinvention of American society* (New York City, NY: Simon & Schuster, 1993); Michael Sandel, *Liberalism and the limits of justice* (Cambridge: Cambridge University Press, 1983); Charles Taylor, *Sources of the Self. The Making of Modern Identity* (Cambridge: Cambridge University Press, 1989) Philip Selznick, *The Moral Commonwealth. Social theory and the promise of community* (Berkeley, CA: University of California Press, 1992).

[8] Mary Ann Glendon, *Rights talk. The impoverishment of political discourse* (New York City, NY: The Free Press, 1991).

essential to it: neutrality requires some basic socio-economic equality and a state that did not interfere in socio-economic conditions, would not be considered impartial, but a very partial state indeed.

Now all these remarks are more or less inspired by intuitions. In what follows I will try to argue in favour of the "European" egalitarian concept of personal autonomy and state neutrality. I will further mainly focus on the problem of legitimate state-paternalism, as discussions on impartiality extend beyond discussions on the morality of state action, to encompass conceptions of "the moral point of view" in a more general (though not integral) way. It is a fundamental characteristic of states that they may threaten or make use of coercive means to enforce compliance with their rules. Particularly this characteristic is essential to understand the very nature of the "neutrality" that is or should be required of modern states.

2. TOLERANCE, PERMISSIVENESS, INDIFFERENCE

The attitudes of Americans toward the homeless, may, from a European point of view appear to be clear signs of indifference, of a lack of care for the poor and the weak. Many Americans, on the contrary, see it as evidence of their tolerance for various ways of life, be it as a beggar on the streets. Now it is one of the characteristics of our times that in discourses – by politicians, public opinion leaders but also social scientists – at this juncture, tolerance is increasingly confused with permissiveness and with indifference. This is a crucial mistake. Thus the European Value Research makes use of a so-called permissiveness-index to measure changing value orientations.[9] It has quiet surprising "indicators" in its questionnaires. As far as "public ethics" are concerned, reference is made to (acceptance of) joyriding, drugs, political murder, threatening non-striking workers, throwing rubbish in public places, driving under the influence of alcohol, buying something which you know has been stolen, not declaring damage done to a parked car, accepting bribes, not paying on public transportation, fighting against the police, lying out of self-interest, evading taxation, applying for social benefits you are not entitled to and not giving back money you found on the street. A surprising list, but it becomes even more so, when we look at the indicators used to measure "permissiveness" as far as "personal ethics" are concerned. Here we find: acceptance of suicide, prostitution, adultery, homosexuality, sexual activity under the age of consent, abortion, euthanasia, divorce and killing out of self-defence. It will be clear that catholic morality is at the roots of these indicators and they are therefore not so innocent. For such a list confuses (on purpose?) three kinds of attitudes. The first attitude is permissiveness towards actions that are of no moral importance (for instance sexual activity under the age of eighteen or the use of illegal drugs). In this sense our culture has

[9] Kerkhofs J. *et al.*, *De versnelde ommekeer* (Tielt: Lannoo, 1992).

become much more "permissive" concerning sexuality, in the sense that all kinds of sexual variations between consenting persons are as such no longer considered an ethical issue. The second attitude is permissiveness towards actions that *are* morally important, but to which, on occasion, one turns a blind eye: it is not nice, nor, however, is it very important. The third attitude is tolerance for actions that are of moral importance, out of respect for the other person. Only this last attitude is really a *moral* attitude. While permissiveness derives from indifference, tolerance derives from a moral norm: the norm of equal respect. Tolerance does not imply respect for the ideas or choices of a person (one has the right to ridicule them). It requires only respect for the persons as free human beings who have the right to make choices.

It is problematic nowadays that a society where institutions are largely based on tolerance, on the norm of equal respect, may be the soil for persons who no longer see see any difference between tolerance and permissiveness, between a moral and an amoral attitude. As a consequence, tolerance itself may be seen as a sign of growing moral indifference. This is highly problematical, for, as sociological research has shown, indifferent persons are often fundamentally intolerant, if their freedom is limited for the sake of guaranteeing equal respect for all.[10]

For this reason, it is important to argue again the case for tolerance and – thus – for neutrality of the state, certainly in light of the fact that many communitarians also seem to confuse tolerance with permissiveness/indifference. I will do so from an egalitarian conception of social justice that is, in my view, the only consistent interpretation of the idea of tolerance and political neutrality.

3. THE NORM OF EQUAL CONCERN AND THE PROBLEM OF IMPLEMENTATION

A consistent ("European") egalitarian is confronted with the question of the legitimate means to implement the norm of equal concern. For however sophisticated his concept of equality may be, he has to answer the question how far a government may go in realising an ethics of equality, more particularly how far state intervention in the private sphere is accepted if this is required to realise egalitarian aims. This is both a question about effective and about legitimate means, in the sense that an egalitarian ideal cannot give a licence to the state to intervene in social life by whatever means it has at its disposal for it may be that such means are either counter-effective or illegitimate.

Ideals of equality that are highly person- and context-related – such as Arneson's equality of welfare[11] or Sen's equality of capability[12] – raise questions

[10] Mark Elchardus and Anton Derks, "The consequences of individualistic challenges in a collectivistic culture", *supra* n 4, 31–57.

[11] R. Arneson, "Equality and equality of opportunity for welfare" (1987) *Philosophical Studies* 56.

[12] Amartya Sen, *Inequality Reexamined* (Oxford: Clarendon Press, 1992).

about: how to gather the relevant information; who should or may gather this information; how to control the implementation of the relevant criteria; and who may or should control this implementation. One of the reasons to prefer rather simple egalitarian rules – such as "equality of income", "equality of primary social goods" or "equality of resources" – could be that, although they do not take account of all morally relevant information, they are better suited as *political* conceptions of justice because they do not rely upon very demanding, perhaps impossible and morally indefensible, methods of information gathering.

There exists an unbridgeable gap between moral conceptions of justice and political or legal ones, a gap that may be understood in terms of neutrality as well: there are limits to what political bodies may legitimately ask from persons, just as there are limits to legitimate state intervention. Even if some information would make the relevant rules more just, it may well be that what is required to find the reliable information for a just application of these rules is unjustifiable. This is not to say that all public rules of justice should be abstract and very general even if this results in grave injustices. It is to say that there are limits to what a "blindfolded Justitia" is allowed to take into consideration and that there is a field which is not the law's business, even though interference within this field would result in a more encompassing application of the rules of equal justice. The eventuality that particular applications of a rule result in deviations from the ideal of equal concern – either in the sense that somebody receives not enough or too much of a relevant good – is in itself no reason to reject the rule, if alternatives to it would imply, if generally applied, graver interference with people's lives or a greater waste of available means.

It is, admittedly, difficult to assess the precise implications of this remark. As is well known, it is central to many libertarian criticisms of governmental interference *per se*, from Nozick's paradigmatic Wilt Chamberlain[13] until the most horrible scenarios of Big Brother watching us all. One may easily get rid of most apocalyptic sketches of egalitarian totalitarianism, but nevertheless, the question of how to realise an ideal of equal justice, which takes account of all relevant aspects of unjust inequality, remains a pressing one. Exactly for this reason, the problem of the limits of state paternalism is integrally related to the problem of how to realise conditions of equal concern.

It should be emphasised that the scope of the discussions treated in this essay is limited in a way that is difficult to justify. For it starts from the assumption that we already know who are the members of the relevant society, to which principles of political justice apply. All arguments, that is, are derived *from*

[13] Robert Nozick, *Anarchy, State and Utopia* (New York City, NY: The Free Press, 1974) 160–4. The general idea is that any "patterned" idea of justice requires permanent interferences with people's lives in order to maintain the "just" pattern. If individuals receive, through personal initiative, more income or wealth than the just pattern accepts, these concepts of justice require either that individuals should not have the right to develop such initiatives or that all income above the just pattern should be taken away from them.

membership and the question which arguments should count as arguments *for* membership is not taken into consideration.[14] Even a superficial view on recent migration on a world scale amply illustrates that this is a very limited approach to the problem of equal justice and political neutrality and, perhaps, the problem of how to apply conceptions of neutrality in the case of refugees, asylum seekers and migrants is much more integrally related to the problem of what the morality of the "impartial point of view" exactly means, than what is taken into consideration here.

4. POLITICAL NEUTRALITY AND THE ENFORCEMENT OF MORALS

4.1. The classic liberal approach

The question of the legitimate reasons to use force was already central in the nineteenth century debate between the views which John Stuart Mill defended in his *On Liberty*[15] and James Fitzjames Stephen's views in *Liberty, Equality, Fraternity*[16] on the legitimacy of state interference. A hundred years later, the debate was reprised by Herbert Hart and Lord Devlin, on the occasion of the publication, in 1957, of the Wolfenden Report.[17] According to this report, it is not the duty of the law to concern itself with immorality as such and there must remain a realm of private morality and immorality which is "not the law's business".[18] A distinction should be made between "immoralities that implicate public interests" and "immoralities that are merely private". Whether an act is a matter of public concern depends on whether it is in itself likely to damage the legitimate interests of third (non-consenting) parties. If it does not, the question of whether the act is "immoral" is irrelevant from the point of view of the criminal law: it is a private act and thus not the law's business. Victimless "crimes" or "immoralities" should not be the concern of the criminal law.

In his debate with Devlin, Hart was a firm defender of this liberal approach to "the proper sphere of the law".[19] Central to this approach is that there are limits to what state power may legitimately enforce. The alleged fact that an act is "immoral" is not sufficient to justify the use of force to prohibit it. It should also be harmful to the legitimate interests of others. People have, that is, a legal right to do (what others consider to be a) moral wrong. What is more, the problem of harm is prior to the problem of an act being immoral or not, for in

[14] Gerald Postema, "Equality as membership" (1990) 19 *Rechtsfilosofie en Rechtstheorie* 155.

[15] John Stuart Mill, *On Liberty* (1859) (Harmondsworth: Penguin, 1971).

[16] James Fitzjames Stephen, *Liberty, Equality, Fraternity, edited with an introduction and notes by R.J. White* (Cambridge: Cambridge University Press, 1967).

[17] John Wolfenden (Chair) *Report of the Committee on Homosexual Offences and Prostitution*, Cmnd 247 (1957) Robert P. George, *Making Men Moral. Civil Liberties and Public Morality* (Oxford: Clarendon Press, 1995) 48–82.

[18] Wolfenden Report, *op. cit.* paras. 61 and 62.

[19] H.L.A. Hart, *Law, Liberty and Morality* (Oxford: Oxford University Press, 1963).

a pluralist society, opinions may diverge on this issue. An act may be harmful, while some may well consider it to be morally right. Central to the liberal (and, in the case of Hart, also utilitarian) approach to "public morality" or "the morality of the rule of law" is not an intrinsic moral valuation of what is right or wrong, but a valuation of acts in terms of their (harmful) consequences for others.[20]

Although this position appears to be clear enough, it nevertheless begs the question of what will be considered "harmful". Central in the classical liberal tradition is the notion of (informed) consent. No harm to a person is done if this person freely agreed with the act. Crude capitalist exploitation could thus be justified in as far as the labour contract was viewed as a free agreement.

That informed consent is not always the final arbiter in defining "personal boundaries" and "harm to others" may nowadays be illustrated by the fact that sharp debates are going on about such issues as surrogate motherhood and organ donation on the one hand and about sado-masochism and midget-tossing "between consenting adults" on the other. While in these former cases, the major reason for making reservations seems to be the presumption that inequalities in power may bias what is considered a "fair" informed consent, the latter cases seem to presume some notion of "human dignity". Thus a Dutch court decided that whether midgets accepted their being tossed as objects in a game, was totally irrelevant: it is against human dignity to do this with human beings, in the same way as it is against human dignity to exploit or discriminate them. Similarly, a Belgian and a British court argued that some sado-masochistic acts, with or without the consent of the victim, should not be allowed as being contrary to human dignity.

To say the least, notions of human dignity are seriously flawed and may be used as "container-concepts" that may moralise and put under the control of the state lots of human activities. For long periods of time, any form of sexual intercourse that was not between married persons, oriented to procreation and taking place in the "missionary position" was considered contrary to human dignity. The theories of Rousseau, Darwin or Freud were condemned on similar grounds. To allow a place for a notion of human dignity in legal state action is to allow extended forms of paternalism.

Yet, on the other hand, the (Kantian) idea that all human beings have a dignity, independent of contingent factors, practices and attitudes (their culture, gender, social position and even their will) which "dishonour" their humanity, lies at the roots of the idea of human rights.[21] And it seems that much of European protective laws (labour law, consumer law) relies upon some notion of human dignity, for they put strong limits on "free consent". Are these laws, therefore, trespassing upon the classical requirements of the "no-harm-principles" and, indeed paternalistic and thus illegitimate and conservative? Let

[20] David Lyons, *Ethics and the Rule of Law* (Cambridge: Cambridge University Press, 1984).
[21] Thomas Hill, *Autonomy and self-respect* (Cambridge: Cambridge University Press, 1991) 169.

us first look at the conservative point of view and ask whether or not interference with socio-economic conditions in terms of "human dignity" contradicts political neutrality.

4.2. Devlin's conventionalism

Devlin attacked the idea that the law should not be concerned with immorality as such and should restrict its interference to cases where harm is done to others. Morals laws may be justified if they aim at preserving social cohesion. Although such laws, which enforce specific moral obligations may, in a secular and pluralist society, not be based on "truth-claims", they may nevertheless be justified in terms of social self-preservation, which depends upon the existence of a shared set of moral beliefs through which people identify themselves with a society as being "theirs". As the threat of social disintegration is a matter of public interest, a state may legitimately use its power to stave off such a threat. Whether or not such a danger exists cannot be decided in terms of "harm"; it also depends upon society's constitutive morality, for example, on whether or not particular acts are widely and strongly condemned as wicked in society and are thus an offence against its constitutive morality.

Devlin does not ground his case for moral state paternalism on the objective truth of some moral beliefs. On the contrary, he explicitly rejects a ("Platonic") justification of morals legislation in terms of its aim to promote "the virtue of the citizenry" as being tyrannical.[22] Devlin relates moral convictions to particular cultures, to conventions these cultures consider to be important. If a culture considers polygamy to be a positive good, then it has the right to protect and promote the practice of polygamy by means of state power, in the same way a monogamic culture does. This is an example he himself gives. Similarly, Devlin should accept that if people from a certain culture are strongly convinced that it is a social duty of young girls to undergo cliterodectomy,[23] then the law, in order to preserve cultural integrity and social cohesion may allow and even enforce this practice.

One cannot, according to Devlin, answer the question of whether an action may cause harm to others, in abstraction from whether it is strongly condemned by the constitutive morality of a society. Even if, for example, homosexual acts between consenting adults in the private sphere, do not harm others, the very knowledge that such acts may freely be committed, may harm the constitutive morality in which people within a society believe. This constitutive morality is a cultural artefact that the legal system nevertheless may legitimately protect.

This account of the legitimacy of legislation in the area of morals is strongly conventionalist.[24] It does not matter whether or not certain acts really do harm

[22] Patrick Devlin, *The Enforcement of Morals* (Oxford: Oxford University Press, 1965) 89.

[23] And see Bibbings, *infra* 139.

[24] Robert P. George, *supra* n 17 at 51.

others, independently from their condemnation by conventional standards. If they *are* firmly condemned by society's constitutive morality as being anti-social acts, they are anti-social acts which, for the sake of social cohesion, may be forbidden. The *reasons* for this condemnation are irrelevant in an account of the legitimacy of certain laws. Whatever the moral beliefs that are shared by the members of a particular society, the fact of them being shared as constitutive for a society's identity, suffices as a ground for legal enforcement.

However, Devlin is not a mere sceptic. Although moral convictions may vary from culture to culture, the right of cultures to preserve their integrity is presented as a universal moral claim. It is a moral right of cultures to protect their constitutive moral beliefs, whatever these happen to be. This position is not sceptical in view of Devlin's non-cognitivist conception of morality as a matter of (shared) feelings, rather than reason. A society, as a "community of ideas", including shared ideas on politics and ethics, relies on such shared feelings as its "common sense". Without such common, fundamental agreement about good and evil, no society could exist.[25]

As Devlin does not refer to the objective truth of a society's values, in order to argue its right to protect them, his approach somehow resembles defences of the principle of toleration in interhuman relations; regardless of what an individual's conception of the good happens to be, the individual has the right to be respected, including the right to express and to live according to his conception of the good, exactly because it is *his* – presumably freely chosen – conception of the good. But this resemblance also destroys Devlin's – and many communitarian – defences of cultural integrity, for a culture may, indeed, have the right to protect its integrity (against "outsiders") but still lacks not yet the right to enforce it on its members. We cannot, that is, argue the case for cultural integrity without arguing the case for individual integrity. As long as the members of a particular culture freely accept and comply with the generally shared moral convictions that constitute their "common sense", no moral problem arises. But if some members of that particular culture oppose some of these conceptions, they have a right to have their integrity respected as well: they may not be forced to "accept" these conceptions.

This point is particularly relevant in all present-day discussions on so-called "group rights" for national or ethnic minorities. Authors such as Kymlicka[26] and Rawls[27] do not only accept particular regulations protecting (the culture, language, traditions etc. of) such minorities, but even go so far as to argue in favour of tolerating practices within such cultures that are fundamentally contradicting individual rights. This is untenable. Of course a "culture" or "group" has the right to protection, but that does not imply that it has also the right to enforce its values or practices *on its own members*. Groups or cultures should

[25] Patrick Devlin, *supra* n 22.

[26] Will Kymlicka, *Multicultural citizenship. A liberal theory of minority rights* (Oxford: Clarendon Press, 1995) 181.

[27] John Rawls, *Political Liberalism* (New York City NY: Ferdinand Knopf, 1993) 29.

both respect democracy and individual rights. They have no right to claim tolerance for practices that they enforce on their members against their will and neither do they have the right to force people to remain members of the group. Group-specific rights, based on cultural differences, can only be invoked as long as the members of the group have democratic voice within the group and do accept freely the values these rights protect.[28] If not, special group rights may justify "a tyranny of traditions" which cannot democratically be challenged and changed because of the existence of these rights, blocking the road of change.[29] Leaders may, in the name of culture or tradition claim authority over their cultural group, while its members would lack the individual rights to leave the group or to change the rules within it.

4.3. Social integration as a value

Returning to Devlin's right of a society to protect it from disintegration, one could attack his position both (1) on the ground that societies do not have a general moral right to protect themselves against social disintegration, (2) on the ground that moral pluralism or tolerance does not, in fact, threaten social cohesion as such. As far as the latter is concerned, Hart argued that even if it is admitted that social cohesion is valuable, it does not follow that changes in moral views do, of necessity, "destroy" or "disintegrate" society, at least not in the strong sense Devlin seems to suggest.[30] Such a point of view would simply discredit any criticism of or changes in existing moral practices and beliefs. As a matter of fact, one cannot maintain that moral changes and moral pluralism within Western societies have disintegrated these societies. Moral views may change and vary without society being destroyed. But, as far as the former is concerned, even if a society would disintegrate because of changes in moral beliefs, one cannot judge such disintegration, independently from the content of the conventional or new moral beliefs. Changes in moral views or the existence within a society of different moral views are not, by definition, "losses". The only "disintegration" Hart would accept as relevant, would be in terms of harm. If new moral views justify practices which do less harm to others than the traditional ones, there is all the reason to welcome such a change, even if it leads to the breakdown of an existing social order. If they justify practices that do more harm, then one has all the reason to resist the change.

[28] Koen Raes, "The ethics of community and the ethics of justice. A misunderstood relationship" in Albert W. Musschenga *et al.* (eds), *Morality, worldview and law. The idea of a universal morality and its critics* (Assen/Maastricht: Van Gorcum, 1992) 191–204; Koen Raes, "Individualist subjectivism and the world as property. On the interrelations between concepts of value and concepts of ownership" in G.E. Van Maanen and A.A.J. Van der Walt (eds), *Property at the threshold of the XXI century* (Maastricht: Maastricht Academic Publishers, 1996) 26–51.

[29] Marlies Galenkamp, *Individualism versus collectivism. The concept of collective rights*, (Rotterdam: Rotterdamse Filosofische Studies, 1993).

[30] H.L.A. Hart, *supra* n 19 at 50.

There is, however, another possible approach both to the meaning of "social cohesion" and to the legitimacy of moral change.[31] One could, as many communitarians have done, interpret "disintegration" not in terms of a total breakdown of some Hobbesian concept of "order", but rather in terms of the erosion of the "integrity" of a culture, upon which the integration of the members of a culture is based. Society is more than a collection of individuals living in proximity to one another in peace. Social cohesion is more than a question of "order". It is also a shared experience, a shared practice. If one conceives persons as integrally related to the culture they belong to, then a disintegration of shared beliefs may, indeed, be conceived as a disintegration of society. This process has been identified, by many authors, as what "modernity" wherein "all that is solid melts into air"[32] is all about. One can hardly deny such processes of disintegration as empirical, historical facts but neither can one deny that modern societies have developed new mechanisms of social integration by means of constitutional protections of the citizens, democratic procedures and the rule of law.

5. DEMOCRATIC OBJECTIVISM

The main question thus becomes whether or not particular, culturally shared moral beliefs, are worthy of protection and even enforcement by the law. And this question cannot be decided separately from either (a) the moral truth of what is protected or enforced under laws dealing with morals; or (b) independent from what the individual members of a society themselves think on this issue. The first position may be called the traditional objectivist one (which Devlin opposed). The second position may be called the democratic objectivist one (which Devlin would have opposed as well). According to the first position, the existence of objective moral values, may in itself offer reasons enough either to protect and enforce generally shared moral values or to change and forbid generally shared moral values, depending on whether these values correspond to objective moral truths; it is the task of a state to protect its citizens against vice or intrinsic wrong. According to the second position, the use of force or coercion always requires specific reasons; the recognition of an objective moral truth is not enough to protect it by means of enforcement.

There is a crucially important difference between "protecting" particular moral beliefs and "enforcing" them. Legal rules may very well protect moral beliefs that are shared within a community, without enforcing those beliefs. This is exactly what the democratic point of view on this issue involves.

[31] Robert P. George, *supra* n 17 at 65.

[32] Karl Marx and Friedrich Engels (1974) (1848), *Manifest der Kommunistischen Partei*, in, MEW 4 (Berlin, Dietz Verlag) 463. English version as (ed. E. Hobsbawm), *The Communist Manifesto* (London and New York: Verso, 1998).

Whether or not certain moral beliefs are objective is, in this view, not enough of a reason to enforce them. The question whether an act is right or wrong and that whether it is right or wrong to interfere are always distinct.[33] This point distinguishes the traditional objectivist position from the democratic objectivist position.

Contrary to Devlin's conventionalism, the traditional justification of morals legislation was based on an objectivist account of moral value. Laws may uphold and reinforce a morality – whether "public" or "private" – precisely in as much as this morality is true. It may be paternalist in order to encourage and even force people to behave virtuously and not wickedly. Although the law should not forbid all vices, it should forbid the more grievous ones, irrespective of whether or not they damage others. They harm the moral character, the real nature of human beings and this is enough of a reason to prohibit them.

A democratic objectivist develops a different approach. Although believing in the existence of objective moral truths, he is (a) fundamentally aware of the possibility that one may be mistaken in what one firmly believes to be objectively valuable (there are no "absolute truths"); (b) not indifferent about the ways possible moral truths are recognised by those for whom they are valid as moral truths.

As far as (a) is concerned, a democratic objectivist denies that there are moral certainties and considers this to be an independent reason not to force values on people even if a lot of evidence points in the direction of them being "true". In an important sense, a parallel may be drawn here with the practice of free inquiry within the scientific community. As free inquiry has proven to be the best available soil to find (always revisable) scientific truth, so a society of equally free citizens may be seen as the optimal soil to find moral truth. This denial of certainty on moral issues should therefore not be identified with moral indifference.[34] Accepting some scepticism is not the same as rejecting the possibility that answers may be right. Rejecting moral absolutism is not the same as embracing nihilism.

As to (b), contrary to traditional objectivism, the question whether or not a value, of whose objective nature one is firmly convinced, is freely to be accepted by a person, makes a morally relevant difference to the democratic objectivist. Thus, whilst Catholics argue (as in the papal *Veritatis Splendor*[35]) that "the problem of who decides is not an ethical issue", a democratic objectivist makes a clear distinction between "the truth of a moral conviction" and "the value of believing a moral conviction". Moral truth is no final reason to enforce it and, what is more, enforcing moral truths upon persons may have as a consequence that belief in them loses its moral value. An enforced moral conviction simply stops being a moral conviction (as an enforced religious faith loses its quality as

[33] William Galston, "On the alleged right to do wrong. A response to Waldron" (1983) 93 *Ethics* 320, 321.

[34] Brian Barry, *Justice as impartiality* (Oxford: Clarendon Press, 1995) 86, 184.

[35] Pope John Paul II, *Veritatis Splendor- The splendor of truth* (New York, NY: Paulist, 1993).

a religious faith). Even though moral values are not simply "chosen" but rather "discovered", it is central to the democratic objectivist position that the free individual acceptance or recognition of value is an essential and not an accidental requirement in valuing its moral standing. The use of force always requires a particular justification. Moral truth is not a sufficient condition for this and even not a necessary condition.

A democratic objectivist is not insensitive to Devlin's conventionalist argument about "social disintegration". But while conventionalists argue against moral pluralism because they consider it to be a sign of such disintegration taking place, from the pluralist point of view, enforcing one particular morality is, on the contrary, seen as a disintegrating social force, which would lead to upheavals, civil war, repression and discrimination.

The neutrality-requirement will strongly favour procedural approaches to public debate and decision-making, guaranteeing all participants equal voice and will thus, because of the "burden of public justification" guarantee more rational solutions as well.

Neutrality follows from the desire to reach agreement with others on terms that nobody could reasonably reject and will be expressed in institutions based on an agreement about the ways disagreements should be settled. Although a desire for civil peace does not necessarily favour neutral political institutions, it may do so if the parties become conscious of the fact that they cannot win the battle by means of force. This is not to say that the parties should give precedence to other (for instance, "economic") issues than the disputed ones. The parties do not have to take their disagreements less seriously. They only have to renounce violence as a means of resolving disagreement. In *this* sense, Rorty is right to emphasise that, in a political culture, democratic procedures ("the way things are said") should have priority over philosophic topics ("what is said") such as "an ahistorical human nature, the nature of selfhood, the motive of moral behaviour and the meaning of human life".[36]

Moral pluralism and state neutrality should not be seen as the enemies of social cohesion and social integration. They may, on the contrary, be the very conditions to counter processes of social disintegration that may end in civil war.

6. POLITICAL NEUTRALITY AND IDEALS OF THE GOOD

It follows from the objectivist case for democracy, deriving from the norm of equal concern, that it is wrong for the government to dictate and enforce a morality to the individual citizen. It is thus not that there is no "fact of the matter" about what forms of life are fulfilling and what forms of life are not

[36] Richard Rorty, "The Priority of Democracy to Philosophy" in Alen Malachowski (ed.), *Reading Rorty* (Oxford: Blackwell, 1990) 279 at 283.

fulfilling, or morally wrong in some other way,[37] but that such enforcement expresses lack of respect for persons as autonomous moral agents and is, because of this, an objective moral wrong. Such respect "requires that we accord them the right to choose a moral standpoint for themselves, however repulsive we may find their choice".[38] If choice and freedom are, in one way or another, regarded as essential components of what it means to act morally, it should also be accepted that persons may make, and have the right to make, the wrong moral choices. The fact that a choice is a morally wrong one is therefore not, in itself, a reason to interfere with it. If someone has the right to perform an act, he is entitled to perform it, even if it is morally wrong and no one has the right to forbid or interfere with it.

This approach needs qualifications (apart from the generally accepted qualifications concerning incompetent minors and the mentally disordered). *First*, it does not imply that no legal enforcement can be legitimate. While recognising "the legal right to do moral wrong", it makes use of the "harm principle" (though not only the harm principle) to draw a line between "the proper sphere of legal enforcement" and the sphere of personal freedom. Protecting individuals (including *future* individuals) against the harmful consequences of other's behaviour is one major task of the law. *Second*, it does not imply that the law may not promote fulfilling forms of life. It is not radically anti-perfectionist. The law may rightly do so, as long as it does not make use of force. And it does imply legal interference in order to guarantee conditions of equal respect and equal liberty, that is, conditions of justice. I will elaborate further on these issues from the perspective of state neutrality.

6.1. The harm principle and justified paternalism

Ever since John Stuart Mill, the "harm" principle, according to which "the sole end for which mankind are warranted, individually or collectively, in interfering with the liberty of action of any of their number is self-protection, and the only purpose for which power can be rightfully exercised over any member of a civilised community, against his will, is to prevent harm to others",[39] has been at the top of the list in a liberal account of state neutrality. Nevertheless (a) it needs amendment and (b) it cannot be the only principle that a neutral government should respect. The principle needs amendment for, as Barry argues, it would entail the illegitimacy of any kind of legislation for the protection of the interests of non-human entities and this can hardly be defended.[40] Harm to

[37] If there were no such thing as a moral wrong, then it would not be wrong for the government to impose moral choices.

[38] Hilary Putnam, *Reason, Truth and History*, (Cambridge: Cambridge University Press, 1981) 149.

[39] John Stuart Mill, *supra* n 15.

[40] Brian Barry, *supra* n 34 at 86.

non-human entities should be taken into account as well. Furthermore, the almost natural way by which Mill restricts his principle to autonomous or competent persons needs qualification, as it does not say anything about how to treat the incompetent, particularly children. Does the curtailment of the "no-harm principle" to competent persons simply imply that *any* paternalism regarding children is justified? And shouldn't there be politically relevant criteria to define the proper sphere of parental and the proper sphere of governmental paternalism? Finally, can one really approach competency in terms of an "all or nothing" matter as if people are either autonomous in all aspects of their lives or the mere objects of paternalist authority in all aspects of their lives? Is competence not rather a question of degree and a question of context in the sense that children – and, as a matter of fact, all human beings – may very well be competent to decide on certain issues while not on others or be competent to decide if certain conditions are met – such as the conditions required in the doctrine on informed consent – while their decision may be deficient if these conditions are not fulfilled?[41] Mill's no-harm principle, that is, is (a) much too anthropocentric and (b) much too much of an "all or nothing" kind.

But does the principle, for all the rest, simply outlaw any intervention "for a person's own good"? According to Barry, paternalism may be justified when there is a disproportion between the harm risked and the good forgone, as is, in his view the case with legislation which obliges people to wear seat belts in cars or helmets on motorcycles.[42] From a similar perspective, one may argue in favour of obligatory health or unemployment insurance: Vanderveer[43] thus interprets justified paternalism in terms of (Rawlsian) distributive justice, where persons in the original position will take account of the chance of their being incompetent or irrational and thus be prepared to "bind themselves" in order to protect their integrity.[44] Such a disproportionality may also be the consequence of time-discounting, the fact that people have the tendency to undervalue risks they are only confronted with in the long-term. This may be an argument for obligatory pension contributions.

Furthermore, a government should not *promote* unhealthy ideals as it should *discourage* racist or sexist ideals.[45] But it does not follow that a government

[41] Alan Buchanan and Dan W. Brock, *Deciding for others. The ethics of surrogate decision making* (Cambridge: Cambridge University Press, 1989).

[42] Brian Barry, *supra* n 34 at 87.

[43] Donald Vanderveer, *Paternalistic intervention. The moral bounds of benevolence* (Princeton, NJ: Princeton University Press, 1986).

[44] And see also John Elster, *Ulysses and the sirens* (Cambridge: Cambridge University Press, 1983).

[45] In discussions on pornography, a lot depends on the very definition of what is considered to be "pornographic" material. Pornography may be defined as (a) a moral wrong, (b) a moral good or (c) a non-moral issue. Thus, "the right to pornography" (as a "liberty", not as a "claim-right") may either be argued *because* it is a moral or non-moral good, or *although* it is a moral wrong. But whether one relates the notion of pornography intrinsically to (the showing/describing of) sexual acts, considered to be morally reprehensible, or uses a morally neutral or positive definition, one cannot escape the task of arguing what exactly makes (some or all) pornography a moral wrong or good. In my view, the main issue is not what should count as a "sexual perversity"(either in terms

may, by the same token, enforce conceptions of the good. The case of smoking can be relevantly invoked here.[46] For a long time, moral objections against smoking were mainly in terms of a puritan anti-pleasure ethics. Since the 1960s, objections against smoking evolved from the value of (personal) health, the fact that smoking harms the smoker. Recently, the ethics of smoking behaviour became more and more a public issue because medical science could prove the significant harmful consequences of smoking on non-smokers.

It will be clear that this last point is a sufficient reason for the government to prohibit the harming of non-smokers against their will and indeed, legislative initiatives in most Western countries develop towards a general ban of smoking in closed, public spaces. Discouraging smoking may even be inspired by paternalist motives (for the sake of the health of the smoker himself), either (a) because most people develop an addictive smoking habit when they are still minors (toning down the informed consent of beginning smokers) and cannot get rid of the habit once they are adults; (b) because most smokers are addicted and admit that they would prefer not to have developed the habit of smoking (raising the problem of weakness of will) and (c) because there is a disproportion and a time gap between the harm risked and the good forgone. All of this is reason enough for a government to have the right to prohibit smokers from harming non smokers (the case of the fetus, harmed by its mother's smoking) and to develop a policy discouraging smoking by means of public campaigns, warnings etc. But it does not give the government the right to prohibit a smoker to smoke "for his own sake", even though his health may be "an objective good".

It could be argued that the "harm" principle itself favours a particular conception of the good, e.g. the utilitarian one, which defines harm as a form of negative utility. But this is not the case. What is considered to be harmful must

of the acts shown or described or in terms of them being shown or described), but what may be considered an abuse of power (as in pornographic material involving children) or a degrading, sexist view on women. Not the sexuality of the context, but power relations define the eventual immorality of pornography. But then again, even if some pornography is morally reprehensible from the point of view of power relations and the norm of equal respect, it does not follow that it should be prohibited, independently from the harm-criterion (e.g. the harm that is done to those who are involved in the production of pornographic material) and (thus) the criterion of informed consent. Admittedly, the case against pornography has been strenghtened by feminist authors such as Catharine MacKinnon ("Sexuality, pornography and method: pleasure under patriarchy" (1989) 99 *Ethics* 314–46) and Andrea Dworkin (*Pornography: men possessing women*, New York City, NY: Women's Press, 1981). If pornography is defined as *intrinsically* sexist, why should the case of pornography be treated differently from the case of racism? If pornography (by that definition) would prove to be directly harmful to those involved in its production and indirectly harmful to its consumers (because it would stimulate aggression against women) wouldn't this be reason enough for it to be banned just as are publications or speech acts instigating racist acts? In my view, the answer does not lie in a defence of censorship, but in questioning the very legitimacy of censorship, whether of sexist or of racist opinions. Particularly in this area, the state should limit its interference by means of prohibition to what directly harms others. Ideals of the good should be promoted by other means than censorship.

[46] Robert E. Goodin, *No smoking. The Ethical Issues* (Chicago, IL: University of Chicago Press, 1989).

be considered bad within a variety of conceptions of the good, including, among others, utilitarianism.[47] Even if it is admitted that conceptions of the good are incommensurable, that does not preclude the possibility of some shared conceptions of what is harmful behaviour. However great cultural diversity may be, there are things which any culture values as a bad thing such as physically hurting someone, the taking of a person's liberty or life, destruction or stealing of property etc. The point is not that all conceptions of what is harmful should overlap – for this is certainly not the case – the point is to found public morality and state action on the prohibition of these kinds of harm that are widely accepted as harmful from different conceptions of the good, not "independent" from such conceptions. Cases against harmful behaviour should be argued for on the ground of good reasons that can be accepted within a variety of conceptions of the good. Nobody should, that is, be able to claim a privileged position for any conception of what is harmful from the point of view of a conception of the good on the basis of the correctness or superiority of that conception of the good.

According to Robert George, the harm principle cannot be the only principle of public morality.[48] This is, indeed, true. A public morality, based on the right to equal concern, justifies many interferences with people's life for the sake of (neutral) justice. Labour law, social security law, consumer law etc. all developed from the aim to protect people from abuses of power, even "against their will" (such as in the protection of minimum wages, obligatory health and unemployment insurance, obligatory clauses in contracts etc.) from the general consideration that circumstances of unequal power relations endanger the personal autonomy of the weaker party. They are protections against unjustifiable (ab)uses of power. But these "democratic paternalist" interferences for the sake of justice, which are justifiable in terms of Dworkin's notions of "endorsed paternalism" and "equal concern" are different from interferences for the sake of some conception of the good as is the case with morals legislation.

6.2. Perfectionism and anti-perfectionism

Rawls' case for a neutral public conception of morality and Dworkin's defence of public policies that are neutral between different conceptions of the good are strongly anti-perfectionist; it is not by using political power that ideals of the good should be spread. However, Rawls' approach leaves room for some state action, based on particular moral ideals. As he developed, in earlier work, the distinction between "justifying a practice" and "justifying a rule or an action falling under it"[49] he argued that societal institutions must be anti-perfectionist, but not that within such institutions, legislative decisions may never reflect

[47] Brian Barry, *supra* n 34 at 141.

[48] Robert P. George, *supra* n 17 at 106.

[49] John Rawls, "Two concepts of rules" (1955) 64 *Philosophical Review* 3–32.

ideals of the good.[50] What is essential to his procedural approach of decision-making processes is that they should be based upon the norm of equal respect. What the results are of such decision-making processes is left open. As long as these decisions respect the general procedural requirements, they should be accepted as just.

Rawls' rejection of perfectionism is motivated by the cautious self-interest of the parties behind the veil of ignorance. Therefore, it is mainly directed against the means that can justifiably be used to implement certain ideals of human perfection. Again, force is what people basically would reject, because it excludes any exit-option.

But exactly because religious toleration is, in Rawls' conception of political neutrality, treated as the "paradigm case", his rejection of perfectionism is too general. His concept of neutrality is strongly determined by a definition of rationality which leaves room only for strategic considerations within his original position, and by the recognition of an absolute veto-right against whatever would possibly transgress whatever conception of the good an imaginary person might possibly have. This is simply too abstract. Would it really be rational for people, inspired by "the highest order desire for justice" to ask for the protection of whatever their ideas, desires, preferences or wants happen to be? Would they not, irrespective of considerations about harm to others, ignore the possibility and the preparedness they might show for changing radically irrational and self-destructive beliefs? It is hardly plausible that the search for justice, by which subjects in the original position are supposed to be inspired, would be that much alienated from conceptions of the good life, that they wouldn't exclude some forms of life as being fundamentally worthless and demeaning. It is not "rational" to ask for "respect" for any want, preference or desire people may happen to have. It is, even within the constraints of the original position, rational to evaluate life options and to exclude some of them on the ground that they are intrinsically degrading, even within a pluralist conception of the good.

For these reasons, Raz denies that a Rawlsian approach to political neutrality is defensible or desirable.[51] He also denies the plausibility of the Rawlsian priority of "the right" over "the good", arguing that it is only possible to ascertain what is right for a government to do if one knows what is good for human beings. According to Raz' liberal perfectionism, governments should be based on a conception of the good, e.g. a conception that understands individual liberty and autonomy as essential to it. A concept of "the right" should not be developed *independently from* any conception of the good: it should *encompass* a plurality of conceptions of the good. Governments should not be inspired by a "politics of neutral concern", but by a politics which protects, supports and

[50] John Rawls, *A Theory of Justice* (New York City, NY: Oxford University Press, 1972) 238.
[51] Joseph Raz, *The Morality of Freedom* (Oxford: Clarendon Press, 1986) 126.

advances personal autonomy. A concern for the dignity and integrity of persons requires moral pluralism, not neutrality or the exclusion of ideals.[52]

Moral pluralism is, as we already argued, not the view that any way of life is as valuable as any other, as long as it is "freely chosen" by someone. First, the class of morally good options may be pluralist and large, but it is not infinite; pluralism is the view that people should have the freedom to choose between valuable options, not between whatever option is available. Second, an option can only count as a morally relevant option (a) if its choice relies upon some idea of *informed consent* and (b) if it can be based on (instrumental or intrinsic) *reasons*, implying that merely wanting something is, as such, not enough of a reason for doing it; allowing for free space to unreflective wants may be *part* of a conception of the good life, but a conception of the good life cannot be *constituted* by unreflective wants or sheer desires. Pluralist objectivism thus requires that a government should provide its citizens not only with basic information but also with primary social goods, resources or capabilities, so that their choices can really count as informed and unenforced choices for which they can give reasons.

It has to be emphasised that even within Raz' perfectionism, which accepts moral ideals as legitimate reasons for action, the legal prohibition of "victimless immoralities" or "choices which do not harm others" is excluded because this would be insufficiently respectful of the value of personal autonomy (not to be confused with moral autonomy). Although Raz thus rejects anti-perfectionism and neutralism, he accepts the harm principle as central in justifications for using coercive means. Not the ends, but the means are illegitimate.

This is compatible with the above mentioned principles of pluralist objectivism, according to which it is the duty of a government to create the optimal cultural soil in which people may, as informed citizens, choose their own ideals of the good. Protecting personal autonomy implies, that is, the protection of immoral choices as well. This is not because they are, as such, worthy of protection, but because one cannot protect personal autonomy and at the same time enforce particular choices upon persons. Raz may criticise the idea of a neutral political morality, but as his case for pluralism makes clear, he is more of an ally than an enemy of the tradition of political neutralism.

Eventually, one could argue that the use of force is not by definition indicative of disregard or contempt for those persons whose preferences or wants are banned. According to George, it may manifest a sense of the equal worth and dignity of those people, if their "preferences" express a serious misconception of their worth and dignity.[53] But what if those people simply do not "get the message"? What is – even apart from the problem of efficacy – won by forcing people to live according to a conception of the good they radically reject or even do not understand? What can be "good" in a life lived without any endorsement

[52] Joseph Raz, *The Morality of Freedom* (Oxford: Clarendon Press, 1986) 127.

[53] Robert P. George, *supra* n 17 at 95.

of its goodness by the subject itself? If a supposedly radically evil or empty life is lived without it harming others, what could be the reason to force other options on the person who values it nevertheless, if all persuasive means have failed? What reason can be given that cannot and will not, by definition, be accepted by the person involved, and yet is sufficiently strong to justify forcing it on him? It is thus, in the field of political morality, not easy to distinguish ends from means, exactly because the means have a direct influence on ends. Whereas enforcing rules of justice can be justified from the perspective of their effects on interhuman (outer) behaviour, no such justification is available if the end is a change in what people think or believe. Moral norms and rules may be enforceable, but ethical beliefs and ideals are not.

Raz rightly emphasises that a government should do more than remain passive regarding conceptions of the good and that it may well promote certain aesthetic, ethical and epistemological ideals. This is, however, not incompatible with the Rawlsian or Dworkinian spirit of political neutrality, which is mainly concerned with the legitimacy of using force. Neither Rawls' procedural concept of political decision-making within the constraints of his concept of justice, nor Dworkin's concept of a politics of neutral respect, exclude perfectionist ideals from governmental policies. What they exclude is certain means to spread such ideals and this is also, from a different approach, Raz' point of view.

George's argument that merely "respecting" whatever "choice" a person has made is not, by definition, an expression of "equal respect", has cogency, for such "respect" could be nothing but an expression of indifference. Not any want, preference or desire can be treated as "a conception of the good" of the person involved, at least not from the point of view of individuals as autonomous persons with a capacity for practical reasonableness. When somebody wants to kill himself, neglects his health, spoils his talents or becomes addicted to a destructive drug, the moral way to respond to such "choices" is not to "respect" them, but to try to convince the other that there are better options available to him and to offer him (material and psychological) opportunities to escape a desperate condition. There is enough evidence to show that people's preferences may be irrational or merely adaptive, because "they know of no better".[54] Simply leaving a person with whatever his choices may be is not a moral attitude. But if a person persist in his choices, after all the evidence to the contrary, and all opportunities to make more valuable options available have been presented and offered to him, and if these choices do not harm others, what else can be done than to accept his choice as *his* and to permit him to live the life he has chosen, or to end it. George's argument is valid if it is meant as a critique of an indifferent liberalism that leaves persons alone and helpless with their uninformed choices in the name of a discourse on human freedom, incommensurability and autonomy. But it does not follow that all means to change a person's point of view are therefore justified. If persuasive means fail, and if the choice is

[54] Amartya Sen, *supra* n 12.

not determined by a lack of socio-economic means, there is no way to change people's attitudes, at least not "for their own sake".[55]

7. THE POLITICS OF EQUAL CONCERN

No calculus is available to settle the problems raised by the concept of egalitarian justice. Whether starting from perfectionist or non-perfectionist ideals, the (legitimate) capacities of a state should not be overestimated and a lot of decisions should be left open to procedural justice within concrete contexts. Inevitably, many applications of the aim to realise conditions of equal concern should be settled, within the formal constraints of the concept of justice, by democratic decision-making, which is itself procedurally constrained. Rawls' meta-ethical approach to justice in terms of fair procedures is thus relevant as well in more concrete contexts.

Democratic objectivism develops mainly a theory of legitimate means, whereas pluralism emphasises that valuations of these means are not independent from goals. Pluralism is not simply the result of strategic considerations, it is also a good in itself, while a culture of equal liberty can be valued as a positive good, as the optimal soil for discovering conceptions of the good. Egalitarianism thus defines the conditions of pluralism and implies that the incommensurability of conceptions of the good is not invoked as an argument against any redistribution. Though conceptions of the good are incommensurable, some means to realise these conceptions are sufficiently widely shared to count as primary social goods, resources or capabilities (although a lot of research on the "quality of life" still remains to be done) of which it can be said that, regardless of what a person's conception of the good is, he will want various things as prerequisites for carrying out his plan of life.[56] This is compatible with the view that there is a multiplicity of human goods and a wide variety of instantiations of those goods. Redistributive schemes concerning certain means to realise a variety of conceptions of the good are thus integrally related to both egalitarianism and democratic objectivism.

Egalitarianism is, finally, not the view that "the common good" is nothing else but the aggregation of the goods of individuals. It recognises the importance of shared interests and shared values within society. But egalitarianism is, contrary to communitarianism, more liberal as far as the state is concerned, leaving room for a variety of communities within the boundaries of political society. Egalitarianism is individualist in the sense that it recognises individual persons

[55] Imprisonment may be justified in terms of the protection of society and in terms of its deterrent effects, but there is only scanty evidence that it contributes in any way to change the prisoner's moral convictions. On the contrary, empirical evidence rather points in the opposite direction. Whatever justifications there may be for punishment, changing "the convictions of the convict" in a moral and not a mere prudential sense, is the least convincing.

[56] John Rawls, *supra* n 50 at 92, 396.

as the primary actors within society, not in the sense that there may not be collective or shared values or in the sense that nothing beyond individual persons can have value. Egalitarianism is both a theory of justification – stating that moral reasons should be good reasons for all persons involved – and a theory of social organisation – stating that human relations should be based on an ethics of equal concern. Concepts of political neutrality should, from an egalitarian perspective, be valued in terms of their contribution to an ethics of equal concern. And this requires, in its turn, that the problem of which conceptions of the good, and which plurality of such conceptions are, in fact, fostered by equal justice should be an integral part of what pluralist egalitarianism is all about.

2

Privacy, Autonomy and Criminal Justice Rights: Philosophical Preliminaries

PAUL ROBERTS*

But he was still the hardy philosopher. As at Barolo, a crowd had gathered round, small at first, but growing all the time, listening to what he was saying. I stood on the fringes and caught some of it. "I read in the newspaper today a very interesting thing," he was remarking. "Always first in the morning when he wakes he reads the newspapers," explained Miss Belli. "I see the Japanese have now invented a special new toilet, the Happy Stool," said Criminale, "It takes what you drop in the bowl each morning and at once makes a medical diagnosis of it." "Bazlo, caro, you are disgusting," said Belli. "In goes your effluent, out from a slot in the wall comes your health report," said Criminale, ignoring this, "Too much vodka last night, sonny, now look what you have done with your cholesterol. Maybe even a needle comes into your rump and puts the matter right." "Bazlo caro, eat something," said Miss Belli, pushing forward a tray of canapés, "All this blasted lovely food and you don't take any!" "After I read this, how can I eat something?" asked Criminale, "You see what it means, there is no secret anywhere any more."

Malcolm Bradbury, *Doctor Criminale* (Secker and Warburg, 1992)

THIS CHAPTER IS mainly devoted to addressing two questions with important implications for the relationship between privacy and criminal justice:

1. ***What is the value of privacy?***
2. ***Is there a (moral) right to privacy?***

* The first drafts of this essay were written during a sabbatical semester spent as Visiting Lecturer in the University of Natal (Pietermaritzburg) School of Law. I would like to record my thanks to all my colleagues and friends in the Maritzburg Law School and the Philosophy Department for ensuring that I enjoyed a very congenial, as well as stimulating and enriching, South African winter with them. Earlier drafts of the paper benefited from being presented at a Pietermaritzburg Philosophy Department staff seminar in September 1998. I am especially grateful for the comments and encouragement I received from Douglas Farland, Ian Jennings and Simon Beck on that occasion. Parts of the paper were later discussed at a contributors' conference organised by the editors of this volume at Gregynog (University of Wales) in October 1998, and at a Durham University staff seminar the following March, and I have sought to take on board at least some of the very helpful and astute comments, queries and objections which participants at those events were kind enough to provide. Finally, I gratefully acknowledge the support of the University of Nottingham International Committee Fund and the University of Natal for their generosity in funding my visiting lectureship.

The word "value" in the first question is intended to bear its full-blooded normative (moral) meaning: that is to say, I want to go beyond the question "What is this value we conventionally refer to as privacy?" to ask "What value does privacy *in fact* have?" This normative inquiry into the value of privacy paves the way to a second, derivative question, namely: "Is there a (moral) right to privacy?" I conclude that there is. The argument will be that a right to privacy is grounded first and foremost in the distinctively (but not exclusively) liberal ideal of personal autonomy.

The device of placing "moral" in parenthesis, being equally tedious for author and readers, will generally be dispensed with, now that its minatory work is done. In this chapter "rights" are *moral* rights, unless otherwise clearly differentiated by an adjectival "legal".

While philosophers might appreciate an inquiry into the existence and value of privacy rights for its own intrinsic merit, my interest is more instrumental, inasmuch as the first two questions are preliminary to a third:

3. What scope might there be – if any – for accommodating privacy rights within criminal justice theory and practice?

This third question is prompted by the thought that privacy, as a value or as a right, is alien to English criminal law. Consult the English criminal lawyer's lexicon of essential concepts and ideas, and there you will find a collection of more or less abstract notions that answer to the traditional needs of criminal litigation. Some of these ideas, like "due process", "reasonable suspicion", or "the privilege against self-incrimination", are components of procedural law. Others – such as "capacity", "causation", "recklessness" or "grievous bodily harm" – are part of the substantive law of crimes. A third set – proportionality, crime-seriousness, mitigation, dangerousness – come into play at the sentencing stage of criminal proceedings. And still other, more general ideas have an institutional life across all three panels of the process-substance-sentencing triptych: "transparency", "integrity", "fundamental human rights" and "justice" are examples. But privacy will not be found anywhere among them.[1]

At the moment of incorporation[2] of the European Convention on Human

[1] While admittedly not a scientific survey, it is noteworthy that none of the following leading English criminal law textbooks has a principal index reference for "privacy": Michael J. Allen, *Textbook on Criminal Law* (London: Blackstone, 4th edn 1997); Andrew Ashworth, *Principles of Criminal Law* (Oxford: Oxford University Press, 2nd edn 1995); C.M.V. Clarkson and H.M. Keating, *Criminal Law: Text and Materials* (London: Sweet & Maxwell, 4th edn 1998); Nicola Lacey and Celia Wells, *Reconstructing Criminal Law: Critical Perspectives on Crime and the Criminal Process* (London: Butterworths, 2nd edn 1998); Alan Norrie, *Crime, Reason and History* (London: Butterworths, 1993); J.C. Smith, *Smith & Hogan: Criminal Law* (London: Butterworths, 9th edn 1999); Glanville Williams, *Textbook of Criminal Law* (London: Stevens, 2nd edn 1983). Since this note was first composed, however, an exception has appeared on the market, reinforcing an underlying premiss of this chapter, that the estrangement of privacy from English criminal law is about to end. Now see Andrew Ashworth, *Principles of Criminal Law* (Oxford: Oxford University Press, 3rd edn 1999).

[2] The language of "incorporation" is difficult to escape, partly because it is so useful and convenient, but strictly speaking the 1998 Act falls well short of full-blooded incorporation of the ECHR

Rights (ECHR) into United Kingdom law, it is particularly apposite to ask whether English criminal lawyers – or any others – need to add privacy to their essential lexicon. It is well known that the ECHR contains a number of articles with significant implications for criminal justice, including, in Article 8, the "right to respect for private life". The Convention will certainly impact on English criminal law and its administration, and there can be no doubt that lawyers who practise in the criminal courts urgently need to get to grips with the relevant articles and their rapidly expanding jurisprudence. But it is also well known that privacy is a problematical idea. As the site of semantic battles between rival conceptions and interpretations, its theoretical foundations are uncertain and its practical limits ill-defined. Some legal commentators are for abandoning the concept entirely.[3] The influence of privacy on criminal law, either as a direct source of legal rights or as a moral, rhetorical or ideological resource in legal reasoning and law reform, has certainly been partial and uneven.

In conclusion, Section III of this chapter briefly indicates some criminal justice applications of philosophical inquiry into the nature and value of privacy, themes which are picked up and elaborated in relation to particular topics and issues by other contributors to this volume. The distinctive contribution of this chapter, however, is to explore some of the philosophical preliminaries that should inform academic legal commentary, and guide legislators, judges and law reformers in their restatement and development of criminal law and criminal justice policy. To this end, Sections I and II, which correspond with the first two of my three questions and comprise the main body of the chapter, develop an argument in moral and political philosophy. It follows that the discussion is not tied to any particular legal jurisdiction or national culture. Quite the reverse. If the argument holds, it applies generally to any place in which individual autonomy and privacy are considered important values. There is certainly no escaping the fact that the value of privacy has varied enormously throughout history, and remains to this day highly culturally variable. However, although what follows is written from a predominantly "Western" liberal democratic perspective, it should not be assumed that privacy has no value for peoples and cultures which typically enjoy less privacy than Dutch people or Britons, anymore than it would be right to assume that privacy has exactly *the same* value for non-Europeans as it does for us. Minute attention to cultural variation (insofar as it survives in the shrinking global village) is beyond the scope of this essay.[4] Suffice it here to say that philosophical arguments are of

into English law. On the constitutional position generally, see A.T.H. Smith, "The Human Rights Act and the Criminal Lawyer: The Constitutional Context", [1999] *Criminal Law Review* 251; David Feldman, "The Human Rights Act 1998 and Constitutional Principles", (1999) 19 *Legal Studies* 165.

[3] Raymond Wacks' uncompromising view, for example, is that "the currency of 'privacy' has been so devalued that it no longer warrants – if it ever did – serious consideration as a legal term of art". Raymond Wacks, "The Poverty of 'Privacy'" (1980) 96 *Law Quarterly Review* 73 at 75.

[4] Some clues about cultural variations in privacy, social control and ontological security might be gleaned from Nobuo Komiya, "A Cultural Study of the Low Crime Rate in Japan" (1999) 39 *British Journal of Criminology* 369.

broad application. In the fashionable modern idiom, this chapter is concerned with questions of fundamental human rights, which for most of the last millennium philosophers called "natural rights".[5]

I. THE VALUE OF PRIVACY

It can be illuminating to approach the problem of privacy's value by an indirect route. To set the scene for our inquiry, and to provide some material with which to conduct it, consider the following six newspaper reports, presented here in slightly edited form, all of which appeared in the English national press during the last few years.

1. *"Internet birth delivers wanted woman,"* The Guardian, *2 July 1998*

"Two weeks ago a woman in a Florida maternity ward – known only as 'Elizabeth' – became a cyber-celebrity by being the first woman to give birth in a live Internet broadcast.

Yesterday the same woman, Elizabeth Ann Oliver, turned herself in on nine misdemeanour counts of passing dud cheques at local supermarkets.

When 40-year-old Mrs Oliver gave birth last month to Sean, her fourth child, thousands of Internet users could not see the broadcast because excessive demand caused the system to crash.

But they did not include the Orange county prosecutors, who saw enough of Elizabeth in labour to be able to identify her as one half of a couple they wanted to interview in connection with $1,300 worth of bad cheques paid to shops in 1989 and 1990.

At the time of the broadcast, it was assumed that Mrs Oliver's decision to be known only by her first name was prompted by a desire for privacy. It has since become clear she had other reasons for wanting to avoid publicity . . ."

2. *"Airport sex pornographers escape jail term,"* The Independent, *16 December 1997*

"The cast of the video *Public Places: Volume 4*, caught being filmed having sex on the bonnet of a car in the short-stay car park at Heathrow's Terminal 4, were yesterday conditionally discharged for 18 months.

Georgette Neale, a 23-year-old former page three girl, and her producer, Vincent Curran, 35, were spotted atop a silver Vauxhall Carlton on a cold November afternoon last year. They were found guilty of outraging public decency by a jury of eight men and four women who reached their decision after watching an eight-and-a-half minute recording of what had taken place.

Remarking on the pair's public performance, Judge Fergus Mitchell told Isleworth Crown Court: 'What I am here to do is to protect the public from that sort of thing. I suppose children have seen everything these days, but people returning form their holidays hardly expect to find that in a terminal car park'.

[5] Cf. John Finnis, *Natural Law and Natural Rights* (Oxford: Oxford University Press, 1980) Chapter VIII.

Neale . . . burst into tears when the judge delivered the verdict. She had turned to blue movie-making after her £1,000-a-month glamour work dried up and she said she had had no idea that the car park scene was illegal until she heard the police sirens.

Curran . . . was warned by the judge that he faced a 'serious' risk of imprisonment.

The actors were being cheered on by a group of builders when car park staff stumbled across the scene and called the police. . . ."

3. "*'Real men' give the game away*," **The Guardian**, *13 April 1998*

"Men who buy bottles of Chardonnay on Thursdays and Fridays have a tendency to put 'something for the weekend' into their shopping trolleys as well, according to Tesco.

'I'll leave you to make the connection,' said a spokesman for the supermarket group, explaining that this was one of the more unusual shopping trends identified via Clubcard, its customer loyalty card scheme.

The spokesman said that although some of the buying links had been predictable . . . others had been more of a shock.

For instance, men who buy nappies are most likely to pick up a six-pack or two of beer. Tesco Clubcard manager Nick Green attributed this to fathers wanting to prove they were 'real men'.

He said: 'Despite advances towards sexual equality, many men still feel embarrassed when they have to buy nappies. They fear people will think them henpecked husbands ordered by their wives to buy the nappies. Proudly placing a six-pack alongside the nappies sends out the message that the man is really a he-man.' . . .

Tesco's 10 million Clubcard members already receive regular mailshots tailored to some extent to their buying habits. . . . The plan is to make this targeting even more suited to individual tastes. . . ."

4. "*They know where you are through your mobile*," **The Independent**, *30 December 1997*

"Your neighbours could be watching you – via a spy satellite which will take detailed pictures to order over the Internet. Meanwhile, Big Brother can track you by your mobile phone. . . .

Within the next few days, Internet users will be able to order photographs showing their house and its environs to a resolution of 10ft, using pictures taken to order from an orbiting satellite . . .

The arrival of the personalised spy in the sky comes through an American company called Earthwatch . . . Its *Earlybird–1* satellite was launched from Russia and just before Christmas was successfully put into orbit, 295 miles above Earth. It orbits about once an hour, adding pictures to a vast database that the company is building up to create a 'digital globe'. . . .

That, though, will be superseded late in 1998, when Earthwatch is launching its *Quickbird–1* satellite. It will be able to distinguish objects 3ft across – detailed enough to see a paddling pool. . . .

The resolution available brings satellite imagery into the hands of anyone prepared to pay at least £200 . . .

Combined with details from mobile phones, this could allow Big Brother to know what you are doing, and trace you, throughout the day. British mobile phone companies have revealed that when required to by court order, they will allow the law enforcement agencies access to their computer data.

This means that someone whose phone is switched on can be tracked around the country, because the phone emits a signal to keep in touch with its nearest 'base station' every 30 minutes. That can also provide evidence, which can be used in court, of a person's whereabouts . . .

For those who have their phones constantly switched on – as terrorists or criminals are assumed to – it is akin to having a homing device in your pocket."

5. *"Judge rules release of television film showing would-be suicide was lawful,"* **The Independent**, *26 November 1997*

"In a landmark judgment yesterday the High Court ruled that a council was within its right to release a CCTV film of a would-be suicide. . . .

Geoffrey Peck says his life has been shattered since a film of him carrying a knife, about to slash his wrists, became an item of public consumption for millions of television viewers.

The footage from closed circuit television was provided by Brentwood Council in Essex. It was shown on Anglia TV and BBC1's *Crime Beat* which has viewing figures of more than 9 million. Mr Peck's features were not properly masked and he was identified by friends, acquaintances and neighbours. . . .

Mr Justice Harrison said he had 'some sympathy' for Mr Peck who had suffered an invasion of privacy which had caused distress and humiliation. The judge said it was a case with important implications for civil liberties and called for 'effective guidance' to be given to prevent any future similar 'undesirable' invasion of privacy. . . .

Mr Justice Harrison said that although the council did have power to distribute the CCTV film to show the public how successful the system was for crime prevention, he felt that with 'benefit of hindsight' the council might want to tighten their guidelines. . . ."

6. *"Secret video reveals parents' brutality,"* **The Independent**, *27 October 1997*

"A controversial secret video operation in two hospitals filmed parents carrying out sadistic attacks on their children. Some of the adults later confessed to killing children in their care.

A team of experts led by cot death expert Professor David Southall will reveal today a shocking catalogue of attacks on babies and young children by apparently caring parents and step-parents.

The secret cameras, which filmed parents suffocating, punching, kicking and poisoning children between the ages of two months and four years were set up in the Royal Brompton Hospital in London and the North Staffordshire Hospital in Stoke-on-Trent between 1986 and 1994. The videotaped evidence led to 33 criminal prosecutions. . . .

All but one of the 39 children attacked were placed in care and it emerged that 12 of their brothers and sisters had died in sudden or unexpected circumstances originally thought to be cot deaths. . . .

Although Professor Southall's methods have been condemned by some families, he believes the use of hidden cameras has been vindicated by the clear evidence of physical abuse. . . .

> All the children videoed had been strongly suspected by paediatricians, social workers and police child protection officers of being in serious danger of life-threatening abuse by a parent or step-parent. . . .
>
> However, his methods have come under criticism in some quarters. Keele University psychiatrists expressed concern about the infringement of privacy and the risk of exposing children to further harm in the surveillance operations. . . ."

Simply to relate these snatched glimpses of human folly and suffering is to know that we live in confused and confusing times, perhaps about values in general, certainly about the value of privacy. These vignettes evoke the gamut of human emotional responses, from mildly amusing prurience to deadly serious fear and pain.

A pregnant woman also conceives the notion that she wants to share the experience of giving birth with any stranger with an ISDN connection, and so many people log on to ogle at her in labour that the system cannot cope with demand. No doubt there have always been exhibitionists and voyeurs. New technologies have, however, revolutionised the scope for indulging both styles of vice far beyond the primitive opportunities available to Lady Godiver and the original Peeping Tom.

But while internet birthing might be the latest spectator sport, having sex in public places is still frowned on by the law, as the tearful Ms Neale discovered nearly to her much greater cost. Now, pornography and other forms of commercial sex are not ordinary sex, and there might be good reasons why the criminal law should differentiate between commercial and non-commercial varieties of sexual activity.[6] But these distinctions were not material here. Curran and Neale could still have been convicted of outraging public decency, and possibly sent to gaol, if they had been over-eager newly-weds passing time before the departure of their honeymoon flight. Judge Mitchell is surely right to observe that people do not expect to see this sort of thing on their return from holiday – certainly not on a cold November day – but nobody who actually saw the performance seems to have been unduly discomposed by it, if the reaction of the cheering builders is any indication. Allow, *arguendo*, that *al fresco* sex is not to be encouraged.[7] That a judge could find himself seriously contemplating a punishment as damaging and expensive as imprisonment still strikes me as puzzling. The offence involves harmless wrongdoing that would have been no crime at all had it been done in the privacy of, say, a fully operational movie studio with scores of film-makers and technicians in attendance. If Neale and Curran were bothering people, could they not simply have been told to get dressed and escorted off the premises?

[6] On criminalising commercial sex generally, see David A.J. Richards, *Sex, Drugs, Death, and the Law: An Essay on Human Rights and Overcriminalization* (Totowa, NJ: Rowman and Littlefield, 1982), Chapter 3.

[7] A concession that is by no means inevitable: cf. Jeremy Waldron, "Mill and Moral Distress", reprinted in his *Liberal Rights: Collected Papers 1981–1991* (Cambridge: Cambridge University Press, 1993) 130: "There is, surely, a debate to be had about the merits of public lovemaking. . .". And compare Brants, 138.

Airport carparks are only one small corner of the modern municipal bazaar in which boundaries between public and private are constantly being blurred. Even the most mundane and prosaic activities are deeply implicated in these trends. Take shopping. Tesco supermarkets know which of their ten million customers buys what and when, and store managers amuse themselves by using detailed evidence of buying trends to construct theories about henpecked husbands and real men. What other information is contained on those harmless-looking credit and store cards that bulk out the wallets and purses of most adults in the United Kingdom and elsewhere? How long until a successful card "swipe" is required before shoppers are even allowed through the supermarket door? This can only be a matter of commercial strategy, since the technology is already here (and in use, for example, on some cash machine booths). All the while, shopping trips to supermarkets, or anywhere else we might choose to go for any other purpose, are being recorded and broadcast by personal homing devices we mistake for innocent cellphones or tracked by spy satellites in the sky.

In still another part of this curious modern world, local councils are queuing up to follow the example of private shopping malls, office complexes, car parks and the like, to fit CCTV in town centres. The rationale is crime prevention, which is often the stated justification for extra-terrestrial surveillance as well. So remember to smile next time you are in town and try to avoid indulging any potentially embarrassing personal habits because, likely as not, you will be on camera.[8] Moreover, it would appear that if English municipal authorities want to give – or sell? – particularly juicy footage to television companies, the only barriers standing in their way are the self-imposed restraints of conscience and the benefit of hindsight.[9] There is certainly no doubting the market potential of this most post-modern genre of *cinema vérité*, in which life *is* art – or, rather, life

[8] Anyone tempted to dismiss these observations as melodramatic should consider the following reports: "Privacy outside the home is almost extinct. The number of closed-circuit television (CCTV) cameras in Britain's public places has now passed 1m[illion], according to industry figures. So dense is the network that in many urban areas people may be monitored from the moment they step out of their front door and be kept under observation on their way to work, in the office and even in a restaurant if they choose to dine out. Over the course of a day they could be filmed by 300 cameras. . . . Among the most 'wired' towns are High Wycombe in Buckinghamshire, Bournemouth in Dorset and King's Lynn in Norfolk. There, the ratio of cameras to people is so high that nobody can escape being filmed unless they avoid shopping, refuse to dine out and never visit the cinema, theatre or nightclubs". Dipesh Gadher, "Smile, You're on 300 Candid Cameras", *Sunday Times*, 14 February 1999; "It became a cliché almost as soon as the ink was dry, but George Orwell was right about Big Brother: he is watching us . . . If you aren't paranoid yet, then read on. It is estimated that the average Briton is snapped up to 500 times a week by security cameras or surveillance videos. When we walk down the High Street, when we visit the cashpoint, when we queue for a nightclub, in stations, waiting rooms, pubs or offices, we regularly come under the camera's cold black eye. Urban-dwellers who spend a day in the open or in public places can, in theory, be tracked constantly. And it doesn't stop there. Public toilets, school showers, shop changing rooms and – thanks to infra-red – even your own bedroom can come under the eyes and ears of the snooper". Barry Didcock, "It's Too Late, Big Brother is Here and He's All Eyes", *The Scotsman*, 14 December 1998.

[9] The unfortunate Mr Peck was denied leave to appeal against the High Court's judgment: *R* v. *Brentwood BC ex p Peck* [1998] EMLR 697 (CA), Lexis transcript 19 February 1998.

is *entertainment* – imitating life. Real-live footage of police car chases, daring rescues by the emergency services, accidents on the motorway, life on board ship or working in an hotel, or even – in one notorious case – two people having sex in a lift[10] scoops big audiences for television companies and turns a brisk trade at the video shops.

To be sure, these new technologies can be applied with great success to unquestionably meritorious ends. Secret cameras seem far less problematic when they are used to expose child abusers, for example. But even here their use is not entirely free from concern. There is something uncomfortable – perhaps even sordid – about covert surveillance, which is not necessarily expiated simply because a particular operation is instrumentally effective. The feeling seems at least in part to be connected with the loss of privacy suffered by targets of surveillance, and by those with whom they associate. Discomfit is further compounded by the worry that the informational fruits of surveillance could be misinterpreted (the camera never lies?), misappropriated or otherwise abused. Friends and relatives of some child abusers caught in Professor Southall's trap complained that the videos did not tell the whole story: "We definitely felt that he had made up his mind and anything we said would be discounted," complained the mother of one woman convicted of poisoning her child to death on the strength of secretly filmed video evidence.

How are we to bring this kaleidoscope of images of the public and private into sharper focus, or sort through the maelstrom of thoughts and feelings these and other similar images inspire? The best sense that I can bring to them appeals to ideas of personal autonomy and individual rights which have been elaborated within the framework of liberal political philosophy.

Privacy and autonomy

This section argues that the value of privacy is best understood as a component of the liberal ideal of individual or personal autonomy. It must be stressed at the outset that the argument from autonomy to be developed here does not preclude the possibility that privacy rights could be grounded in other values instead of,

[10] This video, appropriately enough entitled "Caught in the Act", was brought to us by Barrie Goulding, a small screen film-maker who had already earned his fortune from video compilations of police car chases ("Police Stop!") and capital punishment ("Executions"). The latest project ran into trouble over alleged breaches of copyright in the video footage. See Alex Bellos, "Closed Circuit Video Maker Faces Inquiry as Spy Camera Row Grows", *The Guardian*, 28 November 1995; Jane Thynne, "Spy Camera Film Withdrawn Amid Legal Action", *Daily Telegraph*, 29 November 1995. Goulding fought back, claiming that he had made the videos in order to raise public awareness of the power of CCTV and to generate debate about the need for greater regulation; though his message seems somewhat mixed: "Audiences are drawn like magnets. They are glued to their seats, captivated. The Bill and EastEnders just cannot match this. . . . We are making money, but we also have a message to get across", quoted in Jane Flanagan, "Hypocrisy Out of Control: The Man Behind the Sex in the Lift Film Claims his Motives are Honourable", *Sunday Telegraph*, 3 December 1995.

or in addition to, autonomy.[11] An example will help to clarify this. A person in a deep coma after an accident has no autonomy-based right to privacy, because her current condition precludes autonomous action. At least for the time being, she has no interest in acting autonomously, because, quite simply, autonomous action is impossible for her. However, *this does not prove that she has no right to privacy*, only that her right to privacy – if she has one – must be derived from some other source. Two candidates that spring readily to mind are, first, respect for human dignity and, secondly, the pragmatic imperative of limiting potential abuses of official power by placing restrictions on what people like doctors can do to those unfortunate enough to be afflicted in the manner contemplated. A particular right to privacy might be justified on all three grounds, where it contributes to promoting autonomy, respecting human dignity *and* controlling official power. The argument in this section concentrates on autonomy as the basis of privacy rights, however, both because I think that autonomy is the most important source of privacy-related rights and duties in the criminal justice context, and because demonstrating this claim will be a tall enough order without having to become embroiled in subsidiary issues and arguments that are best left for another day.

A thumbnail sketch of the ideal of autonomy is first required, before attempting to identify privacy's place within it. Although I will elaborate a distinctively liberal conception of personal autonomy, drawing particularly on the work of Joseph Raz,[12] the intimate connection between privacy and autonomy that will be established is not an exclusively liberal concern. Indeed, anyone who recognises personal autonomy as an important moral and political ideal could accommodate this argument within their ethical universe. Most communitarians, for example, agree with liberals that individual autonomy is valuable and worth promoting, but part company with them when it comes to ranking autonomy against other, especially communal, values and ideals ("the common good"). Communitarians might readily endorse the central argument advanced here, that privacy rights serve individual autonomy, though they would tend to value privacy rights less highly than liberals typically do, in accordance with their broader philosophical commitments. On the other hand, there is nothing in this argument for philosophies such as Utilitarianism or National Socialism which, in rejecting individual autonomy as an appropriate focus of moral concern, radically undermine any autonomy-based vindication of privacy rights (and so much the worse for Utilitarianism and National Socialism).[13]

[11] I am grateful to Antoine Mooij for pressing me to make this clarification.

[12] See in particular, Joseph Raz, *The Morality of Freedom* (Oxford: Clarendon Press, 1986) Parts III–V.

[13] Utilitarianism has its superficial attractions, but turns out to be radically destructive of individual autonomy because it "fails to take seriously the distinction between persons": John Rawls, *A Theory of Justice* (New York City, NY: Oxford University Press, 1972) 187. In as much as National Socialism exploited the metaphysical concept of the *Volk* to deny the existence of legitimate individual interests, much less rights, with slogans such as "You are nothing, your *Volk* is everything", it exhibited the same vice. See Markus Dirk Dubber, "The German Jury and the Metaphysical Volk:

The Kantian idea of moral autonomy as "self-determination" is as good a place as any to begin elaborating the conception of personal autonomy I favour. The autonomous life cherished by liberals is the life that can be characterised as (in part) self-determined, self-authored or self-created, following plans and ideals – "a conception of the good" – that one has chosen for oneself. Choice, on this view, is prerequisite to leading a successful, fulfilling and authentic existence according to one's own moral lights. To have an autonomous life a person must be free to deliberate about and choose the projects he or she will take up in life from an adequate range of options accommodating the diversity of human aptitudes, abilities, interests and tastes. In contrast to the value of liberty conceived as the negative right to be left alone, this is an active, "positive" conception of autonomy which requires, as Rawls neatly summarised, the opportunity "to form, to revise, and rationally to pursue a conception of the good".[14] Jeremy Waldron helpfully expands:

> The dominant theme in modern liberalism is that an individual conception of the good life is a plan of life or a strategy for living that an individual uses as a basis for making and reflecting on his more important decisions and for scheduling his enjoyments and set backs (to the extent that he has any control over them). His conception, moreover, defines what is to count as a setback or any enjoyment for him; and it defines for him the things that are most, and least, important in his life.[15]

Autonomy makes a person the sovereign authority over her or his own life, in recognition of the fact that we each have only one life and that what happens in it – what happens to *us* – is our most special and intimate concern. Although political philosophers might sometimes make heavy weather of it, this is a perfectly familiar and comprehensible idea (as indeed it must be to qualify as a compelling personal and political ideal that can be taken to heart by people like us). Ronald Dworkin contributes the following memorable image:

> Each person follows a more or less articulate conception of what gives value to life. The scholar who values a life of contemplation has such a conception; so does the television-watching, beer-drinking citizen who is fond of saying "This is the life", though of course he has thought less about the issue and is less able to describe or defend his conception.[16]

Having a life-plan – or, more accurately, a "plan for living" – is part and parcel of living life "from the inside", to borrow Kymlicka's useful metaphor.[17]

From Romantic Idealism to Nazi Ideology" (1995) 43 *American Journal of Comparative Law* 227, quoting the Nazi jurist Heinrich Lange, at 263.

[14] John Rawls, "Kantian Constructivism in Moral Theory" (1980) 77 *Journal of Philosophy* 517 at 525.

[15] Jeremy Waldron, "Legislation and Moral Neutrality", reprinted in his *Liberal Rights: Collected Papers 1981–1991*, at 161.

[16] Ronald Dworkin, "Liberalism", reprinted in his *A Matter of Principle* (Oxford: Oxford University Press, 1985) 191.

[17] "[N]o life goes better by being led from the outside according to values the person doesn't endorse. My life only goes better if I'm leading it from the inside, according to my beliefs about

Living life from the inside means that people choose plans, projects and commitments which are good – and thus go towards constituting a good life – *for them*. Human beings are psychologically complex creatures with nuanced and idiosyncratic sets of needs, interests, desires and aspirations. Harry Frankfurt is credited with the general observation that people are capable of forming "second order" preferences or desires, that is to say, preferences about what sort of (first order) desires and preferences they would like themselves to have.[18] More recently, Waldron has described a process of reflection:

> whereby the individual stands back and distances himself, from time to time, from his occurrent desires, and determines autonomously whether these are the sorts of desires he wants to be motivated by. In *choosing* his motivations, rather than regarding them as mere afflictions, the individual associates the business of binding his life into a unity with a process of evaluation: each tries to determine a basis for his action that will be *good* by his own lights.[19]

The ideal of autonomy developed thus far concentrates on human beings' *capacity* for self-directed choice, agency and responsibility, which are the mainstays of Kant's ethical system. To this, modern liberal theorists have added the material or socio-political condition that autonomy in the full sense can only be enjoyed in social, cultural and political environments which are conducive to living an autonomous life.[20] Recall the case of the comatose person mentioned briefly at the beginning of this section. She lacked the capacity for autonomy, which, by contrast, the political prisoner of an authoritarian regime still retains (assuming that his captors have not yet subjected him to mind-bending programmes of "re-education" or the like). But the dissident is nonetheless still denied his autonomy, in the full political sense intended here, since his choices and life-chances have been drastically reduced by – imagine, for the sake of a vivid example – indeterminate custodial confinement for holding proscribed heterodox opinions.

This brief overview is enough to stake out a serviceable conception of personal autonomy for present purposes. However, to avoid generating or reinforcing certain misperceptions that often confound a proper understanding and appreciation of liberal accounts of autonomy, several additional points and caveats should be entered before returning to our main theme.

value. Praying to God may be a valuable activity, but you have to believe that it's a worthwhile thing to do. . . .You can coerce someone into going to church and making the right physical movements, but you won't make someone's life better that way". Will Kymlicka, *Liberalism, Community and Culture* (Oxford: Oxford University Press, 1989) 12.

[18] Harry G. Frankfurt, "Freedom of the Will and the Concept of a Person" (1971) 68 *Journal of Philosophy* 5.

[19] Jeremy Waldron, "Legislation and Moral Neutrality", reprinted in his *Liberal Rights: Collected Papers 1981–1991*, at 162.

[20] For an excellent discussion of the meaning of "autonomy", clearly differentiating between Kant's ideas and modern liberalism, see Joel Feinberg, *The Moral Limits of the Criminal Law, Volume Three: Harm to Self* (New York City, NY: Oxford University Press, 1986) chapters 18 and 19. Assistance may also be derived from David A.J. Richards, *Sex, Drugs, Death, and the Law: An Essay on Human Rights and Overcriminalization*, chapter 1.

In the first place, it should be understood that this conception of autonomy, being perfectly compatible with a thorough-going objective morality, lends no support whatever to any brand of moral subjectivism, relativism or scepticism.[21] The idea is that people should choose *the good* (not *anything*) for themselves, and that their choosing what is good *for them* from a range of plural and incommensurable goods is a vital part of a good life. This conception is subjective only inasmuch as what is good for some is not necessarily (as) good for all. (Metaphorically, "one man's meat is another man's poison", but in reality meat is always meat). The moral subjectivist notion that it is good for people to choose *anything at all*, that their choosing *constitutes* the goodness of what is chosen, is no part of the argument made here (poison is poison is poison).

Secondly, there is no implication that a rigid life-plan must be formed at an early stage and compulsively pursued thereafter. Rather, living autonomously is understood to be a continuous and self-conscious process of choice, reflection and reappraisal. Projects may be put aside and new ones taken up on the basis of experience or further reflection, or just because a change can be as good as a rest. One may defer decision-making, even in important matters ("keeping your options open"), rethink one's direction at crucial junctures, or even possibly change course in mid-stream. Yet this is not to say that any commitment that has been incorporated into a life plan can always be lightly avoided, shrugged off or cast aside. To the contrary, it might involve considerable effort and pain to wrench oneself away from old projects and ties and "make a new life" for oneself. Indeed, certain commitments may be so integral to personal identity that they could not be given up except at the risk of complete psychological collapse. (This is the thought expressed when we say things like "ever since his wife left him/ his business collapsed/ his dog died etc., he has been a broken man".) What is crucial about commitments, from the liberal point of view, is that they be freely chosen or accepted, or at least, if not chosen freely in the first instance, that they should later come to be embraced as authentically one's own. Marriage is a good example of the first type of (chosen) commitment, while moral duties owed by parents to their children, and by sons and daughters to their parents, provide examples of the second, unchosen variety.

These examples suggest a third, and final, preliminary note of caution. It is sometimes objected that liberal autonomy is an obsessively individualistic, "atomistic"[22] or even selfish ideal, that it abstracts people from their embedded

[21] For guidance on moral ontology and epistemology, see Joseph Raz, "Liberalism, Skepticism and Democracy" (1989) 74 *Iowa Law Review* 761; Michael S. Moore, "Moral Reality Revisited" (1992) 90 *Michigan Law Review* 2424 and "Good Without God" in Robert P. George (ed.), *Natural Law, Liberalism and Morality* (Oxford: Oxford University Press, 1996); Anthony T. Kronman, "The Value of Moral Philosophy" (1998) 111 *Harvard Law Review* 1751.

[22] See Charles Taylor, "Atomism" reprinted in his *Philosophy and the Human Sciences: Philosophical Papers 2* (Cambridge: Cambridge University Press, 1985). Though some prominent liberals may have been atomists, liberalism need not be. In setting out to salvage Enlightenment values from postmodern assault, Taylor himself has remarked that "Modernity urgently needs to be

social contexts and imagines them to go through life like latter-day Robinson Crusoes. The liberal monad lives in a physically crowded world, perpetually surrounded by other people, but really – the critics accuse – he is emotionally and spiritually always entirely alone and exclusively preoccupied with his own narrow self-interest. Yet this is a travesty of the liberal ideal. A life cannot go well for us without sharing it with other people. We all live with and through others, as companions, friends, lovers, parents, children, work colleagues and so forth. Relationships play a significant role in how others define us, and how we define ourselves. Far from overlooking these elementary facts about our lives, liberalism treats relationships and commitments to other people as paradigmatic examples of the "projects" that make an autonomous life go well.

Personal autonomy, as I understand it, is a thoroughly socialised ideal. It nourishes, and in turn is nourished by, relationships with other people and the wider common good, including, notably, the good of democratic political participation. "Individual" or "personal" autonomy is far from an individualistic, selfish, disengaged or uncaring ideal. Moreover, caring about one's own rights and interests can be an effective way of promoting other people's welfare.[23] Such concern is even sometimes cultivated for expressly altruistic purposes, as where a mother – or soldier – keeps up her strength by eating well the better to defend the interests of those under her care and protection. Another way of putting this is to say that communal values of family and friendship are also well served by individuals whose cultivation of character and self-improvement makes them better parents, partners or friends, as well as more accomplished individuals. Human welfare in social context runs in complex currents of mutual reinforcement.

Now privacy, I want to suggest, is an integral part of this picture. An appropriate degree of privacy is essential for leading an autonomous life in post-industrial Western societies, and anywhere else where personal autonomy is a prevailing ideal. Privacy provides the cognitive, emotional and moral space to contemplate which of the available options might suit one's temperament, tastes and talents, to experiment with new activities and experiences on a trial basis and without fear of ridicule or censure, and to pursue one's chosen projects and commitments without being exposed to avoidable risks of victimisation or unreasonable demands to account for oneself before the galleries of public opinion. What business of yours is it to know what books I read, or the films I watch, or the company I keep? Why should you have access to the contents of my attic, or my fridge, or my stomach, or my trousers, or my mind? Why should I have to reveal them to you if I don't want to? What right have you even got to ask and expect a reply?

saved from its most unconditional supporters . . .". Charles Taylor, *Sources of the Self: The Making of Modern Identity* (Cambridge: Cambridge University Press, 1989) xi. The same might be said of liberalism, as it has been conceived and defended down the ages.

[23] For further elaboration, see Joseph Raz, "Rights and Individual Well-Being", reprinted in his *Ethics in the Public Domain* (Oxford: Oxford University Press, 1994).

The intimate connection I am proposing between privacy and autonomy supplies a plausible rationalisation of the horror we all instinctively feel at the thought of an existence without any privacy at all. This would be a life of constant exposure to the all-seeing eye of judgment, forever denied the blissful release of secret solitude in which to be reconciled with ourselves and whatever divinity we may find in the universe. Gone would be the confidential private moments, experienced alone or in the company of intimates, when life makes some sort of sense, if it ever does. How could I choose freely, indulge myself, try out new things, take chances, while you intently watched my every move, waiting for me to embarrass myself, take a tumble, fall flat on my face? Any society in which people were forced to live in the unremitting glare of soul-searching scrutiny would have a seriously chilling effect on the human spirit of enterprise, endeavour and achievement. Happiness would be fleeting and fugitive; social progress seriously diminished. And the opportunities for leading an autonomous life would be drastically reduced by insecurity, fear, suspicion, self-consciousness and self-doubt, with a plague of secondary vices – prurience, pettiness, envy, posturing, self-righteousness, hostility, and conflict – to follow. Perhaps this apocalyptic vision represents the perfection of Foucault's panoptic society in which the circuitry of power-knowledge is complete?[24] Busybodies and noseyparkers might appear to be in their element, but real men everywhere would need to get sixpacks for their trolleys. Who could lead an autonomous life in such a stultifying and oppressive environment? How would anyone achieve the self-knowledge necessary for an authentic social existence? More radically still: could individual human identity survive this degree of psychological assault?

This, I take it, is something akin to the line of thought that was putting Bradbury's conference-cruising intellectual Dr Criminale off his food, in the quotation I took as the masthead for this essay. Privacy is dead, and autonomy ailing, if there is no secret any more. These are also the thoughts and feelings that George Orwell taps to such memorable effect in *Nineteen Eighty-Four*. Orwell's protagonist Winston struggles to find enough room for the development of an authentic self-identity in the small spaces at the periphery of Big Brother's vision. Winston's profoundly personal struggle leads him to endure manifold discomforts and take risks that ultimately lead to his downfall. The final horror comes with the realisation that Big Brother has the inescapable, mind-bending power to strip away every last vestige of the soul-case and sear its contents with his malignant stare. Identity is eviscerated as the ramparts of the private self are successively breached and trampled down. Once Winston *does*

[24] "[P]rison transformed the punitive procedure into a penitentiary technique; the carceral archipelago transported this technique from the penal institution to the entire social body. . . . The judges of normality are present everywhere. We are in the society of the teacher-judge, the doctor-judge, the educator-judge, the 'social-worker'-judge; it is on them that the universal reign of the normative is based; and each individual, wherever he may find himself, subjects to it his body, his gestures, his behaviour, his aptitudes, his achievements". Michel Foucault, *Discipline and Punish: The Birth of the Prison* (Harmondsworth: Penguin, [1975] 1981) 298, 304.

see five fingers when only four are raised (the focal dramatic moment of the Richard Burton film of the book), his inevitable death is a trivial detail that Orwell only mentions, almost carelessly, in passing.

Today we have the technological capacity to do many of the things that Orwell, writing in 1948, could only dream of, or have nightmares about. Understanding privacy as an essential condition of personal autonomy explains why we should feel uneasy about electronic databanks of personal information, CCTV in town centres, secret videos in hospitals and spy satellites in the sky. These and other modern forms of potentially intrusive surveillance seem threatening and sinister when they invade our "personal space", whatever crime-fighting capacity or other great social benefits may be claimed on their behalf.

Although the privacy-autonomy nexus is, I am suggesting, fundamental to human well-being, the nature of that link must not be exaggerated or misunderstood. Three refinements, or qualifications, should be noted in particular.

First, it is not contended that privacy is an aggregative or fungible good, like Pounds Sterling, so that the more of it one has the better off one must be, in point of autonomy or anything else. A misanthropic and miserly recluse might enjoy a great deal of privacy, but still lead a perfectly useless and miserable life with little opportunity for autonomous choice or action. Privacy, then, is a pre-condition of autonomy, but increases in privacy do not necessarily increase autonomy, and no amount of privacy actually guarantees an autonomous life. The optimum level of privacy must be a matter of degree, and doubtless varies somewhat from person to person and according to social context. But serious privacy deficits, actual or threatened, should be troubling to anyone who values personal autonomy, while the complete destruction of privacy would make an autonomous existence impossible.

Conversely, second, not every diminution of privacy necessarily harms autonomy, or any other valuable interest. Some losses of privacy may be neutral, or even positively beneficial to other values, including autonomy. Exhibitionists who give birth on the Internet might for example increase their autonomy and happiness by relinquishing a measure of their privacy – unless, like Mrs Oliver, they are also fugitives from the law. A loss of privacy in relation to one person or group does not inevitably mean a loss of privacy *tout court* against the whole world. Privacy is relative in that sense, and also a question of degree. One may have more or less privacy *vis-à-vis* different individuals or groups of people across different social settings. Privacy is not something that one enjoys fully at one moment and then forfeits absolutely the next, as though privacy could be switched on and off like an electric light. Nor is it an either/or condition, like pregnancy or clinical death.

The third refinement extends what has previously been said about the objectivity of values generally to the specific value of privacy. To say that privacy is an objective value with a subjective component means that the precise value of privacy to each individual is partly a function of a person's subjective desires and preferences, but that privacy ultimately answers to objective moral truth. The significance of this is that I can suffer a loss of privacy without my knowing it, and that my interest in privacy can be harmed even if I think otherwise. This might in fact have been Mrs Oliver's position (setting aside her problems with the Orange County Sheriff). Although it seems unlikely that Mrs Oliver was reducing her capacity for autonomy by birthing on the internet, her intentional loss of privacy could have negative effects on her personal autonomy, if for example she were to attract a stalker, fall out with her children or suffer embarrassment and debilitating remorse as a result. In any event, Mrs Oliver's own subjective appraisal of the situation would not be conclusive, on the objective conception of well-being advocated here.

II. THE RIGHT TO PRIVACY

If privacy is an essential component of autonomy, and personal autonomy is such a cherished value for liberals and others, does that mean we must have a right to privacy? Alas, matters are not so simple. It certainly is *not* the case that people enjoy rights over everything that is important to them. In order to determine whether there is a (moral) right to privacy we had first better understand what a right is. The most illuminating conception of rights I know is the Interest Theory proposed by Joseph Raz, in these terms:

> Definition: "X has a right" if and only if X can have rights, and, other things being equal, an aspect of X's well-being (his interest) is a sufficient reason for holding some other person(s) to be under a duty.[25]

People being the paradigm and most important case of potential right-holders – "Xs that can have rights" – the question for us becomes: is a person's interest in privacy a sufficient reason for holding other people to be under a duty? One's interest in privacy of course derives from the connection between privacy and individual autonomy explained in the last section. I want now to suggest that this interest *is* sufficient to be a reason for placing others under duties, so that we can and do have a right to privacy, properly circumscribed and understood in ways to be explained in this section.

A useful way to approach the idea of a right to privacy is to see how, in their essential structure as rights-generating grounds of duties, privacy interests resemble or overlap with the negative liberties of traditional political theory. Consider first, by way of contrast, how a positive right to autonomy might be specified. True, a right to have an autonomous life is a conceptual impossibility because nobody else can be under a duty to provide me with something that, by definition, I must do for myself. Only I can lead my life from the inside; nobody

[25] Joseph Raz, *The Morality of Freedom*, *supra* n 12 at 166. See generally, *ibid*. chapters 7 and 8; J. Raz, "Legal Rights" (1984) 4 *Oxford Journal of Legal Studies* 1. An excellent recent overview is provided by Andrei Marmor, "On the Limits of Rights" (1997) 16 *Law and Philosophy* 1.

can coerce me into doing so, for coercion destroys genuine self-determination through external pressure, nor can I be relieved of the fundamentally personal responsibility for leading an autonomous life in any other way. However, it is possible to sidestep this conceptual objection by reconstituting the supposed entitlement as a right to be provided with *the conditions and opportunities* for leading an autonomous life. This right is *conceptually* unproblematic, but has never (to my knowledge) been a moral or political reality in the history of the world. For nobody could claim such a right unless society's material and technical resources were such that the same right could be universalised to everyone, in accordance with the foundational moral norm of equal respect for persons. Once this "merely" contingent, but under current conditions impossibly demanding, material prerequisite is acknowledged, one is obliged to conclude, with Raz, that our mastery over the physical environment has not yet developed to the point where there could be a general right to be provided with the conditions for living an autonomous life:

> A right to autonomy can be had only if the interest of the right-holder justifies holding members of the society at large to be duty-bound to him to provide him with the social environment necessary to give him a chance to have an autonomous life. Assuming that the interest of one person cannot justify holding so many to be subject to potentially burdensome duties, regarding such fundamental aspects of their lives, it follows that there is no right to personal autonomy. Personal autonomy may be a moral ideal . . . But in itself, in its full generality, it transcends what any individual has a right to. Put it another way: a person may be denied the chance to have an autonomous life, through the working of social institutions and by individual action, without any of his rights being overridden or violated.[26]

My interest in a life of boundless opportunity, luxury and fulfilment[27] is not a good reason for placing other people under duties to become my skivvies and servants, or to strive endlessly to create the idiosyncratic public culture in which I would especially thrive and prosper. My interests are no warrant for subordinating other people's life projects to mine. Yet this is essentially what a right to autonomy would entail under prevailing conditions of scarcity, and absent the technological ingenuity to overcome such pragmatic constraints for the foreseeable future (which, admittedly, is not very far into the future, given the quickening pace of technological advances).

Now recall the structure of negative liberty as it has long been conceived in the liberal political tradition. In contrast to any (positive) right to autonomy, the right to negative liberty is neither conceptually impossible nor morally indefensible under contemporary conditions. My interest in being left alone is sufficient grounds for placing others under duties not to molest or interfere with me; and these duties are sufficiently undemanding to be universalised so that, for exam-

[26] Raz, *The Morality of Freedom*, *supra* n 12 at 247.

[27] To give the hypothetical a modicum of plausibility it is necessary to imagine that I am not a university lecturer!

ple, we all have a duty not to invade anybody else's physical integrity.[28] Appealing to negative liberty is one way to construct a justificatory argument for a right to physical integrity; but *not* the best way, which – as also with regard to privacy rights – is to argue from autonomy. In fact, the Interest Theory advocates a multi-layered and dynamic conception of rights, according to which a single right may be the ground of an almost endless number of duties, from which further rights and duties flow. These rights and duties can be described as coming in "waves",[29] or it might be said, less metaphorically, that derivative duty-imposing rights are elaborated through moral arguments which extrapolate from "core" rights and duties.[30] A core right to physical integrity, for example, might include within its derivatives victims' rights to receive compensation, as well as a bundle of criminal justice rights for the state to detect, catch, try and punish offenders in cases where a person's physical integrity has been violated unjustifiably.

The power of general rights analysis can be focused and harnessed to serve our present inquiry. Privacy claims qualify as rights under the Interest Theory if interests in privacy can be delimited with sufficient clarity and precision to give them a similar structure to an interest in negative liberty. Privacy rights must not, on the other hand, assume the structure of an intolerably burdensome right to autonomy. In fact, this condition is quite easily satisfied to the extent that privacy interests converge with negative liberty on a shared core idea of being left alone, free from unwarranted interference.[31] It is no great imposition on your autonomy to be told to leave me alone, while at the same time you, in your turn, benefit from being left alone by me and everybody else to get on with your life. Essentially the same considerations explain the criminal law's preference for operating primarily through negative prohibitions ("don't do *x*, *y* or *z*, but you are free to do everything else"), and its general aversion to omissions liability.

The challenge now confronting the search for a right to privacy is to be able to delineate privacy interests with greater clarity and precision. Some guidance might be found in international human rights norms, especially Article 8 of the European Convention on Human Rights[32] and Article 17 of the International

[28] There are of course well-known limits to duties of non-violence, such as justified self-defence.

[29] Jeremy Waldron, *Liberal Rights*, above n 19 at 212.

[30] "A right is based on the interest which figures essentially in the justification of the statement that the right exists. The interest relates directly to the core right and indirectly to its derivatives. The relation of core and derivative rights is not that of entailment, but of the order of justification". Raz, *The Morality of Freedom*, *supra* n 12 at 169.

[31] Thus, Warren and Brandeis derived their common law right to privacy by generalising from specific instances of the right to be "let alone" already registered at common law: "[T]he protection afforded to thoughts, sentiments and emotions, expressed through the medium of writing or of the arts, so far as it consists in preventing publication, is merely an instance of the enforcement of the more general right of the individual to be let alone". Samuel D. Warren and Louis D. Brandeis, "The Right to Privacy" (1890) 4 *Harvard Law Review* 193 at 205. They added that the underlying rationale was "in reality not the principle of private property, but that of an inviolate personality".

[32] D.J. Harris, M. O'Boyle and C. Warbrick, *Law of the European Convention on Human Rights* (London: Butterworths, 1995) chapters 8 and 9; David Feldman, "The Developing Scope of Article 8 of the European Convention on Human Rights" [1997] *European Human Rights Law Review* 265.

Covenant on Civil and Political Rights, and their associated jurisprudence. One might also undertake comparative analysis of privacy protection in national laws and constitutions.[33] A significant drawback of these strategies, however, is that conceptions of privacy rights in positive law tend to be parcelled up with a certain degree of institutional legal baggage. Allied to the effect of encountering multiple and inconsistent legal definitions, this may serve to confuse in many respects, at the same time as clarifying other matters, which in the aggregate does not necessarily advance the cause of enlightenment. Fortunately help is at hand, in the shape of some excellent academic philosophy and legal writing on privacy interests and rights. In particular, Ruth Gavison has explained the interests protected by a right to privacy in terms of limiting a person's accessibility to others. This seems to me to encapsulate the kernel of the idea we require:

> Our interest in privacy . . . is related to our concern over our accessibility to others: the extent to which we are known to others, the extent to which others have physical access to us, and the extent to which we are the subject of others' attention. This concept of privacy as a concern for limited accessibility enables us to identify when losses of privacy occur.[34]

Gavison breaks down the interest in limited accessibility into three further "irreducible elements" of privacy, which she calls "secrecy, anonymity, and solitude":[35]

> As a methodological starting point, I suggest that an individual enjoys *perfect* privacy when he is completely inaccessible to others. This may be broken down into three independent components: in perfect privacy no one has any information about X, no one pays any attention to X, and no one has physical access to X. . . . A loss of privacy occurs as others obtain information about an individual, pay attention to him, or gain

[33] For example Ian Leigh, "Horizontal Rights, the Human Rights Act and Privacy: Lessons from the Commonwealth?" (1999) 48 *International and Comparative Legal Quarterly* 57; Basil Markesinis, "Privacy, Freedom of Expression, and the Horizontal Effect of the Human Rights Bill: Lessons from Germany" (1999) 115 *Law Quarterly Review* 47.

[34] Ruth Gavison, "Privacy and the Limits of Law" (1980) 89 *Yale Law Journal* 421 at 423. Gavison's approach to privacy is criticised as "arbitrary" by David Feldman, "Secrecy, Dignity or Autonomy? Views of Privacy as a Civil Liberty" (1994) 47 *Current Legal Problems* 41, esp. at 52 and n 49. I do not agree that Gavison's normative argument for a particular conception of privacy interests is arbitrary, except in the trivial sense that a different argument might have been made. The real issue, I suggest, is whether Gavison – and this partial adoption of her argument – is right or wrong. Feldman prefers to give privacy rights a more communitarian or collectivist twist: also see his "Privacy-Related Rights and their Social Value" in Peter Birks (ed.), *Privacy and Loyalty* (Oxford: Oxford University Press, 1997). However, he does not give any example of privacy interests that cannot be accommodated within Gavison's scheme, while his own preferred approach, according to which "[p]rivacy is largely a matter of being able to choose where, when, and with whom to co-operate or to withhold co-operation" ("Secrecy, Dignity or Autonomy?" *supra*, at 51), suffers from the standard objection to "control" or "choice" accounts of privacy: i.e. that privacy interests may be set back by one's own careless or even deliberately self-injuring autonomous conduct, even while one remains fully "in control." If privacy interests are underpinned by an objective conception of welfare, no entirely subjectivist criterion – such as choice or control – will ever successfully capture their essence, though choice might be important in an argument about privacy *rights*. And see n 41 *infra*.

[35] Gavison, *op. cit.* n 34 at 433.

access to him. These three elements of secrecy, anonymity, and solitude are distinct and independent, but interrelated, and the complex concept of privacy is richer than any definition centred around only one of them.[36]

Gavison's insightful analysis can be used to formalise pervasive social fears about the nature of threats to privacy in modern society, fears that are both reflected and reinforced by the newspaper vignettes with which we began. These reflections suggest to me the following working definition of a right to privacy (which, though not fully elaborated or defended here, is intended to be sufficiently robust to clarify the fundamental privacy interests at stake with appropriate precision):

> *The right to privacy is:* the right to be free from (1) unreasonable demands for information, (2) unjustifiably intrusive forms of surveillance, and (3) arbitrary interference with one's person, home, or possessions.

The three limbs of my definition broadly correspond to Gavison's three "irreducible elements" of privacy. Limb (1) accommodates the intuition that privacy is about keeping secrets, as do limbs (2) and (3) to lesser extents. It is patent, however, that privacy can be lost or invaded in ways that have precious little to do with providing information, for example through intrusive surveillance or interference with one's freedom of movement, home or possessions. While all three limbs of my definition could be said to protect interests in anonymity and solitude, limb (2) is most directly concerned with remaining anonymous – one's interest in "disappearing into the crowd" – and limb (3) with protection from interference, the interest in being left alone. It is a virtue of this definition that a right to privacy conceived in these terms is not limited to one's home or, more broadly, to what is loosely referred to as "the private sphere", but extends to places open to members of the public, such as universities, clubs, libraries, shopping centres or telephone booths.[37] It even extends – along with the right to unhindered locomotion – to activities which take place on public highways or in other indubitably "public" fora. As David Feldman rightly observes:

> There are certain situations which are in a sense public (in the sense of being places of public resort, or places dedicated to public purposes under the control of a public authority) but where people properly expect a reasonable level of seclusion. Examples include the sites of disasters, hospital wards, and school premises. The same applies to the cubicles of public conveniences. In such relatively public settings, people conduct parts of their lives which are distinctly private.[38]

[36] *Ibid.* at 428–9 (footnote omitted).

[37] One of the leading cases in US Constitutional criminal procedure decided that a public telephone booth comes within the scope of the Fourth Amendment's privacy protection: *Katz* v. *United States* 389 US 347; 88 S Ct 507 (1967) (US Supreme Ct).

[38] David Feldman, "Secrecy, Dignity or Autonomy? Views of Privacy as a Civil Liberty", *supra* n 34 at 69 and 59–62; and for a general discussion, linking privacy interests in public to significant technological developments, see Helen Nissenbaum, "Protecting Privacy in an Information Age: The Problem of Privacy in Public" (1998) 17 *Law and Philosophy* 559.

The interests involved in the situations contemplated by (1), (2) and (3) are of course not limited to privacy. Being arbitrarily detained or deprived of one's possessions, for example, could involve a multiplicity of harms, including restrictions on freedom of movement and the quiet enjoyment of one's property. The only claim made here is that privacy interests are likely to be among the interests set back, and privacy rights among the rights infringed, on any given occasion. It is not asserted that privacy is necessarily compromised in each and every such case, much less that harm to privacy interests, when it occurs, is always the worst of it. That privacy interests turn out to overlap with other types of interest is, in point of fact, exactly what we should have expected. The proposition that a single act may infringe more than one right, by simultaneously harming two or more protected interests, is – I take it – entirely familiar and uncontroversial (e.g. burglary simultaneously involves trespass, invasion of privacy, and deprivation of property or other harm).[39]

A right to privacy thus defined is universal, since all citizens may enjoy the right equally without placing any individual or social group under intolerable autonomy-diminishing duties. To this extent, in structure, the right to privacy resembles the right to negative liberty: but structural resemblance must not be confused with moral justification. Privacy rights should be justified, not by reference to any negative conception of liberty, but in terms of privacy's unique contribution to the (positive) conception of autonomy sketched in the last section. Autonomy is a richer and more attractive ideal than negative liberty, and therefore supplies a correspondingly superior argument for endorsing privacy rights.[40] The definition of a right to privacy adumbrated here is intended to pick out the realms of "personal space" (with boundaries expanding or contracting according to context) which are essential for the development of authentic self-identity, the capacity for autonomy, and the lived social reality of an autonomous life. In this way, the right to privacy is securely anchored in its ultimate justification, the political ideal of autonomy. And by tying privacy down

[39] A burglar in English law is defined by the Theft Act 1968 s. 9(1)(b) as someone who "having entered into any building or part of a building as a trespasser . . . steals or attempts to steal anything in the building or that part of it or inflicts or attempts to inflict on any person therein grievous bodily harm".

[40] The richer ideal of autonomy is, notably, consistent with perfectionist political principles, and incorporates a more sophisticated account of individual welfare, than does negative liberty. See Raz, *The Morality of Freedom, supra* n 12; Charles Taylor, "What's Wrong with Negative Liberty", reprinted in his *Philosophy and the Human Sciences: Philosophical Papers 2, supra* n 22. Cf. Isaiah Berlin, "Two Concepts of Liberty", reprinted in his *Four Essays on Liberty* (Oxford: Oxford University Press, 1969). Berlin's preference for negative liberty was rooted in his fear of despotism disguised as paternalism. But he was well aware of the dangers of malign neglect, and by no means opposed to state intervention to create the conditions in which negative liberty could be meaningfully exercised. Responding to critics of "Two Concepts of Liberty", he later wrote: "Advocacy of non-interference . . . was, of course, used to support politically and socially destructive policies which armed the strong, the brutal, and the unscrupulous against the humane and the weak, the able and ruthless against the less gifted and the less fortunate. Freedom for the wolves has often meant death to the sheep. . . . The case for intervention, by the state or other effective agencies, to secure conditions for both positive, and at least a minimum degree of negative, liberty for individuals, is overwhelmingly strong". *Ibid.* at xlv, xlvi. And compare Raes, p. 25 in this volume.

to just those realms of "personal space", the definition keeps relevant interests sufficiently narrow to be proper subjects for protection by duty-imposing rights.

Standard objections and popular misconceptions

Someone might accept both the connection between privacy and autonomy asserted in Section I, and the Interest Theory of rights developed and applied here, and yet still be unwilling to concede the existence of a right to privacy. One objection might be that privacy interests can be recognised without being elevated into the subject-matter of a right. The *de facto* enjoyment of freedom from interference with one's privacy is not, assuredly, the same as a right to privacy. Why, it might be asked, is *de facto* freedom not enough? Why must moral rights and duties come into the picture?

The case for a right to privacy has so far rested on: (i) the crucial importance of privacy for personal autonomy; and (ii) the relatively undemanding nature of privacy-related duties: we have seen that this ensures the compatibility of privacy rights with human autonomy and with other important individual and social values,[41] some of which (including, for example, human dignity, family ties, and participatory democracy) derive positive reinforcement from the security of private life. The missing link in the chain of argument, on which this first objection fastens, is the affirmative case for elevating privacy interests into privacy rights.

In the space available, and without becoming embroiled in complex – and anyway inconclusive – questions of moral epistemology, the affirmative case for a right to privacy rests on the following considerations. First, let it be said, there is no grand mystery about the general relations between interests, liberties and rights. From the perspective of the Interest Theory, the question is simply whether an interest is sufficient to place another person under a duty to respect it. As reflected in international human rights treaties like the ECHR and the ICCPR, I suggest that privacy interests are important enough to be grounds of duties, both for government officials and private individuals. As well as following from the analysis of privacy interests undertaken in Section I, this conclusion is strongly intimated by the newspapers vignettes that were quoted *in extenso* at the beginning of this chapter. Privacy interests are highly vulnerable in a world

[41] Privacy's contribution to advancing a broad range of social and political values is stressed by David Feldman, "Privacy-Related Rights and their Social Value," in Peter Birks, *op. cit.* n 34. Feldman asserts that: "Privacy in its sociable form helps us to define and then to defend the social spheres in which we work or play with others. These spheres are more important than those fields in which we operate without others, and are very significantly more valuable than those areas in which we work selfishly against others" (at 22). Nonetheless, when it comes to identifying criteria to determine the scope and limitations on privacy rights Feldman adumbrates a list of distinctly liberal autonomy/harm principle considerations (at 24–5). Since my argument for an autonomy-*based* right to privacy leaves room for social, communal and collective aspects of privacy, there is perhaps little material distance between Feldman's position and mine, though I remain doubtful of aspects of his theoretical analysis.

of CCTV, vast and growing data banks of personal information and spy satellites in the sky. The seriousness of the threat posed to privacy interests in modern society, in conjunction with a proper understanding of privacy's key contribution to human flourishing, justifies mutual duties of respect for privacy. These duties extend, with appropriate modifications in their detailed specification, to a wide range of formal and informal roles and relationships. Professionals such as doctors and lawyers owe privacy-based duties to their patients and clients; employers and employees respectively bear whatever duties of privacy are implied by their particular employment relationship. Officials of all kinds have important privacy-based duties. In the criminal justice context, police officers are not only the most obvious example of state officials with duties to respect privacy, but also demonstrate in their day-to-day activities the manifold ways in which privacy is imperilled by the exercise of official state power. A less familiar but no less important second example is that legislators have duties to enact laws that provide an appropriate measure of protection for privacy interests, and further laws to secure appropriate redress when privacy rights are infringed, as they inevitably will be on occasion. If these and other similar duties have sound moral justifications, as I think they do, this explains why privacy interests are a source of rights, and not (only) liberties.

A different objection to conceding a right to privacy is that privacy is open to abuse, and has in fact been repeatedly abused in the past. Its chequered record has given the right to privacy a bad reputation in some circles. For, it is charged, does privacy not provide a cloak for tyranny and a licence to victimise the vulnerable and defenceless?[42] Is the right to privacy not the reflex defence of choice for sweat-shop factory owners, men who beat their wives and girlfriends, and parents who abuse their children? The work done in recent decades by feminist criminologists and others in beginning to expose the almost unimaginable nature and extent of (mostly) men's violence against women and children in the home gives these questions irresistible force and urgency.[43] Furthermore – as if that were not enough – in these times of "flexibilisation", de-regulation, privatisation and increasing casualisation of the workforce, we are again confronting questions about working conditions and labour exploitation that by now ought to have been consigned to histories of the rabid first phase of nineteenth century capitalism.[44] The feminist-leftist critique of the public/private

[42] The connection is neatly exemplified by chapter 5 of Susan S.M. Edwards, *Sex and Gender in the Legal Process* (London: Blackstone, 1996), entitled "All in the Name of Privacy – Domestic Violence".

[43] The literature is voluminous. See, for example, R. Emerson Dobash and Russell P. Dobash (eds), *Rethinking Violence Against Women* (Thousand Oaks, CA: Sage, 1998); Marianne Hester, Liz Kelly and Jill Radford (eds), *Women, Violence and Male Power* (Buckingham: Open University Press, 1996); Elizabeth A. Stanko, *Intimate Intrusions: Women's Experience of Male Violence* (London: Unwin Hyman, 1985).

[44] In reality, of course, the worst aspects of labour exploitation were not so much left behind, as exported abroad. On the often nakedly direct relationship between criminal justice and economic production in the colonial system, see Bankole A. Cole, "Post-Colonial Systems", in R.I. Mawby (ed.), *Policing Across the World: Issues for the Twenty-first Century* (London: UCL Press,

divide has become (though radicals bristle at the thought of contributing to a new orthodoxy) a received part of the philosophical canon.[45] The argument, in short, is that rights to privacy cannot be allowed if they result in violations of other people's rights to bodily integrity, security, freedom from abuse, good health, safety at work, and to earn a living wage. Found inconsistent with these presumptively more pressing interests, the right to privacy is apparently exposed as sectional ideology, debunked and rejected.

The importance of these considerations, though summarised in necessarily truncated form, must not be underestimated or trivialised. They demand and deserve proper regard. Nonetheless, whatever the wider merits of critiques of the public/private divide, the particular style of objection examined here does not materially weaken, much less defeat, the principled *general* case for a right to privacy. In conclusion to this section, I will expose two baseless misconceptions – one about rights, the other about the value of privacy – on which this unsuccessful objection appears to rest.

A popular misconception about rights is that two genuine rights can never be in conflict with each other. On this view, if an apparent or *prima facie* right to privacy is in conflict with an apparent or prima facie right to, say, bodily integrity, one of these "rights" is an impostor and must give way. Only the superior interest can properly be said to give rise to an all-things-considered right. Yet it would be fatal to any mooted right to privacy if this "winner-take-all" conception of rights were sound. Whenever apparent privacy rights appear to be in direct competition with manifestly weighty interests like bodily integrity or physical security, privacy will almost always appear to be the lesser interest that has to give way. *Ergo*, there is no right to privacy, at least not one of any consequence which could ever derogate from interests in bodily integrity etc.

Viewed through the lens of the Interest Theory of rights, however, this argument is a simple *non sequitur*, since rights conceived as conclusive grounds for duties can, and regularly do, conflict. The harsh ethical reality is that it is not always possible to respect every pertinent right equally, or to discharge all one's duties fully, even when one's acts are unimpeachably well-motivated. Conflicts of duty supply the standard examples of moral dilemmas, as where there are two drowning men but only one lifebelt, so you must choose between the duties of rescue you owe equally to both, though each has the same right to life grounding your duty of rescue. Likewise, the state has duties to respect privacy rights and duties to protect bodily integrity, but there are many situations in which it cannot completely satisfy both. The state, as representative of the political

1999); John A. Arthur, "Development of Penal Policy in Former British West Africa: Exploring the Colonial Dimension," in Obi N. Ignatius Ebbe (ed.), *Comparative and International Criminal Justice Systems: Policing, Judiciary and Corrections* (London, Butterworth-Heinemann, 1996); Colin Sumner (ed.), *Crime, Justice and Underdevelopment* (London: Heinemann, 1982).

[45] See for example, the discussion in Will Kymlicka, *Contemporary Political Philosophy: An Introduction* (Oxford: Oxford University Press, 1990) 247–62. I believe I first encountered the argument in Katherine O'Donovan, *Sexual Divisions in Law* (London: Weidenfeld and Nicolson, 1985).

community, must do the best it can with the legislative, policy, and executive instruments and institutions at its disposal, to strike an appropriate balance between interests and rights which are often competitive and sometimes in conflict. The fact that on some occasions it clearly favours, say, interests in bodily integrity, while in other contexts privacy interests are given greater precedence, shows only that privacy rights and rights to bodily integrity sometimes conflict, not that rights must necessarily be limited to those interests which prevail over all others.

It is tempting to try to explain (away) rights conflict by pointing to the fact that very few rights are absolute. The right to privacy certainly is not absolute, as my proposed definition makes clear: *reasonable* demands for information, *justifiable* surveillance, and *non-arbitrary* interference with person, home or property all fall outside its protection. Perhaps, then, it can be shown that the right to privacy is circumscribed by the boundaries of more weighty interests, such as interests in bodily integrity and security, so that rights protecting these interests are not in conflict with the right to privacy after all?

The suggestion is a helpful reminder that few – if any – rights are absolute, and that apparent conflicts between rights can sometimes be resolved by paying more careful attention to the proper scope of particular rights. On reflection it may be found that one right actually circumscribes or delimits another, as opposed to there being any genuine conflict between them. But this is not enough to salvage the objection presently under examination, as a simple example demonstrates. It is reasonable to postulate that the right to privacy ends at the point where there is "reasonable suspicion" or "probable cause" to suspect that a vulnerable child is in grave danger of harm. This accounts, I think, for the intuition that newspaper story (6) is a relatively easy case in which privacy rights were *not* infringed. But what if there is no reason to suspect any danger or foul play, as there will not be in many instances of child abuse or wife-beating? Random spot checks, unannounced visits, routine searches, blanket surveillance and a whole lot more could reasonably be expected to improve the detection rate (even on the currently accepted, and arguably too narrow, definition of abuse), techniques which are all fundamentally incompatible with the right to privacy, however carefully that right might be parsed or delimited.

Some readers might now be thinking that their scepticism about the existence of a right to privacy has been more than vindicated – and by an opponent! – but this is to forget the lesson of the first section, and so to fall victim to the second misconception I promised to dispel. Privacy, to repeat, is essential for an autonomous life. It is therefore self-defeating for anybody who embraces the liberal ideal of personal autonomy to deny that there is a right to privacy in order to defend a competing right to bodily integrity. For why is bodily integrity valuable? In large part precisely because it is another prerequisite for living autonomously. The implication of finding a common root both for privacy rights and rights to bodily integrity in a liberal conception of well-being, it should be evident, is that bodily integrity would be worth much less (though certainly not worthless)[46] if privacy interests lacked adequate protection. (The reverse relation also holds, of course: a surfeit of privacy would be inadequate compensation for a substantial loss of bodily autonomy). It is certainly much to be regretted that rights always over-extend to situations in which the protection they afford is unwarranted or abused, as well as to situations in which the right-holder's interest in privacy is trivial or non-existent.[47] But this over-extension is an attribute that the right to privacy shares with every other species of right; and while it is possible to reduce the area of over-extension through careful drafting and interpretation, at some point further refinements can only be bought at the cost of excluding meritorious cases from the ambit of the right. No amount of handwringing or denial will alter that conceptual reality, or falsify the moral truth about rights. Unless one is prepared to reject the liberal ideal of autonomy itself, therefore, the right to privacy seems secure, its faults and limitations notwithstanding.

III. PRIVACY RIGHTS AND CRIMINAL JUSTICE

The philosophical inquiry undertaken in this chapter is intended as a contribution to understanding privacy in the context of criminal justice theory and practice. There are, broadly speaking, three dimensions of criminal justice on which privacy rights may bear, namely: (i) substantive criminal law; (ii) criminal investigations, procedure and evidence; and (iii) sentencing and the penal system. It is easy to recite English examples of recent developments in all three areas (and I imagine similar instances can be given for other jurisdictions with no more difficulty): thus, new stalking legislation has extended the ambit of criminal nuisance and harassment,[48] covert surveillance[49] and data banks of personal

[46] A person with no autonomy still has an interest in avoiding the pain or indignity of physical assault, for example.

[47] Being a conceptual truth about all generalisations, this is something that we simply have to learn to live with. See, generally, Frederick Shauer, *Playing by the Rules: A Philosophical Examination of Rule-Based Decision-Making in Law and Life* (Oxford: Oxford University Press, 1991). For remarks applying this general conceptual analysis to the criminal justice context, see Paul Roberts, "Taking the Burden of Proof Seriously" [1995] *Criminal Law Review* 783 at 795–8. Note that the position defended here does not entail the further, controversial claim that there can be a moral right to do moral wrong. The argument is simply that moral rights sometimes provide "cover" for immoralities that are thereby, alas, able to escape prevention or redress: see Robert P. George, *Making Men Moral: Civil Liberties and Public Morality* (Oxford: Clarendon Press, 1993) chapter 4; cf. Jeremy Waldron, "A Right to Do Wrong" (1981) 92 *Ethics* 21.

[48] See, generally, Timothy Lawson-Cruttenden and Neil Addison, *Blackstone's Guide to the Protection from Harassment Act 1997* (London, Blackstone, 1997); Celia Wells, "Stalking: The Criminal Law Response" [1997] *Criminal Law Review* 463.

[49] The limitations of the Interception of Communications Act 1985 are ably demonstrated by Adam Tomkins, "Intercepted Evidence: Now You Hear Me, Now You Don't" (1994) 57 *Modern Law Review* 941. Also see Madeleine Colvin, "Part III Police Act 1997" (1999) 149 *New Law Journal* 311 (26 February). The latest piece of legislation, the Regulation of Investigatory Powers Bill, is, at the time of writing, before Parliament. See Ed Cape, "Regulating Police Surveillance" (2000) 150 *New Law Journal* 452 (31 March), doubting that the Bill would satisfy ECHR standards if enacted without further amendment.

information[50] are increasingly familiar features of criminal investigation, and electronic tagging of offenders[51] and sex offender registers[52] are notable newcomers to the British penal landscape. The confluence of crime prevention, enhanced technological capacity and novel threats to privacy is a common thread uniting all of these developments, and many others besides. Whatever else might be said about the value of privacy, the contemporary significance of privacy rights for criminal justice theory and practice cannot seriously be denied.

The prospects for privacy in the sphere of criminal justice will naturally differ from national jurisdiction to jurisdiction, in part determined by the details of local laws and the strength of legal-cultural support for privacy rights. In Europe Article 8 of the ECHR can only become more influential. England and Wales, Scotland and Northern Ireland, in particular, will shortly be experiencing the full impact of the Convention for the first time, and – if the experience of other Council of Europe members is anything to go by[53] – a steep learning curve is rightly anticipated. To this point, however, it is plain from a common law perspective that privacy has failed to punch its weight in the criminal justice arena. Informed speculation on the reasons for this under-performance might diagnose symptomatology at each of three, sequential stages in the argument for respecting privacy rights: (1) ascertaining the value of privacy; (2) appreciating the nature and significance of a (moral) right to privacy; and (3) establishing privacy rights in law.

(1) Most fundamentally the value of privacy, as a key component of personal autonomy, is not sufficiently well understood, and privacy interests are consequently under-valued. Privacy is often conceptualised and justified in legal and non-legal discourse, not in terms of its contribution to the positive ideal of autonomy, but by reference to a negative conception of liberty. Where this occurs privacy will be weakened and underestimated, because negative liberty is today not an especially attractive political ideal. An undifferentiated and unqualified interest in being "left alone" appears anachronistic in the modern regulatory state, where mutual inter-dependence at close quarters has reduced the relevance of the rugged individualism and separatist ideals cherished by our ancestors in "frontier" societies. Much has changed for the better, and I, for one, would

[50] For example, DNA profiles of potential crime suspects, as regulated by Criminal Justice and Public Order Act 1994, Part IV. See Martin Wasik and Richard Taylor, *Blackstone's Guide to the Criminal Justice and Public Order Act 1994* (London: Blackstone, 1995) 75–8; Mike Redmayne, "The DNA Database: Civil Liberty and Evidentiary Issues" [1998] *Criminal Law Review* 437.

[51] Criminal Justice Act 1991 s.13 provides for offenders" compliance with curfew orders to be monitored electronically. According to Michael Cavadino and James Dignan, *The Penal System: An Introduction* (London: Sage, 2nd edn, 1997) 226–7 the idea originally came from a Spiderman cartoon plot, a nice illustration of the blurred line between criminal justice fact and (science) fiction.

[52] Pursuant to Part I of the Sex Offenders Act 1997 and Crime and Disorder Act 1998 s.2, reviewed by Helen Power, "The Crime and Disorder Act 1998: (1) Sex Offenders, Privacy and the Police" [1999] *Criminal Law Review* 3.

[53] It has been said, for example, that the Convention's impact on national criminal procedure law at first took Dutch lawyers by surprise. Bert Swart, "The European Convention as an Invigorator of Domestic Law in the Netherlands" (1999) 26 *Journal of Law and Society* 38.

rather live in the comparatively sedate and genteel English East Midlands of the twenty-first century than in America's brutal and lawless Wild West of yesteryear. Unfortunately, in the modern world of intensively regulated and intensely supervised social interaction (there is surely more than a passing resemblance to Foucault's "carceral" model) privacy is at risk of being thrown out with the bathwater, unless it can successfully be salvaged and reclaimed for autonomy.

(2) Failure to appreciate the value of privacy naturally leads, at the second stage of the argument, to insufficient regard for the (moral) right to privacy; or even complete failure to acknowledge it. Conflicts between rights are then misunderstood in the ways we have seen: privacy rights are relegated to a subordinate position where they are too easily overridden. The issue becomes framed, for example, as pitting V's right to bodily integrity against D's right to abuse V with impunity; and there is only one possible answer once the question is put in these terms. A different answer would sometimes be forthcoming, however, if the issue were correctly perceived to bear on *everybody's* well-being (including V's), understood – from a liberal point of view – as each person's fundamental interest in leading an autonomous life.

(3) Supposing that, with difficulty, (1) and (2) can be overcome, at a doctrinal level the problem remains one of translating moral rights into legal rights and duties. In order to achieve this it is necessary to be able to define a legal right to privacy so that it is neither too broad nor too narrow. If too narrow, the right to privacy is at risk of becoming wholly subsumed under rights protecting derivative or overlapping privacy-related interests, such as the right to quiet enjoyment of one's possessions, which is protected, *inter alia*, by tort remedies for trespass and nuisance, as well as by the criminal law of theft. In these circumstances the right to privacy ceases to ship juridical freight and is thus rendered redundant as an independent source of legal duties. Yet an over-ambitious right to privacy will be equally ineffectual if its grasp extends too far beyond its reach. This can be seen, for example, in US constitutional law where the "right to privacy" has been stretched to the point where it resembles an inferior, because much less transparent or immediately appealing, legal synonym for personal autonomy. It is not just that an over-extended right to privacy risks being denounced as a disreputable smokescreen for establishing controversial legal entitlements, such as rights to abortion or euthanasia;[54] though that is certainly bad enough.[55] To become used and confused as a functional equivalent of

[54] For sustained critique of the sham neutrality and self-evidence of privacy, see Jed Rubenfeld, "The Right of Privacy" (1989) 102 *Harvard Law Review* 737. A very readable and persuasive introduction to US constitutional law debates on privacy, abortion and euthanasia is Ronald Dworkin, *Life's Dominion: An Argument About Abortion and Euthanasia* (London: Harper Collins, 1993).

[55] I do not mean to say that legal rights to abortion or euthanasia are ill-founded, only that they must be argued for directly, and privacy is not the crux of the matter in either case. To this extent I agree with Michael J. Sandel, "Moral Argument and Liberal Toleration: Abortion and Homosexuality" (1989) 77 *California Law Review* 521 who observes to similar effect that: "The justice (or injustice) of laws against abortion and homosexual sodomy depends, at least in part, on the morality (or immorality) of those practices".

autonomy would be fatal to the prospects of a legal right to privacy, because, as we have seen, there cannot even be a *moral* right, much less a legal entitlement, to lead an autonomous life under prevailing social conditions. Given the narrowness and difficulty of the virtuous middle way, with perils on either side, it is worth considering whether carefully-crafted piecemeal legislation might not be the most effective way of extending legal safeguards to particular privacy-related interests, such as adults' freedom to engage in consensual sexual activity in private.[56] Recent Australian legislation provides one model.[57]

Finally, even if a moral right to privacy, understood as a vital component of personal autonomy, can be correctly identified and translated into positive law, difficult, context-specific questions about the nature and relative priority of competing interests will inevitably remain. I have barely touched upon this very practical dimension of the challenge of privacy rights, but it should be emphasised in conclusion that careful consideration of the value of particular privacy interests, and the weight to be accorded to values and interests which compete with them in concrete settings, is an essential, inescapable feature of moral and legal reasoning about privacy. Filtering privacy claims through the organon of plural and incommensurable values requires highly particularistic, context-sensitive normative judgments, about which generalisations quickly outrun their usefulness.[58]

Two generalisations the usefulness of which I hope to have demonstrated, nonetheless, are: first, that it is necessary to have an informed appreciation of the true nature of privacy interests and rights before any evaluation or balancing against other interests can take place; and, secondly, the reasoning process should be purged of conceptual confusion or error, follow a logical structure and progression, and be transparent to its outcomes. If the arguments presented in this chapter are incomplete and inconclusive in significant respects (which they are), this partly reflects both the generalising nature of the enterprise and the impoverished state of current learning. Though these reflections may fairly be considered preliminary to the main work of giving privacy rights precise substance and form, my aim has been to shine some light on a topic which, for most English criminal lawyers at least, remains the darkest *terra incognita*.

[56] Cf. *R* v. *Brown, Lucas, Jaggard, Laskey and Carter* [1994] 1 AC 212 (HL); *Laskey, Jaggard and Brown v. UK* (1997) 24 EHRR 39 (ECtHR); *Bowers* v. *Hardwick*. 478 US 186; 92 L Ed 2d 140 (1986) (US Supreme Ct).

[57] See Simon Bronnitt, "Legislation Comment: Protecting Sexual Privacy Under the Criminal Law – Human Rights (Sexual Conduct) Act 1994 (Cth)" (1995) 19 *Criminal Law Journal* 222.

[58] On this, at least, I agree with Amitai Etzioni, *The Limits of Privacy* (New York City, NY: Basic Books, 1999).

3

The Public, the Private and the Significance of Payments

PETER ALLDRIDGE

INTRODUCTORY

Criminal law classification

CRIMINAL LAWYERS WHEN engaging in comparative work[1] have been much concerned with the law relating to the attribution of responsibility and the traditional problems of criminal doctrine (the extent of the defence of necessity or mistake of law, impossible attempts and so on) – that is with "decision" or "adjudication" rules rather than conduct rules.[2] It is relatively rare for the issue to arise what conduct is required from citizens[3] beyond being honest in dealing with property and not hurting one another. So the issue "how is it that the legislator does and does not want the citizen to behave?" is seldom debated thoroughly. A more fertile ground for comparisons might be found in the differing behavioural requirements which varying criminal laws impose than rules about the ascription of responsibility.

Theorising in the Anglo-American literature[4] has concentrated on the issues relating to the ascription of responsibility and to offences against "the person" (homicide, assaults, woundings etc.) to the exclusion of the large range of substantive offences which govern various areas of human conduct. The textbooks generally refer to offences of corruption and counterfeiting as property crimes, offences to do with bribery of jurors or blackmail of judges as offences against the administration of justice, offences involving prostitution as morals or

[1] Especially George P. Fletcher, *Rethinking Criminal Law* (Boston, MA: Little Brown, 1978).

[2] Meir Dan-Cohen, "Decision Rules and Conduct Rules: On Acoustic Separation in Criminal Law" (1984) 97 *Harvard Law Review* 625; Paul H. Robinson, "Rules of Conduct and Principle of Adjudication" (1990) 57 *University of Chicago Law Review* 729; Peter Alldridge, "Rules for Courts and Rules for Citizens" (1990) 10 *Oxford Journal of Legal Studies* 487; John Gardner, "Justifications and Reasons" in (A.P. Simester and A.T.H. Smith (eds), *Harm and Justification* (Oxford: Oxford University Press, 1996) 103.

[3] People undertaking specific tasks may be subject to particular regulations, or even to subject themselves to guidance from someone holding such a position as "compliance officers".

[4] Nicola Lacey, "Philosophy, History and Criminal Law Theory" (1998) 2 *Buffalo Criminal Law Review* 295.

public order offences, weights and measures offences as consumer law, offences involving surrogacy or the sale of organs as being areas of medical law, insider dealing as company law, minimum wage legislation as being labour law and so on. These apparently disparate offences can usefully be brought under the head of a "criminal law of markets", and consequently provide grist to the mills of criminal law theorists. Grouping offences in this manner is important because unless crimes are classified appropriately – that is, unless the exact wrong can be identified, which crimes it is like and which it is unlike – then, on a standard liberal account, it will be impossible to label, to compare or to sentence justifiably.

There are some forms of behaviour at the boundary of the private and the commercial (adopting children, donating organs, having sex, keeping secrets, surrogacy) and some others at the boundary of the commercial and the governmental (giving people jobs, entering into contracts with foreign private business persons, influencing foreign public officials, persuading jurors to acquit or convict or voters to vote), which turn upon payment. All these activities are at least lawful, if not laudable, until payment enters, but then they become – in many cases quite serious – crimes. This paper is concerned with markets and exchanges which are criminal in the private sector and lawful in the public sector, or *vice versa*. It is an invitation to consider a group of offences which have hitherto been considered to be separate, to point out salient features which they share and to suggest lines along which further analysis might proceed. The move from the Private to the Commercial to the Governmental is a move from outlawing markets, to embracing the market as the dominant model,[5] to rejecting it again. With growing internationalisation of criminal law and its pressure of homogenisation, one of the questions which recurs is of the relationship between the claims of the international and the claims of cultural difference.

Defining the private in criminal law and criminal justice

There are two ways of drawing a distinction between the public and the private which are germane to this essay.[6] On the whole, criminal law theorists tend to draw the distinction in one way and constitutional lawyers another. To the theorist, the basic idea of the private is that there is:

> . . . a privileged territory or domain over which an individual person or group of persons (for example, a family or a club) have exclusive authority in deciding whether another may enter, and if so, for how long and under what conditions.[7]

[5] With interference from the criminal law (allegedly) to ensure the operation of markets.

[6] And see generally Kay Goodall, " 'Public and Private' in Legal Debate" 18 *International Journal of Sociology of the Law* 445.

[7] D. Feldman, "Secrecy, Dignity or Autonomy? Views of Privacy as a Civil Liberty" (1994) 47 *Current Legal Problems* 41.

This sort of privacy is, on a liberal account, a good and a necessary thing. It is necessary for the establishment of many close relationships. It is necessary for love and intimacy, and for carrying out a range of activities which, were they not performed in private, might give offence. Beyond these instrumental arguments for privacy as benefiting citizens, it also provides an argument for the limitation of the powers of the state. Within the core concept it is necessary to differentiate privacies. In particular, the literature distinguishes between aspects of privacy to do with autonomy, and those dealing with the selectivity with which personal information may be collected, stored and disseminated.[8] The distinction generates different strengths in the claims of privacy that are made.

Now privacy is not an unqualified human good. A substantial body of literature grew up, particularly in the feminist writing about law,[9] in which the idea of the private as the appropriate area for the absence of controls and for less regulated or unregulated self-expression fell into question. Activity in private that was condoned by the state was, so it was asserted, not private (i.e. immune) but rather was state-authorised activity. In particular, oppression and violence that came to be privileged by the fact of its taking place in privacy led to criticism of the standard liberal accounts of the public/private distinction.[10] Put at its simplest, the argument that the private *is* political is one that is set against the traditional liberal position that it is extra-political. In this way those who argued for the maintenance of a public/private distinction were placed in the politically dubious position of being allied to the practitioners of a range of private and indefensible misdeeds,[11] and a theoretical basis was provided for resistance to commodification of the private.[12]

One of the most cherished assumptions of liberal criminal law theory deals with the relationship between the criminal law and the private. It is that criminal law (at least in its purest, non-regulatory guise) is only legitimately directed against "harm". On this view, criminal law need have very little to do with consensual activity of any sort.[13] Nobody is harmed because all contractual activity is consensual. In traditional liberal discourse the classic Wolfenden formulation speaks to the former:

[8] D. Feldman, *Civil Liberties and Human Rights* (Oxford: Oxford University Press, 1993) 357.

[9] (1981) 130(6) *University of Pennsylvania Law Review* contains an important symposium. See particularly Morton J. Horwitz, "The History of the Public-Private Distinction" (1982) 130 *University of Pennsylvania Law Review* 1423 and Duncan Kennedy, "The Stages of the Decline of the Public-Private Distinction" (1982) 130 *University of Pennsylvania Law Review* 1349. See also Ruth Gavison, "Feminism and the Public/Private Distinction" (1992) 45 *Stanford Law Review* 1.

[10] Ruth Gavison, *op. cit.* n 9.

[11] M. Thornton, *Public and Private: Feminist Legal Debates*, (Oxford: Oxford University Press, 1995).

[12] See *infra* 87.

[13] A radical alternative thesis, that the entire body of criminal law is indirectly to protect markets, is derived from the work of Posner. Richard A. Posner "An Economic Theory of the Criminal Law", (1985) 85 *Columbia Law Review* 1193.

> There must remain a realm of private morality and immorality which is, in brief and crude terms, not the law's business.[14]

Following in this tradition are to be found Feinberg's Herculean efforts[15] to prescribe moral boundaries to the criminal law enterprise which depend upon the refinement of notions of harm. Von Hirsch and Jareborg,[16] following Hassamer, have sought to restrict and refine the "harm" principle so as to exclude various remotely occasioned harms from the legitimate use of the criminal law. On this view, criminal law may be the regulatory mechanism whereby markets are kept in order but has no further part to play.

There is an important question of priority as to the relationship between the claim of privacy and the market. It might be that particular matters are private and consequently not the law's business irrespective of whether or not money changes hands, or alternatively, that as soon as money changes hands the claim of privacy is excluded. There is a significant difference between, on the one hand, saying that a claim of privacy excludes the law from considering whether or not there is a payment, and whether, if there is, a regulatory framework could or should legitimately be imposed, and, on the other, saying that establishing that payment excludes a claim of privacy by identifying the activity within a market.

The way in which the distinction between the public and private in the sense generally understood by criminal law theorists, and expressed in this book, is stated is not the same as the way in which it is understood by administrative lawyers, who generally talk in terms of jurisdiction. In their sense "the public" refers broadly to branches of government, and the move from the private to the public was a move from the contractual to the governmental.[17] This is a rather different way of making the distinction, but again it can operate so as to set the boundary at which the criminal law will be invoked. The "private" is now governed solely by contract, not something from which contract is to be excluded. Having the market in private is lawful, but in the public sector it is criminal. It turns out that there are similar groups of crimes to be found at each of the two boundaries of the private and the public.

Locating privacy claims in English positive criminal law

In English criminal law, with the absence of any explicit right of privacy as a starting point, a search for the significance of privacy requires it to be located in

[14] John Wolfenden (Chair), *Report of the Committee on Homosexual Offences and Prostitution*, Cmd 247 (1957).

[15] Joel Feinberg, *The Moral Limits of The Criminal Law* (New York City, NY: Oxford University Press, 4 Vols 1986–1990).

[16] Andrew von Hirsch, "Extending the Harm Principle: Remote Harms and Fair Imputation" in A.P. Simester and A.T.H. Smith (eds), *Harm and Culpability* (Oxford: Oxford University Press, 1996) 259.

[17] And see Goodall, *op. cit.* n 6.

a series of individual prohibitions, from a non-exhaustive statement of which extrapolations may be drawn. First, there is a range of activities that are lawful if practised in private, but not when in public.[18] These include offences to decency,[19] and a number of curious offences involving unlawful gatherings, which may be close to crimes of giving offence.[20] Further offences of dissemination of material are restricted to distribution in public or to the public.[21] Most obviously, there is drunkenness. It is unlawful under English law to be found drunk in a public place,[22] but not, without more, in a private one.[23]

Second, there are offences that might be grouped together as "offences against privacy". These can include thefts of documents or trade secrets, telephonic,[24] postal[25] or other harassment,[26] unlawful telephone taps and unlawful electronic surveillance,[27] offences involving disclosure of confidential information, and (perhaps) racial harassment or domestic violence. One offence that is not tied in so explicit a manner to privacy, yet has developed in such a way as to be inextricably connected to it, is the crime of blackmail.[28]

Third, there are rules of criminal procedure which permit the violation or attenuation of personal autonomy. The significance of a claim of privacy in procedural criminal law is (generally, though not invariably) that there are some privacy interests which may not be invaded, or whose invasion requires particular procedural requirements to be satisfied. The substantive law, if unimpeded by the right to privacy, can affect in a very clear way the development of procedural law, with an obvious argument, which states: "If you are serious about penalising this, that or the other form of conduct, then one of the things you have to accept/embrace is that this is the kind of policing strategy which control over that sort of behaviour necessarily implies". For example, if the importation of drugs is to be illegal, then there must be power to conduct body cavity searches. What can be done procedurally will impact upon what can be prohibited substantively, and what is to be prohibited substantively will impact upon the procedures which are to be adopted.[29]

[18] For kissing in public, see *Masterson* v. *Holden* [1986] 3 All ER 39 [1986] 1 WLR 1017.

[19] Sexual Offences Act 1956 s. 13: Street Offences Act 1959 s.1(1).

[20] Under s. 5 of the Public Order Act 1936 the offence of using threatening, abusive or insulting words or behaviour had to be committed either in a public place or at a public meeting. This condition is not included in s. 4 of the 1986 Act, but s. 4(2) provides that no offence is committed if the person performing the prohibited act and its object are both inside a dwelling (though not necessarily the same one). There is an equivalent provision in respect of incitement to racial hatred: Public Order Act 1986 s. 18(4).

[21] Public Order Act 1986 s.19(3).

[22] Licensing Act 1872 s.12.

[23] No such distinction operates, of course, for drugs.

[24] Telecommunications Act 1984 s.43.

[25] Malicious Communications Act 1988.

[26] Protection from Harassment Act 1997.

[27] Interception of Communications Act 1988, reacting to *Malone* v. *UK* (1984) 7 EHRR 14.

[28] Peter Alldridge, "Attempted Murder of A Soul – Blackmail, Privacy and Secrets" (1993) 13 *Oxford Journal of Legal Studies* 368.

[29] And see Peter Alldridge, *Relocating Criminal Law* (Aldershot: Dartmouth, 2000) chapter 4.

How does the idea of privacy, rooted in information control and autonomy and reflected (more or less) in these areas of law, relate to exchange? If commodification and exchange have no legitimate place in the private sphere of human interaction, it becomes the function of the criminal law (for some reason – maybe just *faut de mieux*) to exclude it from those areas. This has been done in specific areas. After some panics, commercial surrogacy arrangements were made illegal in the UK in 1985.[30] It is a criminal offence to engage in a *commercial* surrogacy agreement,[31] but it is lawful to do it otherwise. The same kinds of issues arose about human organ transplants. After stories in the press about the use of imported organs, legislation was enacted in 1989, outlawing commercial dealings in organs.[32] In these cases the law is used to compel the relationship in surrogacy or organ donation to be one of gift, not an exchange for money.

Regarding the self as property is not unequivocal: it revives the Kantian concern as to regarding persons as property. Radin[33] has continually emphasised that personhood stands as a bar against commodification, and there has followed a debate as to whether or not commodification degrades.[34] It may be accepted that a market valuation is inapt when it degrades what is being valued.[35] One view is that the student of law and economics cannot engage with the person who asserts as a non-negotiable that these matters are not for commodification.[36] Another is that she or he can at least examine the arguments.[37] Duxbury argues that limitations upon the scope of markets are societally and historically contingent[38] and that the argument that markets degrade whatever it is which becomes their subject is one which should be rejected.[39] Markets are not inconsistent with restrictions to minimise exploitation, correct market failures, pursue distributive goals or militate against discrimination.[40] There are, of course, those who would expand the scope of the market. There is a coalition of Marxian and libertarian forces which makes the argument, for example, that

[30] Surrogacy Arrangements Act 1985 s.2.

[31] The suggestion has now been made that the "flexibility" of the rules relating to expenses still allow too much scope for the operation of markets. *Surrogacy. Review for Health Ministers of Current Arrangements for Payments and Regulation*. Report of the Review Team (Cm 4068 The Stationery Office, October 1998).

[32] Human Organ Transplants Act 1989.

[33] Especially Margaret Jane Radin, *Reinterpreting Property* (Chicago, IL: University of Chicago Press, 1993).

[34] And see Richard M. Titmuss, *The gift relationship: from human blood to social policy* (Harmondsworth: Penguin, 1973).

[35] Michael Trebilcock, *The Limits of Freedom of Contract* (Cambridge, MA: Harvard University Press, 1993).

[36] Richard A. Posner, *Economic analysis of law* (New York: Aspen Law & Business, 5th edn 1998).

[37] Neil Duxbury, "Do Markets Degrade?" (1996) 59 *Modern Law Review* 331.

[38] An interesting example is that of life insurance, which was illegal in the US in the nineteenth century because it was regarded as sacreligious to bet on the grim reaper. See Neil Duxbury, "Law, Markets and Valuation" (1995) 61 *Brooklyn Law Review* 657.

[39] Neil Duxbury, *supra* n 37.

[40] Michael Trebilcock, *op.cit.*, n 35.

childbirth should be treated as paid labour.[41] The same kinds of arguments could be advanced in respect of much commercial activity, the behaviour of voters, the behaviour of elected representatives and so on.

In some other examples, the commercial stands explicitly in the place of the public. That is, the law does not say that it is lawful to do something unless it is done *publicly* but that it is lawful to do something unless it is done *commercially*. Without more[42] it is an offence to pick wild flowers only when done for a commercial purpose.[43] Local by-laws against harvesting bait on beaches cannot infringe the right to gather it for personal use.[44] While it is not necessarily a crime to possess obscene articles, it is when they are possessed "for publication for gain".[45] That possession has a commercial purpose has a seriously aggravating role in the case of drugs. Blackmail (in the sense of operating markets in secrets) arose in a form we would recognise in the late nineteenth century.[46] In all these cases the traditional doctrine that motive is irrelevant to criminal liability is challenged. Pick the flowers, or donate the kidney, out of humanity, and be praised: do it for money and be condemned.

As to the second distinction (between the private – in the sense of the contractual – and government) there is a further range of offences of (in effect) creating a market in government. The rule of law cannot operate consistently with a system in which the application of rules is for sale. Before the development of bureaucracy, holding a public office was regarded as a means of generating income.[47] The idea that there may be anything wrong in this came with the development of the career bureaucrat. There developed common law offences of misconduct in public office and extortion by a public servant.[48] The actual offence of extortion was abolished in 1968 but the intention[49] was that the conduct in question should still be covered by the crime of blackmail.[50] General

[41] Susan Sherwin, "All Birthing should be Paid Labour" in H. Richardson (ed), *On the Problem of Surrogate Parenthood* (Lewiston, N.Y.: Edwin Mellen Press, 1987).

[42] The position is different, for example, where the plant is a member of a protected species.

[43] Theft Act 1968 s. 1, s. 4.

[44] *Anderson* v. *Alnwick D.C.* [1993] 3 All ER 613.

[45] Obscene Publications Act 1964 s. 1.

[46] *R v. Tomlinson* [1895] 1 QB 706. See Alldridge, *supra* n 28.

[47] Max Weber, "Bureaucracy" in H.H. Gerth and C. Wright Mills (eds), *From Max Weber: Essays in Sociology* (London: Routledge, 1948) 196, 198 *et seq.*

[48] J.W. Cecil Turner, *Russell on Crime* (London: Sweet & Maxwell, 12th edn 1964); James Lindgren "The Theory, History and Practice of the Bribery/Extortion Distinction" (1993) 141 *University of Pennsylvania Law Review* 1695.

[49] Criminal Law Revision Committee 8th Report, *Theft and Related Offences*, (London: HMSO, Cmnd 2977, 1966).

[50] Abolished by Theft Act 1968 s.31(1)(a). The one case which might not have been covered is the case of the public official who will only do his /her job (issue a licence, a passport etc.) if paid. This may well not amount to blackmail under English law. The technical reason is that a threat to do nothing may not amount to a menace under s.21 Theft Act 1968 even if there is a (contractual) duty to act. Law Commission, Report No. 248: *Legislating the Criminal Code: Corruption* (London: Stationery Office, 1998).

controls upon corruption had to wait until the late nineteenth and early twentieth century, and further reform is afoot.[51]

As to the administration of justice, legislation on bribing magistrates arises very early[52] and the sale of offices has been illegal since the sixteenth century.[53] Juror "knobbling" was a contempt of court from early on but is now also covered by a specific offence.[54] Controls upon the sale of votes had to await the development of the franchise. In England and Wales it is a common law offence to bribe voters in a parliamentary election.[55] It is unlawful by statute to sell votes for local or parliamentary elections.[56] It is not clear whether it is an offence to attempt to bribe, or to bribe, an opponent at a parliamentary election. It is not unlawful for a shareholder to sell a vote for a company meeting, but it is for a director (who owes a fiduciary duty to act in his view for the best interests of the company). Why is it, if it is at least perfectly legitimate and arguably the whole idea, that people should vote out of self-interest, that it is wrong to sell a vote in an election? The literature[57] on representative government is surprisingly unhelpful.[58] The same kinds of issues arise in respect of the question of political party financing.[59]

The laws in question are all either of recent provenance or under current debate. It cannot be said that they are the norms of another place or another time. Bribery as a means of securing contracts overseas was, again until recently a perfectly legitimate way in which to proceed,[60] but is now at the centre of many efforts to control trade on an international basis.[61] It just so happens that many of the areas under consideration are the subject of fairly wide public and quite independent parliamentary debate, so that in the laws relating to surrogacy or party financing a plausible case can be made that they do tell us something about England and Wales now.[62]

[51] See Law Commission, *op.cit.* n 50.

[52] The judicial oath, based upon 8 R II c.3, which was not repealed until Statute Law Repeal Act 1881 (44 and 45 Vict c.59), required that a judge accept no payment from anyone ". . . except meat and drink of no great value". See also 18 Edw III c.4 (1344) for Justices of the Peace.

[53] Sale of Offices Act 1551 (5 and 6 Edw VI c.16); Sale of Offices Act 1809 (49 Geo 3 c.126).

[54] Criminal Justice Public Order Act 1994 s. 51.

[55] *Pitt & Mead* (1762) 3 Burr 1336; 97 ER 861.

[56] Representation of the People Act 1983 s. 113.

[57] For example J.S. Mill, "On Representative Government" in Warnock (ed.), *J.S. Mill: Utilitarianism* (London: Fontana, 1979).

[58] Heather Lardy, "Citizenship and the Right to Vote" (1997) 17 *Oxford Journal of Legal Studies* 75 traces the links between citizenship and the right to vote.

[59] B.J. Levine, "Campaign Finance Reform Legislation in the United States Congress: A Critique" (1997) 28 *Crime, Law And Social Change* 1; I.Ayres and J.Bulow, "The Donation Booth: Mandating Donor Anonymity to Disrupt the Market for Political Influence" (1998) 50 *Stanford Law Review* 837–91. On the reform of political party financing in the UK see Committee on Standards in Public Life, *The funding of political parties* (London : Committee on Standards in Public Life, 1998) and see now Political Parties, Elections and Referendums Act 2000.

[60] Until 1993 deductions were able to be made from liability to tax in respect of foreign bribes. Income and Corporation Taxes Act 1988 s.577A, inserted by Finance Act 1993 s.123, Finance Act 1994 s.141.

[61] *Convention on Combating Bribery of Foreign Public Officials in International Business Transactions* (London: Stationery Office, 1998, Cm 3994).

[62] I assume here that the legal culture of England and Wales is against the use of law as a pious aspiration.

Markets and the hierarchy of exclusionary reasons

It is not the purpose of this essay to address the huge body of literature on the question whether we need markets in babies, blood, organs or secrets.[63] My concern is to examine the inarticulate assumptions about the market and the private which follow from using criminal law to prevent such markets, and to suggest that there may be indicators to be found which can help with comparative analysis of legal systems. The search will begin by seeking rational justifying accounts of the state of the law.

The rhetoric of privacy asserts that what consenting adults decide to do on their own, as judges of their own best interest, is inviolable. The use of money as an exclusionary ("trump") reason, which overrides a claim that individuals pursuing their own preferences should not only not be left alone, but instead should be punished, is by no means an obvious development. I can vote for another person because she or he is white, or for no reason at all, or because of sexual or other attraction, but not because of a gift of money. A person can consent to the transplant of his/her kidney (or refuse to donate it) on the ground that she or he would not let a woman have it, but cannot consent to its removal for money. A buyer for a commercial undertaking, can place a contract with a particular company for any one of those reasons. It may involve doing his/her job badly, or engaging in conduct which will attract condemnation and sanctions in civil courts, but it will not necessarily involve a criminal offence. Payment alters everything: what is a perfectly acceptable and frequently altruistic action becomes a (really quite serious) crime. So far as concerns the production of a rational doctrinally coherent criminal law this does lead to a search for a justifying rationale (in normative terms) for the difference it is that the payment makes. If payment is to provide a ground for intervention then it must be a different order of improper reason for acting than the sorts of improper reasons that do not, in these contexts, give rise to legal intervention. Legislation dealing with discrimination again starts in the public sector and moves towards the private.

The simplest attempt to justify this state of affairs states that what is unacceptable is the money or other payment – that the payment itself constitutes the vice. On this account, it is the fact of payment that is paramount. It is of the nature of the offences under consideration that their gravity[64] is related, if at all, only very weakly[65] to the size of the payment involved. The problem with treating the money or other consideration as being itself the vice is that the difference between proscribed payment and no proscribed payment can be so slight as for

[63] Neil Duxbury, n 37 gives an important corrective to those who would dismiss out of hand the application of arguments about markets in these areas. See also Duxbury, n 38.

[64] Reflected (most obviously) in the applicable sentences.

[65] Compared with thefts and frauds.

it not to be able to support the very serious difference in the consequences. A politician seeking election may make any number of winks and nods and indications that certain groups or people would be favoured upon his/her election, but when a penny changes hands a serious criminal offence occurs. It is difficult to ascribe such significance to so little.

An alternative is to say that payment is a proxy for the real vice. If money is evidence of an improper reason for action, then it is the improper reason, not the money itself, that provides the justification for the deployment of the criminal law. So this line of argument would state that from the point of view of the recipient what is unacceptable is voting, selling one's kidney, being a surrogate mother or giving blood *to get paid*. In English law a right in property implies a right of alienation – and traditionally, the common law right of property implies the ability to dispose, irrespective of any consideration of the motive of the person involved.[66] English law has consequently been loath overtly to acknowledge in any context the idea of abuse of rights (in civil law) or inculpatory motive (in criminal law), asserting among other things the supposed irrelevance of motive to criminal liability,[67] but it has developed[68] many mechanisms for enabling motive to be taken into account.[69] The difficulty here is to distinguish by one order of magnitude this kind of improper motive from others. If this is where the harm lies, then an explanation is needed as to why cupidity is a worse motive than, for example, racism. But this line is the clearest way to a justifying account of the present state of English law. Another way of making the same claim would be to say that criminal law enforcement resources are limited and that there would be insufficient resources for the criminal law to be invoked in all cases of improper motive. The requirement of consideration reduces the class of cases in which there is an offence, and gives the prosecution a clearer and more tangible target, and the citizen is given a clearer idea of what to avoid in order not to commit criminal offences.

Finally, there is the line of least resistance. To the question "what difference does it make that money changes hands?" would come the cynical answer, "It makes no analytical difference – it is some kind of confidence trick or legitimation strategy or false consciousness raising ploy which is employed to make us think that we're in a particular sort of system when actually we're in another". This is an explanation and not a justification, and, if it is correct, then the entire attempt to distinguish between activities for money (criminal) and unpaid (not criminal) should be abandoned.

[66] *Bradford Corporation* v. *Pickles* [1895] AC 587.

[67] And see Mitchell N. Berman, "The Evidentiary Theory of Blackmail: Taking Motives Seriously" (1998) 65 *University of Chicago Law Review* 795.

[68] Joseph M. Perillo, "Abuse of Rights: A Pervasive Legal Concept" (1995) 27 *Pacific Law Journal* 37.

[69] It is difficult to explain decisions in the areas, for example, of mercy killing and accessory liability without recourse to a notion of motive.

Defining the payment

In the criminal offences that deal with conduct that is not criminal unless paid, there is necessarily some kind of definition of what it is which "counts" as the advantage, payment or consideration triggering the criminal sanction. Blackmail is the only case where there is a clear attempt *not* to cover everything possible, and this is probably partly because of the existence of alternative "threats" offences.[70] The definitions are as follows:

Activity	*English law definition of the "consideration"*
Prostitution[71]	"reward"[72]
Organ transplants	"makes or receives any payment"[73]
Surrogacy	"for payment"[74]
Blackmail	"gain or loss" in money or other property[75]
Buying votes	"Money, gift or procurement" references to giving money include references to giving, lending, agreeing to give or lend, offering, promising, or promising to procure or endeavour to procure any money or valuable consideration; and any money, gift, loan or valuable consideration"[76]
Commercial bribery	"gift, loan, fee, reward or advantage"[77] "any gift or consideration"[78] "money, gift or other consideration"[79]
Picking wild flowers	"commercial purpose"[80]

At the very least, a rational comprehensive criminal code would have one definition rather than a number to cover the idea of "getting something for".[81] These definitions are all deliberately set widely. What is striking about them is that there is something that cannot count as "consideration"[82] for these purposes. One of the respondents to the recent Law Commission consultation on corruption was dealing with the definition of the "advantage" which the person

[70] For example procuring sexual intercourse by threats. Sexual Offences Act 1956 s.2.

[71] Prostitution is not itself an offence under English Law, but there is a range of related offences (soliciting, living off the earnings of prostitution and so on) which require a definition of prostitution.

[72] *R* v. *Morris-Lowe* [1985] 1 WLR 29; [1985] 1 All ER 400.

[73] Human Organ Transplants Act 1989 s.1(1)(a).

[74] Surrogacy Arrangements Act 1985 s.2.

[75] Theft Act 1968 s.21 and s.33(2).

[76] Representation of the People Act 1983 s.113(5).

[77] Public Bodies Corrupt Practices Act 1889 s.1(1).

[78] Prevention of Corruption Act 1906 s.1.

[79] Prevention of Corruption Act 1916 s.2.

[80] Theft Act 1968 s.4(1).

[81] With, perhaps a second to deal with the notion of "commerciality".

[82] It is no coincidence that the issue falls close to that of "consideration" in English contract law, as to which see Richard A. Posner, *supra* n 36.

accepting a bribe was to get, and he said, "Even gratification is an advantage".[83] The Commission did not dissent. On its own premise, it should have. In all the transactions under consideration (where activity is lawful unless paid) to include gratification would collapse the distinction which is sought between the area of gift and the area of market.[84] The supererogatory organ donor or surrogate mother, the public spirited MP or councillor or the altruistic voter or the buyer taking a pride in his/her job, and so on, will all receive gratification from the performance of their tasks. That cannot itself be enough to justify the invocation of the criminal law. It must have been as a result of oversight that the Commission was prepared to countenance that line of approach.

The difficulty which the Commission *should* have had with "mere gratification" as supplying sufficient "consideration" points to the underlying issue, which is whether the line between the paid and the unpaid, as a rigid (or even flexible) bifurcation is defensible at all. There is a large realm of our dealings one with another which cannot best be typified in terms either (on the one hand) of a market or (on the other) of individual kindnesses and acts of supererogation. Of course, the absence of a payment does not mean the absence of strings. All the transactions to which I have referred usually or frequently involve some sort of set of expectations – even if it is just the expectation that when this whole thing is over one of the participants will go away. It is difficult to understand them in terms of a naive distinction between gift and market.

Offer[85] argues that the "great transformation" in economic history from customary exchange to impersonal markets is incomplete. Reciprocal exchange pervades modern societies. It takes the form of "gifts", reciprocated without certainty. Reciprocity is driven by the pursuit of "regard". Money is (generally) avoided in regard exchanges, because it is impersonal. Instead, regard signals are embodied in goods, in services, or in time (attention). The personalisation of gifts authenticates the signal. Reciprocal exchange persists in family formation, in intergenerational transfers, in labour markets, in agriculture, the professions, in marketing, entrepreneurship, and also in corruption and crime. Regard exchanges and a favour economy are not susceptible of governance by the clumsy distinction between gift and market. They operate in between. Whether or not a particular transaction is a gift, an "arms length" market transaction or something in between will be culturally determined. And the cultural enquiry will include enquiry into the nature of gift and the nature of obligation.

An important supplementary question which can be answered using Offer's analysis is whether it makes a difference that a particular transaction can be expressed to be for money rather than for money's worth? There is a range of

[83] Judge Rhys Davies QC quoted in Law Commission, Report No. 248 *Legislating the Criminal Code: Corruption* (London, Stationery Office, 1998), para. 5,.41 fn 57.

[84] And see Melvin Aron Eisenberg, "The World of Contract and the World of Gift" (1997) 85 *California Law Review* 821.

[85] Avner Offer, "Between the Gift and the Market: The Economy of Regard" (1997) 50 *Economic History Review* 450.

areas of legal discourse where the issue arises whether or not a financial value can be placed upon a good at all, and even if it can, whether it has the same meaning as the cash. The rule that there are some contracts for breach of which damages are not an adequate remedy, but that they should be specifically enforced[86] is a reflection of just such a set of values. The money is not quite what is sought. Suppose a businesswoman accepts lunch from a business contact: that is fine. If she sits through lunch without eating or drinking and accepts cash in *lieu*, that is potentially corrupt: why? Not because of the respective economic values (which can be identical), but because under those conditions the money is not capable of being a gift, in the way that the lunch can be, so that the recipient can thank the donor yet remain under no further obligation. Issues of cultural difference are clearly important, because the different social meanings ascribed to money as against other goods are societally specific.[87] This is also true of the circumstances in which cash can be an appropriate gift. In Britain, for example, Marks and Spencer tokens are (ridiculous) ways of giving people money while not giving people money.[88] Here, then is the problem of "globalisation" – on the one hand the forces of globalisation call for free markets and the contractual relationship: on the other cultural differences at the local level dictate the meanings of gifts and consequently the range of the intervention which the criminal law is able legitimately to make in relations between consenting adults.

Constructing the rational autonomous individual

Usually the analysis is made in terms of the development of rules relating to the kind of individual whom the criminal law constructs and addresses. It does not take too sophisticated a reading of the relevant texts to generate the inference that a set of issues about class, race, gender and paternalism is in play. Naffine[89] shows that the way in which the law is shaped is a function of the stereotypes that inform its creation. She argues that the law relating to abortion, surrogacy and prostitution is written against a background of patriarchy, and that the Lockean notion of self-ownership is itself a male one. It was never constructed around, and does not apply to women. Consequently the argument from self-ownership has not been allowed to strike at abortion. There is no reason that Naffine's insight need cease at women. Locke's self-owner also owned property, and was white, British and middle class. The rules relating to the establishment

[86] In English law, for a piece of land or a highly specific chattel.

[87] Joongi Kim and Jong Bum Kim, "Cultural Differences in the Crusade against International Bribery: Rice-Cake Expenses in Korea and the Foreign Corrupt Practices Act" (1997) 6 *Pacific Rim Law & Policy Journal* 549.

[88] P. Webley and R. Wilson, "Social Relations and the Unacceptability of Money as a Gift" (1989) *Journal of Social Psychology* 85; J.L. Solow, "Is it Really the Thought that Counts? Towards a Rational Theory of Christmas" (1993) 5 *Rationality and Society* 506.

[89] Ngaire Naffine, "The Legal Structure of Self-Ownership" (1998) 25 *Journal of Law and Society* 193.

of markets in jobs (that the employer is permitted to pay someone to get them an employee but not the employee to get them a job)[90] can be read either as exercises in paternalism or as denying job-seekers choices. The horror stories which generated the legislation outlawing payment for human organ transplants in the UK[91] were of semi-literate Turks being exploited by being paid a few thousand pounds. The middle-class/upper class stereotypes, on the other hand, are those of the parliamentarian or the businessperson. Of course (because they are rational autonomous, honourable and male) they are not going to be influenced in the exercise of their judgment (in passing legislation, speaking to ministers or whatever official position it is which they undertake), simply because somebody has given them a brown envelope stuffed with tenners.[92] That is, not only is it difficult to draw a single boundary between gift and contract, and the public and the private in both senses. Not only is there no rigid bifurcation. There is no bifurcation. There is a radical indeterminacy.

CONCLUSIONS AND AGENDA

Thus far I have been dealing almost wholly with the position in England and Wales. The concern has been with legal definitions. Is it possible to move from that account to any useful comparative account? Comparing sets of rules or comparing social practices can be a barren exercise, informed by what Nelken has dubbed "comparison by juxtaposition".[93] What is there about the current state of the criminal law relating to markets and the private, and the hinterland between markets, gifts and regard exchanges as between jurisdictions which might make it a better indicator of what kind of culture generates it? The area includes two of the major traditional issues treated by doctrinal Western comparative law (the issues of abuse of rights and consideration).[94] It also involves consideration of what are frequently subtle cultural differences. How can we learn about these differences? What kind of thing would need to be known of another jurisdiction in order to advance the account?

The essay has suggested that two things are important. First, the rules of positive law will give an account of the values they enshrine. A given jurisdiction either will or will not allow transplants for money, and whether or not it does says something about the jurisdiction. Second, the culture within which the rules, exchanges and gifts take place should be understood. It is not enough to know that a certain item changes hands: to know that it did so as part of an illegitimate exchange requires access to the cultural meaning of the transaction. By attending to such questions comparative criminal law might avoid some dead ends.

[90] Employment Agencies Act 1973.

[91] Human Organ Transplants Act 1989.

[92] See Dawn Oliver, "Regulating the Conduct of MPs: the British Experience of Combating Corruption" (1997) 45 *Political Studies* 539.

[93] David Nelken, "Introduction", in *Comparing Legal Cultures* (Aldershot: Dartmouth, 1997).

[94] Posner, *supra* n 36.

4

Sovereignty, Criminal Law and the New European Context

LEONARD F. M. BESSELINK

IN THIS ESSAY I shall discuss European law and sovereignty, more especially the role left to the state in penalising certain behaviour, and I shall try to relate that to the issue of autonomy within the private sphere.[1] Many – if not most – of these issues deserve further elaboration in various directions, but some are already more closely examined in other essays in this book. Also for considerations of editorial space, I have therefore opted for the panorama rather than for factual and intellectual detail.

By way of introduction, I first present the problem at issue and a number of brief considerations on sovereignty and the public-private distinction. In the second section I shall turn to a discussion of EU law, by first discussing EC law (primary law on criminal law exceptions to the economic freedoms and secondary law on sanctions) and next the so-called third pillar EU law. With regard to both first and third pillar law, I shall also discuss how institutional aspects of decision-making in Europe affect sovereignty. In the third part I return to the issues of the private and public sphere and of sovereignty.

I. THE STATE, SOVEREIGNTY AND AUTONOMY

The theme of this book questions the possibilities of the state (and the role of various political and legal cultures within certain states) to criminalise certain behaviour in the light of the idea of personal autonomy and respect for the private sphere. It is the relationship between the state and the private sphere/autonomy: to what extent can the state encompass the private sphere: can it extend its power to interfere with what is private and on what assumptions does it or should it do so?

[1] I have been asked to write on substantive criminal law. For that reason matters of procedural criminal law and questions of enforcement, powers of investigation and prosecution – although they clearly have a bearing on matters of substantive law – are not discussed in this paper. The story on those aspects is, especially with regard to European integration, quite different from the one that follows (see also the final remarks in the paragraph on EC sanctions below).

For the sake of this essay I shall narrow the issue down into the question: how far does the state's sovereignty reach? It has become unusual to phrase questions in this type of context in terms of sovereignty. Nevertheless, there may be good reason to do so.

A first reason is of an analytical nature. There is a close semantic resemblance between the concepts of sovereignty and of privacy. The first refers to public autonomy, the second to private autonomy. In this respect the two concepts are analogous. Of course, much depends on what "autonomy" means in these two cases, but even in its respective senses the two concepts can be considered analogous.

The relationship between public and private autonomy is at the centre of the problem of criminal law and the private sphere. The power to punish involves one of the more physical manifestations of the state, notwithstanding the monetarisation of parts of criminal law. Although the theme of the state, the public and the private lends itself to analytical exercises about these concepts as linguistic constructs, we are here dealing with a state substrate in a less pleasant physical reality, which led Hobbes to describe the state, in its very physical capacity, as a monster. The assumption in this essay is that it is sovereignty which inspires that *corpus monstruosum* to impose itself on society; as Hobbes put it, sovereignty is the soul of this leviathan.

This way of representing the state, stands in contrast with how the state is conceived in other contexts. In days of peace and quiet the state, tamed by the rule of law, is often represented in rather harmless terms. That is perhaps most significantly (and surprisingly) so in international relations between European states (outside the Balkan). In the context of internationalisation, Western states have submitted to international standards which are a constraint on their power within each of these states themselves. They have submitted to constraints also through the process of European integration, which has extended into the sphere of criminal law. Hence, also in the context of international relations the question of sovereignty comes again to the forefront.

I shall briefly examine both these internal and external aspects of sovereignty within our broader theme.

Sovereignty

Any treatise which centres on the issue of sovereignty must start with a number of caveats. I have three.

First, it may be pointed out that although in some major European states the issue of sovereignty has been a central concept in politics, constitutional law, public law at large and political and constitutional theory, this is not the case in all corners of the continent. Thus, the Netherlands have throughout political history done without a strong theory of sovereignty. The concept of sovereignty is not articulated as a socially effective prime ordering principle. To this day, it is strange to the political culture and legal theory underlying the system of public law. A leading textbook in Dutch constitutional law – admittedly written by a self-asserted black letter positivist – claims that sovereignty is a virtually meaningless concept in constitutional law in the Netherlands.[2] The political focus has been much more on pluralism and the diffusion of power. For citizens, pluralism was until recently a social fact of everyday life, not so much living under the sovereignty of public authorities. For public authorities it was not so much their assertion of power over subjects, but the brokering of pluralist interests in the exercise of their office. Already in the sixteenth century Althusius laid the foundations of a political and social theory of pluralism. In the twentieth century a similar pluralist concept of sovereignty was philosophicially founded by Herman Dooyeweerd's development of the doctrine of "sovereignty in one's own sphere" – although this philosophical approach, no doubt due to its outspoken Calvinist inspiration, enjoys little attention or adherence these days.[3] Such theories tie in with a society in which a multilayered organisation of large parts of the economy and the idea that as much as is feasible should be left to "self-regulation" of social sectors, are predominant. The absence of strong political notions of sovereignty makes claims such as those of Foucault – to chop off sovereignty's head – strange and irrelevant.

Secondly, the various and often opposed ideological uses to which the concept of sovereignty has been put in political discourse, have exacerbated the problem of what we actually mean when we use the term. I here briefly make a few historical remarks.

The development of the concept in the sixteenth century occurred in the context of the assertion of state-building. It was used mainly in the context of the exertion of monarchical power and the repression of "lower" powers, those of the aristocracy especially. State building in the newly independent Low Countries had to make do with a much looser conception of sovereignty: they failed to agree on which person was to embody their sovereignty, a successor to their previous sovereign lord, the King of Spain, and soon realised that it is not impossible to do without one. As far as sovereignty was concerned, they muddled through for two centuries as a union of self-styled sovereign provincial states, each of which (at least formally) had its own Stadtholder, holding the place of the absent (and non-existent) sovereign. Small wonder that Grotius disengaged the concept of sovereignty from the idea of monarchy. He did, however, analyse the strength of government in relation to the locus of sovereignty within the state – a point from which Hobbes and later writers were to profit.

With the French Revolution, the idea of sovereignty of the people – expressed in various forms in the present day constitutions of many Continental countries – gained the upper hand. It merged with the romantic idea of the nation and led

[2] C.A.J.M. Kortmann, *Constitutioneel Recht* (Deventer: Kluwer, 3rd edn 1998), 67–8.

[3] See especially Herman Dooyeweerd, *A New Critique of Theoretical Thought*, vol. III, *The Structure of Individuality of Temporal Reality* (Philadelphia, PA: Presbyterian and Reformed Pub. Co., 1969).

to the formation of the equally romantic concept of the nation-state. This concept is still surprisingly prevalent – albeit as a problematic notion – in Anglo-Saxon writings. In Germany the concept has constitutional foundations, but it has been notoriously controversial and its discussion is clearly marked by taboo. Notwithstanding fortress Europe disputes and recurrent upsurges of self-proclaimed nationalist feeling, it hardly plays a serious role in political discourse on the Continent (except in the Balkans and some of the countries formerly under the Soviet aegis), probably because it does not answer to political realities.[4] I know all these are sweeping statements, but the concept of the nation-state hardly has a serious role to play in discussions which concern the sovereignty of EU countries in this context. I would therefore like to discard the topic of the nation-state.

Thirdly, sovereignty is a concept which has had too many uses to have analytical value when used in an indistinct manner. In order to clarify the manner in which we speak of sovereignty, we must make some semantic distinctions with regard to the use of the concept in various contexts.

Conceptual distinctions

There are two settings in which the term sovereignty is used: an internal or intrastate and an external or interstate context.

In the first context, sovereignty concerns the locus of power within the state. It may do so in two rather different ways: first, in terms of division of powers between state authorities (in earlier times the monarch versus the "lower" magistrates, in more recent times the primacy of Parliament – hence, the legislature – over the administration, and priority of administration and/or Parliament over the judiciary); and secondly, in the sense of the dominance of the state (and its apparatus) over society. It is mainly in this latter sense that I use the concept of sovereignty when discussing the internal aspect of sovereignty.

In the interstate context, sovereignty is used in two different senses, which I will call the quantitative and the qualitative sense.

The quantitative sense of sovereignty conceives of state sovereignty in terms of a set of powers. The right and power of coinage, of taxation, of punishment, of entertaining exclusive external relations and of organising the defence of the

[4] Even France, where the dominant position is that there is only a French nation and hence there is no official acknowledgement of the existence of ethnic or cultural minorities, most of the matters where the notion of the nation runs into difficulties are resolved along the lines of equality. In other European countries, the nationalist argument is generally a sub-state political phenomenon, although it is uncertain whether this will remain to be the case in what is still Belgium. On the whole, "nationalist" or "semi-nationalist" phenomena are disengaged from the state identity. Cf. J. Habermas, "Citizenship and National Identity" (1992) 12 *Praxis International* 1–19. This disengagement seems to be in line with the status of the right to self-determination in international law, which – put succinctly – recognises its implementation only when sub-national politico-cultural entities have become the object of general repression.

territory – they are the *iura regalia* (as they were called in the Middle Ages and later) which are (sometimes together with other powers) usually considered to be the sovereign rights that, when summed up, constitute the sovereignty of the state. This is a quantitative concept in as much as some of these powers – and sometimes others are added to the list – may to a larger or lesser extent be the exclusive realm of state power. Thus the right to coinage is only one power with regard to the economy, which does not necessarily mean that there should be a national mint, nor even a national currency in order to be a sovereign state.[5] The same may be said about the organisation of the national defence: the right to raise a standing army is not the only and ultimate characteristic which will make or break a state. In the past sovereign states made use of mercenary armies, more recently police forces have been reinforced by commercial patrol guards, while nowadays international coalitions like NATO and to some extent UN peace-keeping forces have in practice a function which is not so different from those of mercenary armies; some modern sovereign states do not have a proper army at all (such as Japan and Germany for a while after the Second World War and a number of miniature states, such as Liechtenstein, San Marino, Andorra – none of which, incidentally, have their own currency either). In short, the sovereignty of a state is a calculus which may lead people to say that a state is in some respects less sovereign than in others. One may even arrive at a point at which the outcome of the calculus is negative: the state ceases to be sovereign.

Clearly, this quantitative approach to sovereignty is predominant in the European Court of Justice's famous *Van Gend en Loos* case:[6] states have limited their sovereignty by transferring powers to the Community legal order. The integrationist discourse of the 1950s and 1960s showed all signs of a conscious drive towards a negative result of the calculus: the eventual eclipse of that dangerous concept of state sovereignty (admittedly a rather naive discourse which failed to take into account the sovereign power which the projected Europe necessarily must gain in a "quantitative" approach by the transferral of power).

The qualitative concept of sovereignty has its roots not so much in the Middle Ages, but in the Renaissance (which in turn links back mainly to Roman antiquity). It centres around the idea of state independence. In public international law it is conceptualised in the principle of the sovereign equality of states. Historically it was articulated in the concept of the *libertas* of the state, the political liberty to shape one's own public society without interference by others. This qualitative concept of sovereignty is not really a matter of more or less sovereign, but of either sovereign or not sovereign. If a territorially organised political entity does not have this quality of being sovereign, it cannot be recognised

[5] For an overview on monetary sovereignty and the implications of the introduction of the Euro for the membership of the IMF, see Rutsel Silvestre J. Martha. "The Fund Agreement and the surrender of monetary sovereignty to the European Community" 30 (1993) *Common Market Law Review* 749–86, esp. 752–66.

[6] *Van Gend en Loos* [1963] ECR 1.

as a state under public international law. In this qualitative sense a state is sovereign or it is not.

It must at this stage be pointed out that the relationship between the qualitative and quantitative senses of sovereignty is a little complicated. The quantitative and qualitative senses interfere with each other. This is so because liberty or independence is implicitly predicated of those powers which (under the quantitative aspect) together make a state sovereign in a qualitative sense. Yet it is useful to make the distinction. The distinction should open the way to understanding why the mere fact of being bound by certain (legal) rules and principles (which clearly limits the power to act in a certain field) in itself does not detract from sovereignty (in the qualitative sense). No author, from Bodin onwards, who has intended to make a meaningful use of the concept of sovereignty has maintained that sovereignty is equal to unfettered power.

I return to the subject of the interrelationship between these two senses of sovereignty at the end of this paper.

The public and the private

I now turn to a brief discussion of sovereignty within the state and concentrate on the distinction between the public and the private.

The erosion of the idea of state sovereignty can be seen as parallel to the erosion of the public domain as organised within the state. This erosion has roots in a certain liberal conception of the state, which distinguishes the public sphere (defined as the sphere which concerns the state institutions and the relationship between citizens and those institutions) from the private sphere (defined as the sphere of private autonomy for the individual and the relationships between individuals). Whereas the free market economy is located in this sphere of private liberty (free society of private economic agents), the state is associated with a household governed by the budget for which the means are provided by the enforcement of fiscal measures, a budget economy which is based on institutions and regulations outside the sphere of free society. The state can only outwardly try to influence the market economy, but is essentially outside it. Empirical evidence is believed to support the idea that piecemeal interventions of the budget economy tend to be counterproductive; more structural intervention leads to a landscape of butter mountains and milk, wine and olive oil lakes. The economic heteronomy of the liberal state is parallelled by its moral heteronomy. State institutions can only govern the world as they find it; it can only legislate to the extent that moral conceptions in society converge. The doctrine of the "neutral" state is predominant in this liberal conception of the state, however impossible it may seem. Although both the economic and the moral heteronomy of the state *vis-à-vis* the market economy and morality need serious qualification, politics and society in Europe seem to have acted upon it: the state has become in many respects a hidden state, present only on the retro-scene, hidden by a dense forest of economic and other non-governmental actors. The state is no longer seen as the maker of society, based on its sovereignty (*societatis factor*) but merely as an actor within society (*societate actor*).

The liberal mood hinges strongly on the emphasis on private autonomy in political contexts. The aim of the state as embodiment of public society translates itself in terms of private objectives. When the ulterior objective of the state is to serve the interests of the private individual, the public good becomes the private good. And in the moral field public morality turns out to be a private thing. Behind this mechanism there is the hypothesis that ultimate liberty is, in *extremis*, the liberty of the solitary individual.

Precisely on this point the republican conception of liberty is offered as an alternative. Republican liberty conceives of the citizen as a person among other citizens within society. What brings people together in public society is not the ultimate furtherance of some privately determined good, but the common cause, the *res publica*. The common good is the *locus communis* of the public domain. Economically, the structure of the "free market" of economic actors is not spontaneous but can only result from state regulation and intervention; one needs to regulate for competition.

Republican notions may tend to be undifferentiated when the state is taken as embodiment of the public domain. When identifying the political as located within state structures, they have difficulty in accommodating intermediate non-governmental structures within society, which may either come to be ignored or may be considered too easily as private affairs. The republican potential is much broader if it is recognised that the public domain in the republican sense need in no way be restricted to governmental structures: non-governmental social structures, far from being private affairs, can very well be aimed at contributing to the common good which constitutes the public realm. This requires a more differentiated concept of the citizen than has sometimes been the case in the classic republican tradition. Also on republican terms, the state may thus lose its claims to prominence and may have to be more on the retro scene than it might have seemed once upon a time.

Both classical liberal and republican conceptions of the state and the public, require reconsideration of the position of the state and recognition of non-governmental actors. Whether one adheres to one conception rather than the other, their analysis of the present situation is not altogether that divergent. This has implications for criminal law. I leave it to other contributors to dwell on issues of (sustained) penalisation of acts within the sphere of private autonomy and private morality. Here I may put forward a number of hesitations as to whether the withdrawal of the state is feasible in the sphere of criminal law. For although the recent literature on criminal law and punishment has not only taken liberal and republican theories into account, but sometimes developed them significantly with regard to various aspects of criminal law,[7] it is still a

[7] Instead of many others I mention the work of Nicola Lacey, especially *State Punishment: Political Principles and Community Values* (London/ New York: Routledge, 1988) and Philip Pettit,

general and tacit assumption that the state is the public body to criminalise, penalise and inflict punishment. Criminal law is not merely part of the public domain; the assumption in both liberal and republican interpretations, is that the state is the body with the required legitimacy authoritatively to decide on punishment, and to provide the instruments for doing so. Although there are liberal and republican variations in the relevant structures of the public domain of criminal law, there are no clear alternatives to the governmental nature of public structures of accountability and responsibility when it comes to punishment. The state's institutions of criminal law may be far from perfect and amendable, but imaginable alternatives in the form of punishment outside state structures raise such acute questions of legitimacy, that they are not even considered. The state's claim to the monopoly of violence has much to do with this.

We must now examine how European integration in the EU framework fits into the picture drawn so far, and to what extent European integration, albeit a predominantly state affair, has a bearing on these developments.

II. EUROPEAN UNION

European integration has most successfully focused on the role of the private sector. The predominance of the economic market hardly needs further elucidation. It has been founded on the economic freedom of movement across borders of goods, services, persons (labour) and capital – freedoms which seem to fit in particularly well with a liberal conception of the market economy. However, the EC illustrates quite clearly how the dominance of the economic market creates the necessity to interfere through fairly massive regulation in establishing market relations which do justice to the idea of a "free" market with a "level playing field" for national and foreign economic agents of various size and nature, and which also takes into account other policy considerations, such as equality between the sexes, protection of the environment, etc. How does this economic process and the process of European integration more generally, affect the sovereignty of the state with regard to substantive criminal law?

Two different aspects should be distinguished: the EC and criminal law (first pillar), and the non-EC EU cooperation (third pillar). I give a descriptive account of how each affects sovereignty. For the first pillar, I sketch the way in which sovereignty may be materially and institutionally affected; for the third pillar, I mainly concentrate on institutional aspects.

notably *Republicanism, a theory of freedom and government* (Oxford: Clarendon Press, 1997) and (with John Braithwaite) *Not Just Deserts: A Republican Theory of Criminal Justice* (Oxford: Clarendon Press, 1990).

The first pillar

It is quite clear that sovereign powers can be more easily limited within the EC than in third pillar cooperation. For a while it may have seemed as if the EC was not affecting the sovereign power of states to determine which acts would or would not be punishable. This is no longer the case. We can distinguish between the limits which Community law imposes on national criminal law, and the activities of the Community itself in the sphere of penalisation through the establishment of sanctions.

Primary EC law and economic freedoms

The official position under EC law is still – in the standard phrase of the European Court of Justice – that "in principle criminal legislation and the rules of criminal procedure are matters for which the Member States are responsible"; but this principle is qualified to the extent that Community law as contained in the founding treaties "sets certain limits to their power" in this field.[8] The main rules of Community law which impose such limits are those set by the principle of non-discrimation within the scope of the treaty between Member States' citizens (Article 6 EC) and the so-called "fundamental freedoms": the economic freedom of movement of goods, services, capital and persons. So the question arises what this exception to the national nature of criminal law amounts to. The broadest possible answer is that the principles of EC law and the economic freedoms have to be respected by national criminal law.

A slightly more detailed account, however, leads almost inevitably to a fairly subtle picture – one which becomes quite complicated if we draw it in terms of exceptions to the national character of criminal law: the picture which is to emerge presently, concerns firstly the exceptions to the rule that criminal law is a national matter (the primacy of non-discrimination and the economic freedoms), next the exceptions to the exceptions (the EC exceptions to the economic freedoms which uphold national criminal law), and finally the exceptions to the exceptions on the exception to the national character of criminal law (the rule of reason, which makes it conditional on proportionality and necessity, that national criminal law is outside the reach of EC law). I will try my best to keep it transparent.

The "exception" to the principle that criminal law is a matter for the Member States is easy enough to explain. European law has precedence over national law; and when it comes down to it, the fundamental economic freedoms of EC law have precedence over national criminal law. From this point of view, enunciating the principle that criminal law is a national affair is a pious genuflection

[8] Most recently, case C–348/96, *Calfa*, 19 January 1999, para. 17; case C–226/97, *Lemmens*, para. 19; case 186/87, *Cowan* [1989] ECR, 195; case 203/80, *Casati* [1981] ECR 2959.

to the Member States, but is in substance not extremely meaningful (yet it shows a sensitivity for the fact that criminal law is usually considered to be one of the sovereign powers of states). In the light of the principles of precedence of Community law it may even be questionable to construct Community law as an "exception" to national sovereignty in the field. In the eyes of many an expert in Community law it would not be correct to speak of Community law in such terms. Community law has in a way superseded national criminal law.

However, things are more complex. The economic freedoms, it should be stressed, are not absolute. They can be legitimately limited on a number of grounds spelt out in the EC Treaty. The most important are in Article 30 (formerly 36) EC: the principle of free movement of goods does not preclude prohibitions justified on grounds of public morality, public policy or public security; the protection of health and life of animals or plants; the protection of national treasures possessing artistic, historic or archaeological value; or the protection of industrial and commercial property; and in Articles 39 (ex 48) (3) and 46 (ex 56) (1) EC on natural or corporate persons, which allows for limitations on grounds of public policy, public security or public health. These explicit exceptions to the economic freedoms in principle also cover criminal law exceptions, in so far as criminal law has the objective of protecting the interests specified.

The exceptions may thus be said to guard against misguided interference in the national criminal law of Member States. But they do not create "nature reserves" for the wildlife called national sovereignty: the ECJ will scrutinise whether the exceptions are legitimately invoked also when this is with a view to apply provisions of national criminal law. Also, the Court has made clear that criminal law restrictions of the economic liberties must comply with the principle of proportionality. Thus, penalties must not go beyond what is strictly necessary, nor may the penalty be so disproportionate to the gravity of the infringement that it becomes an obstacle to the exercise of the economic freedom involved.[9]

The end result of all this is that the ECJ can scrutinise and stop unwarranted interference of national criminal law with the private, mainly economic domain.[10] Here European integration reinforces the private domain of the market economy over the public domain of criminal law.

This conclusion does not apply in the same manner with regard to the so-called "rule of reason" exceptions to the economic freedoms of EC law. These are uncodified exceptions. The "rule of reason" exceptions in essence allow states to take certain measures which do not come within the terms of the codified exceptions but which do prima facie seem to interfere with the economic freedoms. They concern measures which aim to further legitimate objectives of such importance as to outweigh the interests of relevant Community law objec-

[9] *Casati*, *supra* n 8, para. 27.

[10] See for example, C–378/97, 21 September 1999, F.A. Wijsenbeek, in this case the provision of power to imprison EU citizens, who fail to show their passport when entering a Member State, was declared disproportional and hence a violation of the EC freedom of movement of persons.

tives ("mandatory requirements"). Thus measures "reflecting certain choices relating to particular national or regional socio-cultural characteristics" such as Sunday trading restrictions, the protection of the environment,[11] fair trading and consumer protection,[12] protection of the film industry,[13] can be justified, but again provided that they do not discriminate and are proportional. If they are so justified, these exceptions to the economic freedoms which come under the rule of reason, are technically speaking outside the sphere of the relevant Community law.[14] But this is not merely a technical issue. With regard to the explicit exceptions, national criminal law can only play a role under the explicit exceptions under Community law itself which come within the scope of Community law; on the other hand, in cases under the "rule of reason" exceptions, national criminal law is outside the reach of Community law. Under the first category, national sovereignty is precarious; under the second, it is genuinely maintained.

Secondary EC law: EC sanctions

The story of the fate of national criminal law does not end with the sketch of primary Community law we just presented. Community law itself also can be upheld by sanctions. Secondary Community law does in fact call for sanctions in several instances. I shall make a few remarks to draw the outlines of this issue.

The Common Agricultural Policy aimed to sustain agriculture in general and farmers' incomes especially, through strictly regimented market organisations for specific agricultural products. This meant a huge reallocation of income and a concurrent flow of money. This also tends to attract attention to possibilities for unjustified enrichment. As a consequence the enforcement of rules was called for and sanctions for transgression, evasion and fraud were attached to relevant rules.[15] These sanctions oblige national authorities to impose particular financial sanctions for breaches of rules concerning the market organisations, particularly concerning income support under farming schemes[16] and the export refunds scheme.[17] Under Community law these sanctions are considered to be administrative sanctions, although the tendency is to include sanctions with a penal character. The European Court of Justice has confirmed that in

[11] Case 302/86, *Commission* v. *Denmark* [1988] ECR 4607.

[12] Case 286/81, *Oosthoek* [1982] ECR 4575.

[13] Cases 60 and 61/84, *Cinéthèque* [1985] ECR 2605.

[14] *Ibid.*

[15] Of course the European Commission has the power to impose sanctions in the sphere of competition law, but – different from the financial fraud context – this sanctioning is located (almost) entirely at the European level and does not directly touch on national competence to impose penal sanctions.

[16] See Commission Regulation EEC 3887/92 of 23 December 1992, as amended by Regulation EC 229/95 and Regulation EC 1648/95.

[17] Commission Regulation EEC 3665/87, as amended by Regulation EC 2945/94, Regulation EC 1384/95 and EC 495/97.

pursuance of the agricultural policy according to Articles 34 (ex 40) (3) and 37 (ex 43) (2) EC, the Community is competent to impose the sanctions which it considers necessary to ensure effective and uniform administration of the rules concerning market organisations.[18] This must be done taking into account the principle of proportionality.[19] In the final instance it is up to the national courts to judge issues of intent, negligence and *force majeure*, and also they must rule on whether the chosen sanction in a particular instance is reasonable in relation to the infringement, bearing in mind the need to ensure that the aid scheme of the relevant market organisation operates satisfactorily.[20] So Community law attributes a significant role to national courts, but there can be no doubt that the sanctions imposed by Community law cannot be unilaterally discarded by national authorities. To this extent the freedom of the state with regard to sanctions (which may substantially amount to penal sanctions such as fines exceeding the immediate financial advantage derived from fraud) has been limited.

Parallel to the rules which are found in Community legal instruments, the Court of Justice has deduced from Article 10 (ex 5) EC the obligation to penalise infringement of Community law under conditions, both procedural and substantive, which are analogous to those applicable to infringements of national law of a similar nature and importance and which, in any event, should make the penalty effective, proportionate and dissuasive.[21] Whereas the primary Community law which was discussed in the previous paragraph constituted a limitation to the possibility to penalise, we are here confronted with a limitation on the state's power not to penalise certain behaviour. The principle which we are dealing with, however, is not unreasonable or unacceptable in the light of the principle of equality. Given the incorporation of Community law within the national legal orders through which Community law has become part of the national legal orders, it is right that unwarranted different treatment of the punishability of essentially equal cases should not be made. But I hasten to acknowledge that one may have different opinions on what – in applying the Court's *ratio decidendi* – is "similar" and "analogous" in concrete instances; an issue ultimately decided by the ECJ. Also an obvious limitation to the national character of criminal law would be the concept of "effective, proportionate and dissuasive penalties". If this concept were to be considered a uniform standard throughout the Community, without leaving a margin of appreciation to respect the particular penal climate of a Member State, the absolute, uniform conception would seem to be incompatible with the equality between national and EC cases. This is implicit in the principle of non-discrimination in dealing with national penal delicts and similar infringements of Community law. But it should be remembered that non-discrimination in EC law tends to be a one way principle: one is not allowed to discriminate against EC (or foreign Member State) law; but

[18] Case C–240/90, *Germany* v. *the Commission* [1992] ECR I–5383.
[19] Case 181/84, *Man* v. *EBAP* [1985] ECR 2889, para. 20.
[20] Case C–104/94, *Cereol Italia Srl* v. *Azienda Agricola Castello Sas* [1995] ECR I–2983, para. 26.
[21] See for example case 68/88, *Commission* v. *Greece* [1989] ECR 2965, paras. 23–5.

in case of differences between EC and Member State law, directly effective EC law prevails over Member State law. EC law is more equal than national law.

The parallel existence of national criminal law sanctions and Community law "administrative" sanctions raises the question how these two relate, particularly when Community sanctions amount to punitive or penal sanctions. A recurrent principle is that the Community sanctions are not suspended because of prosecution under national law. This principle is present in the Regulations on the market organisations and competition law.[22] Here we have a clear reflection of the fact that citizens are no longer mere state citizens, but are also under the jurisdiction of Community law, including the sanctions part of this law.

In the sphere of competition law, the Court of Justice has announced as a principle of natural justice that if two separate procedures were to lead to the imposition of consecutive sanctions in a single case, any previous punitive decision must be taken into account when imposing the Community sanction.[23] This means that the two legal systems of sanctions to which the citizen is in this case subjected, are to be attuned to each other under the influence of the general principles of proportionality and *ne bis in idem*; these principles are common to the legal systems of the Member States and would seem to require this approach. As such, this state of affairs does not constitute a decisive infringement of state sovereignty, to the extent that under Community law account must taken of the use of national criminal law. Moreover, in case administrative sanctions under Community law are applied, the administrative way of settling transgressions of the law may at the end of the day have priority over the use of the apparatus of criminal justice.[24] This has its advantages (and some disadvantages) over the use of criminal law as an instrument of law enforcement. This needs no further explanation to criminal lawyers.

There is one Community instrument which has tried to solve the issue in a general way. This is Council Regulation 2988/95 EC of 18 December 1995 on the protection of the European Communities' financial interests (the fraud Regulation). This Regulation concerns infringements attributed to an economic operator's acts or omissions that are or could be prejudicial to the EU budget (Article 1 (2)) and applies in a general way to cases of fraud outside those already covered by the instruments of the Common Agricultural Policy, e.g. in the sphere of structural policy, subsidies in the sphere of research, education etc. It provides general framework provisions for the imposition of administrative sanctions. It gives a quite complicated set of rules concerning the relationship between national criminal proceedings and the imposition of Community law

[22] See the Regulation EEC 3887/92, Article 11 (1) and Regulation EEC 3665/87, Article 11 (1) sub-para. 8.

[23] Case 14/68, *Walt Wilhelm* [1969] ECR 1. As far as I know, the matter still has to be decided as to the use of both administrative sanctions and criminal law penalties for the same infringement in cases in which both types are imposed by national authorities.

[24] Solveig Faurholt Pedersen, Thomas Elhom and Lars Kolze, "The effects of Community law on Danish criminal law" (unpublished paper 1998) have shown that this has actually been the major influence of the Community law of sanctions on the Danish criminal law.

sanctions of a penal nature (Article 6). They can be summarised as follows. The rule is that the imposition of Community law administrative sanctions of a penal nature may be suspended if criminal proceedings are initiated for the same infringement. When the criminal proceeding is concluded, the suspended administrative procedures shall be resumed, provided this does not conflict with general legal principles. When a sanction is assessed, then a national penalty imposed for the same infringement must be taken into account.

All this is clearly a compromise text, with all the attendant ambiguities. One thing is clear though: Community law steps back for national criminal law, albeit in theory temporarily.

In conclusion of this brief discussion of Community sanctions and national criminal law under present positive law, I must point out – as was implicit in the above – that the power to impose sanctions is not an exclusive power; the possibility to impose sanctions has not been exhausted by the attachment of certain provisions on sanctions in EC instruments. This, however, again goes one way only: the Member States are in principle free to impose extra sanctions on the basis of their own national criminal law, but they cannot on the basis of their national criminal law frustrate Community sanctions, as this would run counter to the principles of the primacy and effectiveness of Community law.

A few final remarks should be made on tendencies which may in the not too distant future develop the state of affairs beyond what was sketched above as the present positive law. It concerns especially sanctions in the context of fraud which harms the financial interest of the EC. The "fight against fraud", as it has come to be called, is a hot issue. Since Maastricht, Article 209A (now 280) EC imposed the obligation on the Member States to take measures against such fraud and to coordinate their actions and establish cooperation between their competent organs and the Commission. But this has been taken a few steps further than the mere text suggests.

As far as the sphere of substantive criminal law proper is concerned, a Convention on the protection of the European Communities' financial interests (26 July 1995)[25] and two Protocols[26] have been drawn up in the framework of the third pillar. Also a Convention on corruption involving EU and Member State officials (26 May 1997) has been established.[27] All of these require Member States to create criminal offences of fraud (and related acts) which is to the detriment of the Community budget or involves corruption of officials in the EU contexts, all this if and to the extent that such offences do not yet exist in Member State criminal law. These Conventions and Protocols require ratification by all Member States before they enter into force, but to date[28] few Member States

[25] OJ 1995 C 316/49.

[26] OJ 1996 C 313/1; OJ 1997 C 221/12.

[27] OJ 1997 C 195/1.

[28] By mid 1999 Finland, Germany, Austria and Sweden had ratified the first Convention and its first Protocol; parliamentary approval of this Convention is pending in the Netherlands. To date (June 2000) the Second Protocol and the Convention on Corruption have not been ratified by any Member State.

have ratified.[29] To this extent the Member States are still masters over their criminal law.

Community powers are restricted to coordination, cooperation and investigation. But the institutions are pushing the limits. Under the Maastricht version of Article 209 A EC, a Commission unit (UCLAF – Unité de coordination de la lutte anti-fraude) has been set up and is given the task of leading the "fight against fraud". Although it is ultimately dependent on the Member States as far as the prosecution of cases is concerned, it has been given powers of investigation of its own in the sphere of fraud and irregularities under Community law, to wit: on-the-spot-checks and inspections (Regulation 2815/96, OJ 1996, L 292 p. 2). This Regulation – which seems oblivious of the fact that such checks can be an interference with citizens' rights, especially national privacy rights and Article 8 ECHR[30] – has been based on Article 235 (now 308) EC and has set a precedent for criminal law related competence of the EC. The Community powers of investigation and the Community rules governing administrative sanctions may well spill over into the field of substantive criminal law at some stage – perhaps the faster as the ineffectiveness of UCLAF due to its poor organisation and inefficiency, lasts. To remedy UCLAF's organisational deficiencies, it was replaced from 1 June 1999 by a semi-independent unit within the Commission, OLAF (*Office Europeen de Lutte AntiFraude*).[31] But whether this leads to more effective use of present powers, remains to been seen.[32] The rhetoric involved in combating fraud is tough language.[33] It threatens to set the terms of the political debate and decision-making and may make a spill-over into substantive law a natural next step. Criminal lawyers from European universities have already been marshalled in that direction. The so-called Corpus Juris project – an

[29] The Convention on the EC financial interests and the First Protocol thereto has been ratified by Austria, Germany, Spain, the UK, Sweden and Finland. The Second Protocol thereto has been ratified only by Spain and the UK. The Convention on corruption has been ratified by Austria, Spain, the UK, Sweden and Finland.

[30] Under Article 5 "economic operators" are required to grant access to "premises, land, means of transport or other areas, used for business purposes".

[31] See the report of the Court of Auditors mentioned in the next footnote, which reveals that UCLAF was very poorly organised, utterly inefficient and ineffective. Its unnecessary ineffectiveness may be the drive for the equally unnecessary extension of its powers.

[32] See *Rapport de l'Office Europe'en de Lutte Antifraude (OLAF), Premier rapport d'activités opérationnelles, 23.5.2000.*

[33] Thus the Court of Auditors in a recent report on UCLAF (Special Report 8/98, [1998] OJ C 230, para.2. 11–12) complains that the "present arrangements for judicial cooperation are still based on international legislation dating back to the 1950s, when Europe had no common institutions or policies covered by a single budget, when trade and financial flows were a fraction of what they are now and when financial crime was carried out by individuals or gangs, not organised international networks capable of maintaining an outward appearance of legality as is the case today. Moreover, even supposing that all the new instruments were ratified in the short term, a series of measures still have to be taken to enhance the legal basis of the anti-fraud policy. The discontinuity of legal procedures and the disparity between the different Member State systems of criminal justice, notably in terms of the severity and nature of punishment, hinder the effective repression of fraud. There is a need for "radical response to the absurdity, still tolerated though universally condemned, of opening wide our national frontiers to criminals while continuing to shut them against those responsible for fighting crime, despite the risk of turning our countries into crime havens".

exercise at the request of the European Parliament and supported by the Commission – has formulated far-reaching penal provisions of a substantive and procedural nature for the protection of the financial interests of the European Union. It is sometimes presented as the embryo of a future European Criminal Code, although there is no basis in EC law for developing such a code.[34] Long delays (or, in the case of some Member States total failure) in ratifying these Conventions and Protocols, has already tempted the European Parliament to call for the implementation of (elements of) the Corpus Juris on the basis of Article 235 (now 308) EC and 209A (now 280) EC, thus widening the basis for EC competence in the sphere of criminal law.[35]

Finally, mention should be made of the new Article 280 (amending the former 209A) EC introduced by the Treaty of Amsterdam. This provision declares it as a matter for "the Community and the Member States" to counter fraud and other illegal activities affecting the financial interests of the Community. To that effect, the necessary measures may be taken under the procedure of Article 251 (ex 189B) (co-decision of Council by qualified majority and Parliament) for the prevention of and fight against fraud with a view to affording effective and equivalent protection in the Member States. It adds: "These measures shall not concern the application of national criminal law or the national administration of justice". Presumably, this is to keep tightly to the distinction between the first and third pillar competence in the sphere of criminal law. This distinction is real, notwithstanding the reference made under Article 61(e) EC to measures to be taken under the third pillar in the sphere of criminal law (31 (e) TEU) – which is sometimes mistakenly taken to constitute an independent EC criminal law competence in the sphere of Community law.[36] But in the light of what we mentioned above, the suggestion that EC measures in the sphere of sanctions do not concern national criminal law is questionable.

[34] Prominent is the work of Mireille Delmas-Marty, *What kind of criminal policy for Europe?* (The Hague: Kluwer Law International, 1996); "Union Européenne et droit pénal" (1997) 33 *Cahiers de droit Européen* 608; *Corpus Juris portant dispositions pénale pour la protection des intérêts financiers de l'Union européenne* (Paris: Economica, 1997), which also contains an English version; German/French version, published in Köln et al., Heymann, 1998; a Dutch/French version published in Antwerp, Interscientia 1998. Each of the editions is prefaced by an academic of reputation in the relevant language. A version of the Corpus Juris text in English can be found on the Internet at <http://www.eurocep.dircon.co.uk/corpus.htm>. On the Corpus juris Francesco de Angelis (Commission director in charge of the repression of financial fraud) and Rosaria Sicurella (academic), "Vers un espace judiciaire européen?" (1997) *Revue due Marché Unique Européen* 121–37. On similar projects in the framework of the Council of Europe, Ulrich Sieber (presently involved in the Corpus juris project), "Memorandum für ein Europaeisches Modellstrafgesetzbuch" (1997) 52 *Juristen Zeitung* 369–81.

[35] Resolution B4–0457/97 of 12 June 1997, OJ 200/157. See again EP Resolution on criminal procedures in the European Union (Corpus Juris), A4–0091/99, OJ, C 219/106 of 30 July 1999.

[36] Thus (mistakenly) G.J.M. Corstens, "Strafrechtspleging in Nederland na het Verdrag van Amsterdam" (1999) *Nederlands Juristenblad* 803–9; and (correctly) R.H. Lauwaars, (1999) *Nederlands Juristenblad* 1323.

EC law: institutional aspects

Institutional aspects of the decision-making process in the first pillar are relevant for making statements about sovereignty. It does not suffice to stop at the characterisation of the first pillar as a "supranational" construct.

The distinction between primary and secondary Community law (the law of the Treaties and those made by the decisions based thereupon) is relevant here. In a way treaties may always have the effect of limiting to some extent or other the sovereignty of states in certain fields. This is the case when the treaty provisions impose duties on states, especially when they do so in a manner which limits their internal freedom to legislate and govern. This is in the nature of entertaining treaty relationships. As long as the obligations are specific and spelt out in the relevant treaty itself in an unambiguous manner, there is usually a limitation of sovereignty in a delimited quantitative sense and no undue interference with qualitative sovereignty. This may be different with open treaty provisions and with treaty provisions which do not in themselves specify the obligations, but merely function as a basis for taking further binding decisions. Here the decision-making process determines the extent to which sovereignty is at play.

With regard to secondary Community law, the institutional impact of the Commission should not be underestimated. Nor can we neglect the role of the European Parliament, when it has a role to play. But these roles are not always decisive, depending on the legal basis of the relevant decision. Some important decisions are still made by the Council in a quasi intergovernmental context, often on the basis of unanimity. I do not mean to say that decisions taken by unanimity cannot be considered a restriction on a state's sovereignty, nor am I unaware of the dynamics of decision-making, which imply that even unanimous decisions do not always reflect the pooled sovereign wills of the Member States represented in the Council. However, unanimous decision-making by the Council alone, leaves as a matter of normative principle to individual states the possibility of preventing decisions from being taken. In fact, the obstinacy of a Member State, for instance to maintain its own peculiar principles of criminal law and not to offer them up for some ulterior European motive, will decide if and to what extent it relegates its sovereignty in the relevant field; the Member States can have control over their loss of sovereignty in a particular field.

Of the decisions mentioned in the paragraph above, the agricultural market regulations are based on Articles 34 (ex 40) (3) and 37 (ex 43) (2) EC. These are taken on the basis of a proposal of the Commission, by the Council by qualified majority. The broader fraud regulation, however, has been based on Article 235 (now 308) EC, which gives the power to take measures in the framework of the common market, for which no basis can be found in the Treaty but which are necessary for attaining the objectives of the EC treaty. The Council has to decide unanimously, on the proposal of the Commission and the advice of the

European Parliament, and it has done so. As we already pointed out, the Treaty of Amsterdam creates majority decision-making in the context of EC measures against EU fraud.

The third pillar

Cooperation in the third pillar is a field in which on the one hand the allegedly "intergovernmental" character (as opposed to the "supranational" character of the first pillar) might suggest that sovereignty is safer, but on the other hand the field of cooperation in the sphere of criminal law is much broader. Already under the Maastricht version of the Treaty on European Union measures have been taken which touch on the penalisation of certain behaviour. For our purposes the most important feature of the new third pillar under the Treaty of Amsterdam is the "approximation, where necessary, of rules on criminal matters in the Member States" (Article 29 TEU) by "progressively adopting measures establishing minimum rules relating to the constituent elements of criminal acts and to penalties in the fields of organised crime, terrorism and drug trafficking" (Article 31 sub e). Declaration number 7 on Article 31(e) states: "The Conference agrees that the provisions of Article 31(e) of the TEU shall not have the consequence of obliging a Member State whose legal system does not provide for minimum sentences to adopt them".[37]

Under the Treaty of Amsterdam, the objective in the third pillar is one which stresses the common measures to be taken by the Member States, and hence in this sphere reinforces the image of the Union's lack of a competence of its own as distinct from that of the Member States (cf. Article 29 TEU: "[T]he objective shall be to provide citizens with a high level of safety . . . by developing common action among the Member States . . ."). The proposals for granting the Union legal personality have all (at the last minute) failed. It is difficult to come to any other conclusion than that the parties to the Treaty on European Union have not wanted to give legal personality to the Union. Hence, juridical logic implies, the decisions taken in the third pillar must be ascribed not to an entity which is separate from the Member States (the Union) but to the Member States jointly. This assimilates the Union acting within the third pillar to an international conference and the status of their decisions, if they are binding at all, to that of normal treaties under public international law – i.e. the law governing the relations between sovereign states.

[37] Taken together this is a set of rules of which the meaning is at first sight hard to grasp; I find it hard to imagine what is precisely intended with "minimum rules relating to constituent elements of criminal acts"; what does "minimum" mean, and what would be more than minimum in relation to the constituent elements of specific criminal acts? As we shall see, these rules can only be set in framework decisions which are binding as to the results to be achieved but "leave to the national authorities the choice of form and methods"; but what choice can be left?

In the third pillar, the main principle is still that of decision-making in the Council alone on the basis of unanimity. The Amsterdam Treaty has mainly introduced majority voting in relation to decisions of an executive nature which are implemented at the level of the Union (not with reference to the execution of decisions at the Member State level); these decisions may not involve harmonisation (Article 34(2) sub c TEU). The Commission has a right of initiative, but shares this right (contrary to what is the rule in the first pillar) with the Member States. The European Parliament has an advisory power with regard to certain binding instruments only (Article 39).

The normative status of the decisions taken under the third pillar is of some importance. Non-binding instruments do not fetter sovereignty in the way binding instruments do. In principle forms of cooperation which consist in mere consultation, concertation and coordination remain – as far as the consequences for the states' own behaviour internally are concerned – legally covered by national law. However, the regime of public international law does add a legal consequence to consistent behaviour through the doctrine of estoppel: in certain cases states can unilaterally bind themselves *vis-à-vis* other states to certain behaviour; in such cases those states may have to refrain from contrary behaviour towards other states. Thus "resolutions", "declarations", "recommendations", "decisions" to which states have consistently consented may not, by virtue of the nature of the instrument, bind them to the recommended, declared or decided behaviour; but the principle of good faith under public international law may prevent them from acting contrary to what they agreed.

Under the Maastricht version of the Treaty on European Union, the instruments of the common position and the common action were found both in the second and third pillar. The common positions were binding on Member States in international fora (J.2(3), second sentence; K.5). In the second pillar there was an explicit provision that common positions were also binding in national fora (J.2(2) second paragraph), while a similar provision was absent in the third pillar. However, it would seem to be schizophrenic to have to uphold a common position in international fora and not to observe it in national fora.

With regard to the binding nature of common actions, the second pillar provisions under Maastricht were explicit that they were binding (J.3(4)). Again there were no relevant provisions under the third pillar. This has led to uncertainty concerning the status of decisions under the third pillar. Without disclosing its content, the Dutch minister of Justice repeatedly referred in the Netherlands Parliament to an advisory opinion of the head of the Legal Service of the Council, which – in accordance with established Community practice – has remained secret to this day, reportedly because not all Member States agreed with the views expressed.[38] The government of the Netherlands, for instance, initially stated that common actions were not legally binding instruments (discussions in parliament unfortunately focused exclusively on the third pillar) and

[38] Parliamentary documents [Kamerstukken] 1993–1994, 23 490, nr. 10.

changed opinion to the extent that now it considers the language of each individual action to be decisive. Reportedly, Germany and Portugal maintained that all common actions are equally binding.

Even if one were to assert that the instrument of the common action is in principle binding (for this evidence can at least with regard to second pillar common actions be found, and which on the basis of parallelism and the principle of consistency could well be extended to third pillar common actions), this is not the end of the story. Instruments which are in principle binding, can contain non-binding provisions. There are many treaties which under public international law are binding instruments, but which contain provisions which do not create any legal obligations or rights (an example is Article 191 ex 138A) EC). Similarly, most countries will have Acts of Parliament which contain provisions which in themselves do not create rights or duties. On the other hand, the substantive nature of the language employed is decisive under public international law (which is – besides national law – the only relevant category of law in relation to second and third pillar decisions), not the form or name of the instrument. The intent of the states involved, as evident from (primarily) the text of the instrument and (secondarily) the context, is decisive for its legal status and bindingness.[39]

A glance at the various common actions suggests that this instrument has come to be used for more binding texts than is the case for other instruments. Usually, however, the most one can say is that sometimes the Member States, most often the Commission and from time to time the governments take upon themselves certain obligations. So far I have not found a common action that clearly suggests that it has direct effect. This, however, does not preclude the taking of common action which affects citizens directly or indirectly. Dependent on the different status of the second and third pillar in the various Member States, this may create rights within the national legal order.[40]

All this, I maintain, still applies to the Amsterdam Treaty. In an effort to clarify the status of the various instruments in the third pillar, the parallelism between the second and third pillar has disappeared, which may have complicated things. However, some certainty has been established with regard to the instruments mentioned in the new Article 34 (a to d): common positions, framework decisions for the purpose of approximation of laws, decisions for any other purpose, and conventions.

[39] Klabbers, *The Concept of Treaty in International Law* (Dordrecht: Kluwer Law International, 1996); for relevant case law see ICJ, *Ambatielos*, Preliminary Objection [1952] ICJ Reports 28–88; ICJ, *Monetary Gold Removed from Rome*, [1954] ICJ Reports 28; ICJ, *South West Africa*, Preliminary Objections [1962] ICJ Reports 331; ICJ, *Aegean Sea Continental Shelf*, Jurisdiction of the Court [1978] ICJ Reports 39, §§ 95–6; ICJ, *Concerning Maritime Delimitation and Territorial Questions between Qatar and Bahrain*, Jurisdiction and Admissibility [1994] ICJ Reports 14, § 30 juncto 25 and 22.

[40] In monist states like The Netherlands, the validity of the instrument under public international law is in itself enough to create rights and duties for citizens. The UK, however, has never incorporated the second and third pillar into national law; the European Communities (Amendment) Act 1998 consciously only incorporates the first pillar into the UK legal order.

The nature of common positions mentioned in Article 34 (a) is not further elaborated (cf. Art. 37). The "common action" has disappeared as a specific instrument (the words, however, are used in a generic sense in Articles 30 and 31). Instead, the new instrument of the "framework decisions for the purpose of approximation of the laws and regulations of the Member States" has been introduced (34 (b)). "Framework decisions shall be binding upon the Member States as to the result to be achieved but shall leave to the national authorities the choice of form and methods. They shall not entail direct effect", says Article 34 (b). The "decisions for any other purpose . . . shall be binding and shall not entail direct effect" (34 (c)).

Given the experience under the Maastricht Treaty, it is highly unlikely that the summing up of instruments in Article 34 of the Amsterdam Treaty constitutes an exhaustive list. I have little doubt that "conclusions", "resolutions", "recommendations" and other "decisions" of unspecified nature will still be used in the third pillar. Also, the "framework decisions" and "decisions for any other purpose" may well contain provisions that are unclear as to what (if anything) they bind. In itself the possibility remains to decide on instruments, whatever the name, which may create rights and duties outside those mentioned in the Amsterdam Treaty. Given the inflation in numbers of *sui generis* instruments under various names, it is most unlikely that resort will not be had to such instruments. That actually the clearest legally binding instrument in the intergovernmental pillars is one of those (the Mostar "decisions", which concern the administration of the city of Mostar by the EU, and clearly express the intent to create legal rights and obligations also for citizens), is ominous.

III. EU AND PRIVATE SPHERE/ PRIVATE AUTONOMY

A few words about criminal law and the private sphere as a subject matter in the EU. It is quite clear that under the first pillar the criminal law of Member States is affected and may become further affected. So far there has not been, however, anything undertaken which touches directly upon the sphere of private morality. There is some case law on trade in obscene objects, pornography and prostitution. This involved the public morality exception to the freedom of movement of goods and persons. However, the European Court of Justice did not construe this exception any further than that Member States are permitted to make their own assessment of the requirements of public morality within their territories. Ultimately, this case law hinges on equal treatment of goods originating from Member States to goods originating in the importing state, and on the equal treatment of other Member States' prostitutes to those with their own nationality.[41] The primary purpose is to create a market in which goods, services, capital and

[41] Case 34/79, *R* v. *Henn and Darby* [1979] ECR 3795. In this case the Court, however, seemed to allow for an amount of regional variety between Scotland, Northern Ireland, England and Wales in not equally forbidding pornography, but concluded that overall there was a ban; hence an import

persons can freely flow across borders. The economic freedoms which are fundamental to Community law are of course firstly the freedoms of private market agents (private companies and private citizens in their capacity as economic market agents), but are also the freedoms of EU citizens themselves. Criminal law exceptions can restrict those freedoms, not because they are provisions of national criminal law but primarily because and insofar as they serve the interests of an exceptional nature recognised in the Treaty. Criminal law exceptions are not "nature reserves" of national sovereignty, we noticed above; or if they are, they are so under the strict guardianship of the ECJ. This implies that the ECJ can scrutinise and stop unwarranted interference with the private domain of economic agents. The "rule of reason" exceptions are somewhat different: they are more like the wasteland across the borders of Community law. What will happen to *Grogan*-like cases which may involve abortion, euthanasia and other practices which may be called economic services in the sense of Community law, we do not know with certainty. It is not impossible (but uncertain) that the ECJ might in the end also here let the domain of the economic market prevail and hence the sphere of private autonomy. Private morality is then turned into public morality. But perhaps a type of discretion will be left to Member States in this sphere, more or less like the European Court of Human Rights' doctrine of the margin of appreciation when certain issues of public and private morality are involved.

There is a curious contrast between this predominance of private autonomy in the context of the economic market and the force with which some steps have been called for – and have partly already been taken – when it comes to securing the financial interest of the EU itself. Then Commission officials have been provided with powers of investigation which interfere with the private sphere of "economic operators", i.e. companies and citizens engaged in economic activities. Here privacy is not even mentioned in the relevant documents. It is true that similar powers of investigation for the Commission have existed in the sphere of competition law for longer. But interestingly, here the discussion has from the

ban did not discriminate as to the origin of the goods involved. Case 121/85, *Conegate* v. *Customs and Excise Commissioners* [1986] ECR 1007: there existed various restrictions on the obscene objects involved (inflatable "love dolls" and other "sex aids") in the UK, but there was no ban on the production and marketing of them, so in this case an import ban constituted an unjustifiable discrimination. In joined cases 115 and 116/81 *Rezguia Adoui and Dominique Cornuaille* v. *Belgium* [1982] ECR 1665, the Court held: "Although Community law does not impose upon the Member States a uniform scale of values as regards the assessment of conduct which may be considered contrary to public policy, conduct may not be considered as being of a sufficiently serious nature to justify restrictions on the admission to or residence within the territory of a Member State of a national of another Member State in a case where the former Member State does not adopt, with respect to the same conduct on the part of its own nationals, repressive measures or other genuine and effective measures intended to combat such conduct". Presently there is a Dutch case pending at the ECJ for a preliminary decision on whether Polish and Czech prostitutes can claim entrance to the EC to establish themselves as self-employed persons in the sense of the Europa (Association) Agreements, notwithstanding the fact that their professional activities are forbidden by criminal law in their country of origin, and whether prostitution is the provision of services, or a business enterprise in the sense of these Agreements.

beginning been sensitive to interests of privacy and due process.[42] This is in stark contrast to the ferocity of the rhetoric in the context of EC financial fraud. The difference may be that in the first case we are dealing with the enforcement of liberty of private economic operators, whereas in the second it is the protection of the public interest. The first concerns the rules of the game which one group of private operators has to respect towards other economic operators within the market economy; the second is an infringement against public authority, the public fiscal authority within the (supra-)state budget economy – the first is a matter of regulating private business households, the second becomes a matter of crime and criminal law. In the first case, public autonomy is in the service of private autonomy. In the second, public autonomy may be the adversary of private autonomy. Couched in terms of moral justification, public autonomy aimed at the common good is mobilised against the private autonomy that focuses on a morally corrupt egotistic good. But when public autonomy takes the form of criminal law and all its attending powers, it may ultimately be at a cost for uncorrupted private autonomy.

Also under the third pillar, some steps have been taken (and further steps can be expected to be taken when the Amsterdam Treaty enters into force), which involve criminal law and can clearly touch upon the spheres of privacy and personal autonomy. Thus there exist common actions in the sphere of the repression of drug abuse, trafficking in persons and child abuse.[43] These instruments have a strongly rhetorical character and have not had a strongly legal binding significance. Yet, they function as diplomatic contrivances that channel the discussion into a direction where Member State governments are pressurised towards criminalisation, which is not what they would have chosen without the European background. Here again what we have said above applies: the obstinacy of a Member State to abide by its legal culture also in the sphere of criminal law (penalisation and de-penalisation) will be decisive. It needs a strong sense of culture and autonomy for governments, and perhaps more crucially for national parliaments, to show this kind of backbone.

Sovereignty

Some kinds of power have become so exclusively associated with the state for them to be called sovereign powers. Anything which would diminish them,

[42] The ECJ's *Hoechst, Dow* and *Orkem* cases (cases 46/87and 227/88;85/87; 97–99/87; 374/87) have been of primary importance here.

[43] Interestingly, combating trafficking in persons and child abuse are mentioned as objectives in the Amsterdam Treaty in Article 29 [K.1], but not mentioned among the topics on which harmonisation of criminal provisions is to be achieved (cf. the summing up in 34 [K.6](e)). "After the main text was finalized, the Amsterdam Treaty entered into force. Three draft framework decisions have been submitted: on assisted illegal entry (OJ 2000, C 253/6), on fraud in connection with public procurement (OJ 2000, C 253/3), and on the status of victims in criminal proceedings (10387 LIMITE COPEN 54, 14 July 2000)."

diminishes sovereignty. The power to punish and make certain behaviour punishable belongs to that category of sovereign powers. But we do not necessarily have to conclude that that is the end of sovereignty in the qualitative sense. Although certain diminutions of a set of sovereign powers may in the end affect the sovereign quality of the state as such, I do not think European integration within the EU has done so. The most striking developments are in the sphere of the protection of the proper financial interests of the EU. Article 209 A EC (also in the version of Amsterdam) suggests that such developments must be circumscribed to EU-contexts. Although relevant rules may ultimately form part of the national criminal law system, within national systems they are an added element that makes them stand apart as a sort of "federal" criminal law. To the extent that this part of criminal law is distinct from the autochthonous national criminal law, it is an added layer which as such does not immediately affect the autochthonous criminal law. Yet, national law has to take account of this "foreign" element, because it is after all to be enforced at the national level. The impact of this, however direct or indirect, is not necessarily so very different from the social, economic and moral forms of heteronomy with which states and national systems of criminal law are confronted, and on which state legislatures, administrations and judiciaries have to act.

Yet, there is no denying that Member States may have lost their liberty to act or not to act within parts of national criminal law. This is not necessarily a negative development, because it might in some cases also have decriminalising effects that may be welcomed. The liberty to act or not to act has been transferred to another level which for the time being may seem to be outside the reach and control of the citizens. But to what extent are they within the reach of citizens when left to national governments? If there is no clear common EU standard of public morality which is to be enforced or upheld through penalising transgressions, is there really one within Member States? The fates of criminal law at the national and at the European level seem to be more entwined than it might seem at first sight.

5

The State and the Nation's Bedrooms: The Fundamental Right of Sexual Autonomy

CHRISJE BRANTS

INTRODUCTION

THAT "EVERYONE HAS the right to respect for his private and family life, his home and his correspondence", as Article 8 of the European Convention on Human Rights and Fundamental Freedoms (ECHR) has it, is a statement with which few (continental) Europeans would argue, be they lawyers or totally ignorant of the law. To a person like me, trained in the continental legal tradition, it is always somewhat surprising to be reminded – as I was when I read Roberts' contribution to this book – that this is not necessarily the case in the United Kingdom. The great distance between the continental and English legal traditions is always amply illustrated in discussions on privacy, especially in relation to the criminal law. The bland statement: "of course, there is no such thing as a right to privacy here" never ceases to amaze the continental lawyer, while his or her English counterpart is often equally confounded by the answer: "how strange – why ever not?"

Indeed, so entrenched is the notion of a right to privacy both in rights discourse and in the discourse of everyday life in continental European countries, that it is held to be as self-evident as – even a prerequisite of – the pursuit of life, liberty and happiness. Insofar as privacy rights guarantee the inviolability of one's home, one's correspondence (including telephone and other forms of communication) and the right not to divulge intimate information, and provide protection against unwarranted intrusion especially by the state, this is the sense in which privacy (geographical and informational) has always been understood. This is not, however, what concerns me here. For, while there is never total agreement on precisely what the right to privacy entails, it is fair to say that, from a negative right to be free from interference by others in general and by the state in particular in one's intimate affairs, it now has the added dimension of a positive right to determine, develop and express one's personality in all its different aspects – the right to be oneself and do one's own thing.

In everyday life this notion of privacy may owe more to gut feelings than to articulated ideas about a moral right to autonomy, but since it has been taken on board by the European Court of Human Rights there could at least be said to exist a legal basis for a concept of privacy that includes a fundamental human right of individual autonomy. In *Dudgeon* v. *United Kingdom,* for example, the European Court accepted the broad conception of privacy employed by the European Commission, as being the right "to establish and to develop relationships with other human beings, especially in the emotional field for the development and fulfilment of one's own personality".[1] In a number of national jurisdictions too, privacy rights are interpreted as being more than the (negative) right to be let alone; the Dutch Supreme Court, for example, routinely defines privacy as "the right to be one's own, uninhibited self".[2]

In any event, even if the context in which such courts have given their decisions is usually interference in a person's private life by the state and the question of whether they had the right to freedom from such interference, the legal right to privacy has evolved from negative freedom from interference to the right not to be judged on the basis of what one chooses to be and therefore chooses to do, at least in theory. There is indeed a strong theoretical case to be made for a right to privacy based on an individual right of autonomy that encompasses a great deal more than the mere freedom to be let alone, and Roberts has made it elsewhere in this volume.[3] I do not intend to repeat his arguments, although I will elaborate on a number of issues – notably the relationship between rights of autonomy and the fundamentals of democratic society. However, while agreeing with much of what Roberts and others say, I would also contend that the – admittedly strong – theoretical foundations of a moral right to autonomy have little significance if we do not, at the same time, address the issue of what it is that gives the state (or anyone else, for that matter) the right to intervene in situations in which individuals are undoubtedly simply being their own uninhibited selves.

If privacy based on a right of autonomy is so strong as to be regarded as self-evident, it appears to be equally self-evident that privacy rights "can never be absolute", that they only hold good so long as they do not interfere with other interests. There are many decisions by the European Court and by national courts in which the right to privacy is overridden with apparent ease by these "other interests". There are, of course, very few rights that can be regarded as absolute, that cannot be set aside because other rights or interests (or the same right or interests of others) prevail.[4] Nevertheless, privacy rights seem to be

[1] *Dudgeon* v. *United Kingdom*, (1981) 4 EHRR 149.

[2] See Kelk, infra 205, for Dutch case law on issues of privacy and autonomy.

[3] Many others have argued along the same lines – see for a very comprehensive examination of privacy as an inalienable right of every individual, fundamental to Western democracy and the notion of *Rechtstaat*, the Belgian author Serge Gutwirth, *Privacyvrijheid! De vrijheid om zichzelf te zijn* (The Hague: Rathenau Instituut, 1998).

[4] Without wishing to plunge into the deep moral waters of philosophical and religious debate, I would contend that the right to life, for example, is certainly not an absolute right – neither accord-

particularly vulnerable. Part of the problem derives, as Gutwirth rightly points out, from their very self-evidence: ". . . narratives and concepts that can boast unanimous acceptance, are often simply empty shells; everyone can pay lip-service to them, but it need go no further than that".[5] The very fact that we regard privacy rights as self-evident should therefore make us suspicious of such concepts. Yet even if we accept that they are more than empty shells and can be defined as autonomy rights of individuals, that is not really the point – not, that is, unless we can also accept that there is no such thing as society.[6] For privacy/autonomy rights are not problematic because they exist as individual rights, but because, like all other rights, they exist in the context of society and not in a vacuum.

This is the aspect of the right to privacy that I wish to explore and I will do so by concentrating on the sphere of sexual behaviour (including sexual preference). The sexual is more than an intimate part of life, it is part of ourselves and how we choose to experience and develop that part of our existence is not something we expect to have scrutinised and regulated by anyone else (except those with whom we elect to share it). And yet, the right to be oneself *in sexualibus* is the subject of many a criminal case and of several important decisions by human rights bodies on the limits of privacy and the right, indeed the duty, of the state not to refrain from intervention, but on the contrary to intervene in what we commonly consider the most private sphere of all. While the scope of that intervention may differ from jurisdiction to jurisdiction, all of the states of Western Europe, including those that are regarded as (excessively?) libertarian such as the Netherlands and Denmark, criminalise (some forms of) sexual behaviour where the participants would claim to be exercising their right of autonomy and where the justification for state intervention is debatable. While we all seem to agree that there are social limits to the right to do one's own thing, to make one's own choices, to be one's own uninhibited self even when it comes to sex, what do those limits entail and when do they warrant interference by the state, even to the point of criminalisation? Which criteria apply in human rights law, and how are they established and used by the courts? And are these criteria that do justice to individual autonomy as a fundamental human right and the social context within which it is inevitably exercised?

ing to my own moral convictions nor in any legal sense. The European Convention seems to recognise only one right that cannot be the subject of limitations or set aside, even in emergency situations – the right not to be subjected to torture. The apparent definition of the right to a fair trial as a more or less absolute right in Article 6 of the European Convention, is routinely undermined by shifting definitions of what the concept of "fair" means, while of late the European Court seems willing to allow the rights and interests of others, such as victims and witnesses, to prevail over the rights of the defendant that constitute a fair trial. (See *Baegen* v. *The Netherlands*, ECHR 27/10/1995, appl. no. 00016696/90).

[5] Gutwirth, *op.cit.* n 3 at 30.

[6] Margaret Thatcher MP, *Women's Own*, 31 October 1987.

THE PARADOX OF INDIVIDUAL AUTONOMY AND DEMOCRATIC SOCIETY

With the acceptance by courts of a broadening definition of the right of privacy, to include the right to determine, express and develop all aspects of oneself, including one's sexuality, privacy has become a specific legal concept that determines the limits of individual autonomy when it clashes with other rights and interests that have a claim to validity in society. The problem is that the concept of autonomy in a democratic society – or, in continental terms, in a *Rechtstaat* – by its very definition stands in the way of establishing criteria by which to determine how those limits should be set. Basic tenets of democracy are the room it must allow for diversity and plurality and therefore the necessity of curtailing the power of the majority to dictate to minorities the values they should embrace. If autonomy has any significance in a democratic society, it must be the freedom of individuals to live their own (sexual) lives as they see fit and regardless of the religious or moral beliefs or values that govern the lives of the majority. An essential aspect of autonomy and therefore also privacy then, is the right to be different, to be oneself without reference to whether that is appropriate in terms of mainstream beliefs and values – which are also valid, certainly, but no more than equally so.[7] So the legal right of privacy protects an important aspect of what makes us human – the ability to develop and sustain individuality – and that is a highly prized commodity in Western democracies.

If this is the case, then autonomy is both fundamental and in some ways inimical to our Western concept of the democratic *Rechtstaat*, which is dedicated to upholding and securing individual fundamental human rights and the tolerant social context in which they can function. But by its very nature, a right to privacy in the sense of a positive right of autonomy, is unenforceable, and it is much easier for legislators and courts to think of privacy/autonomy in the negative terms of relative freedom from (enforceable) restrictions. "The state", so declared Justice Minister of Canada Trudeau when introducing reforms to legislation on a number of sexual matters, "has no place in the nation's bedrooms".[8] The problem is that, as a generalisation, this is manifestly untrue: forms of sadomasochism, sexual intercourse with underage or same-sex partners, or the solitary enjoyment of certain forms of pornography, which may also take place in the bedroom and be highly autonomous expressions of individuality, are often regarded as very much the state's business, because they are seen as an affront to public morals and can be construed as criminal offences. However, to interfere with individual autonomy in order to uphold public morals or prevent such crimes sits ill with notions of democracy. For in practice,

[7] Cf. Gutwirth, *op.cit.* n 3, 21–43; Rhoda E. Howard, "Gay Rights and the Right to a Family: Conflicts between Liberal and Illiberal Belief Systems" in Peter Baehr *et al.* (eds.), *Innovation and Inspiration: Fifty Years of the Universal Declaration of Human Rights* (Amsterdam: KNAW Verhandelingen, 178, 1999) 111–29, at 114.

[8] Cited in Howard, *loc.cit.*

where else than in the morality of the majority are we to find the substance of public morals or legitimate grounds for criminalisation of "deviant and immoral" (*nomen est omen*) manifestations of sexuality?

This is, of course, precisely the criticism often levelled at (human) rights discourse: it is said to be inherently political, the legislation of majority views or power politics and the protection of privileged groups in society, masquerading as a search for universal and neutral values and the protection of minorities and vulnerable groups; and this is especially the case where rights compete.[9] This has always seemed to me a very English sort of position – or, to put it more neutrally, the sort of position that develops in a legal culture that nurtures a profound distrust of entrenched constitutional rights as the best way of upholding individual rights and liberties.[10] It ignores that rights discourse is also "a valuable form of politics and a significant vehicle for realising the goals of progressive social movements".[11] More importantly, it denies the relatively autonomous discursive power of constitutionally guaranteed rights. Fundamental human rights are part and parcel of modern democracy and they both derive from and sustain it. Without them, we have no way of holding law to its own promises and principles. While rights are often unable to deliver on those promises, this incapacity is not necessarily because they are no more than mere enhancements of already privileged positions or the result of politicians and lawyers playing at rights to hide the "reality of power". The fact that rights are difficult to enforce does not mean they are worthless. This is not to say that politics and power do not influence the practice of law. Of course they do. But just as problematic is the paradox inherent in fundamental human rights, namely that they are individual and in many cases inalienable, yet they do not gain significance until they are exercised in a social context, where they must then compete with equally fundamental and inalienable rights of others. And to return to the subject of this contribution, that paradox is very much in evidence when it comes to a right of privacy that is positively construed as the right of autonomy.

Fundamental individual rights are crucial to democracy. Central to their enforcement – which is of course what counts in practice – is that they are encapsulated in rules and procedures, and therefore clearly defined. Here we encounter another problem with the right of individual autonomy in the social context of the democratic *Rechtstaat*: the essential elements of privacy/

[9] This is the position taken by the Critical Legal Studies movement and also by some feminists; Cf. Sarah Pritchard, "The Jurisprudence of Human Rights: Some Critical Thought and Developments in Practice" (1995) 2 *Australian Journal of Human Rights* 000; on women's rights: Carol Smart, *Feminism and the Power of Law* (London: Routledge, 1989); and on international human rights: Neil Purvis, "Critical Legal Studies in Public International Law" (1991) 32 *Harvard Law Journal* 81.

[10] See on the difference between legal cultural attitudes with regard to the protection of fundamental rights and liberties in the English and in continental European legal traditions: Brants and Field, *Participation Rights and Proactive Policing*, Preadvies uitgebracht voor der Nederlandse Vereniging voor Rechtsvergelijking No 51 (Amsterdam: Kluwer, 1995).

[11] Pritchard, *supra* n 9 at 5.

autonomy – individual freedom, self-determination, the right to make existential choices and to resist power and external influence – mean that "[t]he very essence of privacy defies definition, paradoxically because on the one hand it protects everyone's personal freedom to define it as they will, and, on the other, because such definitions only make sense and have significance in relationship to others".[12] According to Gutwirth, the very impossibility of defining the substance of individual autonomy implies that we cannot therefore endow individuals in law with a subjective right to privacy/autonomy, for to do so would be to establish, regardless of the (social) context, what that right entails and, more importantly, what it does not.

The law can neither give us the right to be autonomous, nor tell us what to do with our autonomy; we have that right as a fundamental human right for the simple reason that we are autonomous human beings and must therefore decide ourselves what it means for us. The elaboration of a subjective right to privacy requires that an individual's process of self-determination be "frozen" in time, conceptually and normatively.[13] This implies, therefore, that the law will determine, not necessarily what we are, but what we should be, whether our own uninhibited self is a correct self, whether our (sexual) individuality is an acceptable individuality. That is our own business, not the law's.

This extremely liberal position,[14] while perfectly compatible with, indeed logically dictated by the nature of individual autonomy as a fundamental right, is nevertheless only tenable if we forget that other fundamental aspect of being human: man is a social being. The right to be different from others if we so choose, to dissociate ourselves from the majority, means nothing if we leave the majority of others out of the equation. The standard way out of this dilemma seems to be to demand that how one chooses to live one's life be "subject only to minimum requirements of law and public order"[15] or be judged only "according to the limits imposed by the democratic *Rechtstaat*".[16] If we agree – and I have yet to find the author who does not – that to have an individual right does not imply that we can always and under all circumstances exercise it in the social context of our relationship to others, then we must not dodge the issue by simply referring to "minimum requirements of law and public order" or the "limits of *Rechtstaat*", but attempt to define what those are and why they may restrict the right of autonomy. At this point it should be noted that geographical criteria are not necessarily as relevant to matters of sexual autonomy as they appear at first sight. If it includes the right to be ourselves and be different from others, then we must be able to be our different selves not only in the privacy of our home but also at work and on the street – although the restrictions of the social context, if only because

[12] Gutwirth, *op.cit.* n 3 at 43.

[13] Gutwirth, *op.cit.* n 3 at 54.

[14] See Alldridge . . ., *supra* 79.

[15] Jack Donnelly, "Non-Discrimination and Sexual Orientation: Making a Place for Sexual Minorities in the Global Human Rights Regime" in Peter Baehr *et al. supra* n 7, 111–29, at 106.

[16] Gutwirth, *loc.cit.*

of the physical presence of others, will be more apparent and sometimes greater in public places. Conversely, it is not possible automatically to shut out the social context of behaviour by closing the door behind us or by joining a "private" club where we can shed our socially imposed inhibitions. And yes, the state does sometimes have a place in the nation's bedrooms: the question is, when?

THE EUROPEAN COURT OF HUMAN RIGHTS ON THE LIMITS OF SEXUAL AUTONOMY

It is at least not difficult to discover what the relevant criteria in practice are, for while Article 17 of the International Covenant on Civil and Political Rights simply grants protection of private life against arbitrary or unlawful interference (leaving the issue wide open to interpretation), the European Convention actually sums them up in Article 8(2): national security, the economic well-being of the country, health or morals, the rights and freedoms of others, the prevention of disorder or crime. Any one of these criteria may determine to what extent a person can exercise the right of autonomy, or, to put it negatively, when the state is entitled to intervene. As far as sexual autonomy is concerned, the debate is usually about morals and crime, although, as we shall see, the issue of health can play an important part and appears, in issues of sexuality, to have become inextricably linked to moral health, or rather, healthy morals.

The European Court has decided many cases in which sexual autonomy was at stake and where individuals have alleged unwarranted interference by the state. On the one hand, there are cases involving criminalisation and/or actual prosecution of forms of sexual behaviour (usually in connection with homosexuality), where criminalisation in itself and/or prosecution constitutes interference and is therefore the issue. On the other hand, there are cases in which individuals claim that other forms of state intervention have prevented them from leading the (sexual) life of their preference – because, for example, they cannot be a member of the armed forces if they are known to be homosexual,[17] or have undergone medical treatment and surgery as transsexuals yet are unable to obtain a birth certificate or passport showing their new gender identity.[18] While all of these issues are dealt with under Article 8 and therefore under the definition of privacy accepted by the Court, namely that respect for private life of necessity includes respect for the "physical and moral integrity of the person"[19] (which is another way of alluding to autonomy and self-determination), even at first sight it is obvious that these are very disparate cases.[20] Although states have often been found in breach of the Convention and individual privacy

17 *Smith and Grady* v. *United Kingdom*, ECHR 27/09/1999, appl. no. 00033985/96.

18 *Sheffield and Horsham* v. *United Kingdom*, ECHR 30/07/1998, appl. no. 00022985/93.

19 *Stubbings and Others* v. *United Kingdom*, ECHR 22/10/1996, appl. no. 00022083/96, para. 59.

20 See David Feldman, "The Developing Scope of Article 8 of the European Convention on Human Rights" [1997] *European Human Rights Law Review* 265.

rights upheld, the structure of Article 8 with its enumeration of grounds for restriction and the reasoning behind some decisions, throw doubt on whether the privacy it guarantees is indeed rooted in a right of autonomy and on whether privacy is always the relevant right on which to decide the issue.

Homosexuality

In three very similar cases, the European Court held that the criminalisation of homosexual behaviour between adults in private was not necessary in a democratic society, and therefore constituted unwarranted interference by the state in the private lives of those concerned. The first case, *Dudgeon* v. *UK*, dates back to the 1970s (the decision was given in 1981).[21] Dudgeon, a homosexual, was arrested after police found documents in his house in Belfast relating to homosexual activities,[22] held at the police station and questioned about his sexual life. At the time, buggery between males and between a male and a female was a criminal offence in Northern Ireland, while there was also an offence of gross indecency between males. The rest of the United Kingdom was already living in the post-Wolfenden era and such conduct between consenting males of twenty-one years and over was no longer an offence.[23] Dudgeon's case was sent to the Director of Public Prosecutions for Northern Ireland with a view to prosecution for gross indecency, but none ensued. Dudgeon claimed that the police questioning was a breach of his (informational) privacy, and also that the very fact that he was liable to criminal prosecution as a homosexual caused suffering and psychological distress and was therefore an unjustified interference with his private life. He consequently also alleged infringement of Article 14 of the European Convention, which forbids discrimination. The Court found that, while the aim of the disputed legislation – the protection of morals in the sense of "moral standards obtaining in Northern Ireland" – was undoubtedly a legitimate one, and while Member States have a margin of appreciation in deciding what is necessary to pursue that aim, in this case there was no pressing social need for criminalisation of behaviour that constituted "a most intimate aspect of private life". Having found a breach of Article 8, the Court saw no reason to examine the claim under Article 14.

The decision in *Dudgeon* is an exceedingly long one, and no fewer than five judges dissented. Both the decision itself and the dissenting opinions provide some interesting pointers to the significance of the grounds for restriction in Article 8, para. 2 ECHR, notably with regard to the question of morals. To these

21 *Dudgeon* v. *United Kingdom*, *supra* n 1.

22 They were looking for drugs, which they also found, although since someone else was charged, apparently not belonging to Dudgeon.

23 The Wolfenden Report (J.Wolfenden (Chair), *Report of the Committee on Homosexual Offences and Prostitution*, Cmd 247) appeared in 1957, advocating decriminalisation, which followed in England and Wales – although with a number of exceptions – in 1967 (Sexual Offences Act 1967); Scotland followed suit in 1980.

we shall return after we have looked at the other two cases, which differ only slightly from Dudgeon – to which the European Court repeatedly refers. In *Norris* v. *Ireland*[24] and in *Modinos* v. *Cyprus*[25] the important difference was that neither complainant was actually the target of criminal justice activity – indeed the relevant provisions criminalising homosexual conduct had not been used against consenting adults for some years in either country, and were in that sense obsolete. Nevertheless, both men claimed that it was the continued existence of this legislation that constituted an unwarranted infringement of their privacy, for they remained legally at risk of prosecution, or at least exposed to the risk and stigma of being the object of a private prosecution. Moreover, the law singled them out as potentially criminally different and therefore contributed to public misapprehension and prejudice towards homosexuality. In this context, Norris alleged (in the words of one of the judges of the Irish Supreme Court), that "in a number of subtle but insidiously intrusive and wounding ways" he had been "restricted in or thwarted from engaging in activities which heterosexuals take for granted as aspects of the necessary expression of their human personality and as ordinary incidents of their citizenship".[26] Although this was too much for the six dissenting judges (out of fourteen) in *Norris* (the mere existence of legislation, they said, did not make him a victim of interference, though they hastened to add that this by no means invalidated *Dudgeon*), a majority did indeed find that criminalisation itself unduly interfered with the private life of the applicant "because of the detrimental effects [it] could have on the life of a person of homosexual orientation".[27] By 1993 and *Modinos*, there was not a single dissenting opinion (if we discount the Cypriot magistrate, whose dissent concerned a technicality and not the essence of the judgment).

So what, one may ask, is the problem? Leaving aside the subsumption of the equality rights of Article 14 ECHR under Article 8, to which I shall return later, it lies not so much in the actual outcome of these cases (with which I happen to agree, although that is hardly the point) as in remarks made by the Court in the course of refuting the governments' claims that the contested legislation was necessary for the protection of morals. The Court explicitly considered the question of the protection of morals as a ground for restricting the rights under Article 8, first when discussing the scope of the margin of appreciation for the UK in determining the necessity (the "pressing social need") of the contested laws and then in considering whether the need was pressing enough. As to the first, the Court reiterated what has long been decided, namely that the margin of appreciation is more extensive where the protection of morals is in issue,[28] for

[24] *Norris* v. *Ireland*, ECHR 26/10/1988, appl. no. 00010581/83; (1991) 13 EHRR 186.

[25] *Modinos* v. *Cyprus*, ECHR 22/04/1993, appl. no. 00015070/89; (1993) 16 EHRR 485.

[26] *Norris* v. *Ireland*, *op.cit. supra* n 24 at para. 10 (vii).

[27] *Ibid.*, para. 46.

[28] Cf. *Handyside* v. *United Kingdom*, ECHR 07/12/1976, appl. no. 00005493/72; (1976) 1 EHRR 737. This judgment was given under Article 10 of the Convention, the freedom of expression, and concerned pornography. Although outside the scope of this essay, the freedom of expression may also in some respects be regarded as embodying a positive right of autonomy.

"attitudes and public opinion in relation to questions of morality differ greatly from time to time and place to place". In the context of Northern Irish society, the government was justified in taking the moral climate in Northern Ireland in sexual matters into account. At the time there was steep opposition to proposed changes in the law. "This opposition reflects (. . .) a view both of the requirements of morals in Northern Ireland and of the measures thought within the community to be necessary to preserve prevailing moral standards. Whether this point of view be right or wrong, and although out of line with current attitudes in other communities, its existence among an important sector of Northern Irish society is certainly relevant for the purposes of Article 8 para.2".[29] The Court also took into account that during the period of direct rule the government was loath to push through new legislation that would offend a large part of the (Protestant) community.

On whether these reasons were sufficient to constitute a pressing social need, the Court had the following to say: "the Court cannot overlook the marked changes which have occurred in this regard in the domestic law of the member States. (. . .) In Northern Ireland itself, the authorities have refrained in recent years from enforcing the law in respect of private homosexual acts between consenting males. (. . .) No evidence has been adduced to show that this has been injurious to moral standards in Northern Ireland or that there has been any public demand for stricter enforcement of the law". And although some members of the public, who regard homosexuality as immoral, might be shocked, offended or disturbed, this did not on its own warrant the application of penal sanctions.[30] These arguments were repeated, *mutatis mutandis*, in the other judgments.

Such reasoning is hardly logical if privacy is to be interpreted as autonomy. How can the moral climate of the community, attitudes and public opinion, let alone what the other Member States of the Council of Europe think about homosexuality, be relevant to the existential right to express one's sexual individuality? What the Court is really saying is that homosexual conduct between consenting adults is acceptable, because a majority in the country, and an overwhelming majority within the community of states to which these countries belong, think it is, or no longer care sufficiently to demand stricter enforcement of the law (a point well taken by the dissenting Cypriot judge Zekia).[31] As to the unenlightened minority who still happen to believe that homosexuality is immoral – well, tough. But if the right in question is a positively defined right to individual autonomy and self-determination, it becomes irrelevant what

[29] *Dudgeon* v. *United Kingdom*, *supra* n 1 at para. 57.

[30] *Ibid.*, para. 60.

[31] Such references to what a majority of states believe to be "normal" are frequent in the case law of the European Court, especially with regard to a positive duty of governments to uphold privacy rights. In the *Sheffield and Horsham* v. *United Kingdom* judgment, the Court referred to the diversity of opinion and practices with regard to transsexuality in the contracting states and was not fully satisfied as to the existence of any common European approach to the problems created by the recognition in law of post-operative gender status." *Ibid.*, para. 57.

lifestyles predominate in society, what religious or other groups believe is immoral or moral, what the majority believes is or is not acceptable. This is the paradox of fundamental rights in a democratic society at work in practice. It bodes ill for other expressions of (sexual) autonomy that are not so "normal" or widely accepted.

Sadomasochism

One such is sadomasochism, and here too the Court has had to decide whether the prosecution of forms of sadomasochism as assault, wounding or causing grievous bodily harm can constitute a justifiable interference with the participants' right to privacy.[32] This case is in some ways exemplary. Not only does it cover the many issues that arise with regard to the exercise of autonomy rights in a social context (public vs. private space, consent, harm, majority vs. "deviant" morality), it also illustrates how weak the right of autonomy can be in practice when it is judged according to the justifiable restrictions of Article 8(2) ECHR.

Over a ten-year period, Messrs Laskey, Jaggard and Brown had engaged with a number of other persons – one of whom was under twenty-one – in (homosexual) sadomasochistic activities, that included branding, beatings, maltreatment of the genitalia with among other things sandpaper and fish hooks, and that resulted in the flow of blood and left scarring. No one, however, ever needed medical attention and there was no indication that the participants in these activities had engaged in them for any other reason than that they chose to do so for the purpose of sexual gratification. The police stumbled upon the case by accident when they found a number of video films during routine investigations into other matters. There was no suggestion that the films served any commercial purpose or had ever been used by others than the participants themselves. The three applicants to the European Court had been convicted and sentenced to quite stiff prison sentences (later reduced on appeal) and eventually saw their final appeal to the House of Lords dismissed by a slim majority (two of the five Law Lords dissenting).[33] The Lords' reasoning, which later formed the basis both for the government's assertion that there had been no unjustifiable interference and for the European Court's decision that prosecution was indeed justified, ran as follows.

Following standard case law, a defence of consent based on a right of individual autonomy, was not available. It was held that in such cases, the criminal law was restraining a practice which is regarded as dangerous and injurious to individuals and which is harmful to society generally and to which consent could not be relevant. ". . . it is not in the public interest that a person should

[32] *Laskey, Jaggard and Brown v. United Kngdom*, ECHR 19/02/97, 00021627/93.
[33] R. v. *Brown* [1994] 1 AC 212; [1993] 2 All ER 75.

wound or cause actual bodily harm to another for no good reason. Thus in the absence of a good reason the victim's consent cannot amount to a defence . . . the satisfying of sado-masochistic desires cannot be classed as a good reason".[34] The participants in this case may not have needed medical attention, but that could have been different, they were not the only practitioners of sado-masochism in England, and in considering the public interest it would be wrong to look at the activities of the appellants only. There could well be other, less responsible and less controlled sadomasochists in the country: when it comes to the public interest, potential for harm is just as relevant as actual harm.

Before the European Court, the UK Government argued along the same lines, contending that the prosecution and conviction of the defendants was necessary for reasons of public health (the risk of harm) but also for broader moral reasons: the behaviour in question undermined the respect which human beings should confer upon each other. Ever cautious about making what it calls "value judgments", the European Court side-stepped the need to say anything about the latter by substantially agreeing with the government on the issue of public health and risk of harm. At the same time, the Court also avoided dealing with the issue of consent, dismissing any reference to *Dudgeon* and *Norris* and merely confirming that the state is justified in intervening in private lives in order to prevent (the risk of) harm. Evaluating the significance of consent, according to the Court, is a matter for the state concerned, a (mitigating?) factor when determining what level of harm or risk can be tolerated.

Arguably the facts in *Laskey* bear little resemblance to *Dudgeon* and *Norris*. But the problem in all of these cases is exactly the same when it comes to autonomy. Again, my argument is not with the outcome (although in this case I happen to disagree), but with the reasoning, including the remark added by the European Court on whether Article 8 was applicable at all. The Court saw no need to determine whether the protection of morals could provide a justification for interference, accepting the government's contention that harm and the risk of harm were sufficiently present and provided sufficient grounds for interference for reasons of public health. But to define what happened in *Laskey* as criminally relevant harm, is to accept what has been called "the homespun moralising of the majority [of the Lords – CB] in *Brown*";[35] it is also to avoid fundamental questions about how harm is defined as criminally relevant in the context of the public interest in a "moral *status quo*". After the reasoning in *Dudgeon* and *Norris*, however, it should come as no surprise that the European Court is not averse to justifying the criminalisation of sexual behaviour on moral grounds, as may be concluded from the final paragraph of the *Laskey* judgment: "[t]his finding, however, should not be understood as calling into question the prerogative of the state on moral grounds to seek to deter acts of the kind in question".

[34] *R.* v. *Brown* (Court of Appeal) [1992] QB 491 per Lord Lane CJ, quoted with approval in the House of Lords by Lord Templeman.

[35] Richard Townshend-Smith, "Homespun morals" (1993) 143 *New Law Journal* 6600, 680.

From *Laskey* we may also learn that the Court considers it quite possible that a person cannot claim protection of his privacy while undoubtedly exercising his autonomy– not because it is overridden by other interests, but because the situation in which it is exercised falls outside the scope of Article 8. "There can be no doubt that sexual orientation and activity concern an intimate aspect of private life", but, the Court goes on to observe, in this case there were specially equipped chambers and video-cameras, this was a group with members, there were as many as forty-four people involved! "It may thus be open to question whether the sexual activities of the applicants fell entirely within the notion of 'private life' in the particular circumstances of the case".[36] The dissenting Judge Petitti was less circumspect: "Not every aspect of private life automatically qualifies for protection under the Convention". Again, this reasoning avoids the crucial question. Forty-four people are quite capable of leading their own sexual lives together, if that is what they choose to do, and if part of the gratification involves video taping, then that is still their choice. That not everything that goes on behind closed doors is automatically immune from state interference (indeed, Pettiti refers to rape within marriage), merely serves to illustrate that geographical definitions of privacy do not always provide relevant criteria for restricting autonomy. *A contrario* there is a parallel here with *Toonen* v. *Australia*,[37] in which the UN Human Rights Committee found that the existence of Tasmanian statutes criminalising male homosexual behaviour constituted arbitrary interference in Toonen's private life (Article 17, International Covenant on Civil and Political Rights) primarily because they did not distinguish between sexual activity in public and in private locations. While many welcomed the decision as at least a step in the right direction,[38] others have pointed out that "[t]he location of gay and lesbian sexual orientation in the private domain doesn't really challenge the notion that homosexuality is immoral (. . .) The message which emanates from the Committee's decision (. . .) is thus one of 'limited tolerance' ".[39]

EQUALITY RIGHTS AND AUTONOMY

Privacy, it would seem, has become a sorely over-stretched concept, both in theory and in positive law. However much we theorise, however many different aspects of private life we define as autonomy, and however much we call for a greater role for the state in promoting rather than simply protecting privacy,[40]

[36] See *Laskey* v. *UK*, para. 36. Since the point was not contested by Laskey et al. or the government, the Court saw no reason to examine this particularly tortured piece of reasoning.

[37] UN Human Rights Committee, A/49/40, Vol. II (1994), Annex IX, sect. EE (226–37).

[38] Cf. James D. Willets, "The Human Rights of Sexual Minorities" (1995) 22 *Human Rights: Journal of the Section of Individual Rights & Responsibilities* 22–7.

[39] Sarah Pritchard (1994) Gay Rights Victory at UN II, June 1994.

[40] A.M. Connelly, "Problems of Interpretation of Article 8 of the European Convention on Human Rights" (1986) 35 *International and Comparative Law Quarterly* 567.

the protection that Article 8 can afford – always and by definition of the restrictions of Article 8(2) – is strictly limited to the protection of negative freedom. Far from being an inalienable fundamental human right, in practice privacy has become a limited subjective right, a conceptual legal tool for determining what (and who) is deserving of protection. This inherent weakness of privacy rights in the field of sexual autonomy has led a number of authors to advocate equality rights, theoretically more logical and easier to uphold. In theory, that is, for as yet neither the European Court nor the United Nations Human Rights Committee have been prepared to examine claims under Article 14 ECHR or Article 26 ICCPR, both of which forbid discrimination. This is despite the fact that the Committee at least explicitly interprets the prohibition on discrimination for reasons of sex as to include sexual orientation.[41] In *Dudgeon* v. *UK* the European Court saw no need to examine the alleged violation of Article 14, regarding the issue as part of and as having been absorbed by the wider issue of privacy. In *Smith and Grady* v. *UK*[42] the Court again did not consider whether there was a breach of Article 14 ECHR; having decided that the discharge of the applicants from the RAF on the sole grounds that they were homosexual (an action fully in accordance with MOD-policy) constituted an unjustified interference with their private lives, the Court considered that a complaint under Article 14 ". . . amounts in effect to the same complaint, albeit seen from a different angle, that the Court has already considered in relation to Article 8 . . .".[43] *In Toonen v. Australia,* the UN Human Rights Committee followed much the same approach.

In his dissenting opinion, UN Committee Member Bertil Wennergren noted that to prohibit sexual intercourse between same-sex partners was to distinguish between heterosexuals and homosexuals and therefore to set aside the principle of equality before the law. That this is also an unwarranted intervention in the right to privacy should, in his opinion, have been deduced from the violation of Article 26 ICPCR.[44] Likewise, Judge Zeika, dissenting in *Dudgeon*, opined that to subsume Article 14 ECHR under Article 8, was to "limit excessively the scope of Article 14 to the point of depriving it of all practical value" (although he came to the conclusion that there had been no violation of Article 14 in the case under consideration). There is indeed a world of difference between the legal consequences of equality rights and privacy rights. For where the legal right of privacy obliges the state to refrain from interference (and any notion of positive duties with regard to respecting private life is embryonic, to say the least), there is no doubt that equality rights impose a positive obligation to act and to ensure that they are upheld. The former may legitimately be subject to and limited by state

[41] It is unclear whether the European Court would do the same, but it is likely given the Court's sensitivity to the majority opinion of Member States; a number of European states, among which are The Netherlands, Denmark, France and Germany, explicitly include sexual orientation in equality legislation.

[42] *Smith and Grady* v. *UK*, *supra* n 17.

[43] *Ibid.*, para. 116.

[44] Cf. Sarah Pritchard, *supra* n 39.

regulation. Equality rights, by definition, may not: all men are equal, some are not more equal than others, just as all human beings are autonomous individuals and some not more autonomous than others.

To consider the right to sexual autonomy as part of the right to privacy means that some forms of sexual expression may be construed as a threat to public health or morals and implies and perpetuates distinctions between acceptable and non-acceptable sexuality. Protection of the privacy of "sexual deviants" may be systematically withheld on those grounds, thereby denying them autonomy and relegating them to less than full rights-holding members of the political community. This is the essence of discrimination. "The logic of full and equal humanity", however, overcomes claims of group inferiority. "Signs of difference from the mainstream that were previously seen as a mark of moral inferiority and grounds for justifiable insubordination, have been excluded from the realm of legally and politically legitimate discrimination".[45] Seen from this point of view, it makes sense to regard equality rights as essential to the right of individual autonomy, for to be disadvantaged or criminalised because one is different from the "normal" majority, is to be prevented from being one's autonomous self.

As Bronnitt points out, equality-based rights discourse has its limitations too. If the division between the public and the private "has played and continues to play, a significant role in concealing and legitimating the subordination of certain groups in society, (. . .) equality rights similarly rest on the public/private dichotomy drawn in liberal theory (. . .)".[46] This argument does not, however, refute the contention that an appeal to equality rights is more appropriate than a claim to privacy rights where it is the state that not only fails to promote equality but actively discriminates through criminalisation or the imposition of other measures. To require of the state decriminalisation of certain behaviour by a sexual minority because it is discriminatory, is no different from demanding that the state require of others that they treat minorities with respect and do not discriminate against them. Legally, therefore, the protection of sexual autonomy afforded by equality rights would seem to be greater than that afforded by the right to privacy. But, however logically attractive the case for equality in order to promote and protect individual sexual autonomy may seem, again we are faced with the paradox of fundamental human rights in a social context. Under the "logic of full and equal humanity" there is no theoretical basis for restrictive intervention in the exercise of equality rights. And unless we argue, like Bertil Wennergren, that discrimination results in a person being deprived of their right to privacy (a perfectly logical and correct argument given the texts of the European Convention and the International Covenant), in which case we are back to square one, there is no legal basis either. By shifting the focus from privacy to equality as fundamental to sexual autonomy, we are simply avoiding the

[45] Donnelly, *op.cit.*, n 15, 96–101.

[46] Simon Bronnitt, "The Right to Sexual Privacy, Sado-masochism and the Human Rights (Sexual Conduct) Act 1994 (Cth)" (1995) 2 *Australian Journal of Human Rights* 1, 4.

issue that must ever arise in a social context, the question of when and why is there a place for the state in the nation's bedrooms?

AUTONOMY AND THE RIGHTS AND INTERESTS OF OTHERS

The paradox that lies at the heart of restricting a fundamental right to (sexual) autonomy is the main reason why it is reduced to a weak, competing bid for negative freedom (or, if we take the remarks by the European Court and Judge Petitti to their logical conclusion, why it may well be no more than a subjective right, the scope of which is defined in law according to what a majority in society regard as moral and immoral).[47] Autonomy lies at the heart of every fundamental human right, for to be human is to be autonomous. And yet there must be restrictions in the way in which autonomy rights are exercised, for to be human is also to engage in social contact with other, equally autonomous beings. Simply to equate sexual autonomy with equality is to ignore certain circumstances that require such restrictions. To reduce autonomy to a component of privacy under Article 8 ECHR, subject to all of the limitations that its second paragraph allows, is to seriously muddle the issue by failing to distinguish between a theoretically justified but unrestrictable right of autonomy and the limited legal right to privacy. Indeed in practice, the European Court, although it refers repeatedly to autonomy as being the right in question, has as yet to find a logical criterion for restricting it. The (threat of) prosecution and conviction of those who willingly and knowingly opt to lead sexually "deviant" lives, i.e. those whose sexual orientation is expressed in ways that are different from what the majority regard as "normal", or may even regard as immoral, is a far-reaching restriction. To justify it by appealing to the protection of morals or harm – defined according to the prevailing moral climate – is to deny the essence of the individual right to autonomy.

The great importance of human rights discourse, is not that an appeal to fundamental human rights carries political weight (although it does that too), but that it provides arguments that allow us to hold law to its own principles. In doing so, it also points to the criteria by which we may judge which restrictions of which rights are justified in the social context in which they are exercised. In the case of sexual autonomy, such restrictions derive logically from the rights and interests of equally autonomous others. It is for this reason that authors have argued that the only logical criterion is harm to those rights and interests.[48] But how do we define what those rights and interests are, and what harm means in matters of sexual activity, without yet again resorting to an appeal to morals? The problem is not that one's partner/s is/are underage or of the same sex, that

[47] Cf. Gutwirth, *op.cit.* n 3, 56ff who argues that one of the risks of defining privacy in law as a subjective right is that the right is then only protected, existent even, if it can be construed as law-abiding, i.e. as "normal".

[48] Cf. Gutwirth, *op.cit.* n 3 at 42 and Bronnitt, *supra* n 46 at 4.

actual bodily harm occurs, that blood flows, that scarring results – all matters than can be objectively ascertained – but the question of whether this is relevant to anyone but the participants. So much has been written about harm and risk of harm as grounds for intervening in the private sphere,[49] that I have no wish to add to that here, except to point out that those who advocate such criteria because they are somehow more objective than "morals", should take a closer look at the government's contention in *Laskey*, not disputed by the European Court, that the risk/harm involved was also a moral risk/harm, and at Judge Pettiti's dissenting opinion on the question of why the protection of the rights guaranteed by Article 8 ECHR did not apply to sadomasochism.

Valverde has predicted that, in the field of sexual morality, the plurality of principles, values and discourses in simultaneous development in post-modern society, will render harm and risk ever more open-ended concepts that, far from being objective, are wide open to moral authoritarianism.[50] Gutwirth also makes this point, although for a different reason: "In modern welfare society, with its perceived necessity to interfere for the common good . . .we have long left the unique individual behind and base our expectations on the average, 'normal' person; all deviants are a threat to the common good, by the very definition of their being different".[51] The notable aspect of *Laskey* in this regard, is that the moral authority to which the government refers is the European Convention itself, which forbids degrading treatment (Article 3) and therefore places a positive duty on the state to act against those whose conduct is degrading.[52] But again, who, if not the autonomous individual, shall decide what is degrading about his or her uninhibited self? The only answer that can be deduced from *Laskey* is: the moral majority. Pettiti is more explicit: calling for regulation of practices of sexual abuse that are "demeaning" even when they do not inflict harm, he ends his rather vehement opinion with: "[t]he protection of private life means the protection of a person's intimacy and dignity, not the protection of his baseness or the promotion of criminal immoralism".[53]

Harm in this sense is not a criterion that logically derives from the notion of (sexual) autonomy as a fundamental human right, for the arguments it provides run contrary to the essential meaning of that fundamental human right in a democratic society. This is not, however, an argument for total relativism and I am certainly not saying that the rights and interests of others are irrelevant or cannot logically be harmed. The essence of autonomy is the right to individual freedom and self-determination, the right to make existential choices and to

[49] See Raes, *supra*, 23.

[50] Mariana Valverde, "The Harms of Sex and the Risks of Breasts: Obscenity and Indecency in Canadian Law" (1999) 8 *Social & Legal Studies* 181–97.

[51] Gutwirth, *op.cit.* n 3 at 71.

[52] There is an interesting parallel here, where in the national debate the British Government appeals to Article 2 of the Convention (the right to life) to justify new measures of detention for psychiatric offenders, especially paedophiles.

[53] Dissenting opinion of Judge Petitti, *Laskey, Jaggard and Brown* v. *United Kingdom*, *supra* n 32.

resist power and external influence. The limits of one person's sexual autonomy derive automatically from the same rights of autonomous others. Seen from this perspective, the question is not whether there is objectively ascertainable physical or psychological damage (although that could play a part), but whether individual behaviour restricts others in their freedom, prevents them from making autonomous choices, takes away their ability to resist power and external influence. The key concepts then are not harm as such, but coercion – violent or otherwise – and consent.

THE LIMITS OF SEXUAL AUTONOMY: COERCION AND CONSENT

The right to make existential choices free from external influence and then to act according to those choices, is an essential part of autonomy, which is another way of saying that autonomous activity is activity to which one has knowingly consented. Participation in sexual activity on the basis of informed consent, cannot therefore justify interference by the state with those who engage in such activity. On the other hand, interference is indicated if participation in sexual activity is the result of coercion, deceit or ignorance about what such activities entail. For in that case there is either no consent, or it has not been knowingly and willingly given.

One of the major inconsistencies in both the *Brown* and *Laskey* decisions was they way in which consent was ruled out as relevant to the issue of justified interference. Despite the fact that harm and the risk of harm in the sense of (serious) injury was the manifest reason given both by the Lords and the UK Government, a subsequent decision under English law reveals that the infliction of pain or even actual bodily harm, is not the issue at stake. In *R* v. *Wilson*[54] the Court of Appeal held that consensual activity between husband and wife in the privacy of the matrimonial home, consisting of the husband branding his initials onto his wife's buttock, is not a proper matter for criminal liability. This despite the fact that Mrs Wilson apparently needed medical attention, for it was the doctor who informed the police. The essential difference between this case and *Brown/Laskey* is not one of geographical privacy ("the matrimonial home"): despite the remark by the European Court on the applicability of Article 8, neither *Laskey* nor the government maintained that these sadomasochistic activities, including the videotaping, were for "public consumption". The difference is that these men were homosexuals, that there were more than two of them, and that this conduct was therefore regarded as degrading, immoral, not in the public interest and the legitimate subject of prosecution.

It would appear that in the field of sexuality, public order and public interest can neutralise consent if it is given for what are considered to be not "good" reasons.[55]

[54] *R* v. *Wilson* [1997] QB 47; [1996]2 CAR 241.

[55] Cf. Nicola Lacey and Celia Wells (1998) *Reconstructing Criminal Law: Critical Perspectives on Crime and the Criminal Process* (London: Butterworths, 2nd edn 1993).

If one wishes to engage in "normal" homosexual activity, as in heterosexual activities that is a good enough reason and consent is crucial, for it distinguishes between sexual contact and sexual abuse, between sexual intercourse and rape. But it also distinguishes between sadomasochism and assault.[56] Whether the participants are homosexuals or not, whether there are two of them or twenty, is of no consequence. What is relevant is whether they, as autonomous human beings, have knowingly consented. "Respecting the right to say yes or to say no to any activity is a crucial part of human rights, and the State, by not allowing one of these options, is denying what is fundamental about being human".[57] Now, that statement by Wadham should be somewhat qualified, for saying yes – or not saying no – is not an unproblematic issue. In discussing *Brown*, Edwards raises two questions: do participants always know what they are consenting to; and how do we tell the difference between consent and submission?[58]

Consent to what?

According to Edwards . . ."sado-masochistic partners have no way of foretelling the degree of bodily harm which will result from their encounters".[59] Now this may or may not be true – although to my knowledge sadomasochism (like any other form of mutual sexual self-expression) is based on trust in one's partner and involves, because of its very nature, an intricate code of signals that will prevent the infliction of pain from exceeding that to which the "victim" has consented. I presume that she means that the risk of harm is sufficient to warrant criminalisation and/or prosecution. Be that as it may, the general issue at stake here is whether the risk of harm warrants state interference in consensual sexual activity of whatever nature. I cannot see why running risks in one's sexual life is different from running risks in any other field. Football and boxing, to name but two apparently perfectly acceptable pastimes, are also risky activities from which (serious) injuries frequently result.[60] In consenting to engage in certain activities, we are accepting that a degree of harm may ensue and therefore consenting to risk.

Likewise, to have unprotected sex could be a risky business, but here too the logic of sexual autonomy dictates that, if a person knowingly entertains the risk of contracting HIV/AIDS, there is no justification for prosecuting the original carrier later. The perspective changes however as soon as coercion or deceit is involved. Bronnitt, almost against his better judgment, reluctantly concludes that "in cases of transmission of a disease which seriously affects the health of

[56] John Wadham, "Consent to Assault" (1996) 146 *New Law Journal* 6672,1812.

[57] Wadham, *loc.cit.*

[58] Susan Edwards, "No defence for a sado-masochistic libido" (1993) 143 *New Law Journal* 406–10.

[59] Edwards, *loc.cit.*

[60] See Bronnitt, *supra* n 46, for a discussion of consent to dangerous sports etc.

another . . . the consent of the other person should be disregarded [for reasons of public policy]". It is a conclusion that seems to me insufficiently thought through as to its implications both in theory and in practice.[61] All sexually transmitted diseases are certainly a matter for public policy, but it by no means follows that consent is no longer relevant as a defence in criminal cases. As in football, there are mutually accepted rules for consensual sexual activity designed to minimise risk. We have not therefore consented to our fellow players ignoring those rules and inflicting serious injury. Neither have we given consent if the other is intentionally exposing us to a risk of serious harm of which he/she is fully aware but that is unknown to us. Then, and only then, prosecution may be warranted. The relevant issue is not the nature of the risk to which a person consents, but whether the other respects the limits of that consent.

I rather suspect that Edwards' problem with consent and risk has more to do with the fact that in rape cases, especially date-rape, consent to risk has often been accepted as a defence where in fact no consent existed. Women who willingly and knowingly accept an invitation to "come back to my flat" are not accepting the risk of being raped – they are accepting the "risk" that the encounter may end with sexual intercourse. That is a very different matter – as indeed most countries in Western Europe (and the European Court) have recognised, in making rape within marriage a criminal offence. If I am right, then Edwards is confusing respect for the right of every autonomous human being to say yes or no, with the fact that (some) men cannot tell the difference. She is also confusing informed consent to risk with the very real problem of distinguishing between consent and submission.

Consent and submission

In matters of sexual autonomy people can be vulnerable for two reasons: because they belong to a "deviant" minority in need of protection against the enforcement of majority morals, or because, for a variety of reasons, they are incapable of giving informed consent to sexual activities. The very existence of the first category logically requires that the limits of sexual autonomy are set at the point where a person is prevented from exercising it. The same applies to the second category. Among the incapable are persons (often, although certainly not always, women) who are coerced or deceived into consenting, because their capacity to consent is blurred by the situation in which they find themselves and by the behaviour of the other, and who feel they cannot say no. There are others of whom we must assume that they are incapable of assessing what consent means. In all of these cases, one person is "overpowered" (not necessarily in the physical sense) and prevented from making autonomous decisions: in the con-

[61] See Bronnitt, "Spreading disease and the Criminal Law", [1994] *Criminal Law Review* 20–34, at 32.

text in which sexual activities take place they are the vulnerable party because there is an inequality of power – either in the specific situation or *per se* – of which the perpetrator takes advantage.

These are the victims of date rapists, of doctors, therapists and teachers for example, who sexually abuse their patients or students, who abuse the trust inherent in the relationship and use the vulnerability generated by the situation to persuade the other that sex is an automatic part of the deal. Again, the limits of sexual autonomy in such cases are not dictated by the sexual nature of the activity involved. It is not sex that is immoral, but the abuse of power. This also justifies setting limits on the age at which consent can be assumed to have been given. (There will of course always be disagreement over exactly what the age of consent should be, although it seems to me that if one is deemed sufficiently autonomous to make other existential decisions such as consenting to medical treatment, then one is also able to decide one's sexual destiny). There is something to be said for the Dutch solution in such cases in which sexual activities in situations where there is an inherent inequality of power are assumed not to be consensual, but only if the victim so indicates.[62]

SEXUAL AUTONOMY, THE PROBLEM OF PUBLIC SPACE AND THE LIMITS OF CONSENT

Accepting consent as the core issue of autonomy means that we no longer need ponder whether the state has a place in the nation's bedrooms. The answer must always be yes: geographical privacy is not an excuse for preventing others from exercising *their* autonomy.[63] It is not the private but the public domain that is the problem, and I have left this matter until last because it vexes me most and indeed, as we shall see, I am unable to take my line of reasoning to its logical conclusion. There are those who argue that causing offence to others' moral beliefs and thereby causing (psychological) distress can be regarded as causing harm and is therefore a legitimate target of state intervention.[64] In so far as this concerns the abstract knowledge that some people willingly and knowingly engage in sexual activities that others (even a majority) find distasteful or immoral, it should by now be clear that this is irrelevant as an argument for state interference. But what about actually being confronted with the (consensual) sexual activity of others in public?

One could argue, as Bronnitt has done, that explicit sexual behaviour could be justifiably restricted, while milder forms of sexual expression could be tolerated, for they are, given changing standards of public decency, unlikely to cause

[62] See Kelk, *infra* 205.

[63] I am by no means unaware of the problems of proving private sexual activities were or were not consensual (and the more so within existing sexual relationships), but that is not the issue here.

[64] See for example, J. Feinberg, *Offense to Others* (New York City, NY: Oxford University Press, 1995).

harm.[65] It seems to me that here too it is not harm (which simply reintroduces the problem of majority morals, for what is harm and who shall determine it?), but consent that we should be looking at – not the confrontation with others' autonomous behaviour as such, but the unwitting confrontation to which no consent has been given. Again, this is the Dutch solution for pornography and explicitly sexual entertainment: provided that readers or spectators are adequately forewarned as to the nature of the material or show and therefore know what to expect, the Dutch Supreme Court assumes that those who buy (tickets to see) it have consented to confrontation with the content.[66] There is no need to resort to the fiction that porn-cinemas or clubs are private space: they are open to all who wish to visit them (and as such are subject to the regulations, including rules on minors and anti-discrimination, that govern other equally public places such as bars and discos).[67]

However, we are still left with overt sexual behaviour on the street, and which ever way I look at it, there seems to be no logical criterion for restriction unless we yet again resort to some standard of generally accepted morality, decency or whatever we want to call it. For this is the one situation in which consent cannot provide a satisfactory solution. I live in central Amsterdam and on Saturday nights in certain areas I am likely to be confronted with many sorts of consensual sexual behaviour, some of which I specifically do not want to see. Of course, I could avoid those areas, but that would limit me in my autonomy. I personally draw the line at, among other things, sexual intercourse, but others may find a display of overt homosexual affection such as kissing or holding hands an affront to their sensibilities and be equally curtailed. Should that be a legitimate reason to forbid such behaviour and even to prosecute those who engage in it?

If lack of consent is the only logical ground for restricting autonomy rights, regardless of what the majority regard as acceptable, the answer must be both yes and no. In the final event, then, I must accept that I too have run up against the paradox of the fundamental human right of autonomy in democratic society.

65 Bronnitt, *supra* n 46.

66 See Kelk, *infra* 223.

67 Child pornography is another matter, for that concerns protection of the vulnerable children, without whom production would be impossible.

6

Human Rights and the Criminalisation of Tradition: The Practices Formerly Known as "Female Circumcision"

LOÏS BIBBINGS

INTRODUCTION

THIS CHAPTER CONSIDERS the legal status of the range of practices referred to collectively as either "female circumcision" (FC) or "female genital mutilation" (FGM). This analysis of the law focuses upon a number of "Western" states (England and Wales, the US, Australia and France) in which some forms of female genital alteration are now criminal offences and examines, *inter alia*, why and how criminalisation occurred, and what practices are currently penalised.[1] The intention is not to present a comprehensive picture of the legal position in each of the jurisdictions considered but, rather, to identify some (common and uncommon) threads in the legal treatment of these practices which have a bearing upon notions of autonomy and privacy.

The aim of this paper is to assess why, by what means, to what extent and in what circumstances criminalisation denies the autonomy of the individual to modify their own or their child's female genitalia. Initially, it is argued that the universalising discourses of human rights (and, in particular, of women's and children's rights) have played a role in influencing and encouraging the criminalisation of FC/FGM in different jurisdictions. Thus, human rights responses to female genital alteration are considered and then compared with the different methods and forms of criminalisation adopted in each jurisdiction.

The analysis of the various criminal laws prohibiting FC/FGM seeks to reveal inconsistencies in the approaches adopted. Thus, the focus here is upon the kinds of modifications or procedures that are potentially encompassed by the criminal law. In addition, some brief consideration is given to the use of prosecution, the relevance of criminal defences, the penalties that a convicted party

[1] I have chosen to focus upon jurisdictions conceived of as "Western" because some of the practices discussed in this chapter are frequently identified as being totally non-Western and this is a crucial point for the direction which my argument will take. However, in using the term "Western" I am not seeking to suggest that this is a unitary concept; rather, for present purposes, it represents a convenient label.

could face and sentencing practice. Other means by which the state "polices" these traditional practices are also discussed in order to illustrate the ways in which personal bodily autonomy can be restricted by non-criminal but possibly more intrusive means.

I begin, however, by briefly considering some socio-cultural definitions and descriptions of FC/FGM to set the scene for the rest of the chapter. Next I move on to look at definitions and responses to female genital alterations in human rights discourses and within the different criminal law jurisdictions.

GENERAL DEFINITIONS OF FC/FGM

It is not my intention to give a full account of the range of practices covered by this terminology because questions of definition and construction are central to my argument. In fact, I am seeking to problematise those definitions that have been proffered within the legal and human rights spheres. However, by way of a brief introduction, a sketch of the way in which the practices under consideration are most frequently described may prove helpful.[2]

In many accounts of the female operations (most of which oppose them), the phrases "female circumcision" (FC) and "female genital mutilation" (FGM) tend to be used as if they described a unified, clearly identifiable practice. Thus, although most writing on FC/FGM takes account of the range of different procedures that are covered by these labels, in analysing the legal or human rights stance which should be adopted towards them FC/FGM is generally viewed as being a homogeneous practice. As a result, the distinction between procedures as diverse as ritualistic circumcision (a symbolic nicking of the skin or blood-letting), the excision of parts of the external genitalia and infibulation (the removal of the clitoris, most of the inner and outer labia – the resultant wound is stitched together leaving only a small aperture for urination, menstruation and penetrative sex) is lost. In addition, the terminology suggests not only a single procedure but, where the word "mutilation" is used, this locates the practices as forms of torture and/or violent bodily injury which are forced upon "victims" by primitive women and men in the name of tradition/culture and religion. To reinforce this view the recent literature upon this subject rightly states that the procedures are most frequently performed upon young girls. The perspective adopted here is clear: the issue of autonomy does not arise or is rejected given both the "barbaric" nature of the practices and the fact that they are visited upon those who are generally judged too young to consent to them.

[2] In doing so a certain amount of generalisation is required. For fuller descriptions of the different physical practices, their consequences and some of the justifications most commonly offered for them see: L.S. Bibbings, "Female Circumcision: Modification or Mutilation?" in J. Bridgeman and S. Millns (eds), *Law and Body Politics: Regulating the Female Body* (Aldershot: Dartmouth, 1995) 151–6; E. Dorkenoo and S. Elworthy, *Female Genital Mutilation: Proposals for Change, Minority Rights Group International Report 92/3*, (London: Minority Rights Group, 1992 – revised edition) 7–15.

In contrast, where the issue of such operations being performed upon adults is concerned, if notions of autonomy are addressed, they are often conceptualised as an aspect of cultural rights or of female adult agency. But even in such contexts free choice tends to be rejected because it is, implicitly or explicitly, viewed as being the result of the "false consciousness" of those involved. Thus those females and males who practise, advocate or choose FC/FGM are, with a varying degree of sensitivity, constructed as cultural dopes who need to be persuaded, taught or forced to see the error of their ways. In short FC/FGM, it is argued, must end.

While the approaches depicted above are not the only views expressed on FC/FGM, they could probably be described as the ones which dominate in the West. Nevertheless, there are those who seek to consider fully whether cultural (or supposedly religious arguments) in support of FC/FGM should, at least in some instances, be respected. Also, some writers seek to distinguish between the different practices in order to decide whether all forms of FC/FGM should be viewed in the same light in human rights and legal terms. Equally, in addressing the question whether adult women (who are fully informed of the consequences of FC/FGM) should be able validly and legally to consent to such operations, the notion of false consciousness has been subject to some critique. For example, Alison Slack's rights-based analysis of the practices addresses all three of these issues:

> Most would probably agree that if an educated, married woman decides to have sunna (mild) operation, it would be her prerogative to do so; and to argue that [this,] under this set of circumstances, is a violation of human rights would be difficult. It is also clear, however, that the rights of a baby girl are being violated when she is infibulated in unsanitary conditions that result in her death. Most people would consider this case to be a violation of the child's human rights.[3]

While one could question who exactly the "most people" she is referring to are, her view is, nonetheless, an important one.

In contrast, those who actually support FC/FGM argue both for its recognition as a cultural right and its protection from (what is often perceived to be) the Westernising force of human rights discourses. They argue, in effect, for a recognition of both cultural and individual autonomy in this context.[4] But these types of arguments tend to be less frequently expressed and, where they do occur, are generally suppressed or attacked particularly in the West as being contrary, for example, to the supposedly univocal voice of human rights or feminist discourses.[5]

[3] A. Slack, "Female Circumcision: A Critical Appraisal" (1988) 10 *Human Rights Quarterly* 437, 472.

[4] For examples see: A. Boulton, "Calls for female circumcision on NHS sparks storm" *Observer*, 14 February 1993; F. Ahmadu, "Rites and Wrongs" *Pride*, April/May 1995, 43.

[5] *Ibid*. However, in France versions of these and related views had a higher profile within the debates on the prosecution of excisers and parents who arranged their daughters' operations. See for example, M. Lefeuvre "Contre la criminalisation de l'excision" (1989) 1 *Bulletin du MAUSS*, 162.

A further point which will be considered in the discussion both of domestic legal and human rights reactions to FC/FGM is the tendency for the practices to be depicted as being completely alien to the Western world. Thus they are tribal traditions of African or possibly of Third World peoples – an (exotic) "other" is thus portrayed as both perpetrator and victim.[6] Overall a picture is painted of an activity which is wholly non-Western in character and, moreover, has no Western equivalent.

Hence, the terms "circumcision" and "genital mutilation" are generally used in the West to refer to a collection of genital modifications which are linked by their supposed "otherness" to the West but which in fact differ considerably. Indeed, perhaps the only unifying characteristic is the fact that in all instances something is being done to the female genitalia. Having said this, some female genital procedures are commonly excluded from these definitions (see below for some examples). These absences are, in themselves, potentially significant. They include procedures which are generally conceived of (often implicitly) as being distinguishable from FC/FGM because of a range of rationales which include the following: they have Western cultural associations; they are or have in the past been located within (Western) medical discourses; because they are in some other respect(s) distinguishable from FC/FGM. Yet, even the notion of FC/FGM as non-Western can be challenged by highlighting instances when clitoridectomy has been performed for medical reasons in England and the US.[7] Further discussion of these definitional issues is included below but, for the moment, what I have mapped here are some threads of the dominant conception of the practices – or at least the one which is most commonly and audibly heard in the West. How then are the practices defined in the sphere of human rights and criminal law and in what ways are these descriptions problematic?

HUMAN RIGHTS, CRIMINAL LAW AND FC/FGM

Human rights conceptions of FC/FGM are particularly significant to a discussion of the criminalisation of these practices given pressures to globally harmonise criminal laws in order to protect individuals and to ensure that states honour their international obligations under the various international models and systems of human rights. Indeed, the work of UN agencies and prominent rights orientated (I)NGOs like FORWARD (Foundation for Women's Health, Research and Development) and Amnesty often have some influence over

[6] See K. Engle's analysis in "Female Subjects of Public International Law: Human Rights and the Exotic Other Female" (1992) 26 *New England Law Review* 1509, 1513–15. In addition, this sense of the "foreign-ness" of the practices is re-emphasised by the fact that they are also frequently linked with Islam; which is characterised as being a distant religion which is repressive of its women "victims". See R.A. Bloul's analysis of this in relation to the wearing of the veil and FC/FGM in France, "Victims or Offenders? 'Other' Women in French Sexual Politics" in K. Davis, *Embodied Practices: Feminist Perspectives on the Body* (London: Sage, 1997), 93, 95.

[7] See E. Showalter, *Sexual Anarchy: Gender and Culture at the Fin de Siècle* (London: Bloomsbury, 1991), 130, 141–2 and n 3 *supra*, 461–2.

decisions to address and possibly criminalise certain activities within different jurisdictions; FC/FGM arguably provides one illustration of this tendency.

Although it has (justifiably) been argued that, in the past, human rights organisations and agencies have often shown a certain reluctance to face the issue of FC/FGM head on, today there are many examples of the conceptualisation of these practices as an interference with female bodily integrity which amounts to torture, and as traditional practices which adversely affect the health and well-being of women and girls.[8] This allows FC/FGM to be categorised as a violation of the rights included within a number of different human rights documents.[9] However, such recognition is not unproblematic in rights terms as many of these documents also grant protection to privacy, religious and cultural rights and this might be taken to suggest that FC/FGM should be afforded some form of protection.[10] Nonetheless, from the late 1970s onwards UN agencies and other rights organisations have become increasingly willing to view, what had previously been referred to as "circumcision", as a mutilation of the female genitalia and an abuse of the women and girls who are affected. As such, it is commonly held that the practices should be eradicated, as cultural or other justifications for their continuance are too inconsequential, given the harm caused. Thus, in this analysis, universalism overturns cultural relativism, cultural or individual autonomy and privacy, even when the procedures are "chosen" by the adult or child they are to be performed upon.

The language of torture is, however, resisted in some instances, or even seemingly apologised for, as it is felt that this would not only be culturally insensitive, and possibly give rise to allegations of racism, but that it would also be strategically foolish. Indeed, it has been argued that condemning FC/FGM too severely or publicly could be counter-productive to the aim of eventually eradicating the practices, as it may occasion a backlash among practising groups who seek to defend their traditions against what they see as interference with their rights to live in accordance with their traditions.[11] Similarly, criminalisation is

[8] The major reason for this reluctance in the past, despite a number of attempts to open UN discussion on "female circumcision" from 1958 onwards, seems to have been a concern that commenting on a particular cultural practice may hold dangers for the human rights ideal. That is that UN agencies or other rights organisations might be criticised for attacking non-Western cultures and/or be accused of racism. For an account of UN progress on addressing FC/FGM see n 2 *supra*, Dorkenoo and Elworthy, 17–21.

[9] For example, provisions which would suggest the need, in human rights terms, to eradicate FC/FGM include: Universal Declaration on Human Rights 1948 (Art. 5); Declaration on Violence Against Women 1993 (Art. 2.a); International Convenant on Civil and Political Rights 1966 (Art. 7); Convention on the Eradication of All forms of Discrimination against Women 1979 (Art. 2(f)); Convention on the Rights of the Child 1989 (Arts. 19.1, 24.3, 37.a); European Convention on the Protection of Human Rights and Fundamental Freedoms 1950 (Art. 3).

[10] See for example, International Covenant on Civil and Political Rights, Arts. 17, 18, 27.

[11] This was to some degree illustrated in 1980 at the UN Women's Meeting in Copenhagen when some Western women attacked clitoridectomy and infibulation as barbaric and primitive practices. Ironically, such pronouncements forced Arab and African women – who had fought against the practices – to feel compelled to defend it. See C.T. Mohanty, A Russo, L. Torres (eds), *Third World Women and the Politics of Feminism* (Indianapolis: Indiana University Press, 1991) 218.

not whole-heartedly advocated as a good strategy towards the goal of eradication. For example, the 1997 joint statement on FGM by the WHO, UNICEF and UNFPA in many respects epitomises this approach.[12] Thus, although the agencies describe the practices as "FGM" and as a "form of violence", they state (contradictorily) that their purpose in doing so:

> . . . is neither to criticize nor to condemn. Even though cultural practices may appear senseless or destructive from the stand-point of others, they have meaning and fulfil a function for those who practice them.[13]

They call for an international and domestic multi-disciplinary, inter-agency approach towards its gradual eradication, in particular, in the sphere of health education.[14] Also they stress the value of supporting resistance from within practising groups rather than necessarily imposing criminalisation upon such peoples.[15] Indeed, assistance is provided by the UN to support this work in different countries.[16]

The latter point is important. Much of the current thrust from human rights discourses to eradicate FC/FGM is wary of advocating criminal law as a solution. Indeed, this is also true of UN efforts towards the elimination of violence against women.[17] Instead, in relation to FC/FGM a less invasive, more gradual approach to the goal of eradication is adopted which suggests that criminal measures should only be used when appropriate, bearing in mind the particular social and cultural context. Also, when used they should be accompanied by other programmes aimed at the sensitive acculturation of practising groups.[18]

What then are the definitions of the operations referred to as FC/FGM proffered by human rights discourses. Perhaps the most all-encompassing description is that given in the joint UN agency statement mentioned above. This defines "FGM" as including a number of classified types of cultural, non-therapeutic procedures, all of which are described as being "irreversible": the excision of the prepuce (clitoral hood), or prepuce and clitoris; the excision of the clitoris with partial or total ablation of the labia minora; the excision of part or all of the external genitalia and stitching/narrowing of the vaginal opening (infibulation). In addition, however a fourth "unclassified" type of FGM is also cited which:

[12] Female genital mutilation: a joint WHO/UNICEF/UNFPA statement (Geneva: WHO, 1997).

[13] *Ibid.*, 1.

[14] *Ibid.*, 13–15.

[15] *Ibid.*, 13–15. This is also perhaps evidenced by the naming of supermodel, Waris Dirie, as UN Population Fund Special Ambassador for the Elimination of Female Genital Mutilation – brought up among a tribe of Somalian desert nomads, she was so altered at the age of five. See UNFPA Press Release on Female Genital Mutilation, 18 September 1997.

[16] *Supra* n 12, 16–19.

[17] For example, see *Preliminary Report of Special Rapporteur on Violence Against Women* (Radhika Coomaraswamy), UN Commission on Human Rights, Fiftieth Session, Agenda 11(a), Report E/CN.4/1995/42, para. 109.

[18] For example, see n 12 *supra*, 15.

> includes pricking, piercing or incising of the clitoris and/or labia; stretching of the clitoris and/or labia; cauterization by burning of the clitoris and surrounding tissue; scraping of tissue surrounding the vaginal orifice (angurya cuts) or cutting of the vagina (gishiri cuts); introduction of corrosive substances or herbs into the vagina to cause bleeding or for the purposes of tightening or narrowing it; and any other procedure that falls under the definition of female genital mutilation given above.[19]

This categorises the performances of a whole range of procedures to the female genitalia as being abuses of human rights – seemingly regardless of whether the female concerned is a child or an adult or whether she is apparently consenting or not. Thus the definition is not limited to the practices which are conventionally described as FC/FGM (ritualistic circumcision, different forms of excision and infibulation). The effect of this is arguably that an area of the female body is portrayed as being, in certain respects, sacrosanct. Thus, although medically justified interventions are acceptable (as long, one would assume, as the rationale is supported by a respectable body of medical opinion and evidence), other activities which are most often not thought of as FC/FGM are apparently also targeted. Indeed, this joint agency statement seems to implicitly make no distinction between all the practices it cites in terms of calling for their eradication. What, in the context of this definition, for example, is the human rights status of genital tattoos (which involve the pricking of the skin), genital piercing and Western procedures such as genital cosmetic surgery, or even sadomasochistic sexual activities which all arguably involve some (cultural) non-therapeutic interference with this part of the female anatomy? Indeed, in some of these alterations exactly the same removal is performed as in certain types of FC/FGM; thus genital cosmetic surgery most often involves the ablation of a part of the labia in order to reduce their size and make them more aesthetically pleasing.[20] The question here is whether the UN agencies' definition of FC/FGM encompasses all these procedures in all circumstances when performed upon the female form. The position in the statement is far from clear on this, although it might be taken to target the "classified" types of modification. Nevertheless, the inclusion of "unclassified" types of FGM within this definition would suggest that in cases of piercing, for example, the adult or child female's consent to such alterations is always overborne because the procedure always amounts to a violation of her human rights. If this is so then notions of female autonomy are completely denied in this context.[21] If it is not, what is it that distinguishes the different genital practices or the ability of adult women, in particular, to be deemed able to validly consent to them? Is it merely that the perceived cultural origins or acceptability in Western eyes of these activities makes a difference in terms of their treatment in practice? Surely, if true, this

[19] *Ibid*., 3.

[20] Such justifications are also very similar to some of the reasons given for FC/FGM. See Bibbings, *op.cit*. n 2 at 155.

[21] One might also question why the female but not the male anatomy is so much in need of protection. See below.

would be an unacceptable and deeply troubling proposition, implying that certain women have agency but "other" women do not, merely on the basis of either their culture or the perceived history of a particular alteration.

As stated above, the UN joint agency definition is probably the broadest. Most other attempts to delineate the compass of FC/FGM stop far short of this. Thus, for example, the non-governmental human rights group Amnesty International in its information pack on "FGM" takes the more limited and conventional definition, stating that it is "the removal of part, or all, of the female genitalia" performed (by implication) for reasons of culture. The practices cited here are infibulation, excision, clitoridectomy and the removal of the clitoral hood. But this document adds:

> In some traditions a ceremony is held but no *mutilation* of the genitals occurs. The ritual may involve holding a knife next to the genitals, pricking the clitoris, cutting some pubic hair, or light scarification in the genital or upper thigh area. (my emphasis).[22]

This definition is particularly interesting as it suggests that the latter types of procedure are not "mutilations" and, therefore, it seems do not constitute FGM. This clearly contradicts the UN joint agency statement which would encompass any cultural and non-therapeutic alteration as opposed to merely a removal of genital tissue.

Thus, the much more limited Amnesty definition of FGM does not appear to question the human rights status of, for example, genital piercing *per se*. However, as we shall see, other definitions of FC/FGM, particularly in the context of criminal law, could be said to, at least potentially, encompass such activities as piercing or cosmetic surgery. Nevertheless, the Western/non-Western distinction seems to stand implicitly or explicitly in most writings about FC/FGM and it is consequently likely that genital cosmetic surgery, for example, is not generally envisaged as being a form of FC/FGM. Nevertheless, given these uncertainties and the problems of definition, the inconsistencies of approach thereby created remain. But, despite this, however FC/FGM is depicted, the practices described by these labels are clearly identified as abuses of human rights by most human rights accounts.

Discussions in human rights discourses have encouraged state action to be taken in the fight to eradicate FC/FGM. In addition, the migration of peoples who continue a tradition of genital alteration has made the practices an issue which Western states have faced within their own borders and not just as something which "other" people do "over there". Indeed, pressure from (I)NGOs, the opinions of professional medical bodies and publicity in the Western media have added to this obligation to "do something" by calling for national policies to be adopted in an attempt to join international efforts to end the practices

[22] *Female Genital Mutilation – A Human Rights Information Pack*, AI Index: ACT 77/05/97 (London: Amnesty International, 1997) (Also available at <http://www.amnesty.org/ailib/intcam/femgen/fgm1.htm>), Section One, 1.

world-wide.[23] Consequently, from the early 1980s onwards a series of Western states have criminalised FGM and, in doing so, particular minority groups in the population are targeted despite the reservations of human rights discourses about using this strategy.[24] Hence, arguably in wishing to be seen to be "doing something" about FC/FGM, some jurisdictions seem to feel that criminal law is an easy way of proving their commitment to human rights in this context, although other policies are often adopted alongside such prohibitions. Indeed, in the jurisdictions under consideration additional measures or educational/outreach programmes have also been established by the state or are granted some state support and/or funding;[25] hence, the multi-pronged approach suggested by human rights discourses has been adopted, albeit to varying degrees.

Moves to criminalise FC/FGM have, however, raised other human rights related concerns about racist laws and the racist policing or implementation of such measures.[26] Also, some in these jurisdictions, while not necessarily defending FC/FGM as a valid cultural practice, have raised concerns about respecting the culture and autonomy of migrant populations and individual women. For example, this is to some extent true in France where there have been calls for the protection of the private choice of those opting for FC/FGM to be performed upon their daughters. For example, the following excerpt from a cultural relativist petition against the criminalisation of FC/FGM illustrates this view:

> [W]e believe it to be our duty to bring to the attention [of our readers] the dangers that any attempt to pass off the practice of excision as intrinsically criminal would cause for the spirit of humanity and democracy . . . Demanding a penal sanction for a custom that does not threaten the republican order and which nothing prevents from being considered as a matter of private choice, as is circumcision, for example, would be tantamount to demonstrating an intolerance which can only create more human dramas than it claims to avoid, and which manifests a singularly narrow conception of democracy.[27]

[23] For example, the work of the campaigning organisation FORWARD provides one such instance of NGO activity particularly in relation to its work in England and Wales. For the World Medical Association's stance on FGM see T. Richards, "Female genital mutilation condemned by WMA" (1993) 307 *British Medical Journal* 957.

[24] However, the joint statement does effectively recognise that in a jurisdiction with only a minority of the population practising FC/FGM criminalisation is not so problematic. *Supra* n 12 at 15.

[25] In Australia, money has been allocated in the Federal budget for community education programmes (M. Swain, "Female Genital Mutilation: An Update" Parliament of NSW Briefing Paper 1/96 (Sydney, Australia: NSW Parliamentary Library, 1996) 14, <http//www.parliament.nsw.gov.au/gi/library/research/bf1–96.html>). In the US at Federal level the Department of Health and Human Services is required to engage in education and outreach to the relevant communities (Pub. L. 104–34, 510, 110 stat. 1321 (1996)). In England and Wales the Department of Health gives financial support to FORWARD (Lord Hunt of Kings Heath, H.L. Debs, col 748, 10 November 1998). In contrast, the French Government's apparent reluctance to give much attention to information, education and support programmes has been criticised (B. Winter, "Women, the Law, and Cultural Relativism in France: The Case of Excision" (1994) 19 *Signs: Journal of Women in Culture and Society* 939, 969).

[26] S.M. Poulter, *English Law and Ethnic Minority Customs* (London: Butterworths, 1986), 157–8.

[27] Lefeuvre *supra* n 5, 162–3. For a discussion of this petition see, Winter *supra* n 25, 951–2. The translation of the petition which I have cited here is that used by Winter.

Similarly, in the French context, the right to a private family life has been defended by Raymond Verdier: "one can measure the extent of the danger of a national penal law which incautiously tries to penetrate the intimacy of families and uncompromisingly imposes our way of thinking and of living on foreigners who do not necessarily share them".[28] Yet there are opposing voices who deny any protection for FC/FGM as cultural practices and claim that, as non-French cultural traditions, they should be afforded no protection under French law.[29]

Generally, though, in the Western jurisdictions in which FC/FGM is now a criminal offence, cultural rights arguments have not figured as prominently as in France. However, where such notions have been raised they have generally been rejected as providing no justification for barbarity; this is especially the case where children are concerned. As a result, the autonomy of those involved and their right to privacy is denied. Thus, in these instances cultural claims offer no protection from criminalisation, at least in the rhetoric of law. Indeed, in the debates in both the UK Parliament and the US Senate little heed was paid to notions of cultural relativism or privacy; rather FC/FGM was graphically described and, consequently perhaps, was perceived to be a barbarous act and an abuse of human rights which needed to be addressed by the criminal law of civilised countries. Here, then, the French context is perhaps distinguishable. This difference may perhaps be said to lie in particularly French notions of respect for cultural diversity, privacy and, as Winter has noted, perhaps even French post-colonial guilt given that most of the perpetrators emanate from former French colonies.[30]

Thus, a number of Western jurisdictions have chosen to criminalise FC/FGM. In some states specific legislative criminal measures have been adopted targeting these practices.[31] Such action has sometimes even been taken despite the fact that existing legal measures prohibiting offences against the person could have been applied at least to circumstances where a child is the "victim" and/or where the excisee does not consent to the procedure.[32] For example, in Australia the Family Law Council's Discussion Paper, "Female Genital Mutilation", concluded that, although it could be argued that theoretically the practice was already illegal in Australia, specific legislation criminalising it combined with community education programmes was necessary in order to work towards the eradication of FC/FGM which, the Council felt, would be deemed an unaccept-

[28] R. Verdier, "Excision, du devoir au crime" *Liberation* 1 July 1991. Translation cited here taken from Winter, *supra* n 25 at 953.

[29] See Winter, *supra* n 25 at 959.

[30] *Ibid.* at 951, 950.

[31] Sweden was the first Western jurisdiction to adopt such a measure: Act 316 of 1982.

[32] Also, it is arguable that for Member States of the European Convention on Human Rights, Article 3 on torture, inhuman and degrading treatment means that states should in their domestic law protect females (children and possibly adults) within their boarders from FC/FGM by having criminal laws which would allow for the prosecution and potential conviction of perpetrators. See *A* v. *United Kingdom*, judgment of 23 September 1998 (100/1997/884/1096) for a comparable approach to the corporal punishment of children.

able practice by most Australians.[33] In response to the Paper, agreements were made between the Federal Government and the State and Territorial Governments to the effect that all jurisdictions would enact legislation banning "FGM" and money was allocated in the Federal budget for community education.[34]

Additionally, in England and Wales, Poulter argued that existing provisions could be used as FC/FGM would constitute an unlawful interference with the "basic right to bodily integrity which everyone possesses under the English law".[35] This is certainly true where a child is concerned – parents can generally only consent to procedures which have a medically beneficial effect upon the girl concerned or possibly to a non-therapeutic operation, provided it is not actually against the child's interest. In addition, it could be argued (more tentatively), as Poulter has suggested, that parents may consent if the operation is against the child's interest but there is sufficient benefit to be gained by others from it and the procedure is not seriously detrimental to the child.[36] None of these grounds apply to the case of FC/FGM. If a benefit to others is claimed for, produced by the operation – namely, the satisfying of "a deep-felt community attachment to traditional customs",[37] the suggestion would most probably be rejected even if doctors performed the procedure in a hospital context; indeed, the WHO and various professional medical bodies around the world have taken a firm stance against the medicalisation of FC/FGM.[38]

Even where the operation is conducted on a consenting adult, it is arguable that, as the common law has, in other instances, limited the circumstances in which consent is a valid defence to an offence against the person, FC/FGM is a criminal offence without statutory intervention.[39] Having said this, of course, there are several advantages in introducing a specific measure criminalising FC/FGM despite the reservations against this course of action. For example, it clarifies the legal position and removes the need for a test case to be brought to establish its status. In addition, criminalisation, according to the UN joint agency statement, "is important both because it represents a formal expression of public disapproval and because it is the means by which governments can establish official sanctions".[40]

[33] See Swain, *supra* n 25, 9–11.

[34] *Ibid.*, 14.

[35] *Supra* n 26, 155–6. Under the Offences Against the Person Act 1861 ss.47, 18, 20 or, where a child under 16 is the "victim" a prosecution under the Children and Young Persons Act 1933 s.1 was also possible. See also K. Hayer "Female Circumcision – is there a legal solution?" (1984) *Journal of Social Welfare Law* 323, 328–9 and R.D. Mackay "Is Female Circumcision Unlawful?" [1983] *Criminal Law Review* 717.

[36] *Supra* n 26, 155–6.

[37] *Ibid.*, 155.

[38] See n 12 *supra*, 8–9.

[39] Of course this is an easier argument to make in the post-Brown climate. See *R* v. *Brown* [1994] 1 AC 212, [1993] 2 All ER 75.

[40] *Supra* n 12 at 15.

What then were the definitions of FC/FGM adopted in the specific measures that criminalised FC/FGM? In 1985 the Prohibition of Female Circumcision Act of England and Wales (the Act also applies in Northern Ireland) made it an offence to "excise, infibulate or otherwise mutilate the whole or any part of the labia majora or labia minora or clitoris of another person" or "to aid, abet, counsel or procure the performance by another person of any of those acts on that other person's own body'.[41] However, procedures are exempted from this provision where an operation is necessary for medical reasons (based upon the physical or mental health of the person) and is performed by a registered medical practitioner.[42] But, for the purposes of these provisions, a doctor, in considering whether an operation is necessary for the mental health of a "person", must take no account "of the effect on that person of any belief on the part of that or any other person that the operation is required as a matter of custom or ritual".[43] Similarly, an alteration performed upon a "person" who is in any stage of labour or has just given birth and is performed for purposes connected with that labour and birth so long as it is performed by appropriate medical personnel is excepted from the prohibition.[44]

This, then, is the definition of female circumcision in England and Wales. The measure represented a significant step as prominent campaigners against FGM see the 1985 English statute as representing a model for other jurisdictions.[45] Indeed, very similar definitions of the prohibited procedure have been adopted in both the US federal and Australian jurisdictions.[46]

[41] Section 1(1)(a),(b). Poulter suggests that the liability of relatives who counsel or procure arises from s. 1(1)(a) and from the Accessories and Abetters Act 1861, not from s. 1(1)(b) which he states only applies to the counselling and procuring of self-mutilation (n 26 *supra*, 156). The drafting of the provision is a little unclear but parliamentary papers suggest he is correct. Section 1(1)(b) was apparently included to target operations on adult women (H.L. Debs, vol 441 col 674). However, a woman who performs an operation on her own body or who arranges for another person to do so does not herself commit an offence under s. 1(1) (H.C. Standing Committee C, col 14, 3 April 1985, col 14 and n 26 *supra*, 156. In addition, presumably liability in relation to attempt, conspiracy and incitement exists in relation to offences under the 1985 Act.

[42] Section 2(1)(a).

[43] Section 2(2).

[44] Section 2(1)(b). Thus re-infibulation may in some circumstances be legal as would, it is assumed, episiotomy preserving whose lawfulness seems to be the aim of this provision.

[45] Although there has been some criticism of potential loopholes in the measure. D. Kogbara, "One Woman's Campaign Against Genital Mutilation" *Ms*. July/August 1993, 18, 19.

[46] Pub.L. 104–208, 645, 110 Stat. 3009–3546 (1996). The practice of FC/FGM on a minor is now a federal criminal offence, unless the procedure is necessary to protect a young person's health. Illegal Immigration Reform and Immigrant Responsibility Act 1996. The statute provides that "whoever knowingly circumcises, excises, or infibulates the whole or any part of the labia majora or labia minora or clitoris of another person" commits an offence (18 USCA 116A). It exempts surgical operations if "necessary to the health of the person on whom it is performed, and is performed by a person licensed in the place of its performance as a medical practitioner" (18 USCA 116(b)(1)). The term "health" is to be interpreted narrowly and "no account shall be taken of the effect on the person on whom the operation is to be performed of any belief on the part of that person, or any other person, that the operation is required as a matter of custom or ritual" (18 USCA 116(c)). A similar exemption to that of the English statute is adopted to encompass procedures performed during or after labour (18 USCA 116(b)(2)). In Australia, see the New South Wales (NSW) Crimes (Female Genital Mutilation) Amendment Act 1994. This Act inserts a new s. 45 into the Crimes Act

The English and US definitions of FC/FGM, although very different from, for example, the UN joint agency statement, are still potentially quite broad. This raises a number of problems similar to those discussed above in the context of some human rights definitions of FC/FGM. Namely, exactly what kinds of genital alteration procedures are encompassed by the criminal provisions? To take England and Wales as an example (as body alteration has received specific consideration in this jurisdiction); what exactly does "otherwise mutilate" mean? Does the provision encompass ritualistic circumcision or activities which fall within the "unclassified" procedures specified by the UN joint agency statement? Is a genital piercing or tattoo a mutilation or could it be legitimately distinguished as an aesthetic alteration akin to, for example, ear piercing, tattooing or even branding?[47] Perhaps the position on tattooing of the female genitalia is most easily resolved. If such activity was held to be included within the phrase "otherwise mutilate", this would contradict the Tattooing of Minors Act 1969 which allows the consensual tattooing of adults – thus presumably genital tattooing is not criminalised by the 1985 Act. However, the position in relation to piercing is less certain. The lawfulness of female genital piercing under the 1985 Act has been raised by the Cardiff Crime Study Group.[48] The argument here was that this matter should be clarified in order to exclude such body piercings from criminalisation (presumably in the case of adults but not necessarily children). However, such consensual piercing is both well advertised by commercial piercers and takes place, as far as I am aware, without occasioning prosecution under the 1985 Act or for any other offence against the person. Nevertheless, a question mark over its legality still remains.

Similarly, what is the status of cosmetic surgery under the 1985 Act? This latter issue was in fact mentioned in the parliamentary debates on the measure in England. It appears that the intention of the Bill's proposer was, following advice/pressure from the medical profession, not to target such procedures, whether purely elective or justified on mental health grounds, as long as the decision to be so altered did not rest upon cultural motivations.[49] Of course, this raises further questions about the types of practices covered by the terms FC/FGM. In practice the distinctions between different procedures made in Parliament and in the wording of the statute seem to be based as much on the

1900 to make the practice of "FGM" a criminal offence. See Supomo, "Female Genital Mutilation Act Commences" (1995) 33 *Law Society Journal* (NSW, Australia) 18.

[47] See *R* v. *Brown*, *supra* n 39, for the legality of consensual tattooing and piercing and *R* v. *Wilson* [1997] QB 47 (CA) in relation to branding. These procedures seem in general to be legal for adults except where sex, or sadomasochistic sex, is implicated in their performance. See L. Bibbings and P. Alldridge, "Sexual Expression, Body Alteration, and the Defence of Consent" (1993) 29 *Journal of Law and Society* 356 and Roberts, "Consent to Injury: How Far Can You Go?" (1997) 113 *Law Quarterly Review* 27. In the US federal context the word "mutilate" is not included: hence only activities which could be described as circumcision, excision or infibulation are prohibited.

[48] Law Commission Consultation Paper No. 139, *Consent in the Criminal Law* (1995) para. 9.3 ftn 4.

[49] M. Roe, H.C. Debs vol 77 col 583–4, 19 April 1985. Also, it was felt that doctors were best placed to decide upon the motivations for cosmetic genital surgery.

reason behind opting for them as the type of operation concerned. Thus, again the cultural origins or associations of a particular form of genital operation seem to be a defining element in deciding what is legal and what is not. Nevertheless, Parliament seemed to accept Roe's view that things were best left in doctor's hands and genital cosmetic surgery continues to be offered to the female consumer in England as it is in other jurisdictions that ban adult FC/FGM.[50]

In Australia, another genital alteration procedure that could be categorised as FC/FGM, has been directly addressed. The Australian Capital Territory Crimes (Amendment) Act (No.3) 1995, which prohibits FGM, thus includes an explicit exception in relation to sexual reassignment surgery.[51] In other jurisdictions that have introduced specific legislative measures the assumption presumably has been that such operations fall within the various medical exception provisions.

In France, as specific offences were not created, the criminal status of FC/FGM rests upon Article 312, para. 3, of the Penal Code concerning a range of violent acts perpetrated against minors. The section that has been applied to FC/FGM provides that "Whoever beats or otherwise voluntarily inflicts violence upon or assaults a child of under fifteen years of age, excluding minor violence, will be punished . . . if there has been mutilation, amputation, or deprivation of the use of a limb, blindness, loss of an eye, or other permanent disability or unintentional death".[52] The definitional issue is very different here because it has been decided that FC/FGM is a violent act encompassed by general criminal law. Thus in 1983 a judgment of the *Cour de Cassation* held that "the removal of the clitoris constitutes a crime of violence resulting in mutilation as defined by Article 312–3 of the Penal Code' it, therefore, seems reasonable to assume that any more extensive ablations will also be encompassed by this Article.[53] In 1987 a second judgment by the *Cour d'Appel* confirmed that FC/FGM was a crime as it involved the removal of a healthy and functional organ although, presumably, ritualistic circumcision may lie outside the ambit of the provision.[54]

A further point needs to be made in relation to the question of the definition of FC/FGM in criminal laws. Some have begun to challenge the range of procedures covered by FC/FGM prohibitions in a very different way. They argue that some practices which are commonly conceived of as being medically beneficial

[50] S. McNamara, "Genital Cosmetic Surgery" *Elle*, December 1993, 174. The Heathwise Medical Group in London offer advice to those seeking cosmetic genital alterations.

[51] Section 5.

[52] Code Pénal, 1983–84, 184. This translation is taken from Winter, *op.cit.* n 25 at 943.

[53] See I. Gillette-Frenoy "L'excision et sa presence en France" (Paris: Edition GAMS, 1992) 32–3. The case related to a severely disturbed white woman who had attacked her daughter's genitalia, but it was clear that it was intended to apply to FC/FGM. See n 25 above, Winter, 944. Later, it was established that infibulation was included within the Code Pénal definition of violence against minors. See Winter, *supra* n 25 at 947.

[54] For an account of the trials see Winter 944–8.

or necessary should be brought into the ambit of such measures. Thus, in the US it has been argued that routine episiotomy in childbirth constitutes FC/FGM at least in some circumstances under the definition given in the North Dakota legislation prohibiting FC/FGM.[55] This claim rests upon recent medical research which, it is maintained shows that this procedure, rather than producing beneficial effects, can actually cause or exacerbate the harm that it is supposed to lessen. This is an argument which could be made in other jurisdictions and it further illustrates the difficulties in classifying what genital procedures are or should be acceptable to the West and are encompassed by the terms FC/FGM.

Having discussed the range of procedures that are criminalised in different jurisdictions, the question of the validity of adult versus child (parental) consent warrants consideration. While human rights discourses tend to view all incidents of FC/FGM (however defined) as abuses of human rights, the criminal jurisdictions under consideration do not necessarily take the same approach. Indeed, there is a marked difference between jurisdictions, with some seemingly implicitly recognising adult female autonomy. Thus, while in Australia, England and Wales and in some US states complete bans have been enacted, at the US federal level only procedures performed upon those under eighteen are explicitly criminalised.[56] In contrast, in France, Article 312 applies to girls under the age of fifteen. Hence there is a conflict here between the approach of different common law jurisdictions. Those jurisdictions that have completely prohibited FC/FGM, have followed and reinforced the dominant human rights conception that all forms of FC/FGM (ignoring for the moment the differences of definition) require complete eradication.

CRIMINAL LAW PENALTIES AND ENFORCEMENT

Thus far this chapter has largely focused upon definitional issues. I will turn next to look briefly at the penalties which a person convicted of performing FC/FGM or being implicated in arranging the operation could face. In this context just one example will be given because of the limits of space. In England and Wales the decision to adopt a specific legislative measure allows an assessment to be made of the sentences that were thought appropriate to cases of FC/FGM. In England the 1985 Act allows a maximum penalty of a five-year prison sentence or a fine. However, as already noted, FC/FGM could have been prosecuted before the 1985 Act under pre-existing measures and could, in fact, probably now be charged under both the specific legislation and other offences.[57] Thus it

[55] J. Hughes, "Episiotomy: Ritual Genital Mutilation in Western Obstetrics". <http:/www.changesurfer.com/Hlth/episiotomy.html>. See also J. McLaughlin "North Dakota's Genital Integrity Law" <http://www.changesurfer.com/Hlth/NDLaw.html>. Female Genital Mutilation 1995 ND Laws Ch. 140.

[56] 18 USCA 116(a).

[57] It is arguable that even now, where severe harm is caused by FC/FGM, charges under ss. 18 or 20 of the 1861 Offences Against the Person Act could be brought. Further where the person

becomes important to look at the sentencing options provided for by other measures in the light of those decided upon by Parliament in the 1985 Act.

One might suggest that the sensitive approach advocated by the UN joint agency statement encourages a tendency to provide lesser penalties for FC/FGM than for equivalent "harms" caused by activities which are criminalised. FC/FGM would probably constitute actual bodily harm, which also carries a maximum sentence of five years' imprisonment.[58] Yet, one could claim that, at least in some instances, FC/FGM could constitute the offence of causing grievous bodily harm or wounding (conceptualised as relating to more serious levels of injury than actual bodily harm) which, if intentional, may result in a life sentence.[59] Thus, it is arguable that, in providing for a maximum five-year prison sentence in cases of "FC', the statutory response is not as punitive as it might have been and it allows for a lesser charge under the 1985 Act even when one carrying a higher penalty may be applicable. As a result, while FC/FGM constitutes a criminal act in England and Wales and thus the autonomy of those choosing, aiding or abetting, counselling, procuring, or carrying out such procedures is rejected or negated because culture and tradition are no excuse for violating a person's human rights, the sentencing options are actually not as severe as they might be. While this leniency may be preferable where it is the families of "victims' who are prosecuted (because of a sensitivity to the future life of the "victim") or the procedure is relatively minor, one might question whether the actual circumciser should benefit from this apparent leniency particularly where infibulation is performed – in such a case perhaps charges under the 1861 Act would be brought alongside those of the 1985 Act.

Having discussed some aspects of measures which criminalise FC/FGM we move on to the question of their implementation. While the criminalisation of a particular activity places limitations upon personal autonomy this restriction has little more than a declaratory or symbolic effect unless the law is applied; although this in itself is arguably of importance. To date, however, France is the only jurisdiction under consideration to prosecute in cases of FC/FGM, yet it has not adopted specific laws.[60] There may be a number of reasons for this. For

operated upon dies a charge of manslaughter or murder would be possible. The 1985 Act does not explicitly exclude this possibility, although, perhaps the implicit definition of FC/FGM in s. 116(a) may be taken to have this effect. See C.M.V. Clarkson and H.M. Keating, *Criminal Law: Text and Materials* (London: Sweet and Maxwell, 4th edn 1998) 125 for a discussion of criminal liability for ulterior offences.

[58] Offences Against The Person Act 1861 s.47. This would theoretically have been the case at least where consent was not present or where the procedure was performed upon a minor. Indeed, even where an adult consented to the operation being performed upon themselves the courts may have decided that their consent was not legally valid as the operation was contrary to public policy.

[59] Offences Against the Person Act 1861 ss. 20, 18 (s. 18 requires intent).

[60] In addition, there has been one trial in the Netherlands. FORWARD (USA) also reports that in 1986 in Atlanta Georgia, DeKalb County law enforcement authorities charged a nurse with child abuse for severing her two year old daughter's clitoris. The woman was not convicted because, it has been suggested, of the difficulty of convincing a jury that this action actually took place. See: <http://www.tggh.net/forward/update.htm>; J. Hansen, and D. Scroggins, "Female Circumcision: US Georgia forced to face medical, legal issues" *Atlanta Journal* 15 November 1992.

example, in England and Wales, where the legislation has been in place for fifteen years, it was recently claimed in a debate on "female circumcision" in the House of Lords that this was, in part, a result of difficulties in locating an exciser even when there is evidence that a procedure was planned or had taken place or a need for a procedure to have actually taken place.[61] This focus upon circumcisers could suggest that proceedings would not be considered in relation to those who arranged the procedure (usually the family), so again this may be taken as evidence of a sensitive approach.[62] More particularly though, there is evidence to suggest that there are other reasons for the non-prosecution. It has been suggested that complaints are rare and when they are made prosecution witnesses are difficult to find and unwilling to give evidence,[63] and that social workers, teachers and legal and medical professionals may be unwilling to get involved, in part, fearing accusations of racism and realising the sensitive nature of posing a challenge to cultural practices.[64] In addition, guidance for these professionals, which is supported by the Department of Health, explicitly states that, where a girl is considered to be at risk of FC/FGM, seeking legal solutions (even in the form of Children Act 1989 protection) may not be an advisable step to take unless completely necessary.[65] Indeed, even where it becomes obvious that an operation has taken place such people may be concerned to deal with the future well-being of the family and may feel that criminal proceedings may actually cause further harm to the "victim" of FC/FGM and so should possibly be avoided. Hence, it is perhaps not wholly surprising that, in England and Wales, the only punitive action taken, apart from investigation thus far, was within professional medical disciplinary proceedings by the judicial committee of the GMC.[66]

In France, as noted above, there were arguments opposing criminalisation based on "the French republican version of the liberal public/private dichotomy" whereby the private sphere is not considered open to public scrutiny unless the national good is under threat.[67] But, following a hard fought campaign spearheaded by feminists, these arguments eventually failed and FC/FGM became a

[61] Lord Hunt of Kings Heath, H.L. Debs col 748, 10 November 1998. The latter comment suggests that inchoate offences cannot be applied in relation to the 1985 Act. Perhaps, however, the reason for not prosecuting in the case referred to by Lord Hunt was that no inchoate offence would fit the facts.

[62] Indeed, some recommend this approach. For example, J.A. Black and G.D. Debelle (both doctors) believe that the 1985 Act should be used against those who perform the operations and not parents who arrange it. "Female Genital Mutilation" (1996) 312 *British Medical Journal* 377, 377.

[63] Lord Hunt of Kings Heath, H.L. Debs col 747, 10 November 1998.

[64] R. Walder, "Why the Problem continues in Britain" (1995) 310 *British Medical Journal* 1593, 1593.

[65] R. Hedley and E. Dorkenoo, *Child Protection and Female Genital Mutilation: Advice for Health, Education and Social Work Professionals* (London: Forward, 1992) 17.

[66] In 1993 a medical practitioner was struck off the medical register in connection with FC/FGM. He did not, however, perform an operation. See Lord Hunt of Kings Heath, H.L. Debs col 748, 10 November 1998 and J.A. Black and G.D. Debelle, "Female genital mutilation in Britain" (1995) 310 *British Medical Journal* 1590, 1591.

[67] Winter, *supra* n 25 at 952. See also Lefeuvre, *supra* n 5, 162–3.

criminal offence.[68] Since then there have been over twenty trials which have involved both parents and excisers.

What, then, can be said about the French trials? In the main initially they involved the prosecution of parents rather than excisers who, it is again maintained, are often difficult to identify or apprehend.[69] Within the trials, notions of cultural relativism, autonomy and privacy recur in different forms. For example, defence strategies often rest partially on the (deeply troubling) notion that those involved are "ignorant Africans" who do not know the law, do not have a good command of French and, consequently, do not know better. Bronwyn Winter has described the phenomenon whereby the testimony of expert witnesses is used to support the view that these people had no choice in their actions.[70] More specifically, this construction of those involved in FC/FGM is supplemented by the notion of culture as a defence to the offence; that individual responsibility is not attributable to those involved because they had no choice but to obey their cultural traditions. Hence, ironically, in supposedly defending their autonomy and privacy, their free choice is effectively denied. Here, the defence of "irresistible force" is argued, where the force in question is cultural. Article 64 of the Penal Code states that: "There is neither crime nor offence when the accused has been in a state of dementia at the time of the act, or when he [*sic*] has been compelled by a force that he has been unable to resist".[71] This could theoretically count as a full defence but in practice it has probably been more useful in relation to pleas for leniency in sentencing. Thus, in France, culture theoretically remains as a possible justification for FC/FGM. However, it is, of course, possible that similar arguments could in the future be raised in trials within other jurisdictions.

What of the result of these French cases? A number of parents and a few excisers have been convicted in relation to the arrangement or performance of FC/FGM. In these instances, the penalties imposed have varied but have often tended to be lenient (particularly where parents are concerned) and have not necessarily reflected the harm caused by the particular procedure. Thus Winter states:

> [T]he history of excision trials in France, far from representing a linear progression towards increasingly harsh sentences and "making punishment fit the crime" (according to which logic, infibulation, with its potentially devastating long-term consequences for women's health, should attract heavier sentences than "mere" clitoridectomy), is more a case of two steps forward, one step back, and even quite a few dodging steps sideways.[72]

Indeed, even when the "victim" dies as a result of the procedure the sentence does not necessarily reflect this.[73] However, it is possible to generalise and to state

[68] Winter *supra* n 25 at 944–5, 951–4.

[69] *Ibid.*, 946.

[70] *Ibid.*, 948–51.

[71] Code Pénal, 1983–4, 50. Translation taken from Winter, *supra* n 25 at 950.

[72] *Ibid.*, Winter 940.

[73] *Ibid.*, 946–7.

that excisers tend to get more severe sentences than parents who arrange the procedures. In fact, parents seem most often to receive suspended prison sentences while circumcisers tend to be sentenced to serve time in prison.[74] While the culpability of these two groups is different, presumably the cultural pressure upon them is not necessarily so distinct. Thus, one could suggest that this is, at least in part, evidence of a degree of sensitivity to the future life of the "victim" and/or her family. In this context it is interesting to note that an exciser recently tried in Paris in relation to forty-eight FC/FGM operations received an eight-year prison sentence (despite the possible maximum sentence of twenty years) while more than twenty parents who arranged the procedures were given suspended sentences.[75]

CONCLUSION

Criminal law, in the instances cited above, intrudes to a varying degree into the private sphere and, in doing so, betrays a blindness towards (non-Western) cultural justifications for FC/FGM. Instead, these practices are, for the most part, conceptualised as crimes of violence which are unacceptable to Western sensibilities. Of course, as has been noted, notions of privacy and cultural rights are not completely absent from the debates around criminalisation and are perhaps reflected in the failure to prosecute, to provide too harsh penalties or impose stiff sentences. Moreover, the specific measures which prohibit FC/FGM, echo and are influenced by Western human rights discourses which have also, in recent years, in this context tended to override custom, autonomy and notions of privacy in order to seek to protect women and female children against traditional practices which are taken to constitute violations of bodily integrity. Yet, despite this similarity of approach (between human rights and criminal law, and between different criminal law jurisdictions), it becomes clear on closer analysis that the definitions of FC/FGM proffered in different contexts vary considerably. Also, such descriptions often fail to take the legal or human rights status of other forms of body alteration into account even when these involve similar or even identical modifications of the female anatomy. Here, then perhaps, we can detect another instance of cultural blindness. Thus, while culture and custom are identified and denied validity in relation to the practices of the "other", they are not necessarily even noted where the practices are "our own".

The latter over-simplified notion is perhaps best illustrated by the case of male circumcision. This procedure is arguably distinguishable from the more extreme forms of FC/FGM – but is it really so different from the most minor forms?[76] If

[74] For example, see *ibid.*, 946–7.

[75] "African woman sentenced for genital mutilation" BBC News Online, 17 February 1999 <http://news.bbc.co.uk>

[76] For example, see comments by Dr L. Miller in C.M. Ostrom, "Harborview debates issue of circumcision of muslim girls" *Seattle Times*, 13 September 1996: "We will cut the whole foreskin off a penis but we won't even consider a cut, a sunna, cutting the prepuce, a little bloodletting [on a girl] . . . medical doctors in this country also do cosmetic surgery on genitals".

the practices are comparable then is not the prohibition of some/all of the most minor forms of the female procedure a form of sex discrimination? Here it could be argued, for example, either that the criminalisation is discriminatory in its protection of the female but not the male, or that the families of male children are able to adhere to their cultural/religious beliefs but those of female children have no such protection of their private cultural lives (and the same could be said in relation to adults where a complete ban on FC/FGM applies). Indeed, some have begun to use the discrimination argument in order to pose a challenge to the legality and human rights status of the circumcision of male minors.[77] In addition, in Australia, the Queensland Law Reform Commission published a research paper on male circumcision in 1993 which suggested that parental consent may provide no defence to male circumcision unless the procedure produced immediate health benefits to a particular child.[78]

Similarly, criticisms could be made in relation to the human rights responses to FC/FGM considered above. In particular, the UN joint agency statement seems to fail to distinguish between a whole panoply of (arguably) very different female genital practices and does not touch upon male circumcision which is simply not seen to be a human rights issue. However, it is, nevertheless, important to note in the human rights context that FC/FGM represents an area where this discourse has denied what were, at least in the past, its traditional boundaries; it has effectively intruded into the private sphere in an attempt to protect women and girl children and has deemed it necessary to comment upon practices which are categorised as being culturally non-Western despite a perceived need to be culturally sensitive.

To conclude, while this chapter has examined human rights and criminal law in relation to culture, privacy and autonomy it is important to recognise that, in particular, criminal law is not necessarily the most intrusive method of social control in relation to FC/FGM nor are the police the people most likely to discover FC/FGM. Thus, arguably, it is professionals such as social workers, teachers, medical personnel and community outreach workers who are likely to suspect or detect that an operation has been or may be performed. Indeed, in France, doctors are also specifically identified as having a duty to inform the police about their suspicions and it is clear that medical and social teams can and do report children at risk or who have undergone FC/FGM – possibly but not necessarily to the police.[79] Equally, it is arguable that it is child law which is

[77] For examples see: Declaration of the First International Symposium on Circumcision, <http//:www.cirp.org/CIRP/pages/riley/nocirc94>; "The International Human Rights Challenge of Genital Mutilation and the United Nations" a 60 page blueprint for global action to eradicate female and male genital mutilation produced by Ecumenics International. See Circumcision Information Network, 1(16) 20 October 1994, <http://www.cirp.org/CIRP/news/cir/1994.10.2>;

C. Price, "Male Circumcision: an ethical and legal affront" (1997) 128 *Bulletin of Medical Ethics* 13.

[78] Queensland Law Reform Commission Research Paper, *Circumcision of Male Infants* (Brisbane; Queensland Law Reform Commission, 1993).

[79] See C. Gallard "Female Genital Mutilation in France" (1995) 310 *British Medical Journal* 1592, 1592–3.

most likely to be employed in such cases. For example, in England protection for a child could be sought under the Children Act 1989.[80] Indeed, it has been reported that, by 1996, in at least thirty instances FC/FGM operations had been prevented by use of the Children Act.[81] Similarly, in the US, alongside the federal prohibition of FC/FGM, other legislative measures and funded outreach projects mean that new immigrants from countries which have traditions of FC/FGM may be subjected to increased observation and control.[82] Thus, the likelihood of some degree of monitoring of "suspect communities" by professionals outside the criminal justice systems and the use of child law proceedings and powers, may be far more invasive, not least in terms of the number of people affected, than the prohibition of FC/FGM in itself. Yet, ironically, this surveillance is sometimes intended to be part of the more sensitive inter-agency, multidisciplinary approach to the eradication of FC/FGM which has been so emphasised in human rights discourses.

[80] See Black and Debelle, *op.cit.*, n 66 *supra* at 1591.

[81] *Supra* n 62 at 377.

[82] US Federal Illegal Immigration Reform and Immigrant Responsibility Act 1996, Pub. L. 104–208, 644, 110 Stat. 3009–546 (1996).

7

Denying Shoah

BERT SWART

No one will have me admit that two plus two make five, that the earth is flat, or that the Nuremberg trial was infallible. I have excellent reasons not to believe in this policy of extermination or in the magic gas chamber (. . .).

I would wish to see that 100 per cent of all French citizens realize that the myth of the gas chambers is a dishonest fabrication, endorsed by the victorious powers of Nuremberg in 1945–46 and officialized on 14 July 1990 by the current French Government, with the approval of the "court historians".

Robert Faurisson[1]

THE AUSCHWITZ LIE

EVER SINCE THE end of the Second World War there have been people who have wanted to deny that millions of Jews and members of other population groups were systematically exterminated by the Nazi regime, that concentration camps were built for that purpose and that the physical destruction of these millions was achieved by such methods as the use of gas chambers.[2] This is often referred to as the "Auschwitz lie". This expression, however, may mean two different, and opposite, things. It may refer to those who would deny the existence of Auschwitz since, in doing so, they are denying well-established historical facts and must, therefore, be liars. It may also be used with the opposite in mind: to make clear that Auschwitz did not exist and that those who would have us believe otherwise are telling lies.

Robert Faurisson, a former professor of literature at several French universities, is one of those who use the expression in its second sense ("dishonest fabrication"). In 1980, he published a book, prefaced by Noam Chomsky, in which he systematically threw doubt on the existence of gas chambers.[3] A year later, he was ordered by a French court to pay the sum of one franc to several private associations engaged in the fight against racism and anti-semitism, for having

[1] Interview in *Le Choc du Mois*, September 1990 no. 32.

[2] See Deborah Lipstadt, *Denying the Holocaust* (New York City, NY: Free Press, 1993).

[3] *Mémoire en défense contre ceux qui m' accusent de falsifier l'histoire: La question des chambres à gaz*, Paris 1980. In his foreword, Chomsky defended Faurisson's right to do so. See also Noam Chomsky, "The Faurisson affair: his right to say it" *The Nation*, 28 February 1981.

stated in a number of newspapers and periodicals that the genocide of the Jews and the existence of gas chambers were part of one and the same historical lie. The court held that, by doing so, he had caused "moral damage" (*préjudice moral*) to these associations and their members.[4] In 1991, the words quoted at the beginning of this paper led a French criminal court to convict Faurisson for having committed the offence of publicly denying crimes against humanity in violation of Article 24bis of the French Freedom of the Press Act (entered into force on 14 July 1990).[5] A year later, another court rejected his appeal. Faurisson filed a complaint with the United Nations Human Rights Committee against his conviction.

Faurisson is not the only French university professor to doubt the existence of shoah. Another well known public figure is the former professor of philosophy Roger Garaudy, who published his book "Les Mythes fondateurs de la politique israélienne" in 1995, and had it reprinted in 1996. The author, a former member of the Communist Party who converted to Islam during the 1980s, attempts an analysis of the development of the ideology and politics of Zionism. The book is mainly a denial of the existence of the Holocaust, which Garaudy also classifies as an historical falsehood, created by a Zionist conspiracy to serve their own political ends. Garaudy described himself not as an anti-Semite, but as an anti-Zionist. In 1988, a French criminal court convicted him of having committed the offence of racial defamation as well as the offence of public denial of crimes against humanity.[6]

The need to deny the dreadful realities of the Second World War is certainly not confined to France, for it occurs both in other European countries and countries such as Canada and the United States. In Germany too, there have been many cases during the past decades in which doubt has been publicly cast on the existence of concentration camps and gas chambers. A salient example from German case law concerns a man who paraded in public carrying a board with the text:

> I, a donkey, still believe that Jews were "gassed" in German concentration camps. I, a donkey, believe the lies about "gassing" and want to pay, pay, pay to Israel. I, a donkey, still believe the propaganda lies of the "victors".[7]

In Europe today, this is no longer a purely national phenomenon. Those who would deny Auschwitz usually belong to political groups that are in contact with each other and form coalitions across national borders. The most prominent example is the right-wing French politician Jean-Marie Le Pen, who, at a political meeting in Munich in 1998, declared that "the mass murder of the Jews is merely an historical detail". On October 26 1998, the European Parliament

[4] Ligue internationale contre le racisme et l'antisémitisme et autres v. Faurisson, Tribunal de Grande Instance de Paris 8 July 1981, *Recueil Dalloz* 1982, 59–64.

[5] Chambre Correctionnelle du Tribunal de Grande Instance de Paris 18 April 1991.

[6] Tribunal de Grande Instance de Paris 27 February 1998, *Le Monde* 1–2 March 1998.

[7] See Bundesverfassungsgericht 27 April 1982, Neue Juristische Wochenschrift 1982, 1803.

decided to withdraw Le Pen's immunity as a member of that Parliament, in order to allow him to stand trial in Germany.[8]

These examples can help us to say something about the apparent need of individuals and groups to deny Shoah. To start with, that need has led to an extensive body of literature with claims to scientific status, on the (non) existence of concentration camps and gas chambers. Internationally, the best known authors in this field are Fred Leuchter and David Irving. This literature aims at denying and repudiating commonly accepted insights of "official" history. The authors call themselves "negationist" or "revisionist", or are referred to as such by others. Their historical accounts rarely approach any level of detachment. The predetermined aim is almost always to unmask dominant historical insights and ideas as deliberate falsifications of the truth, an extensive conspiracy of lies, an historical swindle – a swindle, moreover, in which national governments are systematically involved. It is clear to those who deny Shoah that such lies hide political agendas that have nothing to do with the past, but everything with the present. The aim of the Auschwitz lie, for example, is said to be to force reparations from an innocent and naive German population, or to justify (Western support for) Israeli policies against the Palestinians or Arab nations. And in their turn, to those who resist the denial of Shoah it is clear that this denial in itself derives from a political agenda for the present. In their perception, the aim of those who deny is the acceptance of their own political ideals; political ideals that are rooted in a conception of the world usually barely distinguishable from that of those who caused Shoah in the first place, for which reason the final consequence could well be its repetition. In sum, this debate about Auschwitz is less an historical debate about the past than a political debate about the present and the future.

Almost from the very beginning of the public denial of Shoah, the question has been raised in Europe as to whether this should be a matter of law. Germany and France were the first countries to be faced with this question, but they were not the only ones. During the 1990s, the problem of whether to forbid the public denial of Shoah became the subject of debate within the framework of the European Union. During recent years, also, international bodies whose task it is to monitor compliance with human rights treaties, have been required to examine the question of whether forbidding the denial of Shoah is in itself in accordance with the rights guaranteed by those treaties. This recent internationalisation of the debate is a good reason for again asking whether it is justified and desirable to forbid the public expression of ideas about history that are considered reprehensible, regardless of whether they concern events in Europe during the Second World War, or war crimes, genocide and crimes against humanity in any other historical context – for example in Rwanda, Cambodia or the former Yugoslavia.

[8] See Official Journal of the European Communities 1998 C 328/9, 15, 31–32.

DEVELOPMENTS IN NATIONAL AND IN INTERNATIONAL LAW

A comparative study of national legislation and case law concerning the Auschwitz lie is particularly fascinating, for it shows how much variation there is in the place that societies accord to the freedom of expression and in the cases in and reasons for which they are prepared to accept restrictions of that freedom. In this part of this chapter, I will limit myself to discussing a small number of countries that have criminal legislation under which the denial of Shoah may be a criminal offence – as indeed may the denial of international crimes in other historical contexts. Criminalisation may rest on general provisions of criminal law with regard to the protection of public order, incitement to racial hatred or discrimination, or defamation and libel of individual persons. Developments at a national level are often strongly influenced by the fact that a state is a party to international treaties, especially to the 1965 United Nations International Convention on the Elimination of All Forms of Racial Discrimination. During the 1990s, dissatisfaction with existing general provisions of criminal law led to the introduction of special provisions specifically criminalising the denial of Shoah in several, mainly European countries. France and Germany were among the first countries to take such action. Meanwhile, several others now also have such legislation and it is likely that others will follow in future.

The Federal Republic of Germany is one of the countries where the criminalisation of denying of Shoah has been hotly debated for many decades.[9] This led to several amendments (in 1960, 1985 and 1994) of provisions in the German Criminal Code, culminating in 1994 in the introduction of specific criminalisation of the denial of Shoah. Current German law offers two means of punishing those who deny Shoah: one is an offence against the public peace and the other a form of libel against individual persons. Article 130 of the German Criminal Code, introduced in 1960 and revised in 1994, criminalises incitement to hatred against parts of the population and similar acts as an offence against the public peace (*Volksverhetzung*). Under its first section, it is a criminal offence to incite to hatred against parts of the population, to incite to violent or arbitrary acts against them, or to insult them, maliciously to ridicule them, or to defame them in violation of their human dignity. In all cases the act must be likely to disturb the public peace. The second section deals with persons who disseminate or assist in disseminating writings that incite to hatred; in some respects, the scope of this provision is more limited than that of the first section. The third section, introduced in 1994, contains an independent and specific criminalisation of

[9] For a discussion of German law in the English language see Eric Stein, "History Against Free Speech: The New German Law Against the 'Auschwitz' – and Other – 'Lies'" (1986) 85 *Michigan Law Review* 277–324; Rainer Hofmann, "Incitement to National and Racial Hatred: The Legal Situation in Germany" in Sandra Coliver (ed.), *Striking a Balance: Hate Speech, Freedom of Expression and Non-discrimination* (University of Essex, 1992) 159–70.

denying Shoah: it is a criminal offence to approve of, to deny, or to play down (*verharmlosen*) the genocide committed under the domination of the Nazi regime (*Herrschaft des Nationalsozialismus*) in a way which is likely to disturb the public peace. As well as Article 130, there are also the different provisions of the Code that concern libel against individual persons, namely Articles 185–200. It is interesting to note here that one of them, Article 189, makes it an offence to insult the memory of deceased persons. German courts have long accepted that defamatory language directed against a group of the population may amount to defamation of the individual members of that group. In 1985, the general requirement that a complaint be raised by the victim of defamatory language was dropped with regard to the victims of group persecution under the Nazi regime. The same applies to the victims of any other violent and arbitrary political regime.

In the past decades, both the German Federal Constitutional Court (*Bundesverfassungsgericht*) and the Federal Criminal Court (*Bundesgerichtshof*) have been frequently confronted with the question of whether the denial of Shoah, could, under certain conditions, constitute a criminal offence. Both Courts have often answered in the positive, with regard to both Article 130 and the provisions concerning libel against individual persons.[10] On the other hand, both have also always accepted that merely denying Shoah is not in itself a criminal offence within the meaning of the above provisions of the Criminal Code as they were formulated until 1994.[11] The third section of Article 130 that was introduced in that year has changed that.[12] For an expression to be an offence under Article 130, it must however be likely to disturb the public peace, which also must be the intention of the offender, although no actual disturbance needs to have occurred. It is sufficient if there is a risk of disturbance and the content of that which is expressed determines the risk. For denying Shoah to be an offence under sections 1 or 2 of Article 130, the offender must also have intent to cause hatred or one of the other consequences formulated in these sections. The various articles on libel against individual persons require intent to defame; whether this is the case will mainly depend on the content of an expression and the language used.[13] Content and language will probably also determine whether or not the denial of Shoah constitutes the offence of Article 130, section 3.[14]

In France, restrictions of the freedom of expression are to be found in the Criminal Code as well as the 1881 Freedom of the Press Act.[15] In 1972, when

[10] Cf., *inter alia*, the recent decisions of the Bundesverfassungsgericht of 13 April 1994, *Neue Juristische Wochenschrift 1994*, 1779, and the Bundesgerichtshof of 15 March 1994, *Neue Juristische Wochenschrift* 1994, 1421.

[11] Cf., *inter alia*, Bundesgerichtshof 15 March 1994, *Neue Juristische Wochenschrift* 1994, 1421.

[12] See Daniel Beisel, "Die Strafbarkeit der Auschwitzlüge" *Neue Juristische Wochenschrift* 1995, 997–1001.

[13] Cf., *inter alia*, Bundesgerichtshof 18 September 1979, *Neue Juristische Wochenschrift* 1980, 45; Bundesverfassungsgericht 13 April 1994, *Neue Juristische Wochenschrift* 1994, 1779.

[14] Cf. Beisel, *supra* n 12, 999–1000.

[15] For a discussion of French law in the English language see Roger Errera, "In Defence of Civility: Racial Incitement and Group Libel in French Law" in Sandra Coliver (ed.), *Striking a*

France ratified the UN Convention on the Elimination of All Forms of Racial Discrimination, special provisions criminalising racial discrimination were included in both the Code and the Act; I will concentrate here on the Act. In Article 24 of the Act the new offence of public incitement to racial discrimination, racial hatred or racial violence was introduced. It is not impossible that the denial of Shoah may, depending on the circumstances of the case, be considered to constitute that offence. However, criminalisation of denial was achieved in a special way, which makes the legal situation under French law different from the one under German law in a number of respects.

Ever since the Freedom of the Press Act was adopted, it has not only criminalised public incitement to commit criminal offences but also the public "defence" of offences that have been committed.[16] Article 24 of the Act, as it now reads, establishes this special form of criminal liability with regard to the most serious common crimes. In 1951, the Act was amended to include the public defence of war crimes and crimes or other offences consisting of collaboration with the enemy. In 1987, crimes against humanity were also included; this addition is not restricted to crimes against humanity that occurred during the Second World War in Europe. On the basis of Article 24, courts have sometimes convicted individual persons for publicly defending war crimes or crimes against humanity by denying Shoah. In 1971, the Court of Cassation held that the publication of a text which is likely to incite any reader to judge favourably the leaders of the German National Socialist Party who were convicted as war criminals by the Nuremberg International Tribunal, and which represents at least an attempt to partially justify their crimes, amounts to a public defence of those crimes.[17] Still, existing legislation was believed to be unsatisfactory. In 1990, the so-called Gayssot Act introduced a new Article 24bis. This new provision criminalises any public denial[18] of "the existence of one or more crimes against humanity as defined in Article 6 of the Statute of the International Military Tribunal annexed to the London Agreement of 8 August 1945, which have been committed either by the members of an organisation declared criminal pursuant to Article 9 of the said Statute or by a person found guilty of such crimes by a French or international court". The apparent aim of this new provision is to prevent any discussion in court on history, as well as on the motive or intent of those who deny Shoah.[19]

Other states too have introduced penal provisions specifically criminalising denial of Shoah, which supplement general legislation prohibiting racial dis-

Balance: Hate Speech, Freedom of Expression and Non-discrimination (University of Essex, 1992) 144–58.

[16] Article 24 of the Act uses the word "*apologie*". "*Faire une apologie*" may, perhaps, also be translated by "to attempt to vindicate" as in "*apologia*" and "apologist", but not apology.

[17] Cour de Cassation 14 January 1971, *Recueil Dalloz Sirey* 1971, 101. The case concerns Le Pen.

[18] The French text uses the verb "*contester*", which might also be translated "put in issue".

[19] Recently, the Cour de Cassation held that a minimalisation of the number of persons killed in concentration camps may also constitute a denial if made in bad faith. Cf. Cour de Cassation 17 June 1997, *Recueil Dalloz Sirey* 1998, 50.

crimination. Perhaps the oldest example is Israel, where new legislation was adopted in 1986. One may also mention Austria, Belgium, and Switzerland. There is variation in the way denying Shoah actually constitutes a criminal offence. To give an example: the Belgian Act of 1995, supplementing older legislation on racism and xenophobia, makes it a criminal offence to publicly deny, grossly minimalise, attempt to justify, or approve of the genocide committed during the Second World War by the German National Socialist regime.[20] Other states still rely on general legislation prohibiting racial discrimination. An example is the Netherlands. In 1996, a Dutch court convicted a person for having published a pamphlet, stating that stories about gas chambers in concentration camps are utter nonsense and that showing documentary programmes about them on television is tantamount to deliberately deceiving the population. According to the court, these statements violate Article 137c of the Dutch Criminal Code, which makes it a criminal offence to offend population groups because of their race, their religion, their sex or their sexual preferences. The Dutch Supreme Court upheld that judgment.[21]

In recent years, the denial of Shoah has become a matter of concern to the European Union. In 1996, EU Member States adopted a Joint Action concerning action to combat racism and xenophobia.[22] Among other things it recommends that Member States make punishable as a criminal offence the "public condoning, for a racist or xenophobic purpose, of crimes against humanity and human rights violations", as well as the "public denial of the crimes defined in Article 6 of the Charter of the International Military Tribunal appended to the London Agreement of 8 April 1945, insofar as it includes behaviour which is contemptuous of, or degrading to, a group of persons defined by reference to colour, race, religion or national or ethnic origin".[23] Obviously, there is much in the second category that reminds one of Article 24bis of the French Freedom of the Press Act, although the Joint Action contains a limiting clause not included in the Act. Another important observation to be made here is that the Joint Action does not seem to limit itself to crimes against humanity committed during the Second World War. The first category of conduct to be proscribed may equally apply to crimes against humanity committed in Cambodia, Rwanda, the former Yugoslavia or still other places; here, the influence of both German and French law is, perhaps, visible. Meanwhile, one should not overestimate the (legal) significance of the Joint Action. It recommends criminalisation of denial of Shoah or other international crimes for the sole purpose of facilitating interstate

[20] On Belgian law see G.A.I. Schuijt and D. Voorhof (eds), *Vrijheid van meningsuiting, racisme en revisionisme* (Gent: 1995).

[21] Hoge Raad 25 November 1997, *Nederlandse Jurisprudentie* 1998, 261. On the legal situation in The Netherlands see Reinier de Winter, "De 'Auschwitz-Lüge' na 50 jaar: strafwaardig?" *Nederlands Juristenblad* 1995, 653–9; F. Janssens, "De ontkenning van 'Auschwitz' en de strafwet" (1998) *Delikt en Delinkwent* 565–78; Theo Rosier, *Vrijheid van meningsuiting en discriminatie in Nederland en Amerika*, Ars Aequi Libri, Nijmegen 1997.

[22] Joint Action of 15 July 1996, Official Journal EC 1996 L 185/5.

[23] Instead of "8 April 1945", an apparent mistake, one should read "8 August 1945".

cooperation in criminal matters. A Member State that does not wish to create appropriate criminal provisions is merely obliged to derogate from the principle of double criminality in cooperating with other Member States in the repression of the criminal offences referred to in the Joint Action.

Finally, we must turn to human rights treaties. Their significance for criminalisation of denial of Shoah may be twofold. On the one hand, the question arises as to whether or not their provisions on the freedom of expression allow states parties to make denial a criminal offence. On the other, there is also the question of whether some of them contain an obligation to do so.

As far as the first question is concerned, in 1982 the European Commission of Human Rights already held that prohibiting an individual to display pamphlets describing the killing of six million Jews by the Nazi regime as "a mere invention, an unacceptable lie and a zionistic swindle" may be considered a measure necessary in a democratic society for the protection of others within the meaning of Article 10 of the Convention.[24] Very recently, the European Court also pronounced on the matter in *Lehideux and Isorni* v. *France*.[25] The case is concerned with the question of whether the European Convention permitted France to convict the applicants on the basis of Article 24 of the Freedom of the Press Act, for having committed the offence of publicly defending war crimes and crimes of collaboration by pleading in favour of the rehabilitation of Marshal Pétain, which the Court denied. However, in *obiter dicta* the Court also very briefly turned to the denial of Shoah. It stated that "justification of a pro-Nazi policy could not be allowed to enjoy the protection afforded by Article 10" of the Convention, and that "the negation or revision" of "clearly established historical facts – such as the Holocaust –" "would be removed from the protection of Article 10 by Article 17". Finally, in 1996 the UN Human Rights Committee established under the International Covenant on Civil and Political Rights rejected Faurisson's communication directed against his conviction by a French court for having publicly denied crimes against humanity.[26] The Committee's view is especially interesting because the individual opinions of its members discuss the justifications for making denial of Shoah a criminal offence more thoroughly than the European Commission and the European Court. Together these three decisions constitute a good basis for reviewing the arguments for and against criminalising denial from a comparative perspective.

One may also ask the further question of whether Article 4 of the UN International Convention on the Elimination of All Forms of Racial Discrimination and Article 20 of the UN Covenant on Civil and Political Rights carry an obligation for the contracting parties to criminalise denial of Shoah.

[24] X v. *the Federal Republic of Germany*, Application 9235/81, European Commission 16 July 1982, 29 Decisions and Reports 194 (1982). The application is directed against the decision of the German Bundesgerichtshof of 18 September 1979, mentioned *supra* n 13.

[25] Judgment of 23 September 1998, 38 *International Legal Materials* 30–56 (1999).

[26] *Robert Faurisson* v. *France*, Communication No. 550/1993, Human Rights Committee 8 November 1996, 18 *Human Rights Law Journal* 40–9 (1997).

THE APPROACH OF HUMAN RIGHTS BODIES: ARGUMENTS IN FAVOUR OF CRIMINALISATION

In his complaint to the Human Rights Committee, Faurisson poses as a champion of the freedoms of expression and of historical research. In his view, the 1990 French Gayssot Act makes it impossible for him to cast doubt on the findings and premises of the International Military Tribunal of Nuremberg, by promoting the Nuremberg trial and judgment to the status of dogma. Not surprisingly, he compares himself to Galileo "whose discoveries *were* true, and any law, which would have enabled his conviction, would have been by its very nature wrong or absurd". The French Government, on the other hand, maintain that Faurisson merely expressed his anti-Semitism through the publication of his revisionist theses in journals and magazines and thereby tarnished the memory of the victims of Nazism. Their central thesis is that, by challenging the reality of the extermination of Jews during the Second World War, the author incites his readers to anti-Semitic behaviour.

This debate, as all other debates on the criminalisation of denying Shoah, seems to raise three interrelated questions. Are the participants in a political debate, whether on present issues or past events, bound to respect established facts of a general nature? Conversely, does freedom of expression include a right to ignore, negate, distort or misrepresent facts not about individual persons but about general events? Secondly, if one accepts the proposition that freedom of expression does not include such a right, how is one going to establish what these facts are? Are legislators or courts appropriate bodies to fulfil that task or should one take the view that, since (according to the historian Nuizinga) history is a debate without end, they should have no say in such matters? Finally, if untrue factual statements are not protected by freedom of speech and legislators or courts can indeed be arbiters in these matters, the question remains whether, and when, the false nature of a statement about historical events can be a reason to penalise the person who has made that statement. Applied to the field of racial hatred and racial discrimination in present-day societies, on what grounds may one put untrue factual statements about past events on the same footing with direct incitement to hatred and discrimination of persons because of their race?

To the first two questions German courts have given answers that are in themselves interesting and that have, moreover, influenced the European Commission of Human Rights. In its case law, the *Bundesverfassungsgericht* has always made a distinction between opinions and facts.[27] Freedom of expression aims to protect the expression of opinions. By their very nature, opinions are characterised by a subjective relationship between an individual person and the content of his statement, in other words by the taking of a position. In that

[27] Cf. for example, Bundesverfassungsgericht 13 April 1994, summarising earlier case law, *Neue Juristische Wochenschrift* 1994, 1779.

sense, opinions cannot be shown to be true or false. With regard to factual statements the situation is, however, different. In a strict sense they are not opinions because, here, there is an objective relationship between what has been stated on the one hand and reality on the other; to that extent their accuracy can be determined. Since, however, opinions are usually based on factual assumptions or express judgments on factual situations, freedom of expression must, of necessity, also include the freedom to make factual statements insofar as one cannot hold an opinion without making a factual statement. Therefore, the freedom to make factual statements only ends where these statements can contribute no more to the forming of an opinion. This is the case where factual statements are deliberately untrue or where their false nature has been proven. The implications of this constitutional doctrine for denial of Shoah are considerable. Statements implying that there has been no persecution of Jews during the Third Reich clearly belong to the second category since there is overwhelming historical evidence to the contrary. This approach is also that of the *Bundesgerichtshof*; in its view, therefore, there is no need to produce evidence of the extermination of Jews in gas chambers and concentration camps during criminal or civil proceedings.[28] The approach of both German courts has been followed by the European Commission of Human Rights.[29] It is apparently also at the basis of Article 24bis of the Freedom of the Press Act, which draws its inspiration from earlier French case law. In fact, the reference in this provision to international and national courts is clearly meant to eliminate the need for investigating the truth of certain matters. It is interesting to contrast this approach with that of the Human Rights Committee in the case of Faurisson. At first sight, the Committee does not seem to be at all interested in whether Faurisson could be right in what he had to tell about the extermination of Jews. The mere fact that he spoke of the myth of gas chambers as a dishonest fabrication is in itself enough for the Committee to assume that his conviction on the basis of Article 24bis of the Freedom of the Press Act "did not encroach upon his right to hold and express an opinion" but punished him for having "violated the rights and reputation of others". This suggests a different approach: one implying that the way in which an opinion is expressed, rather than its content, determines its acceptability. However, the individual opinions of several Committee members make it clear that they did not consider Faurisson's statements to be based on serious and bona fide historical research and that this was an important consideration for them in dismissing his complaint.

Meanwhile, the Committee is clearly worried by Article 24bis of the French Act. Taken literally, this provision appears to prohibit any publication that criticises the Nuremberg Tribunal and challenges its findings, including publications based on thorough and bona fide research. To quote the individual opinion of Lallah: "It creates an absolute liability in respect of which no defence

[28] Cf. for example, Bundesgerichtshof 15 March 1994, *Neue Juristische Wochenschrift* 1994, 1421.

[29] *X* v. *the Federal Republic of Germany*, *supra* n 24.

appears to be possible"; and that of Evatt and Kretzmer: "The restrictions imposed (. . .) do not link liability to the intent of the author, nor to the tendency of the publication to incite to anti-semitism". All Committee members consider that such a provision would go too far. If they nevertheless dismiss Faurisson's complaint, it is only after having established that the French courts did not, in fact, rest their conviction of Faurisson merely on his denial of the existence of gas chambers. These courts came to the conclusion that the author's statements, read in their full context, propagated ideas tending to revive Nazi doctrine and the policy of racial hatred and were of a nature as to raise or strengthen anti-Semitic feelings. The Committee respects that judgment. Its criticism of Article 24bis shows an awareness of the need for requiring that a publication is likely to cause harmful effects and is intended to do so, in order to prevent that Article and similar provisions from becoming a licence to prohibit statements which challenge commonly accepted historical truths, or statements which some sections of the public may find offensive and, thereby, from ruling out any open debate on matters of history. Whether, even so, these provisions might produce unintended chilling effects on public debates is a different matter not discussed by the Committee.

What societal interests is the criminalisation of denying Shoah supposed to protect and are these legitimate interests worthy of protection under provisions such as Article 19, para. 3, of the International Covenant on Civil and Political Rights and Article 10, para. 2, of the European Convention for the Protection of Human Rights and Fundamental Freedoms? A review of statutes and case law reveals that the motives for criminalising denial are complex and varied. For analytical purposes one may make a distinction here between denial of Shoah as an offence against individual persons and denial as an act which harms collective goods. In actual practice, however, it is often difficult to separate the two types of justification from each other.

Let us first examine the denial of Shoah as an offence against individual persons. In the case of Faurisson, the Human Rights Committee agreed with the French Government that Faurisson's statements disqualified a whole class of bona fide historians described as liars and swindlers and violated their reputations. More interesting, and more important, is whether denial may constitute an offence against individuals belonging to the group who suffered persecution because of their race during the Second World War. To this question German courts have given an affirmative answer. They assume that insulting or defamatory language directed against a group of the population may amount to defamation of all individual members of that group. They consider the denial of Shoah to be an insult to all those who suffered persecution at the hands of the Nazis, since it amounts to a negation of their human dignity. In this respect, it makes no difference whether or not a person survived the Holocaust. German case law has gone an important step further. It also holds that members of the Jewish community presently living in Germany who have not been the victims of persecution by the Nazi regime, may nevertheless be personally insulted by a denial of Shoah. According to the German courts, they "are entitled, as a component of their personal self-image, to be viewed as part of a group, singled out by fate, to which all others owe a particular moral responsibility, and that is an aspect of their honour. The respect of this self-image constitutes for every one of them one of the guarantees against a repetition of discrimination and a basis for their life in the Federal Republic".[30] Although it places somewhat different emphasis, the French approach to the question is basically similar. According to the French Government, Article 24bis of the Freedom of the Press Act aims at protecting the memory of the victims of Nazism as well as safeguarding the right of members of the Jewish community to live free from fear of an atmosphere of anti-Semitism. The Human Rights Committee agreed with the French Government that denying Shoah may contribute to a reinforcement of anti-Semitic feelings and may thereby constitute a violation of the rights of others.

Finally, we must turn to the recent judgment of the European Court of Human Rights in *Lehideux and Isorni* v. *France*.[31] The Court remarked, *obiter*, that the negation or revision of clearly established historical facts – such as the Holocaust – would be removed from the protection of Article 10 of the European Convention by Article 17. Since Article 17 of the Convention denies persons the right to engage in any activity aimed at the destruction of any of the rights and freedoms set forth in the Convention, the Court apparently sees the denial of Shoah as an infringement of these individual rights and freedoms.[32]

An important aspect of the approaches discussed here is that they "equate" the past with the present: statements about the past are considered to constitute infringements of present individual rights. It also appears from the foregoing that the voicing of opinions that are not directed against any individual person in particular, is equated with the violation of individual rights. The question therefore arises whether there is still a need for criminalising denial of Shoah as an offence against collective interests. Indeed, in many legal systems, the denial of Shoah has been criminalised as an offence against the public order or the public peace; German law provides an example. Again, different justifications may lie at the basis of such penal provisions. One justification may be that denial of Shoah may create an immediate danger of disturbances of the public peace, and therefore be punishable only if there is a clear and present danger that such disturbances will actually occur. Usually, however, this is not a requirement. It suffices that such dangers exist *in abstracto*; in other words, the presumption is that denying Shoah creates these dangers. Often, too, the justifications proffered are

[30] Bundesgerichtshof 18 September 1979, *Neue Juristische Wochenschrift* 1980, 45 (translation by Stein, *supra* n 9, at 303). Cf. also Bundesverfassungsgericht 13 April 1994, *Neue Juristische Wochenschrift* 1994, 1779. The European Commission adopted the same line of reasoning in its decision mentioned *supra* n 24.

[31] *Supra* n 25.

[32] Cf. also Article 5 of the International Covenant on Civil and Political Rights. For the advocacy of racist policies as a violation of individual rights see already the European Commission in its decision of 21 October 1979 in the cases of *Glimmerveen and Hagenbeek* v. *The Netherlands*, Applications 8348/78 and 8406/78, 18 *Decisions and Reports* 187–208 (1980).

of a more general and less tangible nature. For instance, criminalisation is said to aim at the protection of public morals,[33] the promotion of harmonious coexistence of different population groups in society,[34] or the furtherance of principles of tolerance and broadmindedness in a democratic society.[35]

Finally, there is the question of the "necessity" of criminalisation. For criminalisation to be permitted under various human rights treaties it must be shown that forbidding the denial of Shoah is necessary in a democratic society with a view to the protection of rights and reputations of others, or the protection of collective interests such as public order or public morals. In its Communication in the case of Faurisson, the Human Rights Committee, while criticising Article 24bis of the Freedom of the Press Act for going too far in some respects, nevertheless agreed with the French Government that Article 19 of the International Covenant on Civil and Political Rights leaves room for criminalisation of denial. This is in line with the approach by other human rights bodies as well as that of national legislators and national courts that have pronounced themselves on the matter. My general impression is that, once it is assumed that the denial of Shoah may harm individual or collective interests, it is (almost) automatically assumed that criminalisation is necessary. In this respect, it is of course important to point at provisions such as Article 20 of the International Covenant and Article 4 of the International Convention on the Elimination of All Forms of Racial Discrimination. Once denying Shoah is equated with advocacy of racial hatred, dissemination of ideas based on racial superiority, or incitement to racial discrimination, the necessity of criminalisation follows from both provisions.

FREEDOM OF SPEECH IN THE UNITED STATES: ARGUMENTS AGAINST CRIMINALISATION

The approach by the various human rights bodies with regard to criminalising the denial of Shoah seems to reflect the prevailing attitude in European countries. This is not to say that such penal provisions are uncontroversial. There are many who doubt the wisdom of criminalisation. It is, for instance, often pointed out that criminalisation creates a danger to free discussions and free research on important historical issues, a risk that it would be better to avoid. Frequently too, it is said that criminalisation will have no influence at all on those who want to deny Shoah or on their audiences, and that it will simply result in racism becoming less visible and, therefore, more difficult to combat. However, these and other arguments advanced against criminalisation are more often than not presented as arguments pertaining to criminal policy rather than legal principle.

[33] Cf. the French Government in its reaction to Faurisson's complaint.

[34] Cf. UN Committee members Evatt and Kretzmer in their individual opinion in the case of Faurisson.

[35] Cf. the European Commission in its decision mentioned *supra* n 24.

As far as I know, no court in Europe has ever held that the criminalisation of denial is, without more, irreconcilable with the freedom of expression. It is, therefore, important to turn to a country in which, to my knowledge, there is hardly any discussion on the desirability of criminalising denial and in which criminalisation would in all probability be considered an unacceptable limitation of the freedom of expression – the United States. A comparison of the European situation with that in the United States is all the more interesting since it may reveal more general differences with regard to the place accorded to the freedom of expression in a democratic society.[36] I will first try to give a brief summary of some aspects of the prevailing doctrine in the United States with regard to restrictions of that freedom and then attempt to draw some conclusions with regard to the criminalisation of denying Shoah.

While courts in European countries, including the European Court of Human Rights, and in the United States both cherish freedom of expression, there are marked differences in the way they strike a balance between a society's interest in guaranteeing freedom of expression to its members and the interests involved in imposing restrictions. These result from underlying differences in philosophies and as a consequence the freedom of expression is, on the whole, more vigorously protected and less readily abridged in the United States than in Europe. Within the framework of this chapter, the following points seem of particular importance.

The first thing to note is that, although European courts are not unfamiliar with the notion that a government must not be permitted to pick and choose among the views it is willing to have discussed, it is certainly true that courts in the United States and the US Supreme Court in particular, attach more radical consequences to the idea. "Viewpoint-neutrality" is one of the cornerstones on which the case law of the Supreme Court rests. It implies that: "(a)bove else, the First Amendment means that Government has no power to restrict expressions because of its message, its ideas, its subject matter, or its contents".[37] Among the cases in which the Supreme Court elaborated on the importance of viewpoint-neutrality, *R.A.V.* v. *City of St Paul*, decided in 1992, seems of special importance here.[38] The case concerns the constitutionality of the St Paul Bias-Motivated Crime Ordinance forbidding the placing on public or private property of "a symbol, object, appellation, characterisation or graffiti, including, but not limited to, a burning cross or Nazi swastika, which one knows or has reasonable grounds to know arouses anger, alarm or resentment in others on the basis of race, color, creed, religion or gender". The Supreme Court held the Ordinance unconstitutional, since it only proscribed conduct that might give offence to others because of their race, colour, creed, religion or gender, and not

[36] For two comparative studies in this field see Thomas David Jones, *Human Rights: Group Defamation, Freedom of Expression and the Law of Nations* (The Hague/Boston/London: 1998), and Theo Rosier, *supra* n 21.

[37] *Police Department* v. *Mosley*, (1972) 408 US 92, 95.

[38] 505 US 377 (1992).

because of other grounds (such as political affiliation, union membership or homosexuality). The Ordinance therefore proscribed speech based upon its subject matter or content.

The strong emphasis in the United States on viewpoint-neutrality is directly related to certain conceptions and suppositions with regard to the relationship between freedom of expression and the political decision-making process. On the one hand, there is the slippery slope argument: once a government is permitted to exclude certain categories of unacceptable ideas from circulating in the public debate, no one can be sure where this will end. The point is well illustrated by the well known *Skokie* case, which concerned the issue of whether the National Socialist Party of America could be prevented from organising a political demonstration and distributing pamphlets in a neighbourhood predominantly inhabited by Jews, many of them Holocaust survivors.[39] In that case, Justice Decker remarked: "(T)he question is which danger is greater: the danger that allowing the government to punish 'unacceptable' ideas will lead to suppression of ideas that are merely uncomfortable to those in power; or the danger that permitting free debate on such unacceptable ideas will encourage their acceptance other than discouraging them by revealing their pernicious quality".[40] The Supreme Court has left no doubt about the answer: government may not prohibit the expression of ideas "because of disagreement with the message it conveys"[41] or "because society finds the idea itself offensive or disagreeable".[42] On the other hand, strong emphasis is traditionally laid on freedom of speech as a vital requirement for the maintenance of democratic institutions in an open, free and pluralistic society, in which every citizen is entitled to express his own opinions with regard to political matters. To quote Meiklejohn: "The principle of freedom of speech springs from the necessity of the program of self-government. It is not a Law of Nature or of Reason in the abstract. It is a deduction from the basic American agreement that public issues shall be decided by universal suffrage".[43]

In the United States as well as in Europe, freedom of speech does not give individuals the right to defame other individuals. On several occasions, the Supreme Court has held that resort to epithets or personal abuse is not in any proper sense communication of information or opinion safeguarded by the Constitution.[44] Is the same true for group defamation? An affirmative answer to that question was given by the Supreme Court in *Beauharnais* v. *Illinois*, decided in 1952.[45] The case involved a provision of the Illinois Criminal Code making it a criminal offence to disseminate information "which portrays depravity,

[39] *Collin* v. *Smith* (1978) 447 F. Suppl. 676 (N.D. III.).

[40] 447 F. Suppl. 676, 688.

[41] *Ward* v. *Rock Against Racism* (1989) 491 U.S. 781, 791.

[42] *Texas* v. *Johnson*, 491 U.S. 397 (1989) 414.

[43] Alexander Meiklejohn, *Free Speech and its Relation to Self-Government, in Political Freedom: The Constitutional Power of the People* (Port Washington, N.Y.: Kennikat Press [1972, c1948]) 27.

[44] Cf. *inter alia Chaplinsky* v. *New Hampshire* (1942) 315 U.S. 568.

[45] (1952) 343 U.S. 250.

criminality, unchastity, or lack of virtue of a class of citizens of any race, color, or creed or religion to contempt, derision or obloquy, or which is productive of breach of the peace or riots". Writing for the majority, Justice Frankfurter stated that a man's job and his educational opportunities and the dignity accorded to him may depend as much on the reputation of the racial and religious group to which he happens to belong as on his own merits. Frankfurter concluded that speech, concededly punishable when immediately directed at individuals, may also be outlawed "if directed at groups with whose position and esteem in society the affiliated individual may be inextricably involved".[46] However, later developments cast doubt as to whether *Beauharnais* still reflects the law of the land in this respect. In *New York Times* v. *Sullivan*, the Supreme Court severely curtailed the use of group libel laws to impose sanctions on expressions critical of the official conduct of public officials.[47] Speaking for the majority, Justice Brennan deduced from earlier case law "a profound national commitment to the principle that debate on public issues should be uninhibited, robust, and wide-open, and that it may well include vehement, caustic, and sometimes unpleasantly sharp attacks on government and public officials". The question is whether and to what extent group libel laws of the type that was upheld in *Beauharnais* are reconcilable with the principle that debate on public issues should be uninhibited, robust, and wide-open. Whatever the answer may be, one may note that group libel laws are very rare in the United States, a marked difference with the situation in Europe. In 1961, the State of Illinois repealed the controversial provision in its Criminal Code.

As has been shown, in European countries provisions criminalising incitement to racial hatred or racial discrimination, including those on the denial of Shoah, are often justified by stating that they serve to protect public order and public peace. Whether the American Constitution permits such laws was the second important issue decided in *Beauharnais*. The Supreme Court gave an affirmative answer, requiring only that they may be considered to be necessary to promote the peace and well-being within a community. In a number of cases decided later, the Supreme Court has, however, held similar statutes penalising speech as an offence against the public peace unconstitutional for being too vague.[48] Moreover, since *Brandenburg* v. *Ohio*, such statutes have to meet the clear and present danger test.[49] According to the Supreme Court "the constitutional guarantees of free speech and free press do not permit a state to forbid or proscribe advocacy of the use of force or of law violation, except where such advocacy is directed to inciting or producing imminent lawless action and is likely to incite or produce such action".[50]

[46] (1952) 343 U.S. 250, 263.

[47] (1964) 376 U.S. 254.

[48] Cf. *inter alia Ashton* v. *Kentucky* (1966) 384 U.S. 195, with regard to the common-law crime of breach of the peace.

[49] (1969) 395 U.S. 444.

[50] (1969) 395 U.S. 444 , 448.

What conclusions can one draw from the foregoing? It seems likely to me that statutes explicitly limited to penalising the denial of Shoah, such as Article 130, para. 3, of the German Criminal Code and Article 24bis of the French Freedom of the Press Act, would be considered by the Supreme Court to be irreconcilable with the requirement of viewpoint-neutrality. They are limited to criminalising denial of international crimes committed during the Second World War in Europe by specific classes of perpetrators against specific classes of victims. Viewpoint-neutrality would probably require inclusion of denial of other international crimes committed during the same period of history, and possibly also of denial of international crimes committed in other periods and in other places. My second (tentative) conclusion is that statutes in European states that criminalise denial as an offence against the public peace, would, if passed in the United States, run into constitutional trouble for not satisfying the "clear and present danger" test. Moreover, it is hardly likely that the Supreme Court would accept motives such as the "protection of public morals", "the promotion of harmonious coexistence of different population groups", or "the furtherance of principles of tolerance and broadmindedness in a democratic society" as valid grounds for restricting the freedom of expression. These justifications come dangerously close to empowering a government to punish ideas it finds unacceptable and to preventing the truly free flow of information in which all ideas may, as in a market place, enter into competition with each other. More difficult to answer is the question of whether denial of Shoah would have a chance of being accepted in the United States as a form of group defamation. *Beauharnais* seemed to leave room for criminalisation here, but in the light of later developments in constitutional law it is open to serious doubt whether this is still the case.

CONCLUDING OBSERVATIONS

It is not the purpose of this chapter to argue for or against the criminalisation of denying Shoah. My sole aim has been to make an inventory of arguments *pro* and *contra* criminalisation on the basis of a comparative survey of developments in a number of legal systems. Meanwhile, one thing is clear: the denial of Shoah is not an innocent act and those who choose to deny cannot be accused of stupidity. The phenomenon of denial should be taken for what it is: a form of racism as insidious and potentially dangerous as other, more open and direct, manifestations of racism. The question of how the law should react, is, therefore, an important one.

It has appeared from the foregoing that fundamentally different attitudes exist with regard to that question. On the one hand, there are the countries of Europe, followed by international human rights bodies, where the criminalisation of denial is relatively unproblematic. On the other hand, there is the United States, where criminalisation is, as far as I am able to ascertain, not likely to have any chance of being accepted. The differences result from more general differences with regard to criminalisation of speech promoting, in one way or another, racial hatred and racial discrimination.

Obviously, differences in the approach to criminalisation of racist speech are due to different sensibilities and different suppositions with regard to social and political processes, resulting in different models for striking a balance between the freedom of expression and the protection of other societal values and interests. As far as sensibilities are concerned, many European observers are shocked by the comparative ease with which, in their perception, racist speech is accepted and legally protected in the United States to the detriment of those who are its immediate victims as well as society at large. On the other hand, observers from the United States may well have similar feelings when they note how lightly, in European countries, the freedom of expression is sacrificed to all kinds of social interests. Different suppositions about social and political processes also play a part.[51] In the United States, it is an article of faith that democratic institutions depend for their well functioning on almost unlimited freedom of speech. The "danger that allowing the government to punish 'unacceptable' ideas will lead to suppression of ideas that are merely uncomfortable to those in power" is considered to be greater than the "danger that permitting free debate on such unacceptable ideas will encourage their acceptance other than discouraging them by revealing their pernicious quality". Most Europeans are probably inclined to hold the opposite view.

How to explain these differences in sensibilities and in suppositions about reality? While it is obviously quite impossible to give a satisfactory answer to that question in this chapter, a few observations should nevertheless be made. In an article published some years ago Kevin Boyle attributed the differences in attitude with regard to the criminalisation of hate speech to two factors.[52] On the one hand, he supposed that the differences can be explained by the basic characteristics of common law and civil law systems: the First Amendment of the American Constitution reflects the attachment to the English tradition of negative liberty while, in civil law systems, regulation of the freedom of speech by statute is not traditionally associated with restriction and repression. This may be an important factor indeed. But one may also note that many common law countries have, in the past decades, introduced legislation criminalising racist speech: Australia, Canada, and the United Kingdom provide examples. In the matter of criminalising racist speech, the contrast is more between the United States and the rest of the world. On the other hand, Boyle suggests that "explanations for the distinctive position of the United States must include its history as a society born in rebellion against, among other things, censorship. The fact that it was a 'drawing board' society built by immigrants made possible the assertion of new principles of democratic republican order". To that

[51] See Theo Rosier, *supra* n 21, 174–82.

[52] Kevin Boyle, "Overview of a Dilemma: Censorship versus Racism" in Sandra Coliver (ed.), *Striking a Balance: Hate Speech, Freedom of Expression and Non-discrimination* 4–5.

observation, which seems to me to be true, I may add another explanation. The history of Europe in the twentieth century makes it difficult for Europeans to have the same unconditional confidence as Americans in freedom of speech as the basic requirement for well-functioning democratic institutions, and to share America's optimism in this respect. To them it may seem that what may be true for the United States is not necessarily true for Europe as well. After all, the fact that totalitarian regimes have, in the recent past, seized power by the use of democratic means is an important part of the European collective memory. The special sensitvity in Europe with regard to the denial of Shoah, is also due to the fact that these events eventually led to Auschwitz. Unlike the United States, most European nations have to live with the consciousness that the Holocaust occurred on their territories and that the millions of innocent lives taken were those of their own citizens.

8

Criminal Legislation in the Nineteenth Century: The Historic Roots of Criminal Law and Non-Intervention in The Netherlands

C.M. PELSER

1. INTRODUCTION

THIS BOOK DEALS with underlying assumptions in legal cultures concerning the private sphere, personal autonomy and the supposed justifications for state interference through criminalisation and the implementation of substantive criminal law. This contribution approaches the problem from a mainly historical angle, the hypothesis being that present discussions about substantive criminal law and privacy cannot be understood without knowledge of legal history. It was conceived as a preparatory study for broader research into substantive criminal law in relation to the right to privacy in the Netherlands. Although the concept of a right to privacy is a modern one, the lawyers who designed the Dutch Criminal Code – still in force today – during the latter part of the nineteenth century, were already convinced that citizens should be left alone as far as possible. These ideas still influence modern Dutch legal theory, most especially the notion that the criminal law should be used as a last resort only. The question as to the origins of that notion forms my starting point.

Dutch criminal law consists of several areas of criminal legislation,[1] based, since the beginning of the nineteenth century, on a combination of the principles of legality[2] and of codification (preference of codes instead of mere statutes). Codified law therefore dominates the organisation of the legislation. Like that of most civil law countries, the codification itself is bipartite; a Criminal Code

[1] For an overview, see J.F. Nijboer, "Criminal Justice System", in: J.M.J. Chorus, H.M. Gerver, E.H. Hondius and A.K. Koekkoek (eds), *Introduction to Dutch Law* (The Hague: Kluwer Law International, 1999) 383–433.

[2] Both criminal offences and forms of punishment must have a prior basis in law: *nullem crimen/nulla poena sine praevia lege.*

(*Wetboek van Strafrecht*)[3] for substantive criminal law and a special Code of Criminal Procedure (*Wetboek van Strafvordering*) for adjective criminal law, including the rules on criminal evidence and legal remedies in criminal cases. Despite the principle of codification, socio-economic and fiscal criminal law (fields which have expanded enormously since the enactment of the current Criminal Code in 1886), are regulated in separate Acts. However, the Criminal Code has not lost ground because of these developments, being the basis of criminal law in all other areas.

The 1886 Code originates in a draft prepared by a State Commission named after its chair, the State Commission-De Wal.[4] The minutes of the *Commission-De Wal*, the subsequent government Bill and the parliamentary proceedings that followed, form my basic material. I shall be looking at their discussions of state interference through criminalisation in the light of their moderate attitude and the idea that citizens should be let alone. This idea, of course, is not equivalent to a right to privacy, as we understand the concept today. There were no human rights conventions when the 1886 Criminal Code was under discussion. Indeed, the very idea that there could be an appeal to a right to privacy arose only some years later. In 1888, the American judge Thomas M. Cooley observed that privacy is synonymous with the right to be let alone.[5] The issue of privacy arose at the end of the nineteenth century because of, among other things, the invention of photography as part of the onward march of technology, the rise in population and the growing individualisation of society. In their famous article "The Right to Privacy", published in 1890, Samuel D. Warren and Louis D. Brandeis stressed the need for a protection of private life against the excesses of the press.[6] Warren, a Boston lawyer and business man, was reacting against publicity in the "yellow press" about his family's social life, in particular a wedding reception organised by Mrs Warren. In the English and American judicial decisions quoted in their article, Warren and Brandeis recognise a general principle: a right to privacy, the function of which is to protect "an inviolate personality". The authors approach the right to privacy as a split off from the right to life: the right to enjoy life, – the right to be let alone. In determining privacy as a right, the article has been called the most influential ever published.

In the twentieth century, the development of the right to privacy has been affected importantly by Strasbourg case law on Article 8 of the European Convention on Human Rights.[7] The European Convention on Human Rights plays an important role in the Dutch legal system, as the Dutch Constitution

[3] For an English translation, see: *The Dutch Penal Code* (Littleton, CO: Fred B. Rothman & Co, 1997).

[4] "Staatscommissie voor de Zamenstelling van een Wetboek van Strafregt", KB 28 September 1870 (no. 21).

[5] Thomas M. Cooley, *A Treatise on the Law of Torts* (Chicago IL: Callaghan & Co., 2nd edn 1888) 29 (cited by Adam Carlyle Breckenridge, *The Right to Privacy* (Lincoln, NB: University of Nebraska Press, 1970) 1).

[6] S.D. Warren and L.D. Brandeis, "The Right to Privacy" 4 *Harvard Law Review* 193.

[7] See Brants *supra* pp. 117–38.

adopts a monistic approach to international law, allowing courts to apply human rights conventions and to set aside conflicting national legislation.[8] In 1983, the right to privacy was more firmly anchored in Dutch law by its inclusion in the Dutch Constitution. However, because there is no system of constitutional review in the Netherlands and courts are not allowed to test legal provisions against the Constitution, the defence is often forced to refer to human rights conventions.

Despite the increasing significance of the concept of privacy in the twentieth century, a clear definition cannot be derived from Strasbourg case law, or from the "Travaux Préparatoires". In *Niemietz* v. *Germany*, the European Court of Human Rights even admits it would be impossible to attempt an exhaustive definition.[9] Nevertheless Resolution 428 (1970) of the Consultative Assembly of the Council of Europe may serve as a guideline:

> The right to privacy consists essentially in the right to live one's own life with a minimum of interference. It concerns private, family and home life, physical and moral integrity, honour and reputation, avoidance of being placed in a false light, non-revelation of irrelevant and embarrassing facts, unauthorised publication of private photographs, protection against misuse of private communications, protection from disclosure of information given or received by the individual confidentially. Those who, by their own actions, have encouraged indiscreet revelations about which they complain later on, cannot avail themselves of the right to privacy.[10]

From Strasbourg case law we may conclude that the concept of privacy has evolved over the years to more than simply a right to be let alone. In *Brüggemann and Scheuten* v. *Germany*, for example, the basic assumption of the European Commission is that:

> [t]he right to respect for private life is of such a scope as to secure to the individual a sphere within which he can freely pursue the development and fulfilment of his personality. To this effect, he must also have the possibility of establishing relationships of various kinds, including sexual, with other persons. In principle, therefore, whenever the State sets up rules for the behaviour of the individual within this sphere, it interferes with the respect for private life and such interference must be justified in the light of para. (2) of Art. 8.[11]

In *Niemietz* v. *Germany* the European Court observes that:

> . . . it would be too restrictive to limit the notion [of private life] to an "inner circle" in which the individual may live his own personal life as he chooses and to exclude therefrom entirely the outside world not encompassed within that circle. Respect for

[8] See for example, Bert Swart and James Young, "The European Convention on Human Rights and Criminal Justice in The Netherlands and the UK" in Phil Fennell et al. (eds), *Criminal Justice in Europe* (Oxford: Clarendon Press, 1995).

[9] ECHR 16 December 1992, Publ. ECHR Series A vol. 251-B.

[10] *Yearbook of the European Convention on Human Rights* (The Hague: Martinus Nijhoff Publishers, 1970) 62.

[11] Report of 12 July 1977 (Appl. No. 6959/75), Decisions and Reports, vol. 10 (Strasbourg: Council of Europe, 1978) 100–22, § 55.

> private life must also compromise to a certain degree the right to establish and develop relationships with other human beings.[12]

In short, one may say that the current interpretation of privacy includes, besides a passive right to be let alone, also an active right to self-determination. Furthermore, it should be noted that the right to privacy covers many fields and that the scope of its protection differs from field to field.

In the documents investigated for this chapter, we cannot expect to find the modern interpretation of privacy. After all, the 1886 Criminal Code was developed in the second half of the nineteenth century – thus long before the advent of a multiform society and in an era highly different from ours. It was a changing society, but still without cars, planes, computers, much less organised than today. More importantly, the portrayal of mankind and the relationship between the state and the individual, as well as the morals were quite different. Nevertheless, I am convinced that going back to the roots of criminal law will shed light on current substantive criminal law in relation to the right to privacy. The genesis of a code or a statute is interesting in itself, not least with a view to the interpretation of the text of the law. But it is the more interesting if – as in the case of the 1886 Dutch Criminal Code – that code or statute in general appears to be able to cope with the rapid transformation of the society it was designed to serve and with the development of human rights. Either the principles upon which the Criminal Code was based, are not so very different from the concept of the right to privacy which developed later, or the provisions in the Criminal Code leave enough room for new ideas. From what follows, it would appear that both explanations apply. Notions of private, family and home life, physical and moral integrity, honour, reputation, etc., and the general notion of privacy as we know them now, actually did play a part in the discussions (although perhaps less well-articulated), and we may well ask to what extent historical developments influence Dutch attitudes towards contemporary problems.

The structure of this chapter is as follows. First, a situational sketch of the nineteenth century and the making of criminal law in this era is given. Next, the 1886 Criminal Code's leading principles are discussed, whereupon the assumptions of the compilers of the Criminal Code concerning the private sphere and personal autonomy will be analysed. In the last section, the chapter will be rounded off with some conclusions on modern developments in the Netherlands.

2. CRIMINAL LEGISLATION IN THE NINETEENTH CENTURY

In the second half of the nineteenth century, the bourgeoisie[13] governed the Netherlands. The Dutch upper middle class was in general moderate, fairly

[12] ECHR 16 December 1992, Publ. ECHR Series A vol. 251-B, § 29.

[13] I.e., the upper middle class: merchants and the liberal professions (especially lawyers).

advanced and tolerant. The concepts of the Enlightenment were still influential. The nineteenth century can be characterised as a period of transition. In the experience of those who lived through it, it was a definitive farewell to the Middle Ages.[14] In the first decades of this century, agriculture, shipping and trade had been the most important means of sustaining life. Merchandise was carried by boat rather than by cart or wagon over the poor roads; people travelled by stagecoach or tow barge. There was a wide gap between the well-to-do and the working class, which was poor. The years between 1840–50 especially were years of poverty with unsuccessful harvests and food riots.[15] Industrial development was indeed coming up, but at that stage it was no more important than manual work.[16]

After 1850, the economic situation in the Netherlands changed. Official documents from that time refer to a "flourishing" period.[17] Between 1850 and 1870, with the advent of steam, large-scale industry becomes important; post and telegraphy develop, a railway is built; the first modern banks and insurance companies appear.[18] The physical, mental and moral condition of the lower classes in this period, however, remained unchanged. Widespread illiteracy had a lot to do with widespread child labour.[19] Child mortality was high, imprisonment of minors frequent.[20] The state of health of the labour force was poor, due to bad sanitary conditions and an unbalanced diet of chicory coffee with rye bread and potatoes or rice.[21] Alcohol abuse (genever) was common.

With the rise of the bourgeoisie and the growing dualism between state and society during this century, citizens were allowed more and more scope. Under the regimes of William I (1813–40) and William II (1840–9), the Dutch Constitution of 1815 had allowed the sovereign much power, while the rights of the representatives were minute. After the European March-revolutions, the Netherlands underwent important political renewal in the Constitution of 1848. The most prominent change was the introduction of the royal prerogative and ministerial responsibility, and the King was forced to take a major step backwards in favour of Parliament. Moreover, greater contact with the electorate was established through the Second Chamber henceforth elected directly

[14] P-B.M. Blaas, "De onzekere burgerij" (1998) *De Negentiende Eeuw* 1 at 4–24.

[15] I.J. Brugmans, *De arbeidende klasse in Nederland in de 19e eeuw 1813–1870* (Utrecht/Antwerp: Het Spectrum, 10th edn 1975) 214, with reference to J. de Bosch Kemper, *Geschiedenis van Nederland na 1830* (Amsterdam: Johannes Müller, 1882) vol. V, 68, 126.

[16] I.J. Brugmans, *op. cit.*, 72. Whereas in England mechanised production started in the second half of the eighteenth century, in the Netherlands machine-manufacture came into use only much later. The industrial revolution got off to a slow start, much slower than in England, France and Belgium. The starting-point of the modern-capitalistic period in the Netherlands is circa 1870.

[17] *Ibid.*, 215.

[18] *Ibid.*, 218.

[19] S. Sr. Coronel, "In 't Gooi" (1863) *De Gids*. The Compulsory Education Act was enacted in 1900.

[20] Herman Franke, *Twee eeuwen gevangen; Misdaad en straf in Nederland* (Utrecht: Het Spectrum, 1990) 213.

[21] G.E.V. Schneevoogt, "Hygiène" (1861) *De Gids*.

instead of in two or three stages. Because of census-suffrage, the liberals[22] gained a large majority in Parliament.

Until the 1870s, legalism (nourished by liberal notions) dominated legal theory. Law was not seen as providing guidelines for just or moral behaviour but simply as defining a system of reciprocal freedoms, a relationship between equals granting each other, by contract, free space.[23] The liberals thought a good working society would be realised by moral reform of the people and by personal initiative. Many laws were passed under this liberal regime, particularly to consolidate and to elaborate the new polity (e.g. Electoral Act, Province Act, Municipal Corporations Act). But also other important Acts, such as the Postal Act, the Telegraphy Act, the Education Act, the removal of the excise-duties on pork and mutton (a measure to bring meat within reach of the lower classes) and the removal of transit duties, speak to the busy activities of the Liberal Government.

Criminal law was not regarded as especially important.[24] Not only was it given lower priority by the legislature, there was also a lack of academic tradition and expertise. J.E. Goudsmit, chair of the first annual meeting of the Dutch Lawyers Association (NJV) in 1870, spoke of "a lack of a vivid national sense of justice in the field of criminal law".[25] Little was published in this field, and indeed there were as yet no journals on criminal law.[26] At the university, criminal law was only one of several subjects a professor had to teach; the first separate chair for criminal law and criminal procedure was established in 1871.[27]

The first steps towards the current Dutch Criminal Code were taken in those days. After a three-year period of French occupation (1810–13), the Napoleonic Code Pénal, imposed on 1 March 1811, had provisionally remained in force.[28] However, a few important changes were made, drawn from Old Dutch law[29] (e.g. abolishment of general forfeiture of property, abandonment of public executions, reintroduction of public flogging and public exhibition on the scaffold). In 1838, the French *Code d'Instruction Criminelle* was replaced by a Dutch Code of Criminal Procedure. The 1827 draft for a national criminal code however, had been criticised so strongly that the Government withdrew it. The

[22] "Liberal" in the classic continental sense of economic laissez-faire and freedom from state interference in general.

[23] R.J.S. Schwitters, "Vermaatschappelijking van het recht in sociologisch perspectief" in R. Pieterman *et al.* (eds), *Bijdragen tot de rechtsgeschiedenis van de negentiende eeuw* (Arnhem: Gouda Quint, 1994) 205.

[24] See for example, G.A. van Hamel, "De Duitsche Juristendag" 1870 *De Gids*.

[25] G.A. van Hamel, *Inleiding tot de studie van het Nederlandsche strafrecht* (Haarlem/'s-Gravenhage: De Erven F. Bohn/Gebr. Belinfante, 3rd edn 1913) 97.

[26] *Tijdschrift voor Strafrecht* (relaunched as *Delikt En Delinkwent* in 1971) was established in 1886.

[27] A.E.J. Modderman (member of the State Commission) held it in the Law Faculty of the University of Leiden, in succession to his former tutor and chairman of the State Commission J. de Wal, who resigned to devote himself entirely to the preparation of the new criminal code. In 1879, 1880 and 1884 chairs were established in Utrecht, Amsterdam and Groningen respectively.

[28] Article 1 Soeverein Besluit of 11 December 1813, Stb. 10.

[29] Crimineel Wetboek voor het Koningrijk Holland (1809–11).

reunification with the Southern Netherlands under the Vienna Convention of 1815 appeared to be an important hindrance. The (Catholic) Southern Netherlands preferred French law, whereas the (mainly Protestant) Northern Netherlands focused on Old Dutch law. In 1830, Belgium seceded.[30] Under pressure from England and France, King William I finally submitted in 1839. Between 1839 and 1859 several efforts to prepare or to pass a Bill failed, mostly for reasons of substance – e.g. the prison system (1842, 1846) and the Government's authorisation (*exequatur*) for correspondence between the clergy and any foreign power (1847).[31] In 1854, however, an important revision of the adapted Code Pénal took place, which considerably mitigated its harsher provisions.[32] The Government thought it not the right moment to introduce a Bill into Parliament for a completely new criminal code, the establishment of theories being still under discussion.[33]

Finally, in 1870 a State Commission chaired by the Professor J. de Wal of Leiden University, was appointed to formulate a draft Bill with explanatory memorandum.[34] In his recommendation to the King, Minister of Justice Van Lilaar explained that the drawing up of a Bill could be postponed no longer, since the Code Pénal (frequently adapted and therefore now somewhat incoherent) no longer fitted the demands and needs of the day, being out of step with the progress of civilisation and therefore in many respects in conflict with the legal convictions of the Dutch nation. He was not the only person to think so. In his doctorate on the reform of criminal legislation (1863), A.E.J. Modderman refers to "an unscholarly collection of partly draconian, partly incomplete provisions, a travesty of justice, a scorn of civilisation, a denial of the proper interests of the State and its citizens".[35] Referring to the recent abolishment of the death penalty in general criminal law,[36] Minister of Justice Van Lilaar stated that reform should be towards *justice combined with severity*, to which revenge and all tendencies to harshness in the law remain foreign.[37]

The background of the members of the State Commission strongly influenced the design of the Bill. They represented various professional groups and broad judicial experience. Most were liberal.[38] All members adhered to the Classical

[30] Belgium finally replaced the French Code Pénal in 1867.

[31] The power to *amend* proposed legislation did not yet exist. A salient detail is that, after the 1847 Bill foundered on the *exequatur* issue, the right was abolished when the Constitution was amended in 1848.

[32] For an overview, see A.E.J. Modderman, *De hervorming onzer strafwetgeving* ('s-Gravenhage: W.P. van Stockum, 1863) 50–4.

[33] *Ibid.*, 21.

[34] "Staatscommissie voor de Zamenstelling van een Wetboek van Strafregt" KB 28 September 1870 (n. 21). The State Commission consisted of J. de Wal (chair), A.A. de Pinto (secretary), W.F.G.L. François (in 1872 replaced by J.J. Loke), A.E.J. Modderman, M.S. Pols and Jhr. G.J.T. Beelaerts van Blokland (assistant-secretary).

[35] A.E.J. Modderman, *op cit.*, 3.

[36] Law of 17 September 1870, Stb. 162.

[37] Weekblad van het Regt, 3 October 1870, No. 3248, 1.

[38] A.G. Bosch, *Het ontstaan van het Wetboek van Strafrecht* (Zwolle: W.E.J. TjeenkWillink, 1965).

School in criminal law. This school of thought, which finds its origin in the Enlightenment, fits well within the liberal ideology of the nineteenth century. The basic assumption was that exercise of government powers was founded on *le contrat social*,[39] into which citizens were considered to have entered. The most important principles of the Classical School in criminal law are the principle of legality, retribution as basis of the punishment, the principle of culpability and the principle of proportionality.[40]

Forewarned by previous experience, the State Commission took an approach which avoided doctrinal issues. The work, however, took longer than the Commission itself had expected.[41] It required 177 meetings over a period of five years to formulate a draft Bill containing 611 Articles[42] and drafts for the various accompanying laws,[43] all with explanatory memorandums.[44] The draft Bill was much debated, at home and abroad. The general impression was favourable, notwithstanding the fact that the State Commission was not spared severe criticism.[45] Based on the Commission's proposals, a (much reduced[46]) government Bill was introduced into Parliament in 1879. After some modifications, including the penalisation of adultery, major changes in the sentencing system and – again – an important reduction of the number of provisions,[47] the Criminal Code was passed on 3 March 1881 (Stb. 35). Because of problems in harmonising the text with other Acts, it did not enter into force until 1 September 1886. At last the constitutional requirement that general criminal law, the administration of criminal justice and the judicial system shall be laid down in general codes (codification principle) had been met for substantive criminal law.

3. THE 1886 CRIMINAL CODE: LEADING PRINCIPLES

Whereas in the middle of the nineteenth century criminal law was not yet an area for special attention, the legislator of the 1886 Criminal Code did recognise the great value of criminal law, careful lawmaking and a completely new legislative framework.

> (. . .) For the rest, public law, above all criminal law, is as far elevated above private law, as ideals of human nature are elevated above material interests of humanity. And

[39] This school of thought was initiated by Cesare Beccaria's work, *Dei delitti e delle pene* (Milano: 1764).

[40] See Kelk, *infra*, p. 205.

[41] A.G. Bosch, *op. cit.* n 38 at 46.

[42] I.e. 127 more than in the Code Pénal.

[43] Concerning the introduction, transitional provisions and alterations in existing laws.

[44] Ontwerpen van een wetboek van strafregt en daartoe behoorende wetten met toelichting, den Koning aangeboden door de Staatscommissie, ingesteld bij Zijner Majesteits besluit van 28 september 1870, no. 21 ('s-Gravenhage: Gebr. Belinfante, 1875).

[45] A.G. Bosch, *op. cit.* n 38 at 46.

[46] The number of Articles was reduced to 530.

[47] To 472. Most of the omitted Articles would have constituted misdemeanours.

> as for the *legislation*, bad private law can, in general (. . .) and to a greater or lesser extent be de-activated by the citizen; bad criminal law, on the other hand, can poison the moral life of a people, kill freedom, destroy safety, sacrifice the innocence.[48]

According to the ideas at the time "good criminal law" meant reserved law. Nineteenth century liberalism emphasises the solidarity of all Dutch citizens and the equality of all before the law.[49] Outside its natural field of activity (maintenance of order, foreign politics, infrastructure) the government was required to adopt an attitude that allowed citizens to develop in freedom. Contemporary tolerance was also reflected in the criminal law. For the criminal law, Cesare Beccaria's maxim: the maximum of happiness for the maximum number of people, meant, among other things, that prevention of crime is preferable to punishment. Therefore, unnecessary penalisations, which in themselves would create criminality, had to be avoided.[50] Criminal law was seen as a last resort; the ultimate remedy for the most serious norm violations, that were, moreover, recognised as such by common opinion.[51] During the debate on the new Code in Parliament, Minister of Justice Modderman (formerly a member of the State Commission) explained:

> The principle is this: that punishment must be reserved for that which constitutes an *injustice*. This is a sine qua non. Secondly, this must be an injustice, of which experience has shown that it cannot adequately be suppressed by any other means (whereby of course the given social situation must be taken into consideration). The threat of punishment must remain an *ultimum remedium*. Naturally, each threat of punishment meets with obstacles. Every sensible person can understand this presumably without explanation. That does not mean no penalisation, but it does mean that one must always weigh the advantages against the disadvantages of penalisation, and that care must be taken that punishment will not be a cure that is worse than the cause.[52]

Modderman's statement concerned the question of whether or not injustice should be punished. The notion of criminal law as a last resort was reflected in the choice of offences. For example, although the most important function of the criminal justice system was to prevent individuals from taking the law into their own hands,[53] actually doing so was not, as such, a criminal offence. According to all members of the State Commission, it was not only very risky to sum up a large number of actions of very differing gravity in this way, the fact that civil remedies often suffice also had to be taken into consideration.[54] A

[48] Antwoord der Regeering op Verslag der Commissie van Rapporteurs van de Eerste Kamer der Staten-Generaal in H.J. Smidt, *Geschiedenis van het Wetboek van Strafrecht* (Haarlem: H.D. Tjeenk Willink, 1881) vol. I, 18.

[49] Cf. H.J. Smidt, *ibid.* at 21.

[50] C. Kelk, *Studieboek Materieel Strafrecht* (Deventer: Gouda Quint, 1998) 21.

[51] G.A. van Hamel, "De grenzen der heerschappij van het strafrecht" in *Verspreide opstellen* (Leiden: E.J. Brill, 1912).

[52] H.J. Smidt, *op. cit.* n 48, vol. I, 11.

[53] J.M. van Bemmelen, *Het probleem van de doodstraf* (Antwerpen/Amsterdam: De Sikkel/L.J. Veen's Uitgeversmaatschappij N.V., 1948) 9.

[54] Staatscommissie voor de zamenstelling van een Wetboek van Strafregt "1870/1876" (Tilburg: Katholieke Hogeschool, 1976) Notulen I, 294.

specific criterion for determining whether or not an act constituted a criminal offence, which, as Modderman suggested, would also indicate the difference between civil and criminal injustice, is found neither in the Criminal Code itself, nor in the explanatory memorandum.[55] In fact, only at the beginning of the 1970s of the twentieth century did Dutch lawyers start to think seriously about (negative) criteria for penalisation.[56] It is however safe to say that William Blackstone's distinguishing criterion that civil injustice (i.e. infringements merely of particular rights) concerns the individual only and that criminal injustice (i.e. public wrongs which are a breach of general and public rights) affects the whole community, was not fully applied in the Dutch situation.[57]

With reference to the care exercised in considering what ought to be an offence under the new Criminal Code, Minister of Justice Modderman pointed out that, according to existing criminal legislation, a number of acts still went unpunished, "acts of which no one questions that they are deserving of punishment, except perhaps the criminal himself".

> Very many such acts, which are the drawbacks of our "increasing civilisation" and are therefore greatly on the increase, are not criminal offences. To persevere in their impunity, is to allow them even greater scope.[58]

Examples are sexual intercourse with minors under the age of twelve, perjury, laying false information of a crime, and selling goods in the full knowledge that these are injurious to life or health. Accordingly, in comparison with the Code Pénal, the Dutch Criminal Code contained a number of new penal provisions that reflected modern conditions. Under the ruling legalism, the law was seen as the portrayal of social reality.[59] Indeed, the 1886 Criminal Code in its original state can be seen as an image of society in the second half of the nineteenth century. As A.G. Bosch in his memoir on the occasion of the Code's centenary in 1986 explains, the reserved attitude and respect for personal privacy that the bourgeoisie expected of government, led to a decidedly modest code when it comes to penalty clauses. The bourgeoisie was the propertied class, whose interests clearly lay in maintaining existing legal order.[60] The 1886 Criminal Code is directed towards protection of government and contains many offences affecting property. The one-dimensional portrayal of mankind, the good citizen endorsing society, led to an emphasis on provisions for the protection of public order. The Code's structure is striking in this respect. Instead of an order following the natural extension of infringements of rights, beginning with the

[55] *Ibid.*, 3, 116.

[56] L.H.C. Hulsman, "Kriteria voor strafbaarstelling" in *Strafrecht te-recht? Over dekriminalisering en depenalisering* (Baarn: In den Toren, 1972) 80–92.

[57] William Blackstone, *Commentaries on the Laws of England* (Oxford: Clarendon Press, 1765) Book the First, 118.

[58] H.J. Smidt, *op. cit.* n 48 at 98.

[59] A.C. 't Hart, *Recht als schild van Perseus* (Arnhem/Antwerpen: Kluwer Rechtswetenschappen, 1991).

[60] A.G. Bosch, *op. cit.* n 38 at 29.

offences against individuals, offences concerning the organisation of the state, public order and social safety precede those protecting honour, personal privacy, life, body and property rights.[61]

The principle that the state may not be a moralist follows almost naturally from the notion that criminal law must be the last resort.[62] It may not be used to impose morality, for interference with matters of ideology is fundamentally wrong. In the words of Minister of Justice Modderman, the interrelationship between law and morality was as follows: "law and morality are distinct, but not separate".[63] As W.P.J. Pompe explains, law concerns good society, morality good human beings.[64] Society is only affected by overt action that reveals the individual will, by either an act or a failure to act. Only overt action is significant for the sphere of the other, and thus for society. The consequence of this principle is therefore that immoral behaviour cannot constitute a criminal offence unless it is also an *injustice*.[65] The reader should take this observation by the nineteenth century legislator with a pinch of salt. The provisions on public decency were certainly not a mere reflection of such liberal principles. Here the desire to protect young people from immorality prevailed above liberal arguments.[66]

What was considered immoral behaviour? The compilers of the 1886 Criminal Code do not refer explicitly to this question. Their reservations are apparent in the style of the Criminal Code, which excels in simplicity and pragmatism. Definitions of offences are straightforward; motives rarely part of them. The State Commission also avoided, as much as possible, problems of principle; the Criminal Code was not supposed to be a textbook. The same goes for the explanatory memorandum. The compilers were of the opinion that it is not the legislator, but the court that must interpret the text of the law. Therefore, the legislator's vision on morality can be read mainly between the lines.

Despite all such reservation, the 1886 Criminal Code was nevertheless based on Christian morals.[67] Euthanasia, for example, became a criminal offence – in disregard of the right to self-determination – out of respect for human life in general.[68] Furthermore, it follows from the explanatory memorandum that

[61] H.J. Smidt, *op. cit.* n 48, vol. II, 9.

[62] H.J. Smidt, *ibid.*, vol. I, 13, 46.

[63] *Ibid.*, 46.

[64] W.P.J. Pompe, *Het nieuwe tijdperk en het recht* (Amsterdam: Uitgeverij Vrij Nederland, 1945) 54; W.P.J. Pompe, *Handboek van het Nederlandse strafrecht* (Zwolle: W.E.J. Tjeenk Willink, 1959) 2–3.

[65] Contemplating the current compilation of offences, it is clear that morality in general is not the ground of an act deserving punishment. In fact, a lot of (social order regulating) offences are hardly blameworthy.

[66] R.S.B. Kool, *De strafwaardigheid van seksueel misbruik*, dissertation Rotterdam (Deventer: Gouda Quint, 1999).

[67] All members of the State Commission but one, De Pinto who was Jewish, were registered members of the Dutch Reformed Church. However, only Modderman and Beelaerts van Blokland were confirmed Christian. Modderman in particular frequently testified to his liberal Christian principles, which had strongly influenced his beliefs about law. See A.G. Bosch, *op. cit.* n 38.

[68] H.J. Smidt, *op. cit.* n 48, vol. II, 440.

marriage and family life were regarded as cornerstones of society. Yet, the idea of criminal law as a last resort implied that the criminal law could afford only limited protection to marriage and family life. Family and home life as such were not considered rights that required specific protection. Trespass (Article 138 Criminal Code) for example is classified as an offence against public order, although the human right concerned is the inviolability of the home. Entering a bigamous marriage (Article 237 Criminal Code) is classified as an offence against civil status and not, for example, as a moral offence, although because of its links with perjury it is counted among the offences concerning fraud and deceit.[69] Apart from that, the law did not specify the conditions for a healthy married life. Rape during marriage did not become an offence until 1991. Theft and other property crimes during marriage are offences, but cannot be prosecuted (Article 316 Criminal Code). In these cases, civil law takes precedence over criminal law.

The classical offences in the 1886 Criminal Code concern the penalisation of immoral behaviour in itself (e.g. murder, manslaughter, rape and theft). Lottery and fortune telling, on the other hand, were decriminalised, being regarded not as an injustice but merely immoral behaviour.[70] The impunity of this popular amusement is a clear indication that Dutch tolerance does not imply respect for the ideas of a person, as Raes argues in his chapter.[71] During the discussion within the State Commission words like "superstition" and "the wish to eradicate this popular prejudice" slipped out. Still, the majority of the Commission were of the opinion that penalisation is only required if the fortune-teller is committing a fraud. In other words, here we see an example of the classical liberal approach to the legitimacy of state interference.[72] The only circumstances falling within the range of the 1886 Criminal Code are the fortune-teller harming the legitimate interests of others. John Stuart Mill's harm-principle, implying that the only purpose for which power can be lawfully exercised over any member of a civilised community, against his will, is to prevent harm to others, seems to have also been the basic assumption in the penalisation of the moral offences.[73] This led to a very limited penalisation of indecent behaviour, which does not constitute a criminal offence unless others can take offence at that behaviour or are harmed by it. The basic assumption was that criminal law is not concerned with the protection of individuals against voluntary moral corruption.[74]

The requirement that the human will must be apparent in overt action implies that thought and feeling are free. The theory of attempt is specifically based on this principle. As criminal law is concerned only with ideas that are expressed

[69] H.J. Smidt, *op. cit.* n 48, vol. II, 9.

[70] Staatscommissie voor de zamenstelling van een Wetboek van Strafregt "1870/1876" (Tilburg: Katholieke Hogeschool, 1976) Notulen III, 370–371.

[71] Raes, *supra* p. 25.

[72] *Ibid.*

[73] Sexual abuse of young people was excluded. Here the desire to protect prevailed.

[74] A.G. Bosch, *op. cit.* n 38 at 22.

overtly, an attempt to commit an offence does not itself constitute a criminal offence unless the perpetrator has manifested his intentions by initiating the offence (Article 45 Criminal Code). For acts to be considered as initiating the commission of the target offence, it is crucial that, on their outward appearance, these acts are aimed at realising the offence. In older case law, the Dutch Supreme Court required that the act would, without intervention by the perpetrator, lead to the commission of the offence.[75] In this objective theory, attempt and completion more or less coincide, for it implies that everything necessary to commit the offence has indeed taken place. In more recent case law, the Supreme Court applies a less strict, but still objective theory, which requires that an act constitutes a substantial step towards commission of the offence.[76] The overt manifestation of the act determines whether it does so or not, which reasoning on attempt comes close to the standard applied to determine intent.

Although the 1886 legislator adhered to the principle of the state being no moralist, the Code does actually leave room for the implementation of (future) morals. Many criminal offences are couched in vague terms, a legislative technique which has allowed contemporary beliefs about morals and decency to determine the appropriateness of the provision to actual behaviour. A striking example is the use of the word "decency" itself in Articles 239 and 240 Criminal Code. According to the Dutch Supreme Court this term must be taken as a general concept, which can only be defined by taking into account the current opinions of an important majority in contemporary Dutch society.[77] This allowed the term decency to be interpreted in many different ways over the years. Another example relates to the so-called culpable offences and theories of causality. In many definitions of offences, the causing of a particular harm is made punishable either explicitly or implicitly. In these offences, the circumstances under which an act can be said to be the cause of a result are not defined. Article 307 Criminal Code, for example, states: "A person who as a result of negligence or carelessness is responsible for the death of another, is liable to . . ." By defining an offence not as an act, but as a result, the legislator leaves room for the court to determine the appropriateness of the legal provision, for in order to determine culpability, the court must assess the causal connection between act and result. The criterion used by the courts to assess circumstances in which it is reasonable, from a legal point of view, to impute a result to an act or omission, has changed over the years from "foreseeability" to "reasonable imputability".

[75] HR 19 March 1934, NJ 1934, 450.

[76] HR 24 October 1978, NJ 1979, 52; HR 8 September 1987, NJ 1988, 612.

[77] HR 17 November 1970, NJ 1971, 373.

4. THE COMPILERS OF THE 1886 CRIMINAL CODE ON THE PRIVATE SPHERE AND PERSONAL AUTONOMY

Whereas the previous section discusses general principles, this section focuses on the different rights that are protected. I believe that, by analysing these rights, I will further uncover the assumptions of the compilers of the 1886 Criminal Code concerning the private sphere and personal autonomy. We have seen that a preponderance of offences aimed at protecting society and public order rather than individuals, reflects the then prevailing views on society. The protected rights of individuals are honour, personal liberty, life and body, and property, in that order. According to the explanatory memorandum, the rights of individuals are safeguarded "par excellence – never exclusively". Each criminal offence has the rights of society as its object, at least indirectly.[78] To twentieth century eyes, the Code's structure, as set out in the third section, and the choice of protected rights are perhaps somewhat old-fashioned. After all, and particularly since the beginning of the 1990s, the victim has managed to secure a much better position in criminal justice, even, according to some, at the expense of public order.[79] However, for a legislator inspired by the Age of Reason, these are not strange principles, as John Locke maintained that the social contract preserved the pre-existent natural rights of the individual to "life, liberty, and estate", and that the enjoyment of private rights – the pursuit of happiness – led, in civil society, to the common good. The adherents of the Classical School in criminal law considered the enormous government inference, which was needed for the advancement of the public interest, to be a thread to individual liberty. Since freedom is not only a personal interest but also likewise part of the public interest in a fair society, government action requires a special legitimisation, including statutory authorisation.[80]

From the enumeration of protected rights follows, that – contrary to the protection of personal liberty (e.g. slave-running, abduction, unlawful detention) and physical integrity (e.g. murder and manslaughter, grievous bodily harm) – an individual's privacy as such is not a protected right. This is not surprising, considering the classical liberal view that the law is meant to create the freedom to arrange one's life in a particular way. After all, this is negative freedom from interference by others.[81] Indeed, although the right to privacy now forms part of both the European Convention on Human Rights and the Dutch Constitution, the protection of privacy by substantive criminal law is still insignificant. For example, the penalisation of stalking did not arise until Members of Parliament

[78] H.J. Smidt, *op. cit.* n 48, vol. II, 5, 7.

[79] See for example, J.C.J. Boutellier, *Solidariteit en slachtofferschap* (Nijmegen: Sun, 1993). Boutellier argues that since the removal of the traditional religious and socio-political barriers in the Netherlands criminal law needed a new legitimacy, which has been found in the (metaphorical) victim.

[80] C.H. Brants, *Over levende gedachten* (Deventer: Gouda Quint, 1999) 11.

[81] Isaiah Berlin, "Two Concepts of Liberty" in *Four Essays on Liberty* (Oxford: OUP, 1969).

introduced a private Bill in 1997, because the Minister of Justice had refused to do so.[82] Nevertheless, many public order offences in the Criminal Code in fact also affect the privacy of individuals: defamation and discrimination (Articles 137c–137g and 429quater Criminal Code, effective since 1992),[83] trespass (Article 138 Criminal Code) and wiretapping and the appropriation of computer data (Article 139a *et seq* Criminal Code). Other offences such as theft (Articles 310–16 Criminal Code), which protect a particular individual right that in essence concerns property rights, in practice also affect the privacy of the victims. Offences that, according to nineteenth century thinking, affect both the public interest and the interests of individuals (e.g. public indecency, rape and indecent assault),[84] are laid down in a separate section of the Criminal Code. An exception however, was made for the offences against life. Although the State Commission was of the opinion that the penalisation of these offences aims primarily at protecting social order and not the victim, they are counted among the offences concerning the rights of individuals.[85]

It is worth noting that, proceeding from the notion that the foetus has its own development, abortion was made a criminal offence, although even in 1878 the *Raad van State*[86] stressed the fact that this penalisation encroaches deeply on a woman's private life.[87] However, penalisation was hardly effective, since the offence was defined as an offence against life. The Dutch Supreme Court not only required proof that the foetus was alive, but also that the abortionist's intent was aimed at destruction of that life.[88] Therefore, in 1911, a new moral offence was introduced: treating a woman in the knowledge that the treatment could interrupt her pregnancy (Article 251bis Criminal Code). To put the practices of abortionists down, money was made an aggravating circumstance. In 1984, the Termination of Pregnancy Act came into force, which moved abortion to a separate title in the Criminal Code, between the offences concerning life and those concerning bodily harm (Article 296 Criminal Code).[89] Furthermore, the content of Article 251bis was transferred to Article 296 Criminal Code. However, under the Termination of Pregnancy Act and its subsequent order in council, abortion carried out by a physician in a licensed hospital is no longer a criminal offence.

[82] TK 1997–1998, 25 768, nrs. 1–3.

[83] The combination of a figure and a letter indicates that the offence at issue concerns a later addition to the Criminal Code.

[84] H.J. Smidt, *op. cit.* n 48, vol. II, 7.

[85] Staatscommissie voor de zamenstelling van een Wetboek van Strafregt "1870–1876" (Tilburg: Katholieke Hogeschool, 1976) Notulen I, 296 et seq.

[86] The *Raad van State* (Council of State) is the highest independent advisory body to the government. Every Bill is first sent to the *Raad van State* for a recommendation. The *Raad van State* particularly looks at the legal aspects of the Bill. The Government regularly amends Bills on the *Raad van State*'s advice, though it is not obliged to do so.

[87] H.J. Smidt, *op. cit.* n 48, vol. II 444.

[88] For example, HR 24 May 1897, W 6978; HR 29 July 1907, W 8580.

[89] Termination of Pregnancy Act of 1 May 1981, Stb. 257 (into force 1 November 1984).

Although – as here demonstrated by the case of abortion – notions of privacy and private life actually played a part in the parliamentary discussions, there was no clear concept of "privacy" or of any distinction between the "private" and the "public". The members of the State Commission not only refused to formulate a specific criterion to indicate the difference between civil and criminal injustice (see section 3), they were obviously also of the opinion that the meaning of the word "public" differs according to the definition of the offence in which it is used.[90] The members were opposed to the definition "public is everything that is not private", which they had found in Saxon law.[91] It would seem, however, that – for want of anything better – this definition was nevertheless decisive in the end.

In any event, sexuality was in principle regarded as a private matter. After all, the basic assumption was that criminal law should not be concerned with the protection of individuals against voluntary moral corruption. Only when violence was used, defenceless victims like children were concerned or immorality was forced upon others (public indecency) was penalisation considered. Offences like keeping a brothel and homosexual intercourse with a minor[92] date from a later period (1911), when religious parties in Parliament formed a majority and moral corruption was seen as a state matter. The moral offences title,[93] however, contained one striking exception to the principle that the state should not moralise. The offence of adultery,[94] not present in the government Bill, was added before the enactment of the Code. The reason was that all sides, including the Second Chamber, insisted so strongly that Minister of Justice Modderman eventually gave in, out of consideration for national opinion and for the sake of the persuasiveness of the Criminal Code. It is to be noted that he did not wish to make a distinction between men and women, as in French law, his opinion being that the woman could introduce a stranger into the family and "supply superfluous sisters and brothers"; the man for his part could expose his wife and her future children to diseases.[95]

To protect the privacy of victims, the prosecution of some offences is attached to the condition that a complaint has been lodged. This is, for example, the case with the offence of abduction of a bride (Article 281 Criminal Code). In this case, conviction only takes place after the contracted marriage has been annulled.[96] Even when no marriage has taken place, prosecution and the subsequent public investigation can be so painful and harmful for the aggrieved that

[90] Staatscommissie voor de zamenstelling van een Wetboek van Strafregt "1870–1876" (Tilburg: Katholieke Hogeschool, 1976) Notulen II, 173.

[91] Staatscommissie voor de zamenstelling van een Wetboek van Strafregt *op. cit.* Notulen I, 138.

[92] Both offences have meanwhile been abolished.

[93] The moral offences title not only comprises offences concerning sexuality, but also offences concerning morality in general. Examples are the intentional administering of intoxicating drinks (Article 252 Criminal Code) and giving up one's children for begging (Article 253 Criminal Code).

[94] Abolished in 1971.

[95] H.J. Smidt, *op. cit.* n 48, vol. II at 286.

[96] *Ibid.*, 414–15.

the interest of public order in prosecution is easily overridden by the interest of the aggrieved in non-prosecution.

Honour was seen as the highest value and is therefore given a prominent place in the statutory arrangement of protected rights.[97] Deliberately injuring someone's (sense of) honour and endangering it by indiscretion were seen as obvious hindrances to the development of one's liberty. Correspondingly, the series of offences against persons starts with defamation (slander, insult) and violation of secrecy. In the title of defamation, intentionally lodging a false complaint or making a false accusation is a criminal offence. The intention to injure the honour or reputation of a particular person, not the wish to mislead the authorities, is the focus here. Leading principles are (a) no assault without the intent to assault, (b) no slander without evidence of the falsity of the charge and (c) no investigation into truth or falsehood than in cases regulated by law.[98] Without the third principle, the honour of individuals, the peace of families and public decency would be violated, so said the explanatory memorandum. The offender cannot be permitted to subject private acts, the intimate life of the person he has offended against to a public investigation, a public debate and a judicial verdict. With the exception of defamation concerning a public servant during or in connection with the lawful execution of his duties, prosecution is therefore only allowed in case of complaint.

5. CONCLUSIONS ON MODERN DEVELOPMENTS IN THE NETHERLANDS

This chapter has shown that, although the European Convention on Human Rights was still a long way off, in a very simplified form (the right to) privacy did play a part in discussions during the compiling of the Dutch 1886 Criminal Code, if only because couched in terms of the dominant liberalism and moderate views on criminalisation that were the norm at that time. The nineteenth century legislator, although unfamiliar with the concept of a right to privacy, was nevertheless a great believer in the citizen's need to be let alone. The 1886 Criminal Code, at least in its original form, is far from moralistic. In the main, it guarantees negative freedoms. Under the influence of Enlightenment, the individual rights that the Code protects are honour, personal liberty, life and body, and property and above all the right to be free from interference with them by the state.

Although the notion of criminal law as a last resort has been overtaken by modern developments, even today the Criminal Code remains, in essence, a product of the late nineteenth century. Of course, it has been repeatedly adapted to changing circumstances and ideas and numerous penalty clauses have been added. However, the emphasis is still on economic interests, at least those

[97] *Ibid.*, 7.
[98] *Ibid.*, 366.

interests valuable in terms of money. At the time of the Criminal Code's compilation, the major economic resources were agriculture and trade and both are still expressly protected in the Criminal Code. Theft of crops, often of little value, is still a criminal offence, with theft of cattle in the field an aggravating circumstance. Fertile land and planted crops are protected against the appetite or destructiveness of poultry and cattle. Honest trading is stimulated by numerous provisions on fraud and deceit. Means of long-distance transport (waterways, train), on which the nineteenth century economy was chiefly dependent, are protected as well as traffic by land.[99] To these are now added aviation offences, computer offences etc.

The idea that protection of negative freedom suffices has also been overtaken by modern developments. In the beginning of the twentieth century, the rise of social sciences coincided with the development of the Modern School of criminal law. It drew attention to the person of the perpetrator, and influences on criminal behaviour that transcend a person's own free will, to which the citizen is subjected in his actions and which require interventions or measures that are justified by virtue of their expediency. Consequently, some adaptations to the Criminal Code have been introduced that are more directed towards intervention and protection than towards punishment (e.g. hospital order for psychopaths).

The 1886 Criminal Code's underlying assumptions, however, remained unimpaired. Legal theory still has it that criminal law is the last resort. This is remarkable, if only for the fact that classical liberal thinking is now virtually obsolete. Round the turn of the century, the political balance in Parliament shifted in favour of religious parties. But it is equally important that, from the beginning of the twentieth century onwards until the middle of the 1960s, the social and political arrangement which is peculiar to the Netherlands and is known as "pillarisation", deeply influenced a continued "tolerant" approach to crime and criminal law. Pillarisation implies a vertical stratification of society according to religious and secular beliefs. There is some disagreement as to how many pillars there actually were, but in general it is accepted that there has always been a Catholic, a Protestant, a liberal and a socialist pillar and that the groups with religious affiliations were always strongly represented. In itself, despite an apparent live and let live ideology, pillarisation carries the risk of political instability, while it by no means replaces horizontal, class-based social stratification. For this reason, the elite at the top of each pillar, all with an equal stake in the status quo, were much concerned to reach a degree of compromise and to accommodate each other's ideas and pacify any dissent at a lower level. Such politics of accommodation and pacification in themselves require a degree of at least overt tolerance and tacit agreement on non-intervention in matters of ideology where opinions may diverge widely.[100] They also require a good

[99] A.G. Bosch, *op. cit.* n 38 at 29.

[100] A. Lijphart, *Verzuiling, pacificatie en kentering in de Nederlandse politiek* (Amsterdam: De Bussy, 5th edn 1984).

measure of (subtly enforced) confidence in the ability of a (coalition) government to act in the interests of the people as a whole.

This is, to no mean degree, one of the reasons why the notion of criminal law as a last resort has survived. It is supported by the development of the accompanying Dutch system of regulated tolerance. The current 1926 Code of Criminal Procedure starts from the principle of discretionary powers, which are stipulated in Articles 167 and 242. According to Article 167 CCP, the public prosecutor may decide not to proceed with prosecution "for reasons of public interest". A public prosecutor must use this power if he fears that a conviction is unlikely, for example because of inadequate evidence. This is called a technical waiver. However, in the Netherlands a practice has developed in which prosecutions that would certainly have succeeded are nevertheless waived for considerations of policy (policy waivers). These policy waivers are extremely important in the Dutch criminal justice system. While they may be seen to reflect the consideration that criminal law should always be used as a last resort, they are also used for ideological and political reasons, namely that non-intervention prevents social and political conflict in (moral) matters on which society has failed to reach a consensus, and for the more pragmatic reason of preventing the courts from becoming overloaded.[101]

During the second half of the 1960s, religion and secular ideology in the Netherlands began to lose ground as a basis for coherent social arrangements. The attendant de-pillarisation however, did not mean the end of tolerant criminal policies. As critical criminology and legal theory gained ground during the 1970s, the idea of criminal law as a last resort and policies of non-prosecution, formed the basis for new approaches to crime and alternative means of conflict-solving. In politics too, tolerance and accommodation remained the rule, if only because, as yet, no one party has ever managed to gain sufficient majority to govern.

Things began to change from the 1980s onwards, which heralded an era of harsher pragmatisation. A few examples of legislation – with, as forerunner, the introduction of the criminal liability of legal persons in 1976 – are the competence to impose imprisonment combined with a fine (1983) and the penalisation of preparatory acts (1994). There was also a considerable shift in some areas – notably traffic law – from criminal to administrative procedures and sanctions. At the same time, important constitutive concepts long regarded as achievements of the constitutional state (*Rechtstaat*) – such as strict compliance with written procedural rules for the legal protection of suspects and defendants in criminal cases – were more or less relegated to the status of mere technicalities.[102]

Within the framework of this chapter, a highly important change during this period concerns attitudes towards the victim as a legitimate concern of criminal justice. The Dutch criminal justice system is an inquisitorial system and as such

[101] See, for example, Chrisje Brants and Stewart Field, "Discretion and Accountability in Prosecution: A Comparative Perspective on Keeping Crime out of Court" in Phil Fennell et al. (eds), *Criminal Justice in Europe. A Comparative Study* (Oxford: Clarendon Press, 1995) 127.

[102] Law of 20 September 1995, Stb. 1995, 441.

the victim of a crime plays no part in criminal proceedings. As Jörg, Field and Brants explain, the usual way of describing an inquisitorial system implies an investigation of an event with a view to establishing the truth. The state is doubly present in the "fact-collecting" prosecutor on the one hand and, on the other, the impartial and independent judge actively involved in truth-finding.[103] Dutch prosecutors see themselves as magistrates and the public prosecution service is regarded as part of the judiciary.[104] Their professional role is impartial, their concern is the "public interest", with an eye not only for the interests of the victim, being a part of the community as a whole, but also for those of the offender. Nevertheless, during the last decade in particular, victims seem to have extricated themselves from the common denominator of "the public interest". In fact, they have achieved a much better position in the criminal justice system, and that not only in their position as aggrieved party (with a claim to compensation).[105] For example: although the Netherlands has no system of private prosecution, victims have always had a right of complaint to the Appeal Court about decisions of non-prosecution by the prosecutor (Article 12 CCP) – albeit this a procedure is seldom used. In 1996, the Dutch Supreme Court decided in a case of a fatal traffic accident in which surviving relatives complained about the prosecutor's decision to prosecute under culpable homicide instead of manslaughter, that the Appeal Court not only has the competence to assess decisions of non-prosecution, but also, in cases of prosecution, to evaluate whether the penal offence of which the defendant is accused, is the most appropriate.[106] As a result of this judgment, victims are now able to exercise more influence, at least indirectly, on prosecutorial decisions.

Despite the improved status of victims in criminal procedure, until recently, the victim was not usually the main issue in discussions on adaptations of substantive law. While penal provisions were seen as protecting the public interest, offences were seen as legal abstractions, i.e. infringements of the legal order in general. This left no scope for separate individual interests, which were seen as having been absorbed by the public interest. Very exceptionally, in the introduction of penal provisions against (wire)tapping (1971) and in the penalisation of rape within the marriage (1991), the basic assumption was the protection of privacy in relations between individual citizens. In the last decade however, the perception of the criminal offence itself seems to have been changed and to have become, first and foremost, an infringement of the victim's personal rights.[107]

[103] Nico Jörg, Stewart Field and Chrisje Brants, "Are inquisitorial and adversarial systems converging?" in Phil Fennell et al. (eds), *Criminal Justice in Europe. A Comparative Study* (Oxford: Clarendon Press, 1995) 41.

[104] Chrisje Brants and Stewart Field, *op. cit.* n 101.

[105] Law of 23 December 1992, Stb. 1993, 29.

[106] HR 25 June 1996, NJ 1996, 714. The indictment in criminal cases must include information about the fact and about the offence, including the penal provision (Article 261 CCP). Article 350 CCP states that the judge has to decide the case "on the basis of" the indictment, which in fact means that he is literally bound to the charge.

[107] M.S. Groenhuijsen, "Het juridisch tekort in het strafrecht" *NJB* 1996, 1527–37.

Although social tension is ever inherent in criminal offences and prosecution, since the protection of one person's freedom is always attended by restrictions on another's, this new development presents us with questions that, at least on the face of it, may lead to insoluble problems. For example, as the law stands, violence against women in the private sphere falls under the general offence of assault.[108] Some argue however that the special circumstances of this offence require a separate title within the Criminal Code.[109] Feminist writers attribute inadequate legal protection of the private sphere to the fact that the social contract, which forms the theoretical basis of classical criminal law, did not include women.[110] Another example is stalking: the Act making this a serious offence is effective since July 2000. It could be argued that both problems would be better solved through deterrent intervention and protection rather than through punishment. What is more, both problems are on the borderline of civil and criminal injustice, and we may well ask whether civil action in these cases is not preferable. Meanwhile, however, reliance on criminal law as a means of "solving" social problems seems to increase by the year.

How must we deal with questions like these? The 1886 Criminal Code is a paragon of austerity and pragmatism. Consequently, definitions of offences are straightforward and motives behind the crime are rarely relevant, except at the sentencing stage. That goes for violence against women, but also for many other offences. Stalking of the worst kind, for example, can already be prosecuted under the existent offences of threat, attempted murder, trespass, theft etc., and we must ask ourselves whether criminalisation of annoying behaviour as such fits within retributive justice. There is a risk that, in these cases, criminal law will be used to protect and to intervene rather than to punish. Furthermore, by bowing to the (understandable) desire for recognition, we run the risk that all kinds of interest groups will wish to propose or alter offences. In the end, coercive measures could be based increasingly on the pursuit of individual interests. This scenario is not simply hypothetical, for the rise of a multiform society and the fragmented interests of its members are not easily reconciled with the one-dimensional citizen who underlies the 1886 Criminal Code. Besides, a certain moral revival in criminal justice is taking place and, as morality is redefined, victims clamour for recognition. Some recent cases of what has come to be defined (to a great extent as a result of media coverage) as "senseless violence" have, for example, caused public commotion, the more so because onlookers did not intervene or were themselves assaulted when they did. As a result, Members of Parliament have submitted a Bill to aggravate the penalty attached to grievous bodily harm in cases where violence is a reaction to the action of a person "who fulfils his civic duty by trying to call someone to order".[111] Considering that the

[108] Assault against a wedded wife is, however, an aggravating circumstance.

[109] K.D. Lünnemann, *Vrouwenmishandeling strafrechtelijk afgedaan?* (Deventer: Gouda Quint, 1996).

[110] H. Slotboom, "Veilig in de armen van de Staat?" (1994) *Nemesis* 62–74.

[111] TK 1998–1999, 26 295, nrs. 1–3.

existing provisions for such cases are quite adequate, the proposed offence is probably no more than a purely political statement, but for all that the writing on the wall is clear.

Such examples indicate that classical liberal views on criminal law no longer suffice. Positive freedom is now also recognised within criminal law. Increasingly, it is also becoming a means of social engineering: the Bill on "senseless violence" for example, is probably as much an attempt to promote "good citizenship"and solidarity in a fragmenting society as it is a crackdown on violent behaviour. On the other hand, the rejection of stalking laws by the Minister of Justice reveals a still liberal attitude. The Raad van State's advice to move the proposed provision from the title concerning bodily harm to the title concerning personal liberty, makes it quite clear that the initiators themselves were unclear as to the nature of the offence. The criminalisation of annoying behaviour, but in such vague terms that one may well ask whether it infringes the principle of legality, apparently does not fit in with the Code's structure either.

These examples eventually lead to such questions as: must we throw liberal notions overboard and exchange our retributive justice system for a restorative justice system? There is no simple answer, certainly as debates on these topics and the related questions are in full swing in Dutch legal literature. It may not be a matter of choice at all, but a reform along gradual lines; at some point in time we may simply have to accept the fact that we have left retributive justice behind. For what it is worth, I myself (being keen on my privacy and autonomy) am ambivalent at best and I find little comfort in the idea that even postmodernist writers place their ideas within the general concepts of a liberal, democratic and constitutional state.[112] All the same, under the influence of postmodernism, the group of people that see the criminal justice system as deriving its legitimacy particularly from the protection of the victim seems to be growing. I realise that this is not the place to enter into argument with them. I would therefore merely say that opponents of post-modern ideas on the legitimacy of criminal law would argue that there is no need for different concepts, since standing up for the victim is inherent in law enforcement.[113] But even then I have fear that an over-protective state will let itself in for concerns beyond national interest. After all, even within the bounds of liberal concepts there is room for major changes. And I must stress that taking away conflict (solution) from the individual by making it a criminal offence, sits ill with the idea of the individual as an autonomous person.

It should be remembered that the idea of criminal law as a last resort does not mean that criminal law is a repository for hard cases for which other fields of law are not adequate. It means that criminal law must only deal with the most

[112] For example, J.C.J. Boutellier, *op. cit.* n 79 at 202 et seq.

[113] A.C. 't Hart, "Straf, recht en waarden", in: M. Moerings (ed.), *Hoe punitief is Nederland?* (Arnhem: Gouda Quint, 1994).

serious cases ("peaks of injustice").[114] Dissatisfaction with and complaints about the cost and duration of proceedings and enforcement of a court order in civil cases, must therefore lead to alterations in civil law and not to a shift from civil law to criminal law. On the contrary, as the most drastic form of intervention, criminal law cannot be regarded as merely one of the available alternatives. The requirement of Article 8, para. 2 of the European Convention on Human Rights, that interference by a public authority must be in accordance with the law and necessary in a democratic society, presupposes proportionate use of the criminal law, which, in my opinion, precludes protection and intervention as primary objectives of criminal justice. However, I must admit that this is a doctrinal point and even I am not sure whether it will be possible to stand by this opinion in the long run, considering recent changes in society. The fact that both the Bill on stalking and the Bill on senseless violence as an aggravating circumstance have been submitted on the initiative of MPs for example, seems some indication of changing social attitudes to the administration of justice and of a loss of confidence in the criminal justice authorities to ensure that justice is done.

This coincides with the fact that regulated tolerance, for long one of the most striking characteristics of the Dutch criminal justice system, is currently under great pressure. In 1998, for example, suspicions as to the existence of a widespread network of dealers in what is called "baby-porn" were rife. NRC Handelsblad, of old a liberal and influential quality newspaper, violently criticised the traditional approach to criminal justice. Regulated tolerance, it said, for decades an important feature of our overpopulated and strongly divided country, no longer suffices in an era in which the world has become smaller.[115] In relation to other topics too, the legitimacy of criminal justice has been called into doubt, for example, as to whether or not in individual cases the punishment fits the crime. Nevertheless, in comparison with many other Western countries, the Netherlands in general is still tolerant of crime. However, there is always the risk that tolerance will deteriorate into indifference. Seen from that perspective, the aforementioned moral revival is perhaps to be applauded. Anyway, classical liberal views are still so tied up with Dutch criminal law that a fundamental change is most unlikely in the short term.[116] Nevertheless, a stormy future may be forecast, if only because the political unification of Europe has led to ever more criminal law being introduced at a European level. The accompanying political decision-process and inherent compromise could, in the long run, be the definite end to the Dutch idea that criminal law should be only a last resort, a notion which underlay nineteenth century criminal law and has so greatly influenced Dutch attitudes to problems of criminal justice ever since.

[114] D. Hazewinkel-Suringa, J. Remmelink, *Inleiding tot de studie van het Nederlandse strafrecht* (Arnhem: Gouda Quint, 14th edn 1995) 10.

[115] "Porno in de Polder" (NRC Handelsblad, 21 July 1998).

[116] A.W.M. Mooij, "Postmodernisme en gemeenschapsdenken in het strafrecht" in M. Moerings, C.M. Pelser, C.H. Brants (eds), *Morele kwesties in het strafrecht* (Deventer: Gouda Quint, 1999).

9

Consent in Dutch Criminal Law

CONSTANTIJN KELK

1. BASIC ESSENTIALS OF DUTCH CRIMINAL LAW

DUTCH CRIMINAL LAW, as formulated in the Criminal Code of 1886 and other laws, was predominantly conceived according to the principles of the so-called Classical School of criminal law and founded upon the ideas of Beccaria.[1] In keeping with most other continental-European philosophers of the age of Enlightenment, Beccaria called forth a picture of political society in which free citizens – by virtue of a *contrat social* – surrender part of their freedom to a central legislative power, which then exercises the cumulated freedom of all in the name of the sovereign will of the people and on behalf of the public interest. This implies, in particular, protection of the citizen's residual freedom from infringement by fellow citizens, who thus would abuse their own (residual) freedom and must be prevented from doing so. The legislative power has tangible instruments at its disposal, namely criminal law and penal sanctions, but that power is limited by the logic of the requirements of the public interest: not only must punishment be commensurate with the severity of the offence, the individual must know beforehand which infringements upon the freedom of others are forbidden – after all, his own freedom is of essential importance too.

This is the basic value pattern of the Classical School of criminal law, and it implies many things: clearly formulated descriptions of offences in a written Criminal Code (the principle of legality); penal sanctions that are proportionate to the offence; a concept of man as an individual whose behaviour is a matter of choice, governed by his own free will; and as a consequence, individual responsibility and culpability if such behaviour constitutes an offence under criminal law. In essence, these principles still form the core of the doctrine of Dutch criminal law, although there have been many changes in the course of time. In part, these were due to the influence of the so-called Modern School, an international movement which approached the perpetrator from the perspective of behavioural science, and was also more sensitive to the protection of society from individuals viewed as constituting a danger, than to principles of legal certainty.

[1] Cesare Beccaria, *Dei delliti e delle pene* (On crimes and punishment) (Milano: 1764).

In essence, the classical idea of austere and simple law has been preserved in the Netherlands.[2] Descriptions of offences are as brief as possible and rarely differentiate as to motive (Dutch law does not, for example, recognise the *crime passionel* as a separate offence) and wherever possible there is only one legal provision for each offence. Any honourable motive can either be put forward as a defence of justification or addressed in sentencing. The margins within which punishment is stipulated are wide, ranging from general (and extremely low) minima set by law to specific maxima for certain offences. There is indeed a reluctance even to use the criminal law, which is regarded as *ultimum remedium* – the last resort. This is specifically the case with regard to offences against public decency. Beccaria also cautioned against excessive criminalisation, particularly with respect to "indifferent acts that in themselves are neither good nor evil", for this would simply lead to "crimes of a new sort", which would serve no useful purpose.

There is still much in Dutch criminal law that preserves the classical notion of striking a balance between two aspects of the public interest: the protection of individuals from other individuals for the good of themselves and society at large and the greatest possible freedom for the greatest possible number of people. To this end, the functionaries of the criminal justice system are endowed with wide-ranging powers of discretion. The public prosecutor may refrain from prosecution of any offence on the basis of the public interest, while the courts may base their sentence anywhere between the general minimum and specific maximum, after taking into consideration not only the objective severity of the offence, but also the individual circumstances of the offender – a distribution of discretionary powers that reflects considerable trust in the official representatives of the criminal justice system. The acknowledgement of ample freedom for the individual is evident from the way in which such discretionary powers are used and from the considerations that underlie the non-prosecution of offences (either individually or as a matter of policy extending to different categories of law-breaking),[3] lenient sentencing or the acceptance of the defence of justification. There is also a wide range of acts that are not punishable by law, such as attempting suicide, escaping from prison,[4] homosexual acts between consenting adults etc.

In many cases, although an act may seem to constitute an offence under the law, whether it actually is and/or will be prosecuted as such will depend on the relationship between the perpetrator and the victim within the context of their behaviour. For it is the latter that will determine to what extent such behaviour

[2] For a description of the deliberations that led to the Criminal Code of 1886, its basic assumptions and the way in which they still affect Dutch criminal justice today see Pelser, *supra* 181.

[3] See for a discussion of the policy of non-prosecution: C.H. Brants and S.A. Field, "Discretion and Accountability in Prosecution: A Comparative Perspective on Keeping Crime out of Court" in Phil Fennell *et al.* (eds), *Criminal Justice in Europe. A Comparative Study* (Oxford: Clarendon Press, 1995) 127–49.

[4] Quite apart from this the fact remains that assisting the suicide of another person or assisting another to escape from prison are criminal offences, for they promote undesirable results.

should be viewed as constituting a framework within which participants are exercising their right to be autonomous individuals with a claim to privacy. And privacy, it should be noted, is most usually defined in Dutch criminal law as the right to be one's own, uninhibited self – uninhibited that is by interference from others and most especially the state. Lack of inhibition on the part of one individual or group could of course cause offence or (physical or psychological) harm to others. It is for this reason that informed consent on the part of the putative victim plays an important part in Dutch criminal law. Indeed, the combination of autonomy and privacy rights, consent and free will, determines whether the participants can be defined as perpetrator and victim in any sense relevant to the criminal law, for consent implies that both have engaged in behaviour or entered into a situation as autonomous individuals and of their own free will and therefore need fear no interference.

However, there is a problem here in that criminal law does not primarily regulate relationships between individuals but is, also in the light of Beccarian theory, concerned with the relationship between the individual and society as a whole. And society has a stake in those matters that could be defined as matters of public interest because they are harmful and/or offensive – to individuals or to society as a whole. As we shall see when we turn to the areas where consent is relevant in Dutch law, in some cases the rights of the individual take precedence in law over the public interest in the sense that the written law itself either contains no provision criminalising certain behaviour, or specifically exempts acts that would otherwise constitute criminal offences, if the "victim" has consented or can be deemed to have done so. These, however, are the minority. In most cases in which the doctrinal concept of consent plays a part, the act itself is defined as criminal behaviour, but that definition depends on interpretation of the relevant provision in the criminal code or has been modified over the years in case law. If interpretations or case law leave room for doubt in specific instances, whether or not such behaviour will be prosecuted depends on the assessment by the public prosecutor of the circumstances and of the relative individual and public interests involved. What such interests are, however, is also a matter of definition, and this too has changed over the years. The doctrine and practice of Dutch criminal law is perhaps as much to be noted for its continued adherence to its roots in classical theory, as for its ability to cope with social change and with social perceptions of what constitutes the public interest.

2. FIELDS OF CRIMINAL LAW WHERE CONSENT IS RELEVANT

There are different concepts of consent in relation to the question of whether an act constitutes a criminal offence: it may be explicitly required, it may be deemed to have been given if the person concerned did not explicitly withhold it, or it may be implicit in the circumstances of the act. Under Dutch criminal law, consent is relevant especially in the following areas: offences where prosecution is dependent on an official complaint to the public prosecutor; pornography and matters of public decency; sexual acts under duress or involving violence; voluntary submission to violence in general; conduct of the medical profession in general; euthanasia (including assisted suicide) in particular.[5]

In all of these fields, consent by the person who would otherwise be regarded as the victim, may mean that the act is either not a criminal offence, or that the perpetrator cannot or will not be subjected to prosecution. However, it will be clear from the following observations that it is certainly not unrestrictedly true in Dutch criminal law that *volenti non fit iniuria*. All depends on the circumstances and, when seen from a long-term perspective, on changing social definitions of harm and public interest.

a. Offences only prosecuted if a complaint is filed

In 1886 the category of offences for which a complaint was made a necessary condition of prosecution was made wider (i.e. for the prosecution of libel, slander and adultery, although in this day and age adultery no longer constitutes a criminal offence).[6] A complaint filed by the "injured party" is still required in the event of certain crimes, and these fall into two categories There is one group of offences (absolute offences) where a complaint is invariably required and another (relative offences) which can only be prosecuted if a certain relationship (blood or marriage ties) exists between the perpetrator and the injured party.[7]

A complaint is invariably required for: seduction of minors;[8] several other sexual offences (abuse of minors aged twelve to sixteen);[9] gross insult;[10] breach of confidence;[11] abduction;[12] coercion with threat of defamation;[13] extortion or blackmail.[14] The relative offences prosecuted upon complaint include most property offences such as theft, extortion, embezzlement, fraud and vandalism, where a complaint is required if the crime involves a perpetrator and an injured party who are separated, divorced or related to each other. If the offences involve parties who are married to each other, they are excluded from prosecution altogether.[15]

[5] I am leaving aside two issues: the question of consent in sporting activities where injuries may be incurred and the doctrinal question of "necessary consent" – a person other than the perpetrator necessarily contributes to a criminal act, but is not necessarily a criminal participant. It is, for example, not possible to commit bigamy unless there is a new spouse.

[6] The offence of adultery disappeared from Dutch criminal law in 1971.

[7] Title VII, Book I Criminal Code, referring to *absolute en relatieve klachtdelicten*.

[8] Article 248, Criminal Code.

[9] Articles 245 and 147 Criminal Code.

[10] Article 269, Criminal Code.

[11] Article 272, Criminal Code.

[12] Article 281, Criminal Code.

[13] Article 284, Subsection 1, 2, Criminal Code.

[14] Article 318, Criminal Code.

[15] Article 316(1), Criminal Code.

The significance of consent here is twofold, depending on the circumstances. On the one hand, the existence of offences prosecuted upon complaint only assumes, absent a complaint, that it is more in the interest of the injured party or victim to have his or her privacy respected (and his or her dirty linen not washed in public), than in it is to have the perpetrator prosecuted. This is the only way in which citizens can exert direct influence on the decision whether or not to prosecute and where privacy rights of the individual, who, by virtue of a complaint, is consenting to prosecution, override the public interest. On the other hand, the absence of a complaint could well indicate the absence of a victim, because he or she was a consenting party to the offence: there is no abduction, if the abducted person was a "willing victim", no libel if the libelled did not take offence. Indeed, in the case of a complaint by parents or guardians about sexual abuse of minors between twelve and sixteen, the prosecutor is obliged to hear the alleged victim's side of the story in order to establish whether this was indeed abuse and not consensual sex (see below). Finally, although a complaint is formally required to start a prosecution (a dispensable formality now that it is accepted in case law that a report to the police implies a complaint, so that investigation and prosecution may go ahead), there is no guarantee that prosecution will follow, for the Public Prosecutor retains the discretionary power to decide not to prosecute, even if a complaint has been filed.

b. Pornography and matters of public decency

In 1911, Dutch legislation on crimes against public decency was substantially amended to include relatively severe penalties for pornography, homosexual acts, procurement, abortion etc., criminalisations that were completely contrary to libertarian culture as it had existed in the Netherlands up until that time. The then Minister of Justice (Regout) was simply carrying out the wishes of groups representing various religious denominations, and most especially the *petit bourgeoisie*. Their influence had been considerably enlarged by constitutional expansion of the right to vote and they were much opposed to the upper classes' multifarious manifestations of indecency and licentiousness that hid behind a Victorian double morality. As the *bourgeoisie* entered the political arena in some force at the beginning of the century, so too were they able to set the political agenda on a number of issues, of which public decency was one.

The definition of what is offensive to public decency has changed radically since then, most especially in the wake of the so-called sexual revolution of the 1960s. Already in 1970, the Dutch Supreme Court had defined as offensive to public decency "that which is offensive to a majority of the Dutch public",[16] thereby taking into consideration that public sensibilities in this field had changed considerably, given, among other things, that readership of pornographic magazines

[16] HR 17 November 1970, NJ 1971, 374.

was widespread and that a government commission was at that time examining the necessity of decriminalisation. From 1978 onwards, films to be viewed solely by people above the age of eighteen who, before entering the theatre, had been informed in an unambiguous manner of the specific (and possibly indecent) nature of the film, were no longer regarded as pornographic, i.e. as "offensive to public decency".[17] The same applies to written material and illustrations. If readers had publications sent to them at their own request and could be assumed to be aware of the specific nature of those publications, these were not regarded as being offensive to public decency.[18] In 1985, the law was amended accordingly. Pornography only constitutes an offence against public decency if illustrations or objects of an offensive nature are openly exhibited or provided in a public place, or are sent to people who have not requested them. In addition, it is a criminal offence to provide anyone under the age of sixteen with offensive illustrations or objects which can be viewed as harmful to people under the age of sixteen. It is also an offence to produce for distribution or public exhibition or to distribute or openly exhibit illustrations of sexual acts in which someone under the age of sixteen is involved. In 1985, greater legislative restrictions were also applied to the punishable aspect of violations of public decency. This involves public places (which do not include special premises designated by the authorities for the purpose of nude recreation such as sections of public beaches), spots that are accessible to persons below the age of sixteen, and non-public places if members of the public might unwittingly find themselves there.[19]

The concept of consent in all such cases seems to imply that people who, of their own free will, put themselves in the way of pornography have robbed it of its offensive nature, for the punishable aspect of acts, illustrations and performances that are offensive to public decency is limited to unwanted confrontations with material that is offensive to a majority of the Dutch public.[20] We are therefore looking at informed consent as an expression of being one's own uninhibited self, free to enjoy one's own sexuality in whichever way seems appropriate, without outside interference. At the same time, however, youngsters below the age of sixteen are protected from any form of confrontation. It is unlikely that this reflects a notion that those under sixteen are incapable of making informed choices and indeed, when the law was changed explicit reference was made to the importance of not exposing young people to immorality. Here, the protection of the young as a matter of public interest overrides privacy and autonomy rights of young people themselves

The issue of protection of children and young people arises in another way too. Following a number of highly publicised cases in which pornography was linked to child abuse (see below) and considerable international pressure was

[17] HR 28 November 1978, NJ 1985, 93.

[18] HR 30 October 1984, NJ 1985, 293.

[19] Article 239, Criminal Code.

[20] And see the argument that persons depraved and corrupted cannot further be depraved and corrupted: this argument was rejected in England and Wales in *DPP* v. *Whyte* [1972] AC 849.

put on the Dutch Government to tighten up its pornography laws, there has been a move towards criminalisation of what is sometimes known as child pornography. The possession (for one's own pleasure) of pornographic pictures of persons under sixteen has been made a serious criminal offence and many a photo or painting at an art exhibition has been confiscated by the public prosecution service, because its offensive nature was deemed to exceed its artistic value.[21] At the same time, young people are protected against exploitation by penalising producers of and traders in pornography, and recently this has been extended to include anyone in possession of pictures of sexual acts involving persons under sixteen. While the protection of minors from abuse and exploitation overrides the significance of consent in pornographic production and trade, this is not logically the case in mere possession for personal gratification. The official reasoning seems to be that targetting the market will hurt the trade (cf. receiving stolen goods), although changing attiitudes towards paedophilia[22] seem to indicate that increasingly the mere "aberration" of wanting to look at child pornography is reason enough for criminalisation. Moreover, the law as it now stands could include intimate family photos.

c. Sexual acts under duress or involving violence

Various types of situations can be classified as sexual acts under duress or involving violence. First, situations in which people are forced violently or put under pressure to engage in sexual acts, in other words against their will. Secondly, situations in which people are physically hurt for the purpose of gratifying someone else's sexual desire or for mutual sexual desire. While such acts are still defined in the Criminal Code as crimes against public decency, it is generally recognised that it is not the offence against public decency that is their determing characteristic, but coercion, violence and abuse of power. In general, such sexual acts lose their punishable aspect if they are performed with the informed consent of the parties involved. If a physician treats his own wife or girlfriend as a patient, then the sexual contact between them does not entail indecent conduct by a healthcare professional with someone entrusted to his care as a patient.[23] The legislator emphatically excluded this situation.

Interpretation problems can nonetheless arise with respect to the question of just how free people are to willingly engage in certain acts. Contact with minors can also fail to entail indecent conduct[24] if there really is freely obtained consensus. This is not automatically assumed to be the case, as for instance in the

[21] In 1999 in Amsterdam, for example, the prosecution service confiscated a photograph "Father and son" of the American photographer Walter Chapell. It was taken in 1962 by his wife and shows the naked torso of the photographer with an erection, while he is holding his two year old son in his arms. *De Volkskrant*, 6 June 1999.

[22] See Moerings, *infra* p. 245.

[23] Article 249, Subsection 2, 3, Criminal Code.

[24] Article 247, Criminal Code.

case of a twelve-year-old girl with whom a forty-year-old man had engaged in sexual contact, who stated that she had voluntarily entered into an intimate relationship with him, as was clear from their letters.[25] The judgment might well have been different if the age difference had been smaller, for the court seemed to imply that it was the age difference that made informed consent extremely unlikely. Sexual contact between two fifteen-year-olds, for instance, is not viewed as indecent conduct. If it were, parents would be free to file a complaint every time they didn't like their child's boyfriend or girlfriend.

Again, rape is only an offence if it occurs against the wishes of the person who is raped. These wishes are not always clearly stated and a refusal is not always unambiguous. If there is any lack of clarity, the judge will have to deduce consent, or lack of it, from the circumstances of the case, and, if there is any doubt, acquit the perpetrator. In 1987 the Supreme Court confirmed an acquittal for rape because it involved a relationship between a man and a woman that had repeatedly ended and started again. It was the judge's conviction that "after the lengthy relationship between the suspect and the woman, a tug of war that had been going on for years, the suspect was unable to see that the woman really did want to break off with him for good and consequently no longer wished to have sexual intercourse with him".[26]

Until 1991, rape was only punishable outside marriage, but in that year the law was amended to include rape within marriage. On the grounds of the relatively strict principle of legality, in anticipation of the amendment the court still adhered to the words of the law and rape was not assumed, even in a case where the husband and wife were no longer living together and their divorce had already been pronounced but was not yet officially registered.[27] Given the case law on the European Convention on Human Rights (ECHR), there might now be quite a different ruling. In the opinion of the Commission, the principle of legality does not preclude "adaptation to changing circumstances", if there are gradual changes that are in keeping with the essence of the offence and are reasonably foreseeable.[28] These include those on the reprehensible nature of raping one's wife. It is generally far less accepted that being married automatically implies continued consent to sexual intercourse.[29]

In the first instance, sadomasochistic sexual activities could be viewed as grievous bodily harm, or even assault and battery, but they are engaged in to arouse sexual feelings. They thus entail bodily harm for sexual purposes. The

[25] HR 24 June 1997, NJ 1997, 676.

[26] HR 16 June 1987, NJ 1988, 156.

[27] HR 9 February 1988, NJ 1988, 613

[28] *C.R.* v. *United Kingdom* [1996] 1 FLR 434; [1996] Fam Law 275 affirming *R* [1992] 1 AC 599; [1991] 4 All ER 481, given statutory effect in Criminal Justice and Public Order Act 1994 s.142, substituting a new Sexual Offences Act 1956 s.1.

[29] It is intriguing, but outside the scope of this article, why Dutch case law should have lagged behind on this one issue, when there is normally a tendency to adapt to changing public perceptions. A tentative explanation could be that Dutch courts feel free to interpret the law to the advantage of the accused – a typically "classical" attitude – but adhere more strictly to the principle of legality if deviating from it would lead to conviction.

ECHR dismissed a complaint by several British homosexuals that the UK had violated Article 8 of the ECHR. They had been condemned to serve prison sentences on the grounds of a law prohibiting violations of the physical integrity of individuals, even if said acts were committed within the framework of sadomasochistic activities with the consent of both parties. The British authorities defended the prohibition with a reference to health and morality considerations.[30] In the Dutch debate, there is no direct reference to morality. Indeed, here too privacy (being one's own uninhibited self) and autonomy (informed consent) are the guiding principles. The question remains, however, as to whether the end justifies the means, if the person who is subject to such acts has apparently consented to suffer grievous bodily harm. While the essential criminal nature of the act remains – although these are not classed as crimes against public decency but as crimes of violence so that only the "perpetrator" and not the "victim" is punishable – there is assumed to be inadequate reason for prosecution. However, the police and public prosecutor are expected to make every effort to prevent excesses, such as people being beaten unconscious.[31]

d. Voluntary submission to violence in general

People who know full well what the initiation rites will entail and nonetheless decide to join student fraternities, voluntarily submit themselves to certain forms of violence, and consent to undergo aggressive acts there, with whatever injuries might ensue. It is, however, not acceptable for these activities to lead to death, as was witnessed by the so-called "Tres Affair" in 1965, that resulted in the prosecution of senior initiation supervisors for manslaughter due to negligence. In keeping with the tradition of their prestigious fraternity, they had tied a bag filled with soot over a prospective member's head. He suffocated. In 1997, a student died of alcohol poisoning after drinking a litre of Dutch gin in the course of an initiation rite. This was viewed as an accident, but was due reason for the University of Groningen to formulate a special code for initiation rites. The public interest requires that mutilation upon request, for example for purposes of getting a disability pension or being declared unfit for military service, remains punishable as the infliction of grievous bodily harm.

g. Conduct of the medical profession

Medical treatment entails certain acts, the justification of which lies in the consent of the patient or his/her legal representatives if he/she is no longer

[30] *Laskey* v. *United Kingdom* (1997) 24 EHRR 39: see Brants, *supra*, 117.

[31] In Belgium sadomasochism is allowed, but the use of nipple clips and electric current is considered as an act offensive to public decency, although the participants have given their consent. *De Volkskrant*, 25 September 1997.

capable of consenting. In these cases, medical acts cannot be classified as harmful. Some time ago, the Medical Treatment Agreement was legally formulated in Dutch private law, stipulating that the consent of the patient is required for medical treatment.[32] If a physician provides treatment without the consent of the patient, he can conceivably be prosecuted for causing harm. The physician is obliged to respect the confidentiality of the patient, but this does not apply if the patient, by consent, releases him from that obligation.[33] Of course this consent can only be given if the patient has the legal rights the confidentiality refers to.

f. Euthanasia

A specific field where the Dutch physician holds a unique position is that of euthanasia and assisted suicide. Performing euthanasia means acting in such a way as to deliberately terminate the life of another person upon his explicit and serious request. Euthanasia is punishable in accordance with Article 293 of the Criminal Code and assisted suicide is punishable in accordance with Article 294 of the Criminal Code. The legal value that is protected by these stipulations is respect for human life as such. This is why the wish on the part of the individual does not in itself take away the criminal nature of euthanasia or assisted suicide, although compared with homicide or manslaughter it does entail a shorter maximum sentence. In principle, the law does not consider euthanasia to be a matter of concern to the physician alone, and every individual is punishable by law to the same extent. However, increased public acceptability of euthanasia under certain strict conditions has meant that the physician has gradually come to be the only person who can perform euthanasia without being punishable by law. No one else is exempt, not even nurses.[34] Euthanasia has been "medicalised" in the sense that it now falls within the practice of medicine. The enormous technological advances made in recent decades in the field of medicine have considerably lengthened the human lifespan. This in turn has led to an increasing need for euthanasia, particularly on the part of those elderly people who find themselves in a state of constant suffering that they perceive as hopeless and ultimately humiliating. This no longer refers solely to the dying stage, when an extra dose of morphine to kill the pain can also hasten death, which can be referred to as indirect euthanasia. In this case the main purpose is to combat pain, and the side effect is to expedite the termination of the patient's life; such

[32] And compare the position in the law of England and Wales, in particular on the question whether a special exemption for doctors needs to be created. See Alldridge, "Consent to Medical and Surgical Treatment – the Law Commission's Recommendations" (1996) 4 *Medical Law Review* 129–43.

[33] Article 272, Criminal Code.

[34] In March 1995, a nurse was given a two-month suspended prison sentence for giving a good friend of hers, an AIDS patient who was extremely ill, a fatal injection upon his express request and under the supervision of his physician.

treatment has gradually come to be accepted as medical care. There are however growing numbers of requests for active intervention, on the grounds of long-lasting suffering with no hope of relief. In the Netherlands there was initially much opposition to this idea, mainly among traditional Christians and adherents to a code of medical ethics focused on the idea that human life should never be terminated, not even in cases of severe suffering. However, the notion has gradually gained ground though that, in the absence of any other means of alleviation, it can be a cruel and merciless thing to continue a life of severe and long-lasting suffering. At the same time, there is growing recognition of the right of the individual to have a say about his own life.

One of the first Dutch cases of euthanasia to be prosecuted during the last twenty-five years was the *Postma* case, which resulted in a landmark court decision in 1973: a (woman) doctor, upon the express and earnest request made repeatedly by her fatally ill old mother, had administered a lethal injection of morphine. The patient was partially paralysed, incontinent, very hard of hearing, could hardly read and was suffering from a metabolic disorder. The court decided that life-shortening treatment may be justified if certain conditions are fulfilled. In this respect the court did not find it necessary that the patient had entered the terminal stage, but found that there must nevertheless be an incurable disease and unbearable or grave suffering. In addition, the patient must have expressed the will to be released from his/her suffering and the procedure must be carried out by a medical practitioner.

Norms have gradually developed in case law to which the physician must adhere in order to define a situation as an emergency, i.e. as necessity, and thus create the conditions under which he is not punishable by law. This is the case if there is long-lasting, severe suffering with no hope of relief, and if the patient has made a well-considered and long-lasting request for termination of his/her life. A subsidiary requirement is that there no longer is any less drastic way to alleviate the suffering of the patient, and the physician who performs the euthanasia must first discuss the matter with another physician who serves as consultant. These are the rules of due care and diligence in cases of euthanasia.

The Supreme Court has ruled that a justifying necessity may be said to exist if the physician cannot have been reasonably expected to ignore an urgent request to perform euthanasia, consequently ignoring his obligation to respect human life, in a situation that "in accordance with scientifically responsible medical views and in keeping with the norms of medical ethics" can be viewed as necessity.[35] Although a certain form of standardisation cannot be denied (with common medical practice playing a role of crucial importance), the code of medical conduct as such, in the judgment of the Supreme Court of The Netherlands, is not sufficient to give the physician *carte blanche*.

The idea of (arriving at) legalisation of euthanasia arose but, in a political system which embraces both Christian and liberal forces, it proved extremely

[35] HR 27 November 1984, NJ 1985, 106.

difficult to reach consensus on a subject that is so humanly sensitive and that is strongly determined by social attitudes and attitudes towards humanity. For several years parliamentary debates, hearings and proposals followed one after another, but without result. Although, in theory and entirely in keeping with its Enlightenment roots, law in the Netherlands is not found in precedent but in codes and statutes, in practice intepretations of the letter of the law by the Supreme Court to allow a Criminal Code of 1886 to meet present- day social and political requirements does set precedents. Usually, the legislator is quick to take up important changes and to follow with legislation. Not so, however, if the matter is one on which it is very difficult to establish political and social consensus. This is especially the case if moral and ethical issues that arouse strong public feelings are at stake. Then there is a tendency to unload legislative responsibility onto the shoulders of the judiciary. This is an important strategy that allows political stability to be maintained: political parties can manifestly defend the position their electorate requires of them, while all tacitly acknowledge that certain changes (must) take place. In the case of euthanasia, political opinion is strongly divided and an open confrontation over legislation could well have led to political crisis and resignation of the (coalition) government. So while the politicians argued, failed to reach any sort of consensus and periodically shelved the matter, case law on euthanasia evolved and set the standards by which infringements of Articles 293 and 294 Criminal Code were to be judged.

Criteria, comparable to those applicable to euthansia, have now come to apply to situations that can not be strictly categorised as such: the termination of the lives of handicapped newborn babies. They do not have a will of their own, although of course their parents do, and the person who performs the acts would thus have to be prosecuted for homicide. In this case, obviously a great deal of importance is attached to the statements of other experts.[36]

Furthermore it might be useful to mention another case here. A psychiatrist assisted in the suicide of a woman who was suffering from severe mental anguish after the death of both her sons and the end of her marriage. The woman had already tried to commit suicide once, but had not succeeded. The psychiatrist had a number of lengthy face-to-face sessions with her. On the grounds of these talks, he came to the conclusion that she was experiencing permanent and intolerable suffering and could not be motivated to seek treatment. He consulted six other experts about the case. The Supreme Court reversed the decision of the court that had dismissed the case, and introduced an extra requirement of due care. Since it was so difficult to determine the exact nature of the woman's suffering, this requirement stipulated that the physician should have had at least one of the six other experts see the woman in person and investigate himself whether a voluntary and deliberated decision had been made that

[36] HR 28 April, 1989 NJ 1990, 46 and 47 (Baby Ross case). See also the cases of Dr Prins and Dr Kadijk, taken to court in 1995, which were both dismissed.

was not influenced by the woman's disorder, in this case a depression without psychotic features in the framework of a complicated mourning process. The judgment in this case was that the psychiatrist was found guilty but not sentenced to any punishment.[37] The importance of this decision is that bodily suffering was equated with mental suffering albeit under very severe conditions.

Ever since 1994, a report procedure has been included in the Burial and Cremation Act obliging the physician who performs euthanasia to fill in a form with questions about the course of the illness, the well-considered and long-lasting request on the part of the patient or the reasons for the absence of such a request, and the consultations with one or more other physicians. Initially the rules were as follows. After the form was filled in, it was presented to the office of the municipal coroner.[38] The coroner performed an autopsy and reported to the public prosecutor who, based on the findings of the coroner, decided whether the requirements of due care had been met. If so, then no further examination of the report was called for and the physician was assumed to have acted in necessity, i.e. in response to *force majeure*. If not, the physician could be prosecuted by law, in which case the judge in his turn could still come to the conclusion that there was necessity and could dismiss the case.

From a comprehensive evaluation study on the practice and reporting procedure with respect to euthanasia, a report of which was published in November 1996, it was clear that only approximately 40 per cent of all the cases of euthanasia and assisted suicide were actually reported by the physicians. On the other hand, the fact that 40 per cent of the cases were reported at all and that in general doctors agreed that the report-procedure was useful, may in itself be considered a favourable development. The threat of possible prosecution was seen as one of the reasons for the relatively low response. A formalised procedure for the examination of cases by other members of the medical profession beforehand in the form of a professionalised consultation, and a review afterwards by multi-disciplinary committees rather than the criminal justice authorities, came to be seen as the better option.

This would imply even greater recognition of the rules governing the medical profession as the justification for an in itself punishable act of euthanasia. In cases in which the court felt that requirements of due care had not been met, social aspects of the case could be taken into consideration at sentencing.

These ideas resulted in an amendment to the report-procedure as from 1 November 1998. Five regional monitoring commissions have been set up, whose work is to examine the behaviour of a doctor against the criminal law, for euthanasia is still a criminal offence unless the requirements of due care can be shown to have been met. Each commission is multi-disciplinary and has three expert members from the fields of law, medicine and ethics. Each has a secretary trained in law. The procedure is as follows. The doctor who has performed

[37] HR 21 June 1994, NJ 1994, 656.

[38] This course of events is assumed to be not contrary to the *nemo tenetur* principle, see HR 11 May 1993, NJ 1994, 142.

euthanasia must tell the authorities and produce a written report. The municipal coroner, who examines the body of the deceased, checks whether the report is complete and whether the details are clear. The coroner informs the municipal authorities and the public prosecutor of the death, upon which permission for the funeral or cremation is given. The report is then sent to the regional commission.

It is the commission's job to examine the doctor's behaviour in ending a patient's life at his or her request or assisting at the patient's suicide, in accordance with the requirements of due care as these have been developed in case law. The commission may ask the doctor to explain his report more fully, or may seek more information from the coroner, the doctor who was consulted or other professionals involved. The commission reports its findings to the public prosecutor and the regional inspectorate for public health within six weeks of receiving the doctor's report. If necessary, another six weeks is allowed, of which the doctor is informed, while the commission may explain its decision to the doctor in person. This time limit of six weeks means that doctors no longer live with months or even years of uncertainty while the public prosecutor ponders the merits of the case. The chairmen of the commissions meet on a regular basis to exchange information and to attempt to establish common criteria for the whole country by which to judge cases of euthanasia performed by doctors.

The whole procedure also means that it is no longer the public prosecutor, but a multi-disciplinary commission that is first to judge whether a doctor has acted with due care and within the limits of justifiable necessity set by case law. While, in theory, the prosecutor retains full authority to prosecute or not, prosecutors follow the commissions'decisions, unless there are real reasons for doubt (in which case the doctor must be informed of this within a reasonable time). In practice therefore, only if the commission comes to the decision that the doctor has not acted with due care and asks the public prosecutor or the regional inspectorate to examine the case further, could this result in prosecution. It is explicitly not the commission's job to decide on the justification for euthanasia before it has taken place.

The idea is that this multi-disciplinary examination of cases of euthanasia will do most justice to all aspects of the actual case. It certainly seems an improvement on the old situation, in which the coroner gave the first and crucial decision. It would perhaps have been a good idea to include the nursing profession on the commissions, for, certainly in old people's nursing homes they are very close to day-to-day practice. After the first year of their existence, the commissions had decided in an overwhelming majority of cases, that doctors fell well within the limits of due care. The number of reported cases, however, did not rise significantly.

It should not be imagined that these developments imply the decriminalisation of euthanasia. Neither is this to be expected within the foreseeable future. At most, the significance of the criminal justice authorities in the investigative phase has been replaced by a more refined system. Meanwhile, the government have yet again conceived a Bill of law. It gives the commissions the last word on whether or not due care has been exercised. If they report a failure to meet established requirements, they must report this potentially criminal behaviour to the public prosecutor, who may then still decide whether or not to prosecute. So, according to this Bill, euthanasia remains a criminal offence. It will however introduce a written exception[39] for the doctor who performs euthanasia at the patient's request with due care.[40] The requirements set by case law remain of crucial importance.

John Griffiths has advocated removing the investigation of euthanasia entirely from the criminal law and situating it at a local and professional level. In his view, the doctor should report to a local commission from the institution where he works or from the local organisation of which he is a member. Cases should be discussed confidentially with the doctor concerned and a solution found if mistakes have been made or if there are differences of opinion. Only serious cases or repeated infringement of the rules should be reported to the Inspectorate of Public Health and then dealt with through disciplinary measures. The Public Prosecutor should not have access to any information. This would mean that prosecution would be impossible unless private individuals report cases to the prosecution service, and that the official report procedure would no longer be a basis for action. Indeed, Griffiths is of the opinion that euthanasia and assisted suicide should be excepted from criminal law and are matters for the medical profession alone. He bases this on legal developments in which the treatment of pain and suffering with the effect of shortening a patient's life, has come to be regarded as the exclusive domain of medical opinion.

The new euthanasia commissions stop well short of this, but we must assume that their work will have a comparable effect, certainly once the justification for euthanasia performed with due care, has been incorporated in the law. In my opinion, the policy of the commissions should be geared towards doing justice to individual cases and not towards a strictly formal application of standards of due care. The latter seems to be something that Griffiths is worried about, considering the book he has recently published.[41]

All of the above applies to euthanasia at the request of the patient and assisted suicide, but not to any other case in which there has been no request, inevitably, for example, cases involving new born babies. One single, central commission

[39] The problem with a defence of justification is that, should it come to a criminal trial, it places the burden of proof of due care on the shoulders of the doctor. Were euthanasia by doctors – i.e. euthanasia according to the standards and procedural rules developed in case law – to be decriminalised, it would fall to the public prosecutor to prove that such standards had not been met. See: C. Kelk, "Towards the Decriminalisation of Euthanasia in The Netherlands?" in M. Bulterman *et al.* (eds), *To Baehr in our Minds* (Utrecht: SIM-special, 1998) 364.

[40] Previously, a political party of the liberal left, D'66, had devised an alternative Bill, in which the doctor who performs euthanasia or assists a suicide while observing all the established requirements of due care, will no longer be committing a criminal offence.

[41] J. Griffiths, A. Bood and H. Weyers, *Euthanasia and the Law in The Netherlands* (Amsterdam: Amsterdam University Press, 1998).

has been established to deal with such cases, for which there is a certain amount of case law.

In the Dutch situation, there are no doctors who offer their services on a broad scale to those wishing to die, such as "Dr Death" in the United States who was recently sentenced to between ten and twenty-five years.[42] There are sporadic cases of euthanasia in The Netherlands, and doctors regard them as the most difficult part of their job, despite the fact that patients explicitly request, or even beg for, an end to their life.

3. CONCLUSION

In Dutch criminal law, whether or not multifarious acts are punishable by law depends on the consent of the individuals upon whom these acts are performed and/or who are the potential victims (see for example offences that are only prosecuted upon complaint). This fits in with the notion of the greatest possible freedom for every individual to which, in the spirit of Beccaria's concept, the legal system should aspire. Moreover, in the Dutch legal system in general, it is accepted that criminal law should be the *ultimum remedium*, so that restraint is called for in its application. One of the ramifications of this can be that the law may not be applied if the individual, whom the legal system aims to protect, does not wish it to be. However, public interest in protecting certain legal values may override individual wishes. Not every value protected by law is at the citizen's disposal.

Consent under Dutch law therefore requires, first and foremost, that there should be an unambiguous wish or desire, expressed in full consciousness and by someone who has adequate mental faculties and has reached adulthood. Consent is understood as informed consent. These are requirements that should be taken very seriously, particularly as regards euthanasia and assisted suicide and in cases of sexual abuse, especially involving children. The legally protected values involved here are very basic ones, i.e. human life and physical and sexual integrity, particularly of young people who have yet to reach maturity.

It is nonetheless extremely important to guard against moralising by the legal system, a caution already given in 1886 by the authors of the Dutch Criminal Code![43] According to Collins Cobuild English Language Dictionary, "to moralise" means "to discuss or consider a situation only in the ways that it relates to your own beliefs or values of what is right and wrong, and often tell other people your opinions without being asked to". There is thus the risk of the criminal law system exaggerating its protective function and protecting people in essence from their own autonomous will – or rather, preventing them from exercising it. In forcing unwanted protection upon people, the criminal law sys-

[42] *People* v. *Kevorkian* (1999) 601 N.W.2d 99 (Sup Ct Michigan).

[43] See Pelser, *supra* 181.

tem becomes dysfunctional, not only constraining the perpetrator, but also the victim. The decisive factor here is the interest of others, or even the interest of society as a whole, that would benefit from prosecution.

However, it is dangerous to be too quick in granting priority to "public interest" above consent between individuals. An important condition here is that individuals have the approval of others in their immediate vicinity for what, in the first instance, might look like inadmissible or reprehensible conduct. A good example might be the case referred to above of the forty-year-old man who was having a sexual relationship with a twelve-year-old girl. It is a generally known fact that some children mature early and can be attractive in much the same way as adults. So why should a relationship with a much older man necessarily be viewed as child abuse just because of the sizeable age difference? Why should this objective fact in itself make the relationship suspicious or even immoral? Even if the parents find it reprehensible, is that by definition a reason to prosecute the man for child abuse? The present criminal law system does work from that assumption because children under the age of sixteen are not deemed capable of fully comprehending the implications of their acts. It is true that these offences are only prosecuted upon complaint, but if the victim is between the ages of twelve and sixteen, the complaint can be filed by the legal representatives, in other words the parents. In my opinion, the criminal law system should also include exceptions for cases of this kind.

All this is in keeping with the social and cultural climate of modern times. In the past few decades, the image of man as an articulate and responsible individual has come to prevail throughout the Dutch legal system. Nowadays people come of age and are eligible to vote at eighteen. In any number of fields, their explicit consent is required in certain legal procedures, such as voluntary admission to a psychiatric hospital. If the patient objects or if consent is unclear or dubious, the only option is the involuntary admission procedure, with all of the legal guarantees it entails.

I would like to note that consent has even become relevant in Dutch criminal law in sentencing. Alternative sanctions such as community service orders can only be enforced with the consent of the perpetrator. They will otherwise be regarded as forced labour, which is prohibited under Article 4, section 2, ECHR. Even settlement out of court (transactie) by the public prosecutor, which, since 1983, is also applicable to serious offences punishable by a maximum prison sentence of six years, requires the suspect's consent. After all, by consenting the suspect has waived the right to a fair hearing before an independent court and is thus taking the risk that the court might have gone easier on his case, for example by considering extenuating circumstances.

It should be noted that as regards sexual offences, Dutch courts have been inclined towards a broad interpretation of the concept of sexual abuse. In the case of a man who threatened his wife with violence in order to force her to engage in oral and anal sex with a dog, the Supreme Court ruled that this form of sex is to be viewed as sexual abuse in the spirit of the law, since the purpose of legislation in the moral field is to protect the sexual integrity of individuals.[44] Sexual penetration in the sense of rape was also assumed in the case of a man who put and kept his tongue in another man's mouth against his will. The Supreme Court viewed this as an equally severe violation of the man's physical integrity as forced sexual intercourse.[45] Years ago, for the same reason a man who placed an object and not his penis in the vagina of a woman was ruled as having committed rape. If the violation of what the court views as sexual integrity implies broadly interpreting sexual acts as sexual abuse, then the opposite must also apply and what the individual views as the free expression of his own sexual integrity deserves equally broad interpretation.

[44] HR 20 January 1998, NJ 1998, 337.
[45] HR 21 April 1998.

10

Dangerousness, Popular Knowledge and the Criminal Law: A Case Study of the Paedophile as Sociocultural Phenomenon

RICHARD COLLIER

INTRODUCTION

THIS CHAPTER SEEKS to explore those forces which have made it possible to think, visualise and produce the concept of the "paedophile" within contemporary debates around the parameters of the criminal law, personal autonomy and the idea of the "private" sphere. The discussion which follows is based on a reading of a number of incidents which have taken place in Britain during the 1990s around the release from prison of convicted sex offenders. These are events which have been the subject of considerable controversy and public debate, prompting a series of deliberations on a central theme of this book – the use and limits of the criminal law in protecting the public from crime. Via an analysis of the press discourse and government responses to these events what follows is an attempt to capture how understandings of what paedophilia might constitute have become bound up within particular configurations of concepts of childhood, parenthood and of "safe" public/private spaces. The chapter seeks to serve as a kind of prism through which it might become possible to view the shifting relationship between the criminal law and those constructions of dangerousness[1] which, I shall argue, have underscored the emergence of the category of the paedophile within contemporary crimino-legal discourse.[2] What follows does not seek to serve as a legal, institutional history of the paedophile

[1] See further J. Pratt, *Governing the Dangerous* (Sydney: The Federation Press, 1997) 4.

[2] My use of "crimino-legal" here delineates, following A. Young, *Imagining Crime* (London: Sage, 1996), more than simply "criminology" or "criminal justice" or "criminal law" but, rather, ". . . all of these together with the popular discourses that are manifested in the media, cinema and advertising, in order to convey the sense that 'crime' has become (been made?) a potent sign which can be exchanged among criminal justice personnel, criminologists, politicians, journalists, film-makers and, importantly, (mythical) ordinary individuals". (at 2)

and paedophilia.[3] Nor does it present an overview of debates about the gendered nature of the public-private dualism more generally, issues which are well documented elsewhere.[4] It seeks, rather, to map out in a provisional way something of the way in which the circulation of discourses of dangerousness have served within the field of the popular knowledge, the press and official government responses (in the form, for example, of shifts in and amendments to criminal justice policy) to constitute the paedophile as a distinct and *gendered* (specifically, as a particular *kind* of male/masculine) social and legal subject in need of regulation, discipline and surveillance.[5] This chapter detects in the events surrounding the release of convicted sex offenders from prison what I shall argue are some revealing and disturbing aspects of the shifting interface between an (always, already) contingent nexus of (masculine) dangerousness, childhood (innocence) and social order.

1. CONSTRUCTING THE PAEDOPHILE: PUBLIC PROTEST AND THE RELEASE OF SEX OFFENDERS FROM PRISON

> Paedophile hysteria is sweeping the country. Child killers are on the loose. Perverts are everywhere. In terraces and housing estates across the land, vigilante groups are being formed, a righteous citizen's army armed with placards and pickaxe handles to repulse the monsters among us.[6]

There has occurred, at the end of the twentieth century, a fascination with the phenomena of paedophilia, a development reflected in the rapid spread of the term across some diverse cultural artefacts. "Paedophilia" and "the paedophile"

[3] On which see, for example, A. Beech, "A psychometric typology of child abusers" (1998) 42 *International Journal of Offender Therapy and Comparative Criminology* 319; D. Finkelhor, *Child Sexual Abuse: Theory and Research* (London: Free Press, 1984); D. Howitt, *Paedophiles and Sexual Offences Against Children* (London: Wiley and Sons, 1995); Jenkins, *Moral Panic: Changing Concepts of the Child Molester in Modern America* (New Haven: Yale University Press, 1997); J. Morgan, *Child Victims* (Oxford: Oxford University Press, 1992); J.R. Kincaid, *Erotic Innocence: The Culture of Child Molesting* (Durham, NC: Duke University Press, 1998); L. Waterhouse, R.P. Dobash and J. Carnie, *Child Sexual Abusers* (Edinburgh: Scottish Office, 1994).

[4] Note, for example, M. Thornton (ed.), *Public and Private: Feminist Legal Debates* (Melbourne: Oxford University Press, 1995); K. O'Donovan, *Sexual Divisions in Law* (London: Weidenfeld and Nicolson, 1985); C. Pateman, *The Sexual Contract* (Cambridge: Polity Press, 1988); F. Olsen, "The Myth of State Intervention in the Family" (1985) 18 *University of Michigan Journal of Law Reform* 835; S.M. Okin, *Justice, Gender and the Family* (New York City, NY: Basic Books, 1985).

[5] The argument to follow does not imply that the term "paedophile" is meaningless. The questions which need to be asked, rather, relate to the ways in which the term is presently made to signify in particular ways. This is not to negate the discursive purchase of the concept: ". . . on the contrary deconstruction implies only that we suspend all commitments to that to which the term [refers] . . . To deconstruct is not to negate or to dismiss, but to call into question and, perhaps most importantly, to open up a term . . . to a reusage or redeployment that previously has not been authorized". J. Butler, "Contingent Foundations: Feminism and the Question of "Postmodernism" in J. Butler and J.W. Scott (eds), *Feminists Theorize the Political* (New York City, NY: Routledge, 1992).

[6] A. Marr, "The paedophile who has our imagination" *The Independent*, 9 April 1998.

are conceptually distinct. The former refers to a desire, "the condition of being sexually attracted to children";[7] the latter to a *being*, an identifiable figure with its own ontology. Opinion remains divided as to whether the paedophile should be considered as a separate form of sex offender.[8] It seems generally agreed, however, that the vast majority of paedophiles are male,[9] with a racial composition that closely approximates to that of the population itself. Notwithstanding the ubiquity of the term paedophilia in the context of a widespread condemnation of what has been termed the "rediscovery" of child sexual abuse, the positioning of the paedophile within cultural discourses is nonetheless far from straightforward. It has involved, importantly, some frequently contradictory narratives. On the one hand a powerful popular discourse of sexual abuse has been constituted by talk shows, newspaper and magazine articles, television dramas, popular novels and films within the past (at least) fifteen years.[10] This discourse, as we shall see, has positioned the victim/survivor (of abuse) and the abuser in some particular ways. As the subject of a massive entertainment industry, however, and at the same time, the paedophile appears simultaneously as both Other (as a demonised Outsider) while also as being emblematic of a more general collective ambiguity towards the care, protection and sexuality of children affecting (infecting?) the populous more generally. Thus, while some discourses clearly locate the offender "within" rather than "outside" society,[11] notably situating their behaviour within the context of conventional masculine behaviour, others maintain the essential Otherness of the paedophile as a man whose desire and, it is argued, inescapable actions position him, perhaps more

[7] Source: Collins English Dictionary.

[8] On the classification systems for sex offenders generally see D. Fisher and G. Mair, *A Review of Classification Schemes for Sex Offenders* (Edinburgh: Scottish Office, 1998); also D.H. Grubin and H.G. Kennedy, "The Classification of Sexual Offenders" (1991) 1 *Criminal Behaviour and Mental Health* 123–9.

[9] The Government report *Sex Offending Against Children: Understanding the Risk* (London: Home Office, 1999) estimates, summarising research evidence, that around 96 per cent of sex offenders are men, with the majority of the 5 per cent of women offenders working in partnership with a male offender. See further S. Saradijan, *Women Who Sexually Abuse Children* (London: Wiley and Sons, 1996).

[10] R. Kennedy, "The dangerous individual and the social body" in D. Cheah, J. Fraser and J. Grbich (eds), *Thinking Through the Body of Law* (St Leonards, Australia: Allen and Unwin, 1996).

[11] This has been a particular feature of feminist interventions into debates around child sexual abuse: see for example, E. Driver and A. Droisen, *Child Sexual Abuse: A Feminist Perspective* (London: Macmillan, 1989); L. Dominelli, "Betrayal of Trust" (1989) *British Journal of Social Work*; M. Nava, "Cleveland and the Press: Outrage and Anxiety in the Reporting of Child Sexual Abuse" (1988) *Feminist Review* January; B. Campbell *Unofficial Secrets* (London: Virago, 1983). Similar attempts to locate the sex offender "within" society have also underscored approaches to working with men who sexually abuse based on cognitive-behavioural principles: M. Barker "What Works With Sex Offenders?" in G. McIvor (ed.), *Working With Offenders: Research Highlights in Social Work* Vol. 26 (London: Jessica Kinsley, 1996). For many practitioners this intervention takes place within a broad framework influenced by feminism: see further B. Featherstone and E. Lancaster, "Contemplating the unthinkable: men who sexually abuse children" (1997) 17 *Critical Social Policy* 51 at 51.

so than any other category of offender, outside society, beyond reform, redemption and rehabilitation.[12]

The paedophile can, in short, be seen to have become a canonical figure within a broader iconography of masculine dangerousness at the end of the twentieth century. Events surrounding the release from prison in April 1998 of the child-killer Sidney Cooke, although certainly a distinct case in a number of respects, was emblematic of the attitudes towards paedophilia more generally which have encircled debates around the release of sex offenders from prison.

Cooke had become eligible for release in 1998 under prison rules which stipulated an entitlement to a third off sentence for good behaviour; and, as he had been sentenced before the enactment of the 1991 Criminal Justice Act (the provisions of which allow for the supervision of offenders after their release), no restrictions could then legally be placed upon his movements. Thus Sidney Cooke, a convicted sex offender and man who was widely recognised to represent a continuing threat to children, was released from prison among much publicity, two days earlier than intended in order to avoid the mounting public protests which had been planned to time with his release.

Although his status as a convicted murderer made Cooke in many ways exceptional, the events surrounding his release from prison exemplify the constructions of paedophilia which have marked other broadly similar incidents, both prior and subsequent to the release of known sex offenders from prison.[13] In the ensuing debates around the adequacy of existing legal provisions a recurring theme within each of these cases has been a polarisation of the main protagonists into two. For the self-styled "anti-paedophile" protesters and campaigners, discursively positioned as the public, it is a "loophole" in the law which has allowed men such as Sidney Cooke to be released from prison during the 1990s without supervision.[14] This loophole has, in turn, become symbolic of the way in which the entire system of criminal justice is more generally seen to be failing to protect respectable communities from the threat of the paedophile and paedophilia. For the range of agencies involved in the regulation of sex offenders within the criminal justice system, in contrast, it has been the very actions of those who have protested at men such as Cooke's release which has

[12] The tensions this can produce pervade not just media reporting but also the accounts given by offenders themselves: see for example, "The Devil Amongst Us", Force 10 Productions, Channel 4, 8 October 1997. Also D. Birkett, "Monsters with Human Faces", *The Guardian Weekend*, 17 September 1997; "Treatment For Paedophiles", ITV Television, *World in Action*, December 1997; "The Ultimate Taboo" BBC Television *Panorama*, 6 October 1997. On offenders own accounts see further H.G. Kennedy and D.H. Grubin "Patterns of Denial in Sex Offenders" (1992) 22 *Psychological Medicine* 191–6.

[13] Particular concern has been expressed about a number of high-profile lapses of security around the supervision of convicted sex offenders, perhaps encapsulated by the publicity given to the case of Trevor Holland who, in 1996, escaped from custody for forty-eight hours during a supervised day trip to the Chessington "World of Adventures" zoo.

[14] Sidney Cooke had become eligible for release in 1998 under prison rules which stipulated an entitlement to a third off sentence for good behaviour; and, as he had been sentenced before the enactment of the Criminal Justice Act 1991 (the provisions of which allow for the supervision of offenders after their release), no restrictions could then legally be placed upon his movements.

resulted in less, not more, security for the public. The police had for some time, before the release of Cooke, publicly expressed their fears that protests organised by anti-paedophile organisations at the release of such high-profile or "celebrity" child sex offenders might be hi-jacked by "vigilantes".[15] The probation service had sought to highlight the ways in which the use of hostels to secure sex offenders following their release from prison had resulted in reconviction rates which are among the lowest for any group of offenders.[16] The broader growth in the public "outing" of sex offenders in Britain during the 1990s,[17] heightened considerably by the national publicity given to Cooke's release, has been described as "wrecking" attempts to police the movements of known paedophiles. With barely concealed frustration, probation chiefs pointed out [18] how a growing number of hostels were now being forced to close their doors to paedophiles as a result of public demonstrations.[19] Repeated police and ministerial reassurances that the number of offenders who continue to pose a threat

[15] Both police and anti-paedophile protesters sought to distinguish between, on the one hand, the "legitimate" grievances and worries of the "concerned campaigners" and their supporters and, on the other, those "vigilantes" who were routinely presented as hi-jacking otherwise peaceful protests. This is, however, an arbitrary distinction, side-stepping the question of at what point "mothers with toddlers in pushchairs, frightened and angry" might be "turned into a baying mob by their frustration . . ." "Should we listen to the vigilantes?", *The Independent*, 27 April 1998.

[16] The report *Sex Offending Against Children: Understanding the Risk* (London: Home Office, 1999) estimated re-offending rates of 20 per cent, a lower recidivism rate than for most crimes. Sexual crime more generally represents less than 1 per cent of recorded crime (Home Office 1994), although much goes unreported and information on recidivism rates is incomplete. There is, however, no evidence that incidents of paedophilia are more prevalent now than at earlier historical moments. Indeed, some commentators have suggested that contrast with earlier times reveals a significant improvement in the safety and general security of children; on the treatment of sex offenders generally see A. Beech, D. Fisher, R. Beckett and A. Scott-Fordham *STEP 3: An Evaluation of the Prison Sex Offender Treatment Programme* (London: Home Office, 1998); C. Hedderman and D. Sugg, *Does Treating Sex Offenders Reduce Offending?* (London: Home Office Research Findings No. 45, 1996); Marshall, *Reconviction of Imprisoned Sex Offenders* (London: Home Office Research Bulletin No. 36) 23–30; E. Proctor and F. Flaxington, *Community Based Interventions with Sex Offenders Organised by the Probation Service* (London: Association of Chief Officers of Probation); M. Baker and R. Morgan, *Evaluation of Sex Offenders: A Framework for the Evaluation of Community Based Treatment* (London: Home Office, 1993).

[17] Comparison with developments in the USA is instructive in this regard, where the issue has for some time had a high profile. Under variations of what was introduced in New Jersey as "Megan's Law", many states now allow public access to a register of paedophiles, with some posting names, pictures and addresses of paedophiles on the Internet.

[18] The Association of Chief Probation Officers issued a report at the height of the furore over Cooke's release detailing over 40 serious incidents from around the country in which public disorder had hampered attempts to keep sex offenders under supervision (*Exercising Constant Vigilance*, HM Inspectorate of Probation Report, 28 April 1998). In one case the police had to evacuate residents and staff from a hostel when it had been surrounded by a crowd of 400 people angry about the presence of a sex offender (who was in fact not there). G.Smith, "Vigilantes get 'upper hand' ", *The Guardian*, 29 April 1998.

[19] At least ten probation and bail hostels, as a direct result of Cooke's release, refused to accept sex offenders released from prison early specifically because of the fear of attacks from local residents. In effect, hostel managers were refusing to take in sex offenders, not because they could not handle or cope with them but because of fears of the local community "doing something very stupid to the hostel and the staff there": *The Guardian*, 29 April 1998. Guidelines had previously been issued by the Chartered Institute of Housing concerned by the growing number of councils apparently refusing to house paedophiles: *The Guardian*, 3 March 1998.

to children following release from prison remains small[20] was contradicted by what the public *felt* to be the "truth" of the threat of the paedophile and the inadequacy of the law and the criminal justice system to offer any protection from such a threat.[21]

In seeking to make sense of such events it is important to recognise how such public concerns around paedophilia can be contextualised or viewed in different ways. Paedophilia exists as a discursive practice already constituted by both the popular media and official discourses in some different, though at times overlapping, ways. An iconic figure such as Sidney Cooke, for example, was readily located in relation to other infamous crimes of the same genre, albeit that his was a particularly horrific example of paedophilic intent allied to murderous impulse. The extensive media coverage the case of Cooke continues to receive in Britain has served, on one level, to highlight and bring to public attention what was already by 1998 a well-established debate about sex offending with its own trajectory, *dramatis personae*[22] and political and legislative history.[23] In this debate some

[20] As of April 1998 an estimated 430 sex offenders were living in approved probation hostels in England and Wales, convicted of a range of "sex crimes" ranging from charges of minor indecency to "a few predatory paedophiles" such as Sidney Cooke (Source: Graham Smith, Chief Inspector of Probation: "Vigilantes get 'upper hand' ", *The Guardian,* 29 April 1998). Of these around 150 men were due to be released from prison in the next two years, among whom about six were deemed to be "as dangerous as" Sidney Cooke. *The Independent*, 7 April 1998.

[21] The strength of feeling evident in the demonstrations may, in part, have reflected a heightening of concern following well publicised events in Belgium, where a failure to maintain a secure hold on Marc Detroux, had resulted in public outcry.

[22] Cooke was not the first sex offender whose release from prison was to become a "cause célèbre" during the 1990s: note, for example, the release of Graham Seddon in 1997: "Outrage as deal merely delays pervert's release", *The Daily Mail*, 15 June 1997. Also in 1997, and among much publicity, two convicted sex offenders in North Wales brought a test case at the High Court (subsequently lost) questioning the legality under Article 8 of the European Convention on Human Rights of the police practice of informing residents when an offender released from prison had moved into a particular area: *The Guardian*, 1 July 1997: *R v. Chief Constable for North Wales Police* ex p AB [1997] 3 WLR 724. See R. Mullender, "Privacy, paedophilia and the European Convention on Human Rights: a deontological approach" [1998] *Public Law* 384–9. This case was to be the catalyst for the setting up of the organisation PARASOL (Parents Aiming to Right Abysmal Sex Offender Laws).

[23] Note, in particular *Sentencing and Supervision of Sex Offenders: Consultation Document* (London: Home Office, 1996); The Sex Offenders Act 1997, Part I of which requires the registration of convicted offenders within specified time limits and gives the police the power to arrest anyone who had not signed up by the deadline facing, if guilty, a fine of £5000 or a six month prison sentence. The Cooke case encapsulated the broader problem of tracking those offenders who were to be released from prison but who were beyond the reach of the Sex Offenders Register set up by the 1997 Act. It has been estimated that, although 2,200 convicted people were originally identified as needing to be on the list, by September 1997 less than 800 had come forward; that is, around two thirds of offenders required to sign up to the list had failed to report to the police. The 1997 Act also allows for British courts to try nationals for crimes committed overseas, in an attempt to address the problem of "sex tourism". Note also the Crime and Disorder Act 1998, section 2 of which creates "Sex Offender Orders" and sections 58–60 of which introduce extended post release supervision for sexual and violent offenders. Section 2 provides for the police to apply for an order against any sex offender whose present behaviour in the community gives the police reasonable cause for concern that such an order is necessary to protect the public from serious harm. Orders are preventative and require sex offenders to register under the 1997 Sex Offenders Act. On the provisions of the 1997 Act, see R. Henham "Child Victims and Sentencing Policy for Violent and Sexual Crimes" *Web Journal of Current Legal Issues* (1997) 5 Web JCLI. Henham argues that the common perception

familiar questions about retribution, reform and rehabilitation, just desserts and due process have coalesced around the issue of the problem of "what to do" with sex offenders released from prison. Both the media coverage and subsequent political responses can be seen to fit many elements of classic moral panic theory, not least in terms of the projection of public fears and fantasies onto a specific individual or group via a language of societal crisis. Nonetheless, the paedophile ill-fits any mantle of a vulnerable, "unfairly maligned" "folk-devil".[24] He embodies an Outsider status which few would seek to reconstitute or reclaim as, in any sense, "victim". In marked contrast to such views a few voices suggested that a "paedophile hysteria" was now "sweeping the country,"[25] seeking to defend the rights of convicted offenders.[26] The majority of the British press, however, united in seeing the concerns of anti-paedophile groups as being (generally) legitimate and as, at the very least, raising some fundamental and legitimate questions about the relationship between the criminal law, the role of the state and the state of the nation. "It is not the habit of liberal newspapers to stand up for a baying crowd", declared *The Independent* newspaper, capturing what was to become the general mood, but "if a dangerous paedophile turned up at any neighbourhood slammer, free to walk, every local parent would be, to go to the root of the word, vigilant".[27]

Notwithstanding the very public and visible nature of this debate, epitomised by the spectacle of the police station, courtroom and rooftop demonstration,[28] the riot and the various performances (to camera, to press) of politicians and anti-paedophile spokespeople, the phenomenon of paedo*philia* itself appears as that most "private" of crimes in the way in which it transgressed normal codes of justice and due process. Men such as Sidney Cooke, and those like him whose release from prison was by April 1998 anticipated,[29] were seen as threatening precisely *because* they could be "anywhere", undetectable, unknowable and unseen. And, therein, between what was both "seen" and "unseen",[30] lies, I now

that social protection is achieved through the sentencing policies of the courts is both simplistic and inaccurate. Evaluation of the protection actually offered by existing legislation and appellate guidance confirms the lack of any coherent sentencing policy to deal with child victims.

[24] See further E. Goode and N. Ben-Yehuda, *Moral Panic: The Social Construction of Deviance* (Oxford: Blackwell, 1994); A. Hunt, "'Moral panic' and moral language in the media" (1997) 48 *British Journal of Sociology* 629–48; A. McRobbie, *Postmodernism and Popular Culture* (London: Routledge, 1994).

[25] A. Marr, *op. cit.* n 6. Also "Paedophiles should have rights as well", *The Guardian*, 1 July 1998.

[26] On the broader legal framework see R. Mullender *op. cit.* n 22.

[27] *The Independent*, 27 April 1998.

[28] For example, in June 1999, following a 24,000 signature petition and among much publicity, anti-paedophile protesters broke into Nottingham jail to protest against plans to house released sex offenders in the prison itself. The aim of the protest had been "to show that as we could get in, they [the paedophiles] could get out": *The Independent*, 19 July 1999. On issues raised by the Nottingham case, L. Brooks "You expect to be beaten up. You know society hates you. And you're terrified of yourself", *The Guardian*, 21 June 1999.

[29] See n 20 *supra*.

[30] Note, for example, the depiction of a perceived public duty to "make visible" the paedophile and paedophilia by the dissemination of information about their whereabouts: "Exposing the guilty is a public service", *The Guardian*, 10 June 1997. On the relation between the seen and unseen, A. Young *op. cit.*n 2 at 112.

wish to argue, something of the dilemma which the crimino-legal domain has faced in responding to the phenomenon of the paedophile.

2. THE DANGEROUS INDIVIDUAL: RISK, POPULAR KNOWLEDGE AND THE RULE OF LAW

Constructing an interpretative genealogy from something as diffuse and complex as press discourse is notoriously problematic. Yet newspaper usage of the term "paedophile" has undoubtedly had an influence on both academic and official governmental interventions in this area throughout the 1990s. This is not to say that newspapers have initiated linguistic change so much as ". . . push[ed] the language along further in the direction in which it was already going".[31] And just as sociologists have been ascribed some responsibility for the pervasive use of "moral panic" within the media,[32] the present ubiquity of the term "paedophile" has become enmeshed within diverse representations of a range of questions around (among others); "moral decline", "family breakdown", the parameters of adult and child sexuality, the changing nature of childhood, the breakdown of community and, in particular, a perceived failure of the state to protect its citizens. The disturbances which followed the release from prison of Sidney Cooke, as well as other convicted sex offenders, have not only raised the profile of an already established debate therefore. They have prompted a series of meditations on issues far beyond the scope and content of the criminal law. Although some potent and familiar associations of paedophilia and public panic would appear to have had a permanent effect on the moral language used by the media in the late twentieth century, the contours of any specific event are by no means fixed. As such, it is possible to locate within these representations of the paedophile not only a certain homogeneity and continuity with well-established ideas about sex offending; they also, revealingly, indicate some significant *shifts* within a discourse of the dangerous individual which itself has a number of implications for developing an understanding of the relationship between popular knowledge, the public/private divide and the rule of law.

The dangerous individual, risk and the fear of crime

The figure of the paedophile, I have suggested above, occupies a special place within contemporary discourses of dangerousness.[33] As an individual who will

[31] J. Aitchison, *Language Joyriding: An Inaugural Lecture* (Oxford: Clarendon Press, 1994) at 19, quoted in A. Hunt, *op. cit.* n 24 at 630.

[32] *Ibid.*

[33] A central concern within the history of "dangerousness" has been the question of how the concept has historically been used to classify offenders who frequently, but by no means necessarily, suffer "from mental abnormalities [and] who demonstrate a propensity to repeat their crimes and thereby put at risk the well-being and security of others": J. Pratt, *op. cit.* n 1 at 1. The concept of

(inevitably) repeat (his) crimes the paedophile appears, perhaps more so than any other offender, to be a man who speaks the Truth of his being *through* his crime(s). As an affront to the "right to life" of the modern subject he exemplifies many aspects of the idea of the dangerous offender as an individual who puts at risk the security and well-being, not just of other individuals, but of society and sociality itself. The increasing visibility of representations of the paedophile can thus itself be seen as revealing of some broader developments in/around the concepts of dangerousness and the meaning of social change. Encircling concerns around the release of convicted paedophiles from prison has been, in particular, a range of anxieties associated with the "fear" of crime more generally.[34] These are fears which connect, Hollway and Jefferson have argued, not just to the realities of becoming a victim of a specific crime, but also to broader historical, socio-political formations in which questions of order and control – and the very meaning and experience of "crime" and the "fear of crime" – have each been socially and politically constructed within an overall context of *risk-management*.[35]

The literature on fear of crime has, Hollway and Jefferson suggest, tended to be conceptually undeveloped, pitched largely at a descriptive, empirical level.[36] However, this idea that risk may be managed or, more specifically, regulated (by appropriate use of legal sanction) is of considerable use in seeking to make sense of the grievances, protests and arguments of those who have objected so vociferously to the release of convicted sex offenders from prison. Fear is here conceptualised as ". . . not simply a quantity, of which one possess larger or smaller amounts: rather it is *a mode of perception*, even perhaps a constitutive feature of personal identity".[37] Following Beck's[38] influential analysis of risk, in which risk is seen as a central analytic tool for understanding ways of dealing with the hazards and insecurities introduced by modernity and late modernity, and in seeing risk itself as being "written into" the social forms of contemporary capitalist societies, the transformations ". . .of the routines of everyday life and the pleasures that they have brought" are here seen to have created "new uncertainties, risks and fears".[39] From such a perspective the threat to sociality

dangerousness, drawing on Foucault's influential text *The Dangerous Individual*, has been seen as legitimating the medical and legal regulation of a range of particular individuals perceived to be, in one way or another, "dangerous". Recent scholarship from within this Foucauldian tradition, notably informed by the key theoretical terms of risk and governance, has sought to explore in particular how the criminals who constitute the risk of dangerousness are themselves governed and constituted at particular moments.

[34] See further W. Hollway and T. Jefferson, "The risk society in an age of anxiety: situating fear of crime" (1997) 48 *British Journal of Sociology* 255–66 at 256.

[35] W. Hollway and T. Jefferson, *ibid.* at 257.

[36] See R. Sparks, "Reason and unrealism in "left realism": some problems in the constitution of fear of crime" in R. Matthews and J. Young (eds), *Issues in Realist Criminology* (London: Sage, 1992); Hollway and Jefferson, *ibid.*

[37] R. Sparks, *op. cit.* n 36 at 14: quoted in J. Pratt, *op. cit.* n 1 at 2: my emphasis.

[38] U. Beck, *The Risk Society* (London: Sage, 1992).

[39] J. Pratt, *op. cit.* n 1 at 150.

represented by the paedophile becomes more understandable. The risks focused on in the fear of crime discourse have tended "to have had individual identifiable victims and individual identifiable offenders which makes them *knowable*".[40] Yet the figure of the paedophile constitutes a risk which is, at once, both "knowable" *and* "unknowable". Convicted offenders such as Sidney Cooke are identified criminals. They have been punished, their sentence served. Yet at the same time the crime which they embody – paedophilia – continues to appear as fluid, slippery and evasive. As a desire, an intended and possibly realised action, it is undetectable by an individual's own cognitive means. This takes on a particular significance in a context in which paedophilia (and, implicitly, the paedophile) increasingly appear as a ubiquitous phenomena, potentially penetrating all spheres of life;[41] for example, via the Internet[42] into the school,[43] the charity and voluntary organisation,[44] the home, the children's bedroom and other (constituted as "safe") spaces, in so doing transcending the boundaries of the family, community and state.[45] Thus, while attempts may be made to expunge the body of the paedo*phile* from society, in the form of expulsion from the community into which he is to be introduced on release from prison, the danger and risk of paedo*philia* appears much more evasive, powerful and threatening, a hazard which cannot be confined to any particular time, space and locale. Indeed, in the context of the legal regulation of cyberspace and in the laws of international relations – in relation to sex tourism for example[46] – it is the very public space which has encouraged the promenade of bodies which can be seen to have created this ". . . suburban criminal [who] blends in with the environment": "We have convinced ourselves that 'they' are everywhere, in scout troops, schools, any institution involving children".[47] The "criminal life support system" of the paedophile may be less visible than other offenders, but it would also appear to threaten most acutely that basic trust which residents feel for others who live in (their) community, embodying for many a "down-

[40] W. Hollway and T. Jefferson, *op. cit.* n 34 at 260: original emphasis.

[41] A point encapsulated in headlines such as "Nightmare on *Any* Street", *The Guardian*, 10 June 1997, my emphasis.

[42] This issue was to receive considerable attention following a series of arrests in September 1998 in Britain, the United States, Germany, Portugal, Italy, Australia, Austria, Belgium, Finland, France Norway and Sweden resulting from the (chance) police discovery of the "Wonderland Club". The technological sophistication of this child pornography group was widely described as shocking and led to calls for greater regulation of Internet usage and provision. Note also responses to the arrest and conviction of the celebrity Gary Glitter in Britain on charges relating to possession of child pornography downloaded from the Internet.

[43] "Schools ignoring classroom sex abuse", *The Independent*, 26 June 1999.

[44] The National Criminal Intelligence Service reported evidence in July 1999 that paedophiles were joining aid agencies in order to facilitate access to children overseas, stating that this problem now has the potential to become as serious as that of "sex tourism": "Paedophiles Infiltrate Aid Charities", *The Guardian*, 22 July 1999.

[45] At the time of Cooke's release, concern had been expressed about the ability of "the determined paedophile . . . to target children through school e-mail addresses": "Paedophiles targeting pupils via the Internet", *The Independent*, 10 April 1998.

[46] "Child sex tourists escape UK law", *The Independent*, 13 July 1998.

[47] A. Marr, *op. cit.* n 6.

side" of urban life in a world in which strangers are encountered on public streets and in places which, increasingly, pose profound and unsettling questions about possible dangers and personal harm.[48]

The political effects to which these particular representations of risk and dangerousness have been put during the late 1990s in the context of sex offending has involved the development of a moral agenda in which men who sexually abuse children are routinely homogenised (as "paedophiles") in a way which negates consideration of diversities between offenders, and in so doing works against strategies and programmes of intervention based on a recognition of such difference.[49] As a result theoretical engagement with the differences *between* individual men has been accorded little attention in these debates although, as Featherstone and Lancaster suggest, a recognition of such difference is vital if initiatives designed to reduce offending are not to reproduce much of the divisiveness of contemporary social and penal policy.[50] Popular knowledge, typified by the widespread use of the terms "evil" and "human wickedness" in the press, has promoted a construction of the paedophile as a "monster" or "grotesque" which has served to establish a distinction between categories of "sex offender", which has in turn involved a valorising of the paedophile and a passing over of the abuse of children and adults in other contexts (for example institutionalised abuse).[51] Thus, and in transforming the paedophile into

[48] D.Karp, G. Stone and W. Yoeb, *Being Urban: A Sociology of City Life* (New York: Praeger, 1991).

[49] B.Featherstone and E.Lancaster, *op. cit.* n 11 at 61, argue that the present stereotyping of men who sexually abuse children involves a process through which the individual is being reduced to the sum total of a few characteristics, attitudes or behaviours allegedly possessed or exhibited by anyone falling into that particular category.

[50] There has been a tendency within dominant approaches to men who sexually abuse children, B.Featherstone and E. Lancaster (*ibid.*) argue, to portray perpetrators as a homogenised mass, indistinguishable from other men. Probation officers and social workers are accustomed to working with those who are at the margins of, or outside, commonly accepted moral discourses and over the last decade there has been a growth in probation and social services involvement in treatment initiatives with men who sexually abuse: see further M.Barker and R. Morgan, *op. cit.* n 16. This has, Featherstone and Lancaster suggest, involved the production of an agenda within the criminal justice system which has served to legitimate the treatment of one group of offenders in ways different from others solely on the basis of a perceived risk reduction.

[51] Indeed, one result of the construction of the paedophile as a "special case", deserving "special laws", has been that serious sexual assaults on adults are themselves routinely seen as less deserving of public concern (notwithstanding the fact, for example, that convictions for rape have fallen from 24.4 per cent in 1985 to 8 per cent in 1994). The relative lack of public and media interest in the judicial inquiry into institutionalised sexual abuse at Children's Homes in North Wales has stood in marked contrast to the case of Cooke. Compare also with the case of Frank Beck, ("Britain's most notorious child abuser", *The Independent on Sunday*, 12 April 1998), who had been sentenced in 1991 to five terms of life imprisonment for sexually abusing children while he was manager of children homes for Leicestershire County Council. It was estimated that he sexually and physically abused some 200 children: see further, M. D'arcy and Gosling *Abuse of Trust: Frank Beck and the Leicestershire Children's Homes Scandal* (London: Bowerdean, 1998). On 31 April Eric Taylor, age 78, a priest who sexually abused young boys was jailed for seven years (*The Guardian*, 1 May 1998). The 1997 report of Sir William Utting chronicles accounts of widespread poor education and health, high rates of mental illness, bullying and intimidation, and the threat of "sexual terrorists", men who it argues still work in the care system preying on young, vulnerable victims: It is estimated that nearly five thousand care workers and former care workers are now on a government "black-list",

something "beyond human" and in rendering his actions emblematic of an inhumanity beyond comprehension and understanding, the expunging of the broader social context can itself be seen to have served to erode any collective responsibility for understanding and challenging the individual and social forces that have produced such an event. Moreover, and to take the argument forward, in this process the moral encoding of the allocation of risks surrounding the release of convicted paedophiles from prison would itself appear to have brought to the surface, in a strikingly clear way, the way in which a discontinuity or collision between different rationalities has informed a profound rupture between ideas of "popular" knowledge and the rule of law within late modernity. This point requires clarification.

Popular knowledge and the rule of law

In the debates which have surrounded the release from prison of convicted sex offenders during the 1990s the discursive power of what we might term a "popular knowledge" of the paedophile and paedophilia has been considerable. Such popular knowledge, as outlined above, can usefully be understood, Kennedy has suggested,[52] as the knowledge which people have acquired in their everyday lives, rather than by specialised study and training. Implicitly, it has historically been assumed that the mob, the mass, "the public" exists as the site of or for such "popular" knowledge.[53] The crimino-legal domain has itself historically been marked, Kennedy argues, by a hierarchical opposition whereby scientific knowledge has tended to be recognised as the standard by which such popular knowledge has been adjudged, in various ways, to be "naive".[54] Psychiatric and legal discourse, in particular, have been seen as formed independently of such "popular" views, making their own particular claims to scientific status. And yet, Kennedy argues, this opposition between the expert and the popular has itself tended to encourage a perception of popular, medical and legal knowledge as discrete fields, each with nothing to do with the other (notwithstanding the fact that everyday life attests to the ways in which they have everything to do with each other). Within the conditions of late modernity, crucially, it is this very hierarchical opposition through which such a knowledge formation has

all having received convictions or police cautions: *The Independent*, 20 November 1997; "Care system fails children" *The Guardian*, 20 November 1997: N. Davies "Public figures named in paedophile ring", *The Guardian*, 15 October 1997, November 1997; also J. Snow, "Scandal of the true abusers", *The Guardian*, 6 June 1996. Note also "Priest jailed for sexual abuse of boys", *The Guardian*, 1 May 1998; "Nuns abused hundreds of children", *The Independent on Sunday*, 16 August 1998.

[52] *Op. cit.* n 10.

[53] V. Walkerdine, "Subject to change without notice: Psychology, postmodernity and the popular" in S. Pile and N. Thrift, *Mapping the Subject: Geographies of cultural transformation* (London: Routledge, 1995) 324.

[54] R. Kennedy, *op. cit.* n 10.

been constituted which has itself been disturbed as popular knowledge has come to be ascribed an increasing power and authority while, at the same time, the status of "rational" legal discourse has, in a number of respects, become increasingly ambivalent.

This shift between the popular and the rational-legal is apparent not just in the dialectical relationship between the popular media and contemporary criminal justice policy, whereby politicians increasingly appear to speak directly "to" the public through an engagement with, for example, the tabloid press.[55] It is also central to the way in which, following Lyotard,[56] late modern cultural formations appear to have surfaced the limits of a rationality which hierarchises discourses based on a criteria of Truth *per se*. This can be seen as having a particular relevance for contemporary concerns around the legal regulation of the paedophile. The debates which have taken place about the release of convicted child sex offenders from prison, as outlined above, exemplify aspects of the ways in which the position of law has become increasingly contested in relation to popular knowledge. Indeed, in a number of respects the discourse of "the public" would now appear to be on a par with – if not to supersede – official discourse within this particular context. It was precisely a concern to address (redress) "the power of the popular" which underscored the attempt by the British Government, in July 1998, to distribute information packs to all parents about the "reality" of the threat and risk posed by the paedophile as a direct response to the case of Sidney Cooke. The dissemination of such "expert knowledge" was required, it was argued, to counter the series of prevailing myths which had surfaced about the paedophile and paedophilia. We have seen above how the "mass", the self-styled "vigilantes", did not seek to measure discourses of dangerousness according to any criteria of Truth as a representation of reality. Rather, a *pre-existing* popular knowledge of the paedophile spoke to collective experiences of fear, risk and anxiety in ways which clearly could not be calmed by appeals to the "professional" credentials of official agents (whether the police, the probation service or government ministers). In relation to paedoph*ilia* such popular knowledge had already produced a "true" criminal identity, an ontology of the paedophile. Yet it was this knowledge which was itself, in turn, to become operative for the very social institutions and practices of the criminal law which were seeking to respond to the problem of "what to do" with the paedophile.

Popular knowledge of the paedophile fed into, and served to legitimate, the very feelings of despair and helplessness which were being so powerfully expressed by those who could not understand why such men were being released

[55] Witness, for example, in 1998 the British Home Secretary Jack Straw writing a column in *The Sun* newspaper during the controversy surrounding payments to the "child-killer" Mary Bell. Straw defended his intervention into the debate via tabloid newspaper on British television by making explicit reference to the fact that his predecessor, Michael Howard, had himself increasingly chosen this forum to articulate his own views on a range of subjects.

[56] J.F. Lyotard, *The Postmodern Condition* (Minneapolis: University of Minneapolis Press, 1984).

from prison in the first place. Thus, although "flawed" in a number of respects, it nonetheless functioned to supersede, and to make claims to Truth more powerful than those other discourses which were simultaneously seeking, in contrast, to (re)position the paedophile as within society, as part *of* the social. Popular knowledge, despite its lack of professional credentials, came to serve in debates around the release of convicted sex offenders from prison ". . . as an authoritative discourse in relation to the objects and domains it produces and addresses".[57] It is now arguable, indeed, whether paedophilia can be rationally interpreted and discussed as a (relatively modest) social problem at all,[58] as a powerful discursive category of the paedophile has become "a special case" in which "the normal rules of justice do not apply", serving to short-circuit otherwise ostensibly liberal sensibilities by legitimating appeals for preventative custody (locking up someone for something they might do).[59] It is an issue, moreover, which in turn has informed some broader concerns around public safety and the limits of the criminal law. Leaving aside the question of whether the indeterminate sentences subsequently proposed by the British Home Secretary would be considered lawful by the European Court, such categorisations, I have argued, serve not only to negate an individual offender's own responsibility for his act; they also obscure "the complexity and ambiguity of actual men's lives and their actions".[60] Within this dominant ontology such men appear to be both responsible *and* irresponsible for their actions. Yet "if sex offenders are totally responsible for their behaviour, then why not shoplifters and burglars?".[61]

Addressing the fear of crime has, of course, historically involved the state in a balancing of individual rights with questions of public protection. The power of any particular discursive construction of the paedophile has been such that, if it has not (and cannot) be owned by the political executive, then it can certainly be shaped by different political rationalities as an object amenable to programmatic intervention. From such a perspective, the protests surrounding the release of convicted sex offenders from prison can be seen to illustrate some of the ways in which ideas of dangerousness have themselves been given sustenance by fears and insecurities which are able, at particular moments, to out-

[57] R. Kennedy, *op. cit.* n 10 at 188.

[58] *The Independent*, 27 April 1998.

[59] In July 1999 the Government subsequently announced provisions for the indefinite "preventative detention" of people with untreatable personality disorders, commonly described as "non-violent psychopaths" (*The Independent*, 20 July 1999). Although the stated aim has been to allow doctors to detain individuals who they believe will not respond to treatment, many organisations (including MIND, Liberty and the Law Society) maintained their opposition in principle to the detention of individuals who had not committed an offence.

[60] B.Featherstone and E.Lancaster, *op. cit.*, n 11 at 52. If it is the case that any punishment designed to reform the paedophile has to be adapted to the individual, to their motives and inner-will, then it is also necessary, Featherstone and Lancaster suggest, to know why s/he did what they did, "how they became the person they are".

[61] K. Buckley, "Masculinity: The Probation Service and the Causes of Offending Behaviour" in T. May and A. Vass (eds), *Working With Offenders: Issues, Contexts and Outcomes* (London: Sage, 1996) at 97, quoted in B.Featherstone and E.Lancaster, *op. cit.* n 11 at 54 .

weigh doubts about the level of state power necessary to protect the individual from any specific risk.[62] The popular knowledge of the dangerous paedophile can be seen to have made possible and legitimated power/knowledge projects which, in a number of respects, run counter to the "legislative ambitions of philosophical reason". In the remainder of this chapter I wish to consider how this popular knowledge of the paedophile has also involved a particular *gendered* narrative in the way in which it has served to constitute and cement an understanding of the social bond via the establishing of particular norms of conduct and criteria of Truth. What concerns me in what follows is *why* it should be that the figure of the paedophile should come to have assumed such a contemporary significance within discourses of dangerousness in the way in which it (he) transgresses the bonds of sociality.

3. CHILDHOOD, PARENTHOOD AND GENDER: (RE)CONSTRUCTING THE PAEDOPHILE AS OTHER

> There cannot be a parent, faced with lengthy news reports about paedophilia, who does not ask themselves if they want to know that much detail or whether it is their duty to read on and face the terrible reality for their children's sake.[63]

Throughout the 1990s familiar conflations of ideas about family life and socio-economic privilege have pervaded accounts of respectability, security and public safety with regard to the relationship between children and crime[64] (the murder in 1993 of the two-year-old James Bulger continuing to have an especial significance in this regard). The ontological importance given to the heterosexual "family" as an institutional source for the preservation and reproduction of moral order has itself been central to a discursive construction of the Social *per se* within modernity.[65] It is a particular mythologising of locale, however, which has informed constructions of Britain's "dangerous places" as communities associated with high-profile crimes against children. And in the context of child sexual abuse it has been a particular mapping of the safe/dangerous "space" of

[62] The initial response of the Home Secretary, Jack Straw, to the case of Sidney Cooke had been to give consideration to new measures to enable sex offenders to be locked up "indefinitely". He commissioned a study by officials from the Home Office and Department of Health into whether there was a need for further provisions to deal with "dangerous personality disordered offenders" such as paedophiles. In Straw's words, ". . . at the moment paedophiles can be imprisoned indefinitely only if they have committed the most appalling of offences. A new sentence would allow dangerous paedophiles to be detained indefinitely after their first offence", *The Independent*, 7 April 1998. On 5 May 1998 the Home Secretary announced emergency measures to identify paedophiles whose release from prison would be likely to spark such demonstrations and that a working group would be formed to assess the release of paedophiles and identify those who are likely to trigger public concern. In addition, from 2000, judges will be able to take expert advice on the sentencing and release of sex offenders and the threat they represent to the community.

[63] *The Express*, 15 April 1998.

[64] See R. Collier, *Masculinities, Crime and Criminology* (London: Sage, 1998) chapter 3.

[65] J. Stratton, "Serial Killing and the Transformation of the Social" (1996) 13 *Theory, Culture and Society* 77–98 at 78.

(men's) crimes against children which has become increasingly contested and problematic.

Vulnerable childhood, anxious parenthood and the dangerous masculine

> Do you live in fear for your children? Send us your stories. We will be publishing a dossier later this week.[66]

Surrounding debates about the paedophile and paedophilia during the 1990s has been a construction of parenthood itself as a perpetual state of anxiety and vigilance. Within both the press and governmental discourses referred to above parenthood increasingly appears as an ontologically insecure state in comparison with previous historical periods; "Can there be a parent in the land who does not fear for their children? Fear to let them walk on the streets, play their games in the parks or stand too long at the school gate lest they get molested, mugged or abused".[67] For some commentators, parents have become the "unwitting jailers" of their children,[68] a lack of play,[69] restricted autonomy and increasing pressure to educationally succeed[70] widely seen as having deleterious consequences for child, parents, family life and society as a whole. Yet at the same time a general belief continues to be expressed that, by a number of criteria, childhood today is fraught, unsafe and permeated by new, previously unimaginable, dangers.[71] As the body of the child appears permeable, porous and essentially vulnerable, to be reached in all kinds of ways, implicitly child*hood* itself appears as a pre-discursive ontological state. It is something which once existed but is now said to have been "stolen"[72] – "Childhood as we once understood it, no longer exists: instead, there is only the vague unease of an extended adolescence that seems to start at five and finish not at all".[73] This

[66] *The Express*, 15 April 1998.

[67] *The Express*, Editorial, 15 April 1998. In 1999 the "Full Stop" campaign by the charity the National Society for the Prevention of Cruelty to Children met with considerable criticism for the way in which it was seen as heightening anxieties while encouraging over-protective behaviour on the part of parents: *The Observer*, 8 August 1999.

[68] "Britain is becoming a generation of battery children . . . Parents frightened of crime are keeping youngsters cooped up like hens for their own safety", *The Express*, 15 April 1998; "Parents make their kids too soft to survive", *The Observer*, 1 August 1999. This issue resurfaced during 1999 following the announcement that a major supermarket chain in Britain was planning a pilot electronic tagging system, based on a combination of anti-shoplifting technology with surveillance devices used to track criminals released from prison with the result that the very technology used to police the movements of paedophiles is now being used to protect children.

[69] See for example, the Mental Health Foundation report *Too Safe For Their Own Good*. (September 1999) "NSPCC accused of fuelling parents fears", *The Guardian*, 9 August 1999; "Lack of risk in play damaging children", *The Guardian*, 24 June 1999.

[70] See for example, "Play is out, early learning is in", *The Guardian*, 23 June 1999.

[71] Children growing up in the 1990s are widely seen to be more likely to be involved in crime, to face poverty living in a lone parent household than those who grew up in post-War Britain; "Children experience the pros and cons of modern life", *The Guardian*, 14 January 1999.

[72] "Whatever happened to childhood?", *The Independent on Sunday*, 18 July 1999.

[73] *The Express*, 15 April 1998.

phantasm of childhood-lost has encircled a range of anxieties around the relationship between paedophilia, risk, youth crime[74] and the parameters of the dangerous masculine within Western cultures.

To clarify. From their Post-Enlightenment positioning as an unequivocal source of love, recent sociological accounts of childhood[75] have presented the child within late modernity as signifying both a "nostalgia" for an innocence-lost[76] and, notably in the form of the criminality of (male) youth, a heightened sense of social breakdown and moral dislocation. Yet if the essential innocence of the child has served to, as Jenks puts it, ground a sense of sociality at a time of intolerable and disorientating change, it is the abuse and destruction of such innocence which has come to strike powerfully at the remaining vestiges of the social bond. In such a context it is perhaps unsurprising that what should result should be general expressions of collective pain at the loss of social identity.[77] However, that all this should then be seen as an affront, first and foremost, to the institution of family and to the very idea of the heterosexual familial(ised) social itself becomes revealing given the way in which a complex range of social, cultural and economic reconfigurations are now connecting the "fragmenting" heterosexual family to concerns about, and reinterpretations of, men's dangerousness. It is to be remembered that, central to the cultural impact of feminisms, this reassessment of men's dangerousness has involved a reappraisal of male sexuality and the relationship between men and children as increasingly contested phenomenon. This changing relationship between men and children itself *pervades* questions which have a direct bearing on perceptions of the paedophile, paedophilia and of masculine risk more generally; how is an understanding of the "dangers of men", as it were, to be guarded against? What is considered to be a safe/dangerous male presence in the lives of children in the light of such knowledge that the majority of men who sexually abuse are known to their victims? What are the acceptable/unacceptable boundaries of physical intimacy between men and children, whether in the family or in public institutions-settings?[78] Each of these questions

[74] Note the merging of sex offending with the youth crime curfew provisions within the Crime and Disorder Act 1998.

[75] See for example, U. Beck, *op. cit.* n 38; U.Beck and E. Beck Gernsheim, *The Normal Chaos of Love* (Cambridge: Polity, 1995); A. James, C.Jenks and A. Prout, *Theorizing Childhood* (London: Polity, 1998); A. James and A. Prout (eds), *Constructing and Reconstructing Childhood* (London: Falmer Press, 1990); C. Jenks, *Childhood* (London: Routledge, 1996); J. Qvortrup, "Childhood and Modern society: a paradoxical relationship?" in J.Brannen and M. O'Brien (eds.), *Childhood and Parenthood* (London: Institute of Education, 1995); J. Qvortrup, M. Bardy, G. Sgritta and H. Wintersberger (eds), *Childhood Matters: Social Theory, Practices and Politics*, (Aldershot: Avebury Press, 1994); J. Brannen and M. O'Brien (eds), *Childhood and Parenthood: Proceedings of the International Sociological Association Committee for Family Research Conference* (London: Institute of Education, 1995).

[76] C. Jenks, "The Postmodern Child" in J. Brannen and M. O'Brien (eds), *Children in Families: Research and Policy* (London: Falmer Press, 1996).

[77] C. Jenks, *ibid.* at 20.

[78] 'British men fear to touch children", *The Observer*, 25 July 1999, reporting a study which found that British men were, in comparison with other European countries, seen to have a distorted or negative view about family life, with a clear link being made to coverage about child sexual abuse. UK advertisers have themselves been advised to be wary of using images of men with children.

run through debates about the legal regulation of child welfare across diverse domains, notably (thought not exclusively) in relation to institutional contexts such as the play group, the nursery and the primary school, where the presence of men tends to be discursively positioned as potentially, if not as at times inherently, problematic.[79]

It is, in short, in the light of these *adult* investments[80] that the betrayal of the child, encapsulated in the breach of trust represented by child sexual abuse, would appear to be so deeply felt. The presence of the paedophile in the midst of the community raises questions about the way in which men's relationships to/with children are themselves being (re)framed. For, ultimately, what does the ontology of the paedophile, as outlined above, say about "normal" men? What does it reveal about a masculine subject which has *already been* constituted as Other to "everyday" child care practices, beyond a primary men/child nexus of economic provider and socialising role model (though this is not to say that these constellations of the men/child relationship are not undergoing profound changes)? Ultimately, and given the centrality of the figure of the child to the familial(ised) experience of the material and emotional dependencies which surround heterosexual relating more generally, it is perhaps unsurprising that it should be in negotiations around the security of children that the dangers associated with men's physical presence/proximity to the child should become such a contested and problematic issue – not just in relation to "law and order" but in relation to questions of sex difference, gender and the "public sphere" more generally.[81] In a context in which ". . . the enhanced interest in men's relationship to children and of men in children" grows,[82] and where the construction of (hetero) masculinities are being subjected to increasing critical scrutiny, I have suggested that the iconic status of the child has become the disputed territory around which a more general assessment of the contribution of men to the social is taking place.

In such a context ideas about men's sexual abuse of children which had hitherto been understood in colloquial, familiar terms – the "flasher", the "stranger

[79] See further, C. Skelton, "Sex, Male Teachers and Young Children" (1994) 6 *Gender and Education* 87–93.

[80] A recurring theme in the work cited at n 75 *supra* has been to surface the emblematic status of the child as the ". . . last remaining, irrevocable, unexchangable primary relationship. Partners come and go. The child stays. Everything that is desired, but is not realisable in the relationship, is directed to the child . . . The child has become the final alternative to loneliness that can be built up against the vanishing possibilities of love. It is a private type of re-enchantment, which arises with, and derives its meaning from, disenchantment" (U.Beck, 1992 *op. cit.* n 38 at 118, quoted by C. Jenks, *op. cit.* n 75 at 20). The child of postmodernity ". . . is now envisioned as a form of 'nostalgia', a longing for times past, not as 'futurity'. Children are now seen not so much as 'promise' . . . as primary and unequivocal source of love, but also as partners in the most fundamental, unchosen, unnegotiated form of relationship. *The trust that was previously anticipated from marriage, partnership, friendship, class solidarity and so on is now invested more generally in the child*". (C. Jenks, *op. cit.* n 75 at 19: my emphasis).

[81] See further, A. McMahon, *Taking Care of Men: Sexual Politics in the Public Mind* (Cambridge: Cambridge University Press, 1999).

[82] C. Jenks, *op. cit.* n 75. at 20.

at the school gate" – re-emerge as part of a different language, a different narrative of social (dis)order.[83] They are questions about a "crisis" of public safety, of risk management, a breakdown of the family and, less visibly though increasingly, about the nature of male sexuality. The crisis of order represented by the regulation of the body of the paedophile may have deep historical roots. And the construction of the paedophile as Other (to "family" men, to the heterosexual community) would certainly *appear* to cleanse the social body through the sacrifice of a particularly dangerous individual.[84] Yet at the present moment the concepts of the child, parenthood and paedophilia are each being transformed in the face of changing sexual subjectivities, cultural formations and political realignments, in ways which have served to ask some profoundly disturbing questions about the nature of "normal" masculinity and male sexuality in the first place.

4. CONCLUDING REMARKS

The re-organisation of the patterning of relationships deemed familial within late modernity has, I have argued in this chapter, been inextricably bound up with the crisis of order represented by the phenomenon of the paedophile. I have sought to trace a discursive bifurcation between, on the one hand, a criminalised/dangerous public sphere "polluted" by the presence of the paedophile; and, on the other, a crime-free, presumed "safe" (for children, for adults) "private" familial existence. In surfacing and undermining the dualism through which the idea of the paedophile as "stranger" to the family has been constituted, and in surfacing the sexed (as different) experiences of community, solidarity and "family life", the taken-for-granted nature of men's location within the social *per se* is itself disturbed. The dominant discourse, in which a pathologising of male sexuality is focused on the paedophile as dangerous Outsider to the family, has served to divert attention from the frequently problematic nature of the presence of men *in* the lives of children, whether in their capacity as (biological or social) fathers or as caregivers to children and as welfare workers across a range of institutions and organisations. Underscoring contemporary conversations about the changing relationship between men and children has been a consciousness, an implicit awareness, of how men constitute potential threats to the safety, integrity and autonomy and, ultimately, to the lives of children. These are threats which cannot be confined to the extra-familial domain,

[83] A rich vocabulary exists, known to adults and children alike, through which to depict the paedophile. The "flasher" and "stranger at the school gates" are immediately recognisable figures within this iconography, denoting a *particular type* of man: "When I was growing up in Worthing, on the South Coast, the arrival of longer spring evenings meant freedom: lambs in the fields, buds on the trees and flashers behind the bushes . . . Now it's more difficult. The twin perils of modern Britain – traffic and perverts – have made every parent feel justly overprotective", Maeve Haran, "novelist and mother of three", *The Express*, 15 April 1998.

[84] See further on this notion of "sacrifice" A. Young, *op. cit.* n 2.

although it is significant how at present hitherto subjugated knowledges are articulating the point that "strangers" have been a significant problem in the lives of many young men and women, boys and girls for years in terms of sexual abuse in locations such as the youth club, the school, the church, children's homes and so forth.[85] It remains, nonetheless, within the parameters of the (hetero) sexual family that the rupture between men and children is presently being most rigorously and pervasively experienced. The representation of the paedophile as an unproblematic Other would appear to restore some order to a (familial) community/sociality which is being displaced as an institutional source for the preservation and reproduction of moral (sexual) order. And in so doing that which is considered dangerous about men has itself moved somewhat closer to (the) "home".

The category of the paedophile, I have argued, is neither a statistical artefact not a political property. It is, rather, a sociocultural phenomenon. In the suggestion that there is something new and distinct about paedophilia, that it is a "new kind of crime", it has been widely assumed that crime more generally has "transformed itself and mutated". In so doing a space has opened up for much speculation about the dark side of "human nature". Yet a more plausible and resonant reading of the emotions roused by events surrounding the release of sex offenders from prison can be found, I have argued, in locating representations of paedophilia in relation to broader transformations in the discursive experience of the social. Ultimately, the framing of debates around the legal regulation of the body of the paedophile transcends the sphere of crime and criminality. They draw on wider shifts in cultural configurations of sex/gender through which understandings of "dangerous masculinities" are presently being (re)constituted. The reconstitution of paedophilia at the end of the twentieth century has served to surface not simply the way in which "dangerousness" has itself been given a continuous momentum by the fears and anxieties attendant on modern life;[86] within a context in which danger *per se* is increasingly recognised as a sexed/gendered (masculine) phenomenon,[87] the high-profile release of known sex offenders from prison has contributed to a collective fear of danger, the events surrounding such releases participating in the production of domains of objects and rituals of truth which have supported a particular disciplinary apparatus. The debate about "what to do" with the problem of the paedophile has reproduced ideologies of normality and criminality, sanity and madness, good and evil, psychopathology and sociopathology each of which have constituted the norms by which we judge the conduct of ourselves and others. Yet as Hollway and Jefferson argue, it is necessary to present a more complex psychical dimension to the construction of "fearful" subjects in a context where social explanation can itself so easily become a "psychic reality".[88] Certainly, what is

[85] See n 51 *supra*.
[86] See further J. Pratt, *op. cit.* n 1.
[87] R. Collier, *op. cit.* n 64.
[88] See further W. Hollway and T. Jefferson, *op. cit.* n 34.

required is something more complex than the representations of "false consciousness" on the part of the "unruly mob" or "the mass". It may well be that the fear of the paedophile is a particularly "apt discourse"[89] within the modernist quest for order, the paedophile constituting a risk at once knowable and potentially controllable (that is, via the physical removal of the paedophile from a geographical area) while, importantly, presenting a blameless victim (the innocent child). Ultimately, however, the paedophile is neither outside society nor wholly reducible to it, neither totally powerful nor the victim of forces beyond his control. In seeking to "reflexively re-configure the relationship between the social and subjectivity"[90] the case of the release of sex offenders from prison can be seen as illustrative of a broader phenomenon whereby the sociality of men's crimes as the actions of *men* is more generally routinely effaced. That this is a question which traditional political and criminological discourse appears incapable of addressing itself says much about contemporary understandings of the relation between crimes, criminality and understandings of the social.

89 *Ibid.*
90 T. Jefferson, "Review" (1996) 36 *British Journal of Criminology* at 323.

11

The Fight Against Sex with Children

M. MOERINGS

1. INTRODUCTION

IN RECENT YEARS, society has begun to think very differently about the sexual intimacy of adults with children: the development from relative tolerance to (almost) a hate campaign against anyone who does not express a negative opinion on sex between adults and children as a matter of course. The development from considering it quite natural for parents to take showers together with their children to teachers' fear of being accused of sexual abuse if they place a comforting hand on a child's shoulder.

Let there be no misunderstanding: I am against the indecent assault and rape of children and also sexual contact with young children in dependency relationships, such as between father and daughter or sport instructor and pupil. However, I wish to argue in favour of a more balanced approach, in which attention is paid to the differences and in which, for example, exploratory sexual play among children is not equated with sexual abuse. Nor should photos depicting naked children be lumped together with child pornography. Furthermore, although certain acts should be strongly condemned, this does not mean that all forms of social ostracism and isolation of adults who abuse children should be accepted, if only because they will most likely be ineffective, or more aptly stated, counterproductive.

By using a number of examples, I wish to show how unbalanced the reactions are to sexual acts involving children. The official justification for the condemnation of such sexual contact and pornography in which children are involved is the protection of juveniles. The assumption is that sexual contact with children and child pornography result in harm to the (emotional) development of the child. Such is undoubtedly true of sexual contacts with children in the nature of indecent assault or rape, but, in my opinion, the harm caused by contacts which are less obviously involuntary, such as sex with children between the ages of twelve and sixteen, or by pictures or videos of naked children, is less evident. The (possible) harm to the child may well be used as an argument, by the government as well, but, partly under the influence of international pressure, there is also a wish to prohibit such sexual contacts and images because they are contrary to prevailing morality, which goes beyond the protection of the child. I wish to illustrate that in the social and political debate, certain aspects are not being brought out into the open or are not sufficiently elucidated. I will also show[1] that the parole service, through its director, is arrogating itself a questionable role.

2. BACK TO THE CLOSET

In the 1960s and 1970s, Edward Brongersma, Upper House member from the PvdA (Labour Party), who was known to have sexual contacts with juveniles, was able to argue on television in favour of understanding and acceptance of love and sexual relationships between adults and children. During the last years of his life, at the end of the 1990s, he had gone more or less underground. And in 1998, the hate campaign conducted against him, which included breaking the windows of his house, caused him to decide to expedite his death. The board members of the trust that manages his estate were at a loss as to what they should do with the large collection of child pornography he wished to preserve for posterity for scientific purposes. The Public Prosecution Service has recently tried to make things easier for them by instituting a judicial inquiry into whether the collection may be preserved for scientific purposes or should be destroyed at least in part.

In the 1970s and 1980s, the Martijn Society actively championed the interests of paedophiles and published a magazine with photographs of children. I do not know if the association still exists, but in any case it has proved impossible to contact its members. They have gone *back to the closet*. During the last two decades, the psychologist Sandfort has done extensive research into the experience of sex by juveniles, also with adults. His conclusions are extremely balanced. For example, he makes a distinction between voluntary and involuntary sexual contacts of juveniles, also with adults. Such voluntary sexual contacts – which in itself is not surprising – result in a more satisfying sex life at a later age than involuntary contacts. Through this type of findings alone, he has made himself suspect and has been branded by various media as a propagandist for sex with children and associated with child pornography networks.[2] There is no nuance whatsoever in many media and in the minds of many people regarding the subject of sex with children. Even approaching the theme scientifically can make a person suspect. Not only is the bringer of bad tidings stoned, but so too is the bringer of balanced tidings.

[1] Section 11, *infra*.

[2] T. Sandfort, *Het belang van de ervaring. Over seksuele contacten in de vroege jeugdjaren en seksueel gedrag en beleven op latere leeftijd* (Utrecht: Homostudies, 1988) 182.

3. REACTIONS OF SOCIETY

The last thing I wish to do is defend sexual abuse of children, but I do wish to emphasise that a balanced discussion about sex in which children are involved in any way has been impossible in recent years. The taboos surrounding sex with children, or at least the increasingly restrictive climate being created, are defended in the interest of (the protection of) the child. I do not want to cast any doubt on the importance of the interests of the child, but I do suggest that the positions of the public and the media are not inspired only by that: in my opinion, the protection of the child is being used and to a certain extent abused for repressive reactions and measures that discredit by definition men – who are the exclusive subject of the public debate – with an erotic interest in children. They are the scapegoats of contemporary society. All the "evils of sex" are projected onto them. Furthermore, the distinction is blurred between paedophilia – feeling sexually attracted to children – and paedophile abuse. The media repeatedly mention paedophiles where "paedophile sex offender" is meant. The media confirm and reinforce the idea that a paedophile is not just someone who is sexually attracted to children, but is by definition a man who sexually abuses children. Paedophiles are modern-day scapegoats. The designation of scapegoats distracts attention from other acts of people themselves that cannot bear the light of day.

Public opinion is actively sweeping politicians and legislators along in this unbalanced current. The fear of men who violate children – although there are also women who cannot leave children alone – runs deep and leads to reactions having little to do with social reality. For instance, a new swimming pool has been made "paedophile-proof": corners of the swimming pool which are difficult to see are checked for men who might touch children in an indecent manner. A jacuzzi is a bad idea because no one can see where groping hands are going. Emotions are burning, even though they are not based on anything but rumours. They will not be contained as long as it is not 100 per cent certain that they are founded on quicksand. And maybe not even then.

In a village in the northern Netherlands, parents accused teaching staff of mass sexual abuse. Sex cellars were said to exist where these atrocities took place. Police investigations did not reveal any traces of this. Sufficient reason to close the investigation, but the village continued to be seized by the alleged sexual abuse of the children. The vast majority were nevertheless convinced that the stories had been made up, but a minority led by the parents of the children who had told the sex stories continued to believe that the teachers had enticed their children into sex cellars in order abuse them. Ultimately, in 1999, the judicial authorities decided to have an investigation carried out by TNO (Netherlands Organization for Applied Scientific Research) into the existence of these cellars. As expected, this investigation did not produce any results. It is doubtful whether this has reassured the parents concerned.[3]

Although social unrest was initially limited to sexual activities of adults with children, in recent years indecent assaults and rapes of children by their peers or older pubescent juveniles and adolescents have also attracted attention. Pawing in swimming pools, in particular, has received broad coverage in the press.

Adolescents are believed to commit 30 to 50 per cent of the sexual abuse of children.[4] Victims of under age sex offenders are mainly young children. Fifty to 60 per cent of their victims are younger than ten years of age.[5]

The intention is not to make light of actual indecent assault, let alone rape, but a social hypersensitivity has been created that also labels what was considered until recently to be sexual play among children as "indecent assault". Take, for example, the story which made the front page of the (regional) press that a fourteen year old boy had indecently assaulted a child of seven.[6] What appeared to have happened was that an adolescent pulled down a child's bathing suit and pinched his penis. After hearing about this, the parents immediately reported it. The teenager was picked up by the police and interviewed. Because he was German, the German police were called in, who offered the boy a professional counselling programme. A current affairs series on television was devoting attention in the same period to unwanted sexual contact in swimming pools. In addition to a few serious incidents, a pinch in the behind was considered a form of indecent assault. Incidents in swimming pools, certainly including a few serious ones, have resulted in the abolition of mixed swimming at any swimming centre during school outings. Reactions remain bitter, even after the sentence has been served. An Amsterdam man who had served a sentence for violent sex with children was harassed at home to such an extent that he had to flee and ultimately move house.

Early in 1999, the mayor of a village was able to express public sympathy for a "people's court" to which young people from his municipality had subjected a fellow resident who was sentenced because he could not keep his hands off a child. He had been guilty of sexually tinted caresses, for which he was sentenced to community service. The young people considered this punishment too light. The mayor could sympathise with that, because everyone in his small municipality is accustomed to hard work.

In such stigmatising actions, it apparently makes little difference *what* someone has done with children. The distinction between sexually tinted touches, as in this village, and the brutal rape by the man from Amsterdam hardly seems to matter: "They have to keep their hands off our children".

[3] *Telegraaf*, 17 November 1999.

[4] M. Boelrijk, *Minderjarige zedendelinquenten en het strafrecht. De strafrechtelijke aanpak van minderjarige plegers van seksuele delicten*, diss (VU, Amsterdam: VU uitgeverij, 1998) 18.

[5] *Ibid.*, 55–6.

[6] *Dagblad de Limburger*, 31 July 1999.

These examples make it clear that public reactions, fuelled by various media, are not always in proportion to the extent of harm done to the child's interests, or are partly inspired by other reasons and feelings. Naturally we have been confronted with the atrocities of Dutroux, in which various children were brutally murdered after having been severely sexually abused. Horror and indignation run deep.

We shall also see that in politics, the administration of justice and law enforcement – partly implicitly – other considerations than the pure protection of the child are playing an increasingly greater part. I will illustrate this on the basis of Article 247 of the Penal Code that criminalises sex with children between the ages of twelve and fifteen, and on the basis of the child pornography article (Article 240b Penal Code). Violent sex with children, such as indecent assault and rape, are only mentioned incidentally because the fact that they harm the interests of the child is not challenged.

4. SEX WITH CHILDREN AND THE CRIMINAL STATUTES

The assumption in criminalising sexual acts in general is the lack of free will on the part of one of those involved. Irrespective of their age, people are protected against threats to that free will, for example in the event of indecent assault and rape, in which physical integrity is violated. With respect to children, it is assumed that they are not yet able to determine their will, also because they cannot fully assess the consequences of their behaviour. They need extra protection against abuse of that incapacity. That is why committing lewd acts with children under the age of sixteen is punishable.[7] Under certain circumstances, this also applies to sexual contact with a child of sixteen or seventeen, if an abuse of power is involved.[8] Anyone who has sex with a child under twelve years of age may be prosecuted without a complaint from the victim or his/her legal representative. If sex with a child aged twelve to fifteen is concerned, the suspect can only be prosecuted upon receipt of a complaint.[9] A minor of that age category can decide herself whether she has sex with a boy or man (let us continue to use the example of a girl who has sex with a boy, although the same applies to homosexual contact). If this sexual contact takes place against her will, she can report it and file a complaint. The girl does not have to do this by herself. Her parents, and under certain circumstances the Child Care and Protection Board,

[7] Dutch Criminal Code, Article 247 para. 1.

[8] Apart from that, sexual contact between two adults can also be punishable in the event of abuse of power, for example by a doctor who starts a sexual relationship with a patient. This theme is dealt with comprehensively by R.S.B. Kool, *De strafwaardigheid van seksueel misbruik* (Deventer: Gouda Quint, 1999).

[9] Please note: We are discussing the criminalisation of lewd sexual acts with children. If the acts can be classified under indecent assault or rape, the articles in question are applicable and prosecution can also be instituted without a complaint.

may file a complaint independently if they consider the contact to be undesirable. However, the intention is that the minor child is heard regarding the desirability of prosecution before the public prosecutor takes a decision. This does not mean that the public prosecutor will adopt the young person's position. The requirement of a complaint also implies that sexual contact remains a risky undertaking for the adult. If the child consents to the contact, but later comes to regret it when the relationship is broken off and love has possibly turned to hate, he or she can still file a complaint. This could be the basis on which to prosecute the adult years later, with due observance of the period of prescription.

(a) Indecency is time-related

The law refers to the prohibition of lewd acts with children and not to sexual contacts *pur sang*. The spirit of the times may enter the picture and influence the opinion of the court as to the existence of lewd behaviour. Or stated more aptly: lewdness implies the commission of a sexual act in contravention of a socio-ethical standard, contrary to morality. According to contemporary Western standards, a seventeen-year-old boy is completely free to have sex with his fifteen-year-old girlfriend. A more complicated and sensitive issue is a relationship between a young girl and an obviously older man.

A man of forty had a relationship with a thirteen-year-old girl. The girl had consented fully to the relationship. She was in love with him and also went to bed with him. When the girl's mother found out about it, she filed a complaint with the police. The man was prosecuted and convicted of having committed lewd acts with the girl. The Hoge Raad[10] held that that the man's sexual acts were lewd. The fact that there was an intimate love relationship between the man and the girl did not make a difference. In relationships such as that with a forty-year-old man, according to the Hoge Raad, minor children are unable or not sufficiently able to oversee the implications of their acts and to determine their will freely. They must be protected against undesirable influence on their will. According to established case law, if the age difference is negligible, there is no question of lewdness. But the tide may turn. We only have to think of the sexual play in the swimming pool which is now seen in a very different light from that of several years ago.

(b) Abolition of the complaint requirement

When lewd acts are committed with minors from twelve to sixteen, a prosecution may only be instituted after the victim or his/her legal representative has filed a complaint. This also makes a prosecution possible as a result of a

[10] HR 24 June 1997, no. 105.005.

complaint, for example from the parents, while the child him or herself had consented fully to the contact, which could become apparent when the child is interviewed in person.

The complaint requirement was introduced in order to strike a balance between the child's right to experiment and develop sexually and the protection of the child against sexual abuse. In actual practice, the complaint requirement[11] has not proved to function adequately. For instance, assistance agencies and investigation authorities state that the requirement of a complaint hinders the ability to prosecute. This allegation sometimes seems to be inspired more by emotions than by knowledge of the facts. The comment has been made that in cases where parents are (co-) perpetrators of lewd acts with their child, the complaint requirement offers less protection to the victim, or that lewd acts of teachers with their pupils cannot be combated without a complaint. This is absolutely untrue. No complaint has to be filed in such cases. The public prosecutor may prosecute *ex officio* on the basis of Article 29 of the Penal Code, which, among other things, criminalises lewd acts of a parent with his minor child or a teacher with his minor pupil. In the case of sex within certain obvious dependency relationships, no complaint is required for prosecution. Nor does the heartfelt cry cut any ice of an expert detective in sex cases, who remarks that the complaint requirement hinders the detection of child molesters.[12]

The complaint requirement will continue to apply for some time to sexual contacts with very young male or female prostitutes. At present, this makes it difficult to take action against Dutch tourists in Asian countries who have sexual contacts with children under sixteen years of age, although a few men have been prosecuted in The Netherlands for such a sex offence in a foreign country.[13]

Arguments have been put forward for abolition of the complaint requirement in such cases because very young (male and female) prostitutes will not usually be very quick to file a complaint, as their livelihood would be at risk or they could come under pressure from pimps and traffickers in women. From 1 October 2000, simultaneously with the abolition of the general ban on brothels, the complaint requirement for the commission of sexual acts with a juvenile prostitute, male or female, will cease to apply. The age for prostitution will be increased to eighteen.[14]

In the meantime, there is also a proposal to abolish the complaint requirement in other sex cases involving children from twelve to sixteen. Instead of the

[11] J. de Savornin Lohman et al., *Betere en adequate rechtsbescherming door de nieuwe zedelijkheidswetgeving? Evaluatieonderzoek naar de effecten en doelbereiking van de nieuwe zedelijkheidswetgeving*, (Utrecht: Verwey-Jonker Instituut, 1994) 95.

[12] *Ibid.*, 94.

[13] A Dutchman had sexually abused two child prostitutes in the Philippines. The girls filed a complaint in the Philippines. Reference 000. And compare Peter Alldridge, "The Sexual Offences (Conspiracy and Incitement) Act 1996" [1997] *Criminal Law Review 30*; "Sex Offenders Act 1997 – Territoriality Provisions" [1997] *Criminal Law Review* 655.

[14] Press release, Ministry of Justice 28 December 1999.

complaint requirement, if the police obtain knowledge of possible abuse, they will be obliged to give the child the opportunity to tell his or her side of the story: "Such a rule ensures that prosecution will follow where it is appropriate, and will not be instituted if this is prompted by the child's interests".[15] This rule may be an improvement, insofar as the child actually has a veto right and, otherwise than at present, the public prosecutor may not prosecute on the initiative of the parents who, for example, are against their daughter having a sexual relationship with a man of whom they do not approve.

Even though there are a few sound arguments for abolishing the complaint requirement, as we have seen, the social debate is partly fuelled by spurious arguments that misrepresent the facts.

5. CHILD PORNOGRAPHY IN THE CRIMINAL STATUTES

In the fight against child pornography, which mainly serves to protect the child, other issues are playing an increasing role. The criminalisation of the distribution of child pornography, introduced in 1986, was amended drastically once again in 1996. The maximum sentence was originally three months. It is now four years. By increasing the penalty, it is now possible to apply coercive measures such as pre-trial detention and searches of premises. This should enable a more effective fight against child pornography. The scope of the article has also been widened. The production, shipping in transit, export and stocking of child pornography has been made punishable. Traditionally, the distribution of child pornography has involved the operators of sex shops and post order dealers, but it also includes the modern-day Internet distributor. The reason for amending the article was the increasing unrest concerning the sexual abuse of children.

Until the amendment, "having child pornography in stock" was linked with the intention to distribute it or display it in public. Since the introduction of the new statutory provision, this intention has been dropped, although the term "having in stock" has been maintained. The explanatory memorandum shows that the term has been extended to "simply having available" or "possession". The private individual who has a child pornography magazine in his possession for his own gratification is also included under this provision. That was later denied by the minister: possession "indicates plurality and has an outwardly directed connotation".[16] The two positions are not compatible, and that is why the Hoge Raad wished to provide clarity. According to the Hoge Raad, the rationale of the criminal provision is the protection of young children against sexual abuse of which they could be victims. Therefore, it chose the broader interpretation, which comes down to the fact that "having in stock" also means

[15] Memorandum 1999, 26. This was also one of the options proposed by J. de Savornin Lohman et al., *Het functioneren van het klachtvereiste in de zedelijkheidswetgeving* (5 volumes) (Utrecht: Verwey-Jonker Instituut, 1998) vol. 5, 60–1.

[16] See note 't Hart to HR 21 April 1998, NJ 1998, 782.

having a picture in one's possession, even the possession of one or more pictures for private use.[17] It could be argued, although the Hoge Raad did not explicitly follow this line, that where there is a demand for such material, there will also be a supply. This stimulates production and distribution. Such an argument was indeed put forward in the Lower House, where a comparison was made with receiving stolen property: the market must be tackled in order to prevent the underlying criminal offence.

Such interpretations are in keeping with the spirit of the times, in which the assumption of the protection of the child is maintained without restrictions, regardless of whether this is actually involved. If the legal protection of the accused was also taken as an assumption, the Hoge Raad's position might have been different: through the conflicting possibilities for interpretation, to which the legislator itself has contributed, it would not be clear to the accused whether or not he was allowed to have child pornography in his possession. This is contrary to the principle of legal certainty, which guarantees that no one can be convicted of behaviour, the punishability of which is up for discussion because of conflicting statements from the legislator. The Minister of Justice has meanwhile promised that legislative consequences will be attached to the judgment of the Hoge Raad.

(a) The rationale behind the child pornography article

The rationale behind the criminalisation of child pornography is the protection of the child against sexual abuse. The purpose of the article is not to prevent children or adults from seeing sexually stimulating visual material.

Child pornography must involve an image or video of a child obviously younger than sixteen who is involved in a sexual act.[18] Merely posing nude does not constitute such an act, according to the Hoge Raad. The image must be intended to arouse sexual desire. That is why photographs by the photographer Mader in which boys posed nude in a way in which their sex was depicted explicitly were not labelled as child pornography. The photographer wanted to record the different stages of sexual development in an artistic manner. Nor were nude photos by the same photographer in which a boy was depicted in natural surroundings in a relatively natural pose considered to be pornography.[19] A later ruling shows that the dividing line between what is and is not child pornography is extremely thin. This involved photographs of a boy who had taken on a pose in which his penis could be seen clearly in a slightly swollen state. This was not "simple nudity". The pose constituted an act which was

[17] HR 21 April 1998, NJ 1998, 782, with note by 't Hart.
[18] Penal Code, Article 240b.
[19] HR 6 March 1990, NJ 1990, 667.

sexual in nature because of the way in which and the situation in which the sex organ had been photographed.[20]

In my opinion, the criterion applied by the Hoge Raad that a sexual act exists if sexual excitement is apparently intended is much too broad. Excitement can happen in countless ways and in an innocent manner, argued 't Hart.[21] Advertisements are full of it. It does not matter what kind of fantasy an image or photo arouses in the viewer. If this were otherwise, not only innocent holiday photos of naked children would be considered child pornography, but also cute, spontaneous-looking children with clothes on, who can arouse sexual desires in certain people, such as the youth photo of a male or female singer, with which people gratify themselves. The point of departure in this case law is the degree of harm to the child, as explicitly intended by the legislator. Harm can consist in the young person being compelled either to take a position or to commit or tolerate a sexual act that is harmful to him or her, or in the fact that the publication of the act is harmful to the young person. It is incidental that the image was mainly produced and circulated to excite others.

Making recordings of naked children at home or at the nudist camp does not fall under child pornography. Nor can books in which innocent pictures of children are accompanied by pornographic texts be viewed as child pornography. Visual material produced with the aid of computer animation, in which children are depicted in a more than lifelike manner in the most provocative positions, is not child pornography either. No child was involved in its production, and by definition its interests cannot have been harmed. The former Minister of Justice, Sorgdrager, urged that in amending Article 240b of the Penal Code, the position should be maintained that child pornography must require a depicted act which is harmful to the young person involved in it.

Meanwhile, only a few years later, the current Minister of Justice, Korthals, expressed a different opinion. He is convinced, whether or not under international pressure, that through the development of technology, the justification for criminalisation can no longer be sought exclusively in the protection of children against actual sexual abuse. "Justification can also be found in the prevention of harm resulting from the circulation of visual material that suggests sexual abuse".[22] Precisely because of the wide distribution via the Internet, the police and public prosecution service cannot be expected to prove that children are depicted in the material discovered.

The minister puts forward an argument that is important in relation to the problem of proof, but I sense rather strongly that such images simply "should not be allowed". This no longer concerns the pure protection of the child, but such images are in conflict with moral consciousness as such, which should be reflected in criminal law.

[20] HR 4 December 1990, NJ 1990, 312.
[21] Note 't Hart to HR 6 March 1990, NJ 1990, 667.
[22] Memorandum 1999, 25.

We have not yet gone as far as in the United States, where self-appointed moral censors were able to get Benetton, which – it cannot be denied – has a reputation when it comes to shocking, provocative advertisements, to stop its advertising campaign for children's underwear. The advertisements showed two innocent children in decent underpants. According to the champions of morality, if you looked closely you could see the outlines of two children's penises through the underwear. According to them, the photographers could not have had any other intention but to arouse sexual desire. Benetton capitulated, although for purely commercial reasons.

Schuijer rightly raised the question a few years ago whether the public prosecution service will exercise restraint in prosecuting. He is uneasy when referring to a manual of the Board of Procurators General. The instructions it contains in respect of what does and does not fall under the definition of child pornography are so vague that it could include very many images.[23]

Meanwhile, it appears that Schuijer was right. In the summer of 1999, the public prosecution service confiscated several photographs on exhibition in an Amsterdam artist's society. These were nine photographs of sitting, semi-reclining and standing boys, whose sexual organs were visibly illustrated. Some of them were taken over a hundred years ago and have often been exhibited all over the world, including in the much more prudish United States, without any commotion. In one of them, that of Walter Chapell, a nude man with an erection is standing, holding a very young child on his arm.

The question that the public prosecution service wants to have answered by the courts is the extent to which these are sexual acts or illustrations in an erotic context, which are (were) harmful to the boys. Is the public prosecution service really upset or does it need case law that can give direction to future enquiries into child pornography, in which the ultimate object is the protection of the child and not the prevention of pornography itself? Or is it?

In the meantime, the Amsterdam District Court sitting in chambers has ruled that this does not constitute child pornography, even in the case of the "father and son" photo. The Court sitting in chambers agreed with the public prosecution service that the combination of the man with an erection and the child could give the photo an unnatural character. Given the fact that the man is actually the child's father, and the photo was taken by the mother, this is a different matter. Moreover, the photo focuses on the father's hands and it does not appear from the photo that the child can see his father's erection (sic! MM). The baby is also unrecognisable.[24] The son, now almost forty years old, has made it known that he does not have any problem with the photo.

The public prosecution service has brought an appeal from the court's ruling before the supreme court. In the public prosecution service's view, it is not

[23] J. Schuijer, "Schieten op een bewegend doel: de nieuwe kinderpornowet" (1997) *Delikt en Delinkwent* 443–5.

[24] District Court Amsterdam RK 9999/3597.

relevant whether or not the children enjoyed being photographed. "Posing in this unnatural way disturbs a child's normal sexual development. This has meanwhile been proved", according to the press officer of the public prosecution service. "We think that the court is using the wrong criteria".[25] I would like to know what the grounds are of the public prosecutor's allegations. He is undoubtedly concerned about the undisturbed sexual development of children, but doesn't his feeling also play a part that such images are contrary to public decency?

The elements of Article 240b Penal Code leave room for a broad interpretation. This open description[26] applies to "a sexual act" but also to "having child pornography in stock". Optimists, or pessimists, depending on your own moral convictions, believed for a long time that the possession of pornographic magazines for one's own enjoyment did not fall within its scope. The Hoge Raad proved them wrong in 1998 by ruling that the possession of any images for one's own gratification fell under the concept "having in stock". This has left the door wide open for far-reaching criminal intervention.

(b) Increasing the age limit for child pornography

Under prevailing legislation, child pornography must involve a child apparently under the age of sixteen. The word "apparently" indicates that the victim's age does not have to be proved, but must be estimated on the basis of the image. This could result in no prosecution or conviction if the victim is estimated to be sixteen or older, even if he or she is actually younger. But the reverse could also occur.

At the international level, pressure is being exerted through lobbies at conferences and through conventions to increase the age limit to that of majority, eighteen. The ILO Convention Concerning the Prohibition and Immediate Action for the Elimination of the Worst Forms of Child Labour will oblige parties, among other things, to provide that "the use, procuring or offering of a child (a child under eighteen) for the production of pornography" are criminal offences. Ratification of this Convention by The Netherlands will entail amendment to the child pornography article.[27]

As a consequence of increasing the age limit to eighteen, after the statutory amendment, a picture of a seventeen-year-old boy with an erection, which can now still circulate freely on the market because he himself had consented to this, will be subject to confiscation. Is the picture forbidden because it is harmful to the boy concerned? No, according to common opinion at the time the photo was

[25] *Het Parool*, 15 June 1999.

[26] This is not uncommon in moral legislation, precisely to give the court the opportunity to determine the interpretation of the elements partly on the basis of developments in ideas concerning society and morality.

[27] ILO Convention June 1999, listed in Memorandum 1999, 24–25.

taken. This is a departure from the interest of the child to be protected in favour of moral indignation that the photo is so shocking and contrary to moral views, even if this is not (yet) or only reluctantly acknowledged.

A curious discrepancy also continues to exist between, on the one hand, the rule enabling immediate prosecution for the possession of pornography picturing a child (in future) under the age of eighteen, regardless of whether or not the child has consented (Article 240b Penal Code), and on the other hand, the rule of Article 247 Penal Code. According to the latter provision, prosecution may only be instituted against sexual contact with a child under that age (provided he/she is aged twelve or older) if it is clear that the young person did not consent. This discrepancy also makes it clear that the child pornography article involves more than protection of the young person in question. Testing exclusively against the harm to the young person is being increasingly abandoned, even though public justification for faster and easier action under criminal law follows strongly on this concept.

6. THE ENFORCEMENT OF SENTENCES AND ITS AFTERMATH

In legislation and case law, we are witnessing a development in which the point of departure is protection of the child, but in which, whether or not under the influence of international pressure, abstract moral influences can also be recognised. This development is more strongly visible in the manner in which punishment and social ostracism are being demanded for those guilty of sexual abuse of children. These reactions are inspired by feelings of indignation and retaliation, but they are so fierce and extreme that it is very doubtful whether they serve the interests of the child, let alone those of the perpetrators.

The number of detainees in pre-trial detention on suspicion of lewd acts with children or involvement in child pornography has risen sharply, as I have been told by prison directors. And an employee assured me that the number of suspects of paedophile contacts under psychiatric examination in the Pieter Baan Centrum has also increased in recent years. Whereas a few years ago such suspects were the exception in the houses of detention, there are now special sections in various institutions where sex offenders are placed for the sake of their own safety.

The explanation of this growth is certainly not just the increased number of cases of sex with children but, in my opinion, also the social sensitivity to them. The criticism of, for example (Protestant) school governors who kept such matters within the confines of their comprehensive schools, may perhaps have resulted in more and earlier reporting. Whereas suspects of less serious sex offences were sometimes sent home after a police interview, nowadays this is virtually unthinkable and the choice is made to impose pre-trial detention.

Within the prison hierarchy, sex offenders are on the bottom rung of the ladder, and fellow prisoners would prefer to throw them off altogether. Whereas swimming pools are being made paedophile-proof by avoiding corners that are difficult to see when they are built,[28] the showers and toilets of prisons have corners hidden from the view of the guards, where sex offenders can be attacked. "Bullies", who are respected in prison, get furious at someone who cannot keep his hands off children – it could also be their children.

The development outlined above has most likely led to a larger number of reports. Rough figures from the CBS[29] (Central Bureau of Statistics) for 1997 show that the number of rapes and indecent assaults registered by the police had remained the same compared with previous years. The number of other sex offences had, however, more than doubled in comparison with the preceding year (from 1094 in 1996 to about 2600 in 1997). Unfortunately, a further breakdown is not possible because of the manner of registration by the police, but it seems to me that they are very likely to include a considerable number of sexual offences involving children as the victims. The explanation could lie in the increased sensitivity of society and concomitant greater willingness to report such offences.

Larger numbers of reports lead in turn to more prosecutions and convictions. After having served out their prison sentences or hospitalisation orders, these sex offenders return to society. The neighbourhood where such a sex offender came from is not happy about his return, or takes action to prevent this, the most decent case of which was bringing interim injunction proceedings against such return. Nor are harder actions shunned, such as breaking windows or threats of violence. Sometimes the actions are aimed against sexual abuse such as rape and indecent assault, but can also be taken against a man who had limited himself to sexually tinted caresses. Naming and shaming is already very common in the United States.

This is witnessed by the American *Megan's Law*. This law, named after the girl who was murdered by a paedophile who had previously made more victims, was enacted as early as three months after the murder, partly thanks to the fierce battle fought by the victim's mother and the great national unity on the matter, through which any critical remark by opponents was resolutely brushed aside. Not only the police and municipality are informed when a convicted paedophile wishes to take up residence once again in the neighbourhood, but citizens throughout the United States have also had the right since 1996 to know if anyone convicted of a sexually tinted offence comes to live in their neighbourhood. Even the Internet is available to answer the question whether a former child molester is living in the neighbourhood. More than other offenders, men who have attacked children remain stigmatised upon their return to society, which is due in no small measure to the image formed in the media. For instance, the man

[28] *Algemeen Dagblad*, 13 January 1999.
[29] Police statistics CBS 1997.

who raped and murdered the seven-year-old girl in Assen was labelled by the largest morning newspaper in the Netherlands, the *Telegraaf*, as "the Monster of Assen". The court where he was tried became a guarded fort. In the courtroom, the accused was separated from the public by bullet-proof glass. He was sentenced to life imprisonment.[30]

(a) The questionable role of the probation service

Experts such as therapists, who emphasise that it is very difficult if not impossible to cure paedophiles of their illness, also play an important part in forming their image. At most, they can be taught to suppress their sexual feelings. The official recidivism figures are about 25 per cent, but they emphasise that these figures are actually considerably higher. A large number are able to conceal their reversion to the old pattern. These experts estimate that approximately two/thirds re-offend.[31] It is unclear to me how reliable such estimates are. They do, however, lead a life of their own. By taking this position, such therapists – who would be considered by many to be realistic at least – choose in favour of the protection of society. They could be forgiven, but this applies to a much lesser degree to the way in which the general director of the Netherlands probation service, Van der Valk, put himself in the spotlight. Over a year ago, he argued for the lifelong incarceration of sick paedophiles in special psychiatric wards and for an effective pre-selection of incurable paedophiles. Several hundred paedophiles, 30 per cent of the total group, are so seriously ill that they cannot be treated. "Then, as a society, you have to decide to protect children against these people for good".[32]

Now he advocates making instruments available to the probation service for the supervision of paedophiles who are released which would enable mandatory hospitalisation or treatment to be imposed if they constitute a danger to society. A court would not even have to be involved.[33] Furthermore, preventive hospitalisation should be possible for such people, according to Van der Valk. For their own good, even before they commit any criminal offences. In my view, for the protection of society, he wants to give the probation service a more definite place once again in aftercare. However, he seems mainly to be anticipating the interests of concerned neighbourhood residents. It is food for thought when the head of the probation service, who is obliged to make efforts for the resocialisation of offenders and has built up a long tradition in doing so, argues in favour of measures including more exclusion of this specific category. "His ideas signify

[30] *Telegraaf*, 18 August 1999.

[31] J. Frenken, "Seksuele misdrijven en seksuele delinquenten" in van Koppen, D. Hessing en H. Crombag (eds), *Het hart van de zaak, psychologie van het recht* (Deventer: Gouda Quint, 1997) 205.

[32] *De Volkskrant*, 9 December 1998.

[33] W. Baardemans,"Reclassering wil bevoegdheid voor dwangopname bij monitoring" (1999) 6 *Reclassering* 4–8.

a fundamental turnabout, towards selective incapacitation of a large group of people", according to Ippel.[34]

What I am seriously concerned about is that, the probation service, which has the task of rendering assistance and monitoring whether its client is keeping to agreements, is, according to Van der Valk, also the body that must take the decision to lock someone up if things go wrong or threaten to go wrong. In this way, he puts the individual probation officer in the judge's place.

At present, the (civil) court, which is required to balance the interests of society with those of individual citizens, decides on mandatory hospitalisation in an institution. Above all, let's keep it that way.

(b) Lifelong monitoring and social isolation

In taking his position, the director betrays the humane tradition of the Netherlands probation service.[35] In doing so, he also fuels the idea of excluding paedophiles, who are able to return to society, lifelong from jobs in which they associate with children, such as teachers or sport instructors who are suspected or convicted of sexual contact with their students and pupils.[36] The Netherlands scouting organisation, Scouting Nederland, has a blacklist of names of people who have been guilty of sexual abuse. How did they obtain this information? Is it reliable?

Under pressure from the media and public opinion, the Minister of Justice is seriously considering the central registration of sex offenders. Bodies that have a lot to do with children, such as schools and children's homes, could then consult a databank to see whether an applicant or employee has been convicted of a sexual offence.

Please note, this goes much further than a certificate of good behaviour (VOG), which can be denied to an applicant because he has a criminal conviction. The statutory rule of "the certificate of good behaviour", as it is persistently referred to in popular language, provides the possibility to exclude convicted persons from certain jobs for eight years. Employers may require job applicants to submit a certificate of good behaviour. They must request them from the mayor of the municipality in which they live. The mayor may refuse to issue the certificate, taking account of the nature of the conviction in relation to the job for which they have applied. If the applicant is unable to submit such a certificate, the employer will know that the applicant has a police record. He

[34] Ippel, Seks, vrijheid, vervolging. Kinderporno en pedofilie als "zuiver kwaad": de noodzaak van nieuwe nuchterheid in J. Blad et al. (eds), *Crimineel Jaarboek* (Nijmegen: Ars Aequi Libri, Coornhert-liga, 1999) 148.

[35] Ippel, *op. cit.*, 149.

[36] This discussion was revived as a result of the report *Kinderporno en kinderprostitutie in Nederland, de stand van zaken*, compiled by the working group child pornography and child prostitution in The Netherlands, ChildRight World Wide/TransAct Utrecht, 1998. However, this working group does not argue in favour of mandatory statutory registration of offenders, 81.

will not be informed of the actual reason for refusal of the certificate, which prevents scapegoating.

Meanwhile, a new Bill has been in preparation for several years that is intended to replace the current Judicial Records and Certificates of Good Behaviour Act.[37] This will meet the wishes of, for example, volunteer organisations that organise holidays for foreign children with Dutch families for improved screening. The circle of agencies that may request such a certificate will be extended considerably to, for example, sport clubs and youth organisations such as Scouting Nederland. The assessment period will also be extended: a possible ban from certain jobs for twenty years, instead of a maximum of eight years as is now the case. Therefore, the future Judicial Records and Certificates of Good Behaviour Act already offers more possibilities to exclude sex offenders, without stigmatising them permanently, for example as child molesters.

A databank would go much further, because interested parties could find out what an applicant was convicted of. It would be even more suspect if information could be divulged that someone was only *suspected* of not being able to keep his hands off children. Fortunately, the policeman suspected of abusing his minor daughter was ultimately cleared, and walked away with a well-deserved large sum of money after a fight lasting several years with the highest judicial officials; otherwise, if such a bank had existed, he might never have been allowed to work with children again. After all, as remarked discreetly by a high judicial official, there was no proof that he had not sexually abused his daughter.

It must be proved that sexual abuse actually was committed. It is notoriously much more difficult to establish unequivocally. The policeman in question, who has meanwhile fled the country, is very much aware of this. He himself is apparently afraid that he will never be able to forget his past, even though he has been formally cleared of all blame. The chance of stigmatisation and ostracism would increase considerably through the existence of such a databank. Furthermore, such data can lead a life of its own and be used for blacklists. People *merely suspected* of a sexual offence could be sentenced for life.

In my opinion, a databank as described above is completely unnecessary, as long as due care is taken in issuing or refusing certificates of good behaviour. By establishing a databank, the government would increase the stigmatising effect. Such a cure is worse than the disease. The argument that mayors are now too generous in issuing certificates of good behaviour should not be a reason for creating such a register, but at most is cause for critical examination of the VOG procedure.

The call of society is becoming increasingly louder and reaching ever further. For instance, pressure groups are arguing in favour of informing neighbourhood residents if a former sex offender wants to live in the neighbourhood.

The "Stichting registratie opgespoorde pedofielen (Strop)" (≠ society for the registration of traced paedophiles) wants to open a website where concerned

[37] *Bijl. Hand.* II, 1995–1996, 24 797, nos. 1–2.

Dutch people would be able to test the vicinity of their homes for the presence of former sex offenders in their neighbourhood. Strop wishes to have a record of all convicted paedophiles. Dutch people could enter their address via the website. If a registered paedophile lived within a radius of 2500 metres, the word "yes" would appear. The intention is that the resident will take this data to the police in order to obtain more information on the person involved. If the police refuse to give it, the society will see whether it can provide such information itself.

The Minister of Justice is not completely prepared to meet the demands of neighbourhood residents to be informed of the return of paedophile sex offenders, but he has decided to inform the authorities. The pivotal point in the provision of information will be the public prosecution service, which will be given the authority to provide the police and the mayors, and if desired also the victim, with information, to prevent them from being confronted unexpectedly with the perpetrator. But would the victim be less afraid to meet the perpetrator on the street after a message from the minister? Moreover, there would be more of a temptation to mobilise the neighbourhood.

Neighbourhood residents would be able to exert strong pressure on the police with the information obtained from the Internet. Certainly in small communities, it would not be long before the "child molester" is spotted. There is then a good chance that such a man would not have any more life in that neighbourhood. He would be stigmatised and socially isolated. This would not help his social integration, but would be counterproductive. Being labelled as a child molester would increase rather than decrease the chance of re-offending (secondary deviance).[38]

It looks as if Bolsward, a town in Friesland, has indeed succeeded in preventing escalation. Neighbourhood residents there have agreed in consultation with the municipality that the probation service, the neighbourhood policeman and the neighbourhood residents will keep an eye on a man who was convicted of sexually abusing children in the neighbourhood.

For therapeutic reasons, it may, of course, be in the interests of both the victim and the offender that he does not take up residence in the vicinity of his victim. For example, the requirement may be set on conditional termination of a hospitalisation order that a person must not return to the neighbourhood where he committed his offence. The same requirement could also be set in granting leave to a sex offender sentenced to imprisonment. A requirement to move house after serving the sentence or measure may not be imposed legally. This could only be compelled by way of a street ban imposed by the civil court.

[38] In the labelling approach, this is called secondary deviance, a term derived from Lemert: the deviant behaviour is continued because of the social reaction that makes a life in accordance with social standards impossible, see R. van Swaaningen, "Kritische criminologie", in: E. Lissenberg et al. (eds), *Tegen de regels III, een inleiding in de criminologie* (Nijmegen: Ars Aequi Libri, 1999) 202–4.

7. PAEDOPHILE SEX AND CHILD PORNOGRAPHY IN THE LIGHT OF MORALITY AND LAW

We have seen from the foregoing that the government has included the moral views on sex with children in the criminal statutes. When does the government have the right to do this? Individual freedom of action is central to the classical liberal tradition. The government may only encroach upon it in order to prevent harm to others. A century and a half ago, this was expressed aptly by John Stuart Mill:[39] "The only purpose for which power can be rightfully exercised over any member of a civilised society against his will is to prevent harm to others". Children require extra protection because they are not able to determine their own will. This paternalistic approach can also be found in 1980 in the final report of the advisory committee on sex legislation, the Melai Committee: "The importance of protecting the personalities of children and juveniles is directly opposed to the decriminalisation of sexual contacts between adults and children".[40]

In the debates of the last few years surrounding criminalisation and the enforcement of child pornography and paedophilia laws, the issue of protection of the child always emerges: the child that cannot and may not decide by itself on sexual contact with adults. It is protected in order to prevent damage to its own (sexual) development. The point of departure of this argumentation can be recognised as a liberal approach or possibly the more contemporary postmodernist attitudes towards morality. Because, despite the great differences between the liberal and postmodernist approach,[41] these agree to the extent that they both centre on the freedom and autonomy of the individual. The individual may only be restricted in his choices and personal development if this is harmful to others. Harming the person or the good of others constitutes the justification for taking (lawful) action against the autonomous behaviour of another and subjecting it to restrictions.

Children, however, are not in a position to determine their will with respect to sexual contacts with adults. Such contacts with children under twelve years of age are punishable because it is assumed that they are harmful to their (sexual) development. They must be protected against this. The liberal point of departure for children is supplemented by a paternalistic approach. The same sort of reasoning applies to the criminalisation of child pornography: children are sexually abused for its production, they are placed in unnatural positions for recordings or the context in which things happen is unnatural.

[39] J.S. Mill, *On Liberty* (1859) in G. Dworkin (ed.), *Morality, Harm and the Law* (Boulder, CO: West View Press, 1994) 9.

[40] Final report of the advisory committee on decency legislation, (The Hague: Staatsuitgeverij, 1980) 33

[41] In the classical liberal view, the acts of autonomous people result in a common morality. According to the post-modernist approach, the autonomous acts of the individual will result in a multiform morality. A common morality is lacking precisely in our multiform society.

It is in keeping with this tradition that when the child pornography article was amended, the former Minister of Justice, Sorgdrager insisted that a child must actually be involved in the production. Virtual child pornography does not meet this requirement. It is also in line with this that, according to Sorgdrager, the possession of child pornography for private use does not fall within the scope of the article.

Since 1995, the attention of society for sex in which children are involved has increased, and social abhorrence of it has grown accordingly. This has had its repercussions on politicians and law enforcers. The concept of harm as the touchstone for criminalisation and judicial action has been extended. It is to be expected, although the minister will first await international developments, that virtual child pornography will also come under the criminal statutes.[42] Even though no flesh and blood is involved in the production, its distribution and display suggest sexual abuse, which reinforces the idea that such manners of acting are allowable. It could function as an example. Also looking at child pornography, purely to gratify one's own desire, has meanwhile been punished by the Hoge Raad. It could be reasoned, although the Hoge Raad did not explicitly follow this line of reasoning, that where there is a demand for such material, supply will follow. This stimulates the production and distribution. A similar argument was used in the Lower House, where the comparison was made with receiving stolen goods: the market must be tackled to prevent the underlying criminal offence.

When the protection of children is involved, it is becoming increasingly difficult to understand and justify the social and political discussion of these matters exclusively from a liberal, and where children are concerned, paternalistic view of morality within the law.

Discussions about the criminalisation of child pornography are being fuelled increasingly by the apprehension and indignation that exist in society regarding this issue. Communal thinking is entering the picture more and more. This does not start from the individual, whose autonomous acts can only be restricted by legal action if his acts affect the freedom of others, in this case children, to act. Society is concerned about certain acts. It expresses such concern in the criminal statutes. This is defended by the argument that the majority of society have such opinions, and it is defensible on the basis of democratic principles to include them in the law. Such majority thinking starts from an incorrect concept of democracy because it ignores the position of minorities in society.

Another variation of communal thinking emphasises that human beings are social beings, living in social relationships. It is from this that they derive their identity. This argues in favour of an extensive common morality that expresses itself on all types of substantive questions of life. Such morality binds people together. It is necessary for social cohesion. It is the lubricant of society. This

[42] Memorandum 1999, 25.

morality is laid down in laws.[43] Violation of these laws goes against the social order, which it endangers.

The criminalisation of acts (in certain countries) such as gambling, the use of drugs, abortion,[44] prostitution, homosexual contact and pornography is defended on the basis of such communal thinking, even if it only involves adults who fully consent to such behaviour. Inclusion of these victimless crimes in the penal code is defended from this point of view.

As far as sex is concerned in which children are involved in one way or other, communal thinking clearly emerges in the broader interpretation of the element lewd acts with children between the ages of twelve and sixteen.[45] Nowadays, this sometimes includes acts between children that were previously dismissed as sexual play. Also the extension of the concept "sexual behaviour of children" to an image of a child that is sexually exciting testifies to the fact that establishing the (possible) harm to the child has been abandoned in determining whether or not child pornography is involved.

I can only see the plans to include the images of a sexual act of a young person up to eighteen years of age – this is now sixteen – under child pornography in this perspective as well; and the abolition of the requirement for the young person (between twelve and sixteen) involved in the sexual act to file a complaint is also in keeping with this, unless the new rules are formulated in such a way that the young person will have a right to veto the prosecution when he or she is heard.

A curious discrepancy also remains between, on the one hand, the rule that enables immediate prosecution for production or possession of pornography in which a child (in future) under eighteen years of age is depicted, irrespective of whether the young person has consented[46] and, on the other hand, the rule of Article 247 Penal Code. According to the latter provision, prosecution may only be instituted for sexual contact with a child under that age (if twelve years of age or older) if it is clear that the young person did not consent. This discrepancy also makes it clear that the child pornography article involves more than the pure protection of the young person involved.

Testing only against the harm to the young person is being abandoned more and more, even though public justification for quicker and easier action under criminal law is strongly in line with this concept. The protection of the child is also cited in defending draconian punishments and measures, such as lifelong internment of child abusers. This also applies to the continued monitoring of perpetrators who have been released by the police or even by neighbourhood residents. These measures, which are proposed from society and are being seriously considered (in part) by the government, do not guarantee the safety of

[43] See P. Beirne and J. Messerschmidt, *Criminology* (Fort Worth, TX: Harcourt Brace College Publishers, 2nd edn 1995) 179 ff.

[44] In respect of abortion, it could be argued that the foetus, the unborn child, is the victim.

[45] Dutch Criminal Code, Articles 245 and 247.

[46] Dutch Criminal Code, Articles 240b.

children and may even be counterproductive. Social ostracism and stigmatisation could even endanger the social order.

From a more liberal viewpoint, restraint is not only expected from the government if acts do not harm anyone, but even when they do, the rules, punishments and measures that may be imposed should be helpful. The harm or problems as a consequence of certain behaviour must not be surpassed by more problems as a result of the rules and penalties intended to combat and prevent the harm.[47]

[47] For such utilitarianism within the liberal vision, see: T. de Roos, *Strafbaarstelling van economisch denken* (Arnhem: Gouda Quint bv, 1978) 33–49.

Index